Traditional CAKES & PUDDINGS

ANN NICOL AND HILAIRE WALDEN

Traditional
CAKES & PUDDINGS

ANN NICOL AND HILAIRE WALDEN

First published in 2002 by
New Holland Publishers
(UK) Ltd
Garfield House
86-88 Edgware Road
London W2 2EA
United Kingdom
London • Cape Town
• Sydney • Auckland
www.newhollandpublishers.com

Designed and edited by
Anness Publishing Limited
Boundary Row Studios
1-7 Boundary Row
London SE1 8HP

ISBN 1 84330 424 4 (hardback)
ISBN 1 84330 426 0 (paperback)

Editorial Director:
Joanna Lorenz
Art Director and Designer:
Peter Bridgewater
Project Editor:
Jennifer Jones
Text Editor:
Norma McMillan
Illustrations:
Vana Haggerty
Photographer:
Kulbir Thandi
Home Economists:
Steven Wheeler and
Jacqueline Clarke

2002 EDITION:
Editorial Co-ordinator:
Emily Preece-Morrison
Production:
Marion Storz
Editorial Direction:
Rosemary Wilkinson

Printed in Malaysia by
Times Offset (M) Sdn. Bhd.

5 4 3 2 1

CONTENTS

Serve a delicious looking, smelling and tasting honest-to-goodness pudding and watch people's faces light up. A good pudding of some sort is the best way to end any meal on a high note. It does not have to be heavy or rich, require a long time slaving over a hot stove, and a large portion does not have to be eaten. 'Pudding' covers a wide range of dishes, but the one thing they all have in common is that they are not delicate, fanciful desserts, so none is overly expensive or complicated to make. Home-made cakes are simply very special. They are signs of love and affection for family and friends, which no shop-bought cake, however luxurious, can duplicate. There is nothing quite like the unmistakable aroma of baking in a house, or the satisfaction gained from laying a tea table with home-made good things, or baking and giving your own cakes.

In the following pages you will find recipes for many different occasions, to suit all tastes and budgets, which take into account the time and degree of skill needed to prepare them. We all lead busy lives these days, and many people say they have no time to bake. But it is always worth making the time, and some very quick recipes indeed are included.

This book is for both new and experienced cooks, and a simple step-by-step approach to each recipe is used. Cakes and puddings for every occasion are included and there are tips and hints to help if something goes wrong.

*T*HE BASICS

$\mathcal{T}$HE BASICS

There are a few basic rules to observe before you start. Selecting the best ingredients and using appropriate equipment are important factors in ensuring the success of a recipe, and some guidelines are given here.

$\mathcal{A}$ NOTE ON INGREDIENTS

EGGS

Eggs are used widely. They can add lightness to, thicken or set a pudding, help raise a cake and provide richness and flavour. For baking cakes, use 4–5 day-old eggs, which have lost a little moisture, and stick to the size specified in the recipe if possible. Eggs should be used at room temperature to achieve the best aeration. Don't use cold eggs straight from the refrigerator, where they should be stored, but take them out to stand at room temperature 30 minutes–1 hour before use. If using eggs in puddings where they are not cooked, take care — use fresh, good quality eggs. Because of the risk of salmonella poisoning, raw or lightly cooked eggs should be avoided by ill or elderly persons, young children and pregnant women.

It is a good idea to break the eggs one at a time into a bowl before beating them into a mixture, just in case one egg is not sound. This is also a good idea when you are separating a lot of egg whites and wish to keep out any specks of yolk or pieces of shell.

FATS

Fat gives a richer flavour to cakes and puddings and improves the keeping qualities. Butter and hard or block margarine are interchangeable, but butter gives the best flavour and should be used wherever possible. Unsalted butter is specified because it is generally better quality and fresher than salted butter, which is usually reflected in the taste. Soft tub margarine is only suitable for an all-in-one type cake recipe; if it is used for creaming, the mixture will become too wet. Always use fats at room temperature.

Oil is sometimes called for in recipes, and mild flavoured oils like vegetable or sunflower are best to use.

CREAM

The richness of creams, in ascending order, is single, whipping, then double, and they can often be substituted for one another, as when making custard-type mixtures, depending on how rich you want a recipe to be. An exception is when cream has to be whipped, when only whipping or double cream can be used. Chill cream for whipping, use cold equipment and proceed cautiously, as cream can quite suddenly become curdled. For folding into mixtures, whip until the cream is thick enough just to form floppy peaks. If it is to be piped, it should be whisked until the whisk leaves stiff peaks when lifted from the cream.

SUGAR

Sugar is not just for sweetness; it also influences texture and the choice of sugar can affect flavour. Always use the type of sugar stated in the recipe. Bear in mind when cooking mixtures to be served cold that they will taste sweeter when hot than when cold.

CASTER SUGAR: this is the best white sugar for most baking as it creams easily with butter and dissolves easily and quickly into the mixture.

DEMERARA: this sugar is granular and mainly used for decorative purposes or for cake mixtures where the sugar is dissolved over heat. It can also help make puddings moist.

SOFT, LIGHT AND DARK BROWN SUGARS: these cream well and are often used in fruit cake recipes, where rich flavour and colour are needed. Muscovado is the best soft dark brown sugar, as it is naturally unrefined and has an excellent rich flavour and dark colour.

GRANULATED: this is a coarser white sugar which is not really suitable for baking as it does not dissolve easily. It is used for frostings and boiled icings.

ICING SUGAR: this white sugar is very fine and powdery. It is used mainly for decoration. Keep in a dry place and always sift before use as it tends to form lumps in storage.

VANILLA SUGAR: vanilla sugar adds a subtle softness to the flavour of a pudding. Simply pop a vanilla pod in the sugar and keep it in an airtight container. Leave the sugar for about 5 days before using it. When the sugar has been used, add some more — the vanilla pod should remain effective for up to a year.

FLOUR

PLAIN AND SELF-RAISING: flour provides the structure that makes a cake, so the right choice is vital. Self-raising flour is used for plain cake mixtures that contain no fruit and it has raising agents mixed into it. Richer cakes that do not need raising agents are made with plain flour, or plain flour plus a small amount of a raising agent. If a recipe calls for self-raising flour and you have none, use 2½ tsp baking powder to each 225g/8oz plain flour.

STRONG PLAIN FLOUR: cakes baked with yeast need strong flour, as it enables the dough to stretch further. It gives a light open springy texture to the cake.

WHOLEWHEAT AND WHOLEMEAL FLOURS: these contain all the bran from the wheat and give good texture, flavour and fibre to cakes. Good in rich fruit cakes, you may need to add a little extra liquid, as the bran absorbs more of this.

RAISING AGENTS

These produce a light texture in cakes and it is important to be very accurate when measuring them out.

BAKING POWDER: this is a ready-made mixture of bicarbonate of soda and cream of tartar. When liquid is added, the baking powder effervesces and produces carbon dioxide, and the heat of the oven expands these gas bubbles to give the cake an airy texture.

BICARBONATE OF SODA: this is a raising agent with a gentler effect. It is sometimes used to give heavy or spicy mixtures a lift. It must be measured accurately as too much will give a bitter aftertaste.

CREAM OF TARTAR: this is a fast-acting raising agent: it begins to work the moment it is in contact with liquid. Always bake a mixture as soon as possible after adding cream of tartar or its effect will be reduced.

Dried vine fruits are usually bought pre-washed and cleaned, but you may well find large pieces of stalk in some packs, so it is worth picking them over. Unless they are to be cooked in a liquid, all dried fruits benefit from an initial soaking in water, orange juice, or an alcohol such as sherry, rum or brandy, to plump them up, but make sure to pat them dry in a tea towel or kitchen paper before use or they will sink in a mixture. When cooking other dried fruits, use only enough liquid to cover them. Store all dried fruits in airtight containers in a cool, dry, dark place.

Glacé and crystallized fruits like cherries should be washed in warm water to remove their syrup before use, or the sugary coating will dissolve on cooking and drag the fruit down. Toss whole cherries in flour before baking to stop them from sinking. If pieces of candied peel are too sticky to be easily chopped, sprinkle them with a little of the flour from the recipe in which you are going to use them.

NUTS

Nuts add flavours to mixtures, and when chopped they add texture, and when they are ground they make mixtures moist. Nuts have a high oil content, so become stale and rancid quickly and lose flavour. These reactions occur more rapidly once the nuts have been removed from their shells and with even greater speed after they have been chopped or ground. So, where possible, buy nuts in their shells, or at least whole, keep them in the freezer, or a cool, dark, dry place for no longer than 1 month, and chop or grind them when you need them. Keep them cool while handling them, and when grinding them, do so in small amounts and take care not to overwork them.

TO PEEL ALMONDS: put the nuts into a bowl, pour over boiling water, leave for a few minutes, then remove the nuts; the skin should slip off easily.

TO REMOVE THE THIN, BITTER INNER SKIN OF HAZELNUTS: place the nuts under a low grill or in a low oven until the skin dries and cracks, then tip the hot nuts into a clean cloth and rub until the papery skins come off.

TOASTING AND ROASTING NUTS: this enhances the flavour of nuts as well as adding a new dimension to it. Spread the nuts on a baking tray and place under a medium grill or in an oven set to 180°C/350°F/Gas 4 for 10–12 minutes, stirring occasionally, until the nuts have darkened evenly to the required degree.

CHOCOLATE

Chocolates vary not only in their quality but also in their sweetness. For the finest, most intense chocolatey flavour, use good quality confectioners' or bakers' chocolate, chocolat pâtissier, or the least sweet, darkest bitter type you can find. Bakers' chocolate may sometimes be referred to as cooking chocolate; chocolate-flavoured cake covering can also be euphemistically referred to as cooking chocolate as well, but it is quite a different product and to be avoided if you are hoping to make a good pudding or cake.

Store chocolate in a cool, dry, dark place. For information about melting chocolate, see pages 306–307.

$\mathscr{C}$AKE BAKING — SECRETS OF SUCCESS

CAKE TINS

Always use the size of tin specified in the recipe, or the cakes will turn out peaked, cracked or sunk in the middle. Choose good quality, rigid tins that will last well. Jumble sale and charity shops are good places to pick up really strong, old cake tins that only need a good scrub.

PREPARING TINS: tins without a non-stick finish should be greased and lined before use; non-stick tins need only a light greasing. Apply a thin film of melted margarine using a pastry brush, or rub a margarine paper round the tin with your fingers.

Line deep tins round the base and sides. To do this, cut a piece of greaseproof or non-stick silicone paper big enough so that when folded double it will be about 5 cm/2 inches wider than the tin depth. Fold up the folded edge of the strip about 2.5 cm/1 inch and snip with scissors along the folded portion in a slanting direction. Grease the tin and line the sides with the strip, with the snipped edge on the bottom, lying flat. The lining should stand about 2.5 cm/1 inch higher than the rim of the tin. Place a round of paper on the base of the tin to cover the snipped edge. Greaseproof paper should be greased, but non-stick paper does not require this.

To line sandwich or shallow tins, place the tin on a sheet of greaseproof paper and trace round the tin with a pen. Cut out the shape, which will fit the base exactly, grease the paper and then put it in the tin.

Lining a round cake tin:

Cut non-stick paper into double-strip wider than tin depth. Make slanting cuts along top of strip, then place round inside edge

Cut a circle to fit base and insert

Lining a cornered tin:

Use tin as guide to cut paper piece, larger all round

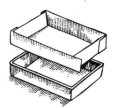

Fold edges up around tin, then fit snugly inside

Brush paper lightly with oil or butter

TEMPERATURES AND OVENS

Always preheat the oven in good time before you start to bake, and arrange the shelves before placing the cake in the oven. Heavy and rich fruit cakes will need low temperatures, and take longer to cook. If the oven is too hot the outside will burn before the inside has had time to cook. Lighter mixtures need hotter temperatures and faster baking times.

The new types of fan-assisted ovens circulate hot air round the oven, and they heat up very quickly, so reduce the temperature by 10% of what the recipe states. You may even need to reduce the cooking time. Get to know your oven and follow the manufacturer's instructions.

How to tell
WHEN A CAKE IS COOKED

☞ The centre of a cake is the very last part to bake, so cook for the time directed, then test the centre. For a sponge mixture, do this by pressing lightly with a fingertip: the cake should only give very slightly. If it feels springy, and no imprint remains, the cake is done. It should also have shrunk a little from the sides of the tin.

☞ Small cakes should be well risen, golden and just firm to the touch when pressed lightly.

☞ Lift large fruit cakes from the oven and listen to them! If the cake is not fully cooked, there will still be a bubbling or sizzling noise in the centre.

☞ To test creamed or fruit cakes, insert a very thin warmed metal skewer into the deepest part; it will come out perfectly clean if the cake is cooked. (To warm a skewer easily for testing, place it between the tin and the paper lining for a few seconds.)

Test creamed and fruit cakes by inserting a skewer

Cooling cakes

☞ All freshly baked cakes are very fragile whilst still warm, so leave them in the tin for at least 3 minutes before turning them out.

☞ Rich fruit cakes are very pliable when newly cooked, so leave these in the tin for longer. Very rich fruit cakes, like wedding cakes, should be left in the tin until completely cold.

☞ Loosen sponge cakes from the sides of the tin with a palette knife, then turn on to a wire rack. Immediately flip over on to another wire rack to prevent the top of the cake from being marked with a criss-cross pattern.

☞ Set delicate sponges, still in their tins, on a damp tea towel for a few minutes before turning out, and they will slip out more easily.

Leave cakes in tin for 3 minutes before turning out

*Turn sponge cakes on to a wire rack.
Flip on to another rack to avoid marking the top*

$\int$TORING AND FREEZING CAKES

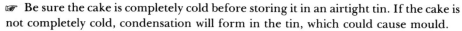

☞ Be sure the cake is completely cold before storing it in an airtight tin. If the cake is not completely cold, condensation will form in the tin, which could cause mould.

☞ Keep cakes with fresh cream fillings and icings in the refrigerator.

☞ Store cakes and biscuits separately, or the biscuits will go soggy.

☞ If you do not have a large airtight tin, invert a Pyrex bowl over the cake, being sure the bowl rests flat on the cake plate or work surface, and it will keep just as fresh.

☞ Store un-iced rich fruit cakes in their baking papers. Prick the surface of the cake and brush with a little brandy, then overwrap in clean greaseproof paper and seal with sticky tape. Overwrap again in a double layer of foil, and tape up tightly. Before icing and decorating wedding and Christmas cakes, keep them in storage for 6 weeks minimum, ideally 4 months, to mellow the flavour and produce a really rich moist texture.

☞ Fatless sponges will keep for 1–2 days only; Genoese sponges, 3 days; Victoria or creamed sponges, up to 1 week. Light fruit cakes will store in a tin for 2–2½ weeks, and rich fruit cakes a month or much longer if not cut.

☞ Each recipe gives freezer notes, but most undecorated cakes will freeze well. Overwrap in freezer film or bags or foil, trying to exclude as much air as possible. Unwrap before thawing, and allow plenty of time to thaw at room temperature.

$\mathcal{G}$UIDE TO
BETTER BAKING

$\mathcal{T}$here are various methods of baking. These are the main ones used in this book:

THE CREAMING METHOD

This is used for sponge and fruit cakes where the amount of fat is equal to all, or half, the weight of the flour. The key to success is lengthy beating of the fat with sugar to form a fluffy, light foundation into which the whole eggs or egg whites can be lightly beaten. Heavier ingredients, such as flour, nuts or dried fruits, are lightly folded into the creamed mixture. When adding the eggs, break them into a bowl and beat with a fork, then add to the creamed mixture slowly. If they are added too quickly, or they are too cold, the mixture will curdle. Adding a little flour with each addition of egg will help prevent the mixture separating at this stage.

THE WHISKING METHOD

This is used for light sponge-type cakes such as Genoese and angel cakes. Eggs are whisked with sugar until a thick ribbon will form when the whisk is lifted away. Flour and melted fat or oil are gently folded into the thick foamy mixture, which must be baked immediately or the air beaten in will be lost. To produce a good volume of air in the mixture, it must be warm. Place the mixing bowl over a pan or bowl of hot water, or gently heat the bowl and sugar first if using a table-top mixer. To achieve a golden crust, dust the cake tins after greasing with half flour and half caster sugar.

ALL-IN-ONE METHOD

Cakes made by this method are so quickly mixed, it is important not to start before you have heated the oven properly. All the ingredients are placed in one bowl and quickly beaten together. Soft tub margarines are the best fat to use in these cakes, and extra raising agent, usually baking powder, is needed, even if self-raising flour is used. Do not leave the mixture to stand before baking as the raising agent will start to work immediately.

RIGHT (from top to bottom): Rich Fruit Cake (see page 96), decorated with fondant icing (see page 164) and flowers (see page 179); Twelfth Night Cake (see page 99); Chocolate Yule Log, or *Bûche de Noël* (see page 50).

THE MELTED METHOD

This is used for cakes like gingerbread and honey cake. The fat and sugar, treacle or honey are gently heated together until melted, then cooled and beaten into the dry ingredients. The mixture must be beaten well with a wooden spoon at this stage, to develop the gluten in the flour. A raising agent and, usually, an egg are needed to add lightness. Because of their high sugar content, these cakes take longer to bake. It is imperative not to open the oven door for at least the first 45 minutes of baking, or the cake will collapse. Melted cakes are quick and easy to make and ideal for introducing children to baking.

OVEN TEMPERATURE CHART

°C	°F	Gas Mark	Temperature
110	225	¼	Very cool
130	250	½	Very cool
140	275	1	Very cool
150	300	2	Cool
160/170	325	3	Warm
180	350	4	Moderate
190	375	5	Fairly hot
200	400	6	Fairly hot
210/220	425	7	Hot
230	450	8	Very hot
240	475	9	Very hot

NOTES ON CONVERSIONS

The recipes in this book give ingredients in metric and imperial measures. It is important to follow only one set of measures, and never to mix them, as they are not exact equivalents.

The table below shows the equivalents used in this book.

25g	1oz
50g	2oz
75g	3oz
100g	4oz
150g	5oz
175g	6oz
200g	7oz
225g	8oz
250g	9oz
275g	10oz
300g	11oz
325/350g	12oz
375g	13oz
400g	14oz
425g	15oz
450g	16oz (1lb)
675g	1½lb
900g	2lb
1kg	2¼lb

All spoon measures are level unless otherwise noted. Spoon measures used are based on metric spoons: 1 tablespoon = 15ml, 1 teaspoon = 5ml.

LEFT (from top to bottom): Mocha Nut Squares (see page 89); Baklava (see page 87); Easy Cupcakes and Butterflies (see page 82).

$\mathscr{S}$PONGE AND LIGHT CAKES

CHAPTER ONE

*T*he key to making successful cakes by the creaming method is thorough beating of the fat and sugar, to give the cake a good base and to incorporate as much air as possible. Start by using butter or block margarine at room temperature or soft tub margarine, which are easier to cream. Use a balloon whisk, wooden spoon or electric mixer and beat vigorously until the mixture becomes pale and fluffy, and almost doubles in bulk. When well creamed, most mixtures will be very pale in colour, and soft and floppy in texture. It is then easy to incorporate the eggs, or egg yolks. Beat these in one at a time to prevent curdling the mixture, then fold in flour or nuts with a large metal spoon using a figure-of-eight motion, trying to keep in as much air as possible.

Cakes produced by the whisked or Genoese method have a lovely light texture, but do need skill to prepare. For the Genoese method, whole eggs and sugar are whisked together until a trail or ribbon forms when the whisk is lifted. The whisking is done in a bowl set over hot water to help thicken the mixture, and the use of an electric mixer really helps, as this mixture needs beating for a long time until the correct consistency is achieved.

SPONGE AND
LIGHT CAKES

CLASSIC VICTORIA
SANDWICH

*This cake was made in the time of Queen Victoria, when only butter
was used. Butter does give a rich colour and flavour to a plain
cake, so do use it if you can. The secret of a sponge cake is in the
creaming so always ensure the butter and sugar mixture is really
light and fluffy. I learnt this by experience when I had to make 200
Victorias for a TV flour commercial!*

- 175 G/6 OZ BUTTER OR
  BLOCK MARGARINE,
  AT ROOM TEMPERATURE
- 175 G/6 OZ CASTER SUGAR
- 3 EGGS, SIZE 3, AT ROOM
  TEMPERATURE, BEATEN
- 175 G/6 OZ SELF-RAISING
  FLOUR, SIFTED
- FEW DROPS VANILLA ESSENCE,
  OR 1/2 TSP GRATED LEMON ZEST
- ICING SUGAR, TO DREDGE
- **FILLING:**
- 4–5 TBSP RASPBERRY JAM
- 150 ML/1/4 PINT WHIPPING
  CREAM, WHIPPED

1 Set the oven to 180°C/350°F/Gas 4. Grease and base-line two 20cm/8inch round
sandwich tins.

2 Put the butter or margarine in a bowl and beat until very soft, using an electric
mixer if possible. Add the sugar and beat together until the mixture is light, fluffy
and pale in colour.

3 Beat in the eggs, a little at a time, adding a teaspoon of the flour with each
addition to prevent the mixture from curdling. Gently fold in the remaining flour
with the essence or zest and 1 tbsp water.

4 Divide the mixture between the tins and spread level. Bake in the centre of the
oven for about 30 minutes or until well risen, light golden and firm to the touch.
Leave to cool in the tins for at least 3 minutes, then turn out on to wire racks to cool
completely. Peel away the lining paper when cold.

5 Place the base of one cake on your prettiest serving plate and spread with
raspberry jam; cover the underside of the other with whipped cream and sandwich
together. Sprinkle with sifted icing sugar and serve immediately.

TO FREEZE: *Wrap unfilled sponges in foil. Keeps for 3 months.*

Illustrated opposite page 33

GENOESE SPONGE

*This is a very light sponge that keeps well, providing a good base for
a decorated special occasion cake. Add the butter very gradually in
a slow thin trickle to avoid making the cake heavy.*

- 3 EGGS, SIZE 2
- 75 G/3 OZ CASTER SUGAR, STORED WITH A VANILLA POD
- 65 G/2½ OZ PLAIN FLOUR
- 1 TBSP CORNFLOUR

- 40 G/1½ OZ BUTTER, MELTED AND COOLED
- FILLING AND TOPPING (SEE STEP 7)

1 Set the oven to 180°C/350°F/Gas 4. Grease and base-line two 18cm/7inch sandwich tins or one 20cm/8inch round deep cake tin.

2 Place the eggs and sugar in a heatproof bowl and set over a large saucepan of hot water. Whisk until very thick and pale, and firm enough to leave a ribbon trail when the whisk is lifted. This will take about 6–7 minutes using an electric mixer at medium speed. Remove from the hot water and continue whisking until cool.

3 Sift the flour and cornflour together. Gradually fold half into the whisked mixture using a large metal spoon.

4 Gradually fold in the melted butter alternately with the remaining flour mixture, using as light a touch as possible or the butter will sink and the cake will be heavy.

5 Pour into the tin(s) and bake above the centre of the oven for about 25 minutes for the sandwich tins and 35–40 minutes for the deep cake tin. The cakes should be well risen, firm to the touch and just beginning to shrink away from the sides of the tin.

6 Leave to cool in the tin for about 3 minutes, then turn out on to a wire rack to cool completely. Peel away the lining paper when cold.

7 Cut the larger cake into two or three horizontal layers. Sandwich with filling and decorate (see Icings and Fillings, pages 156–71, and Cake Decoration, pages 172–87).

TO FREEZE: *Wrap unfilled cake in foil. Keeps for up to 2 months.*

ALL-IN-ONE
SPONGE CAKE

*This is the easiest and quickest sponge cake to make. As the cake is
not beaten for long, you need to add baking powder for extra
lightness. The cake freezes well, retaining all its moisture.*

- 175 G/6 OZ SELF-RAISING FLOUR
- 1 TSP BAKING POWDER
- 175 G/6 OZ CASTER SUGAR

- 175 G/6 OZ SOFT TUB MARGARINE
- FEW DROPS VANILLA ESSENCE
- 3 EGGS, SIZE 3, BEATEN

1 Grease and base-line the tin of required size (see chart below). Set the oven to
180°C/350°F/Gas 4.

2 Sift the flour and baking powder into a bowl, then add all the remaining
ingredients.

3 Beat together with a wooden spoon quickly until combined. Do not overbeat or
the mixture will become wet. Add the chosen flavouring variation if required (see
opposite).

4 Spread the mixture in the tin and bake according to the chart below or until the
sponge is light golden and springy to the touch. Leave to cool in tin for about 3
minutes, then run a knife round the inside of the tin and turn the cake on to a wire
rack to cool completely. Decorate when cold.

TIN SIZES & COOKING TIMES
20cm/8inch round deep tin: 50 minutes – 1 hour
two 18cm/7inch sandwich tins: 30 minutes
15cm/6inch square deep tin: 50 minutes
20cm/8in ring mould: 40 minutes
900g/2lb loaf tin: 50 minutes
23cm/9in shallow slab tin: 40 minutes

TO FREEZE: *Wrap undecorated in freezer bags or foil. Keeps for 3 months.*

QUICK VARIATIONS
FOR ALL-IN-ONE
SPONGE CAKES

CHOCOLATE CHIP

Fold 100g/4oz small chocolate drops into the basic mixture.

LEMON

Stir the grated zest of 2 lemons and 1 tbsp lemon juice into the basic mixture.

ORANGE

Stir the finely grated zest of 2 oranges and the chopped, seeded flesh of 1 orange into the basic mixture.

GINGER

Finely chop 3 pieces of preserved stem ginger in syrup and add to the basic mixture.

CHERRY

Wash, drain and chop 100g/4oz glacé cherries and fold into the basic mixture with 25g/1oz ground almonds.

WALNUT

Fold 75g/3oz chopped walnuts into the basic mixture.

BUTTERSCOTCH

Use only 100g/4oz caster sugar to make the basic mixture. Melt 75g/3oz cream toffees with 1 tbsp golden syrup in a small pan or in the microwave oven. Leave to cool, then add to the mixture.

MOCHA

Replace 2 tbsp flour with cocoa powder. Dissolve 1 tbsp instant coffee powder in 2 tbsp boiling water and cool, then add to the mixture.

MARBLED CHOCOLATE AND ORANGE

Divide the basic mixture in half. To one half add 1 tbsp cocoa powder dissolved in 1 tbsp boiling water and cooled. To the other half add 1 tbsp orange juice and 1 tsp finely grated orange zest. Place alternate tablespoons of the mixture in the tin, then draw the spoon through the mixture, swirling it as you go to create a marbled pattern.

ℒEMON MADEIRA CAKE

This classic cake keeps well for up to a week in an airtight tin, and provides a good base for novelty cakes as it cuts firmly. Originally it was decorated with a strip of citron peel on top, but this is very difficult to obtain these days.

- 175 G/6 OZ BUTTER, AT ROOM TEMPERATURE
- 175 G/6 OZ CASTER SUGAR
- 3 EGGS, SIZE 3, BEATEN
- 175 G/6 OZ SELF-RAISING FLOUR
- 75 G/3 OZ PLAIN FLOUR

- FINELY GRATED ZEST OF 1 LEMON
- 1 TBSP LEMON JUICE
- 1 THIN SLICE CITRON PEEL (OPTIONAL)

1 Grease and base-line a 20cm/8inch round deep cake tin. Set the oven to 170°C/325°F/Gas 3.

2 Beat the butter and sugar together until light, fluffy and pale in colour. Gradually add the eggs, beating well after each addition. Add a teaspoon of flour if the mixture begins to curdle.

3 Sift the flours together, then fold into the mixture with the lemon zest and juice.

4 Spoon into the tin and level the top. If using the citron peel, place in the centre. Bake in the centre of the oven for about 1 hour and 10 minutes or until firm to the touch. Leave to cool in the tin for 10 minutes, then turn out on to a wire rack to cool completely. Peel away the lining paper when cool.

𝒪LD ENGLISH SEED CAKE

This is a variation of Madeira cake which has been baked here for over 300 years. It was always served with a glass of sweet wine for morning refreshment in Victorian times. What a shame the habit has died out.

Follow the Madeira cake recipe above, omitting the lemon zest, juice and citron peel. Add the following with the flours: 1 TBSP GROUND ALMONDS, 1 TBSP CARAWAY SEEDS AND 2 TBSP MILK.

TO FREEZE: *Freeze the cake whole or in slices, wrapped in freezer bags. Keeps for up to 3 months.*

TIP: *Any leftover stale pieces of Madeira cake are excellent used in trifles. Sprinkle with a little sherry before use.*

Illustrated opposite page 32

$\mathcal{A}$NGEL CAKE

If you ever have a surfeit of egg whites and are wondering what to do with them, make an angel cake. It is fatless, delicate and totally delicious. You really do need a large tube or ring cake tin, however, as if the angel cake is baked in an ordinary tin, the outside will dry out before the middle sets.

Turn cake out by inverting tin over a funnel

- 75 G/3 OZ PLAIN FLOUR
- 50 G/2 OZ CORNFLOUR
- 100 G/4 OZ ICING SUGAR
- 1 TSP CREAM OF TARTAR
- FEW DROPS VANILLA ESSENCE
- FEW DROPS ALMOND ESSENCE
- 10 EGG WHITES, SIZE 3
- 175 G/6 OZ CASTER SUGAR
- TOPPING (SEE STEP 6)

1 Set the oven to 190°C/375°F/Gas 5. Have ready an ungreased 25cm/10inch tubular or ring cake tin.

2 Sift the flour, cornflour and icing sugar together.

3 Take a large bowl and scald it with boiling water to ensure it is completely grease-free. Dry thoroughly, then add the cream of tartar, essences and egg whites. Whisk, preferably with an electric mixer, until the egg whites form soft peaks. Whisk in the caster sugar, a little at a time, and continue whisking until the mixture forms stiff peaks.

4 Fold in the flour mixture one-quarter at a time. Be careful not to overmix. Spoon into the ungreased tin, trying to ensure there are no large air bubbles.

5 Bake in the centre of the oven for about 45 minutes or until the cake lightly springs when touched with a fingertip. Remove from the oven and invert the tin on a wire rack over a funnel. Leave to cool upside-down in the tin, until completely cold.

6 Gently run a palette knife round the sides of the tin to release the cake, then turn out on to a serving plate. Serve the cake plain, or covered with seven-minute frosting (see page 166) or Italian meringue (see page 168), decorated with a thinly sliced lime and served with a sharp fresh raspberry sauce.

Not suitable for freezing.

Illustrated opposite page 128

*Pour caramel on to cake
and smooth over*

Mark cake into eight sections

DOBOS TORTE

*This gâteau is named after its creator, Dobos, a famous Hungarian
pâtissier from Budapest. It makes a really spectacular centrepiece
for a party.*

- 5 EGGS, SIZE 3
- 175 G/6 OZ CASTER SUGAR
- 150 G/5 OZ PLAIN FLOUR
- 50 G/2 OZ SHELLED HAZELNUTS,
CHOPPED AND TOASTED,
TO DECORATE
- **CARAMEL GLAZE:**
- 150 G/5 OZ CASTER SUGAR

- **CHOCOLATE CREAM:**
- 100 G/4 OZ DARK PLAIN
CHOCOLATE
- 225 G/8 OZ UNSALTED BUTTER,
AT ROOM TEMPERATURE
- 3 EGG WHITES, SIZE 3
- 150 G/5 OZ ICING SUGAR,
SIFTED

1 Take six sheets of non-stick silicone paper, each large enough to line a baking
sheet. Draw a 20cm/8inch circle on each sheet of paper. (An easy way to do this is to
trace round a saucepan lid.) Line one or more baking sheets with paper. Set the oven
to 200°C/400°F/Gas 6.

2 Place the eggs and sugar in a heatproof bowl and set this over a large saucepan of
hot water. Whisk until very thick and pale, and firm enough to leave a ribbon trail
when the whisk is lifted. Remove from the heat and continue whisking until cool.

3 Sift one-third of the flour over the mixture and fold it in, then continue with the
remaining flour in the same way.

4 Carefully spread one-sixth of the mixture on to each lined baking sheet inside the
drawn circle, making a neat round. Bake for 6–8 minutes until golden brown. Loosen
from the sheets and trim any edges while still warm, then leave to cool on the paper
on wire racks. Re-line the baking sheets, and bake six layers in total.

5 Take the round with the best and flattest surface and place it on an oiled baking
sheet. Put the caster sugar into a small, heavy-based saucepan and heat gently,
without stirring, until it melts and turns a light brown. Immediately pour the caramel
over the cake round on the baking sheet, spreading it out with an oiled palette knife.
Mark into eight sections, then trim the edges. Leave to cool and set.

6 To make the chocolate cream, place the chocolate in a small heatproof bowl and
set over a pan of warm water, until the chocolate has melted. Set aside to cool slightly.
Beat the butter until pale and fluffy, then beat in the chocolate until well combined.

7 Place the egg whites and icing sugar in a heatproof bowl set over a pan of hot
water and whisk until thick. Stir 2 tbsp into the chocolate mixture to soften it, then
fold in the remainder.

Illustrated opposite page 33

8 Fill a small piping bag fitted with a star nozzle with a few tablespoons of the chocolate cream. Sandwich the cake rounds together with two-thirds of the remaining chocolate cream, using the caramel-glazed cake for the top. Spread the sides of the cake with the remaining chocolate cream, then press the chopped nuts neatly on to the sides.

9 Pipe the chocolate cream into a neat star border all around the top of the cake between the caramel and the hazelnuts.

Not suitable for freezing.

ALL-IN-ONE BIRTHDAY SPONGE

I call this a birthday sponge because I've been called on to make so many cakes at the last minute, and you can mix this one up in a trice. The evaporated milk helps keep it moist, so you can bake it the day before, or freeze it and ice it later when you have more time.

- 100 G/4 OZ SOFT TUB MARGARINE
- 100 G/4 OZ CASTER SUGAR
- 170 G/6 OZ SELF-RAISING FLOUR
- 2 EGGS, SIZE 3, BEATEN
- 3 TBSP EVAPORATED MILK
- ½ TSP VANILLA ESSENCE, OR FINELY GRATED ZEST OF ½ LEMON
- FILLING AND TOPPING (SEE STEP 5)

1 Set the oven to 190°C/375°F/Gas 5. Grease and line a 20cm/8inch round deep cake tin.

2 Place all the ingredients in a large bowl and beat with an electric mixer for 2 minutes, or for 3–4 minutes by hand, until smooth and creamy.

3 Spoon into the tin and spread level. Bake for about 45 minutes or until firm to the touch in the centre and pale golden.

4 Leave to cool in the tin for 5 minutes, then turn out on to a wire rack and peel away the lining paper.

5 When cold, split and fill with cream or jam, and cover with buttercream, frosting or fondant icing (see pages 170, 166 or 164).

TO FREEZE: *Wrap unfilled cake in foil. Keeps for 3 months.*

$\mathcal{T}$ IPSY CAKE

This cake doubles up as a wonderful pudding. You could cheat and make it with bought sponge cakes, but the home-made ones really taste best.

- GENOESE SPONGE CAKE (SEE PAGE 23), BAKED IN TWO 18 CM/7 INCH SANDWICH TINS
- 4 TBSP APRICOT GLAZE (SEE PAGE 169)
- 25 G/ 1OZ AMARETTI BISCUITS, ROUGHLY CRUSHED
- 25 G/ 1OZ PLAIN CHOCOLATE, COARSELY GRATED
- 25 G/ 1OZ FLAKED ALMONDS

- 4 TBSP GOLDEN SYRUP
- 2 TBSP AMARETTO OR OTHER ALMOND LIQUEUR
- 2 TBSP TIA MARIA, KALUHA OR OTHER COFFEE LIQUEUR
- 300 ML/½ PINT WHIPPING CREAM, SOFTLY WHIPPED OR 1 QUANTITY SEVEN-MINUTE FROSTING (SEE PAGE 166)

1 Split the two sponge cakes in half horizontally, and spread the bottom layer of each with apricot glaze. Roughly chop the other 2 layers into large pieces. Divide the pieces into three portions. Mix the amaretti biscuits into one portion, the chocolate into another portion, and the flaked almonds into the third.

2 Gently warm the golden syrup in two separate bowls set in a pan of hot water. Add the almond liqueur to one and the coffee liqueur to the other. When the syrup is liquid, pour the almond syrup over the cake and almond mixture and stir; pour the coffee syrup over the chocolate and cake mixture and stir.

3 Place one glaze-covered cake layer on a serving plate. Cover with the soaked and plain cake pieces alternately and pat together neatly, then place the other jam-covered layer on top, glaze side down. Press together, then chill for 4 hours to firm the cake.

4 Cover the cake with cream or seven-minute frosting, swirled roughly round the top and sides. Decorate with fondant, frosted or real flowers (see pages 179–81 or 185) to serve.

Not suitable for freezing.

Illustrated opposite page 32

$\mathcal{B}$ATTENBERG CAKE

This sponge cake, made from coloured squares, makes a popular addition to the tea table. It originated in Germany, when Prince Henry of Battenberg married Beatrice, one of Queen Victoria's daughters (the name changed later to Mountbatten).

- 100 G/4 OZ BUTTER, AT ROOM TEMPERATURE
- 100 G/4 OZ CASTER SUGAR
- 2 EGGS, SIZE 3, BEATEN
- FEW DROPS ALMOND ESSENCE
- 100 G/4 OZ SELF-RAISING FLOUR, SIFTED
- PINK FOOD COLOURING

TO FINISH:
- 3 TBSP RASPBERRY JAM
- 4 TBSP APRICOT GLAZE (SEE PAGE 169)
- 225 G/8 OZ ALMOND PASTE (SEE PAGE 160)

1 Set the oven to 180°C/350°F/Gas 4. Grease and base-line an 18cm/7inch square cake tin.

2 Beat the butter and sugar together until light, fluffy and pale in colour. Add the eggs gradually, beating well after each addition. Add the almond essence, then gradually fold in the flour with a metal spoon. Divide the mixture in half and colour one half pink with the food colouring.

3 Spoon the plain mixture in one half of the tin, divide with a strip of foil, making a neat line in the middle, then spoon the pink mixture on the other side. Smooth the top level, then bake in the centre of the oven for 30–35 minutes or until firm to the touch in the middle. Cool in the tin for 3 minutes, then turn out of the tin, remove the lining paper and leave to cool.

4 Divide the cake down the middle into a pink half and a white half, then cut each half in half lengthways to form four oblongs. Brush two long sides of each piece with raspberry jam and stack them on top of each other to form a chequerboard pattern.

5 Brush the four long sides of the cake with apricot glaze, leaving the ends free. Roll out the almond paste into a rectangle to fit the length of the cake and four times the width of one side. Place the cake on the almond paste and press it round to cover all the sides. Make a fluted ridge on the top edges by pinching the paste between your thumb and forefinger. Score a diamond pattern on the top with a sharp knife.

TO FREEZE: *Wrap finished cake in foil. Keeps for 3 months.*

Illustrated opposite page 33

Cut both cake colours into four oblongs

Stack alternate colours, securing with jam

Roll almond paste into a rectangle and wrap over

Pinch paste on top edges to flute

Spread sponge base
with warmed jam

Roll up from the short end

When rolled, cool on
a wire rack

RIGHT (from top to
bottom): Tipsy Cake
(see page 30); Old
English Seed Cake (see
page 26); Swiss Roll
(see above).

$\mathcal{S}$ WISS ROLL

A Swiss roll can double up as a useful pudding, served with cream
or fromage frais and fresh fruit. It can also be made ahead and
filled just before serving.

- 3 EGGS, SIZE 2
- 100 G/4 OZ CASTER SUGAR
- 100 G/4 OZ PLAIN FLOUR

- 6 TBSP WARMED JAM
- ICING SUGAR, TO DREDGE

1 Brush a 33 × 23cm/13 × 9inch Swiss roll tin with melted margarine. Cut a piece of greaseproof paper 5cm/2inches larger than the tin all round. Place in the tin, snipping the corners to fit, then brush the paper with melted margarine. Set the oven to 200°C/400°F/Gas 6.

2 Place the eggs and caster sugar in a heatproof bowl and set over a saucepan of hot water. Whisk, using an electric mixer if possible, until very thick and pale, and firm enough to leave a ribbon trail when the whisk is lifted. Remove from the heat and continue whisking until cold.

3 Sift half the flour into the mixture and fold in with a large metal spoon. Fold in 1 tbsp warm water and then the rest of the flour.

4 Pour into the prepared tin, spreading the mixture evenly into all the corners. Bake for 7–10 minutes until golden and firm to the touch.

5 While the cake is baking, make preparations for turning it out: wring out a clean tea towel in hot water and spread it out on a work surface. Spread a sheet of greaseproof paper on top of this and sprinkle with caster sugar.

6 Turn the cooked cake out of the tin directly on to the sugared paper. Working quickly, while the cake is still hot, peel off the lining paper and trim away the crusty edges. Spread with the warmed jam to within 1cm/½inch of the edges.

7 Roll up from a short side, using the paper to help guide you. When completely rolled up, leave covered in the paper to stop the cake from unrolling. To serve, remove the paper, sift icing sugar lightly over and slice.

How to fill with cream instead of jam:
Roll up as above, but without the jam and rolling the sugared paper inside, to prevent the cake sticking to itself. Leave to cool completely. When cold, unroll very carefully, trying to avoid cracking the cake, and remove the paper. Spread with ¼ pint/150 ml whipped cream, or cream and small pieces of fruit, and roll up again carefully.

TO FREEZE: *Wrap unfilled cake in foil. Keeps for 3 months.*

Illustrated opposite

WHAT WENT WRONG?

☞ **THE CAKE HAS A DOMED TOP:**
This happens if the mixture is not creamed enough, or the cake was baked in too hot an oven or on too high a shelf in the oven.

☞ **THE SPONGE HAS A CLOSE, DOUGHY TEXTURE:**
This happens if you add too much egg, fat or flour, or too little raising agent. Inadequate creaming or beating or underbaking can also cause this.

☞ **SPECKLES ON TOP OF THE CAKE:**
Insufficient creaming could cause this, because the sugar remains undissolved before baking; or insufficient sifting of ingredients together.

☞ **A CRUSTY RING FORMS ROUND THE SIDES:**
Over-greasing the tins can cause this.

☞ **HOLES OR TUNNELS FORM IN THE CENTRE OR THE TEXTURE IS UNEVEN:**
This can be caused by overmixing or uneven mixing when folding in flour. A mixture that is too dry can trap pockets of air and this will also happen if the raising agent and flour are not properly sifted together.

☞ **WHISKED SPONGE IS VERY SHALLOW AND DOES NOT RISE:**
This happens if the mixture is not whisked sufficiently, or it is baked in too cool an oven.

☞ **THE TOP SINKS IN THE MIDDLE:**
This can happen if the mixture contained too much raising agent, the fat and sugar were overcreamed, or soft tub margarine was used (only use this for quick all-in-one mixes). Using too cool an oven or opening and slamming the door during baking can also cause this.

☞ **SWISS ROLL IS THIN AND BADLY RISEN:**
The mixture did not contain enough air, due to insufficient whisking.

☞ **SWISS ROLL CRACKED WHEN ROLLED:**
The cake was not rolled quickly enough before cooling, or the crusty edges were not trimmed off.

LEFT (from top to bottom): Dobos Torte (see page 28); Classic Victoria Sandwich (see page 22); Battenberg Cake (see page 31).

CHOCOLATE CAKES

CHAPTER TWO

*C*hocolate came to us from the New World in the 16th century, and the craze for it has never left us. Smooth and rich in texture and flavour, chocolate is loved by almost everyone, including the gods – its Greek name theobroma cacao *means 'food of the gods'. It was considered as great a luxury as gold by the Aztecs and was served to the men only at the court of Montezuma. Female members were forbidden it, possibly because of its reputed aphrodisiac powers! It still has very romantic connotations today, as is seen by the popularity of chocolate cakes and chocolates on Valentine's Day.*

The flavour of chocolate blends beautifully with many spices, fruits, liqueurs and cream to form the most decadent of luxuries – chocolate cake! Served for morning coffee, lunch, tea or as a pudding, eaten day or night, it is the most self-indulgent treat ever.

CHOCOLATE
CAKES

Melt chocolate in a
double saucepan

WORKING WITH
CHOCOLATE AND COCOA

Chocolate needs to be pampered and treated with respect; if not, it will show its prima donna-like qualities and become temperamental and obstinate and refuse to co-operate. Be gentle with it and it will comply with your every wish.

FOLLOW THESE RULES FOR SUCCESS:

☞ Always buy the most expensive chocolate available. Price is a good indication of quality and the flavour of real chocolate far outweighs the economic gains of the cheaper varieties, which may not contain real cocoa fat.

☞ Store chocolate and cocoa in a cool, dark place. Wrap opened chocolate tightly in foil, and it will keep almost indefinitely. Use cocoa powder within a year as it tends to taste musty after this.

☞ To melt chocolate successfully, place the broken pieces in the top of a double boiler over warm but not hot water. If you do not have a double boiler, put the chocolate in a small heatproof bowl over a pan of warm water. Make sure the pan or bowl containing the chocolate is completely dry – water and steam are the enemy while the chocolate is melting (you can, however, melt chocolate with milk, butter or water as long as these are added to the pan with the chocolate – see below). Also make sure the base of the pan or bowl does not actually touch the water. Heat very gently, melting without stirring, for about 10 minutes. If the chocolate reaches a temperature higher than blood heat, it will lose its sheen on cooling.

☞ If the chocolate gets too hot and starts to stiffen, stir in a little vegetable margarine – not butter.

☞ If chocolate comes into contact with water or steam it becomes a thick rough mass that will refuse to melt. This can be corrected by stirring in a little vegetable oil or margarine, 1 teaspoon at a time, until the mixture becomes smooth again. This is an emergency measure though, and may alter the final balance of the recipe.

☞ Combine the melted chocolate with other ingredients while it is warm and easy to pour. Try to keep other liquids at the same temperature, as a liquid hotter than the chocolate, or ice cold, will cause the cocoa butter to separate and make the chocolate lumpy.

☞ If chocolate is melted together with milk, butter or water, the process can be done directly over a gentle heat in a heavy-based pan, but you will need to stir and watch it all the time.

☞ White chocolate is the most difficult to work with. It helps to grate it finely first, and keep the heat very low when melting. If white chocolate starts to 'tighten', add a few drops of boiling water to smooth it.

☞ Cocoa grains need to be cooked for the full flavour to emerge, so blend to a paste with boiling water before adding to a cake mixture.

☞ Don't substitute drinking chocolate for cocoa powder, as this contains sugar and milk powder and will spoil the flavour of a cake.

☞ Chocolate can be successfully melted in a bowl in the microwave oven. Use short bursts of power to avoid over-cooking, depending on the amount of chocolate being used.

SACHERTORTE

This is one of the world's most popular chocolate cakes and should be served simply, covered in chocolate icing, with the word 'Sacher' piped across. Use only the finest quality dark chocolate for this cake.

- 150 G/5 OZ PLAIN CHOCOLATE
- 150 G/5 OZ UNSALTED BUTTER, AT ROOM TEMPERATURE
- 150 G/5 OZ CASTER SUGAR, STORED WITH A VANILLA POD
- 6 EGGS, SIZE 2, SEPARATED
- 150 G/5 OZ PLAIN FLOUR, SIFTED

- 6 TBSP APRICOT GLAZE (SEE PAGE 169)
- 50 G/2 OZ MILK CHOCOLATE
- **CHOCOLATE ICING:**
- 175 G/6 OZ PLAIN CHOCOLATE
- 4 TBSP BLACK COFFEE
- 175 G/6 OZ ICING SUGAR

1 Grease, base-line and flour a loose-based 20cm/8inch round deep cake tin. Set the oven to 180°C/350°F/Gas 4.

2 Break up the chocolate and melt it gently in a heatproof bowl set over a pan of warm water, or in the microwave oven. Cool slightly. Beat the butter with half the sugar until light, fluffy and pale in colour. Beat in the melted chocolate, then the egg yolks, one at a time.

3 Whisk the egg whites until stiff, then fold them gently into the mixture with the flour and remaining sugar. Spoon into the prepared tin and level the top. Bake for about 1¼ hours or until a skewer inserted into the middle comes out clean. Leave to cool in the tin for 10 minutes, then turn out on to a wire rack to cool completely.

4 If the cake has domed, slice a thin layer off the top to level it. Cut the cake horizontally in half. Heat the glaze and use 2 tablespoons to sandwich the layers together. Spread the rest of the glaze over the top and sides of the cake.

Cut cake horizontally in half

5 To make the icing, melt the chocolate with the coffee in a small heatproof bowl set over a pan of warm water. Gradually sift in the icing sugar, beating well. Working very quickly, spread the icing over the top and down the sides of the cake, using a large palette knife. The icing will thicken as it sets, so make sure all bare patches are covered and smooth. Place the cake on a serving plate and leave the icing to set for about 2 hours.

Sandwich layers together with warm glaze

6 For the icing melt the milk chocolate in a small heatproof bowl set over a pan of warm water, then place in a greaseproof paper piping bag (see page 182). Snip off the end, then pipe the word 'Sacher' on top of the cake. Leave to set for 30 minutes.

TO FREEZE: *Open-freeze decorated or undecorated, then store in a rigid container. Keeps for 3 months. Thaw for 4 hours before serving.*

Illustrated opposite page 49

Spread chocolate icing over glaze with a palette knife

ℬROWNIES

MAKES 12

Brownies keep nicely moist in an airtight tin for 4–5 days, and are ideal for freezing.

- 150 G/5 OZ BLOCK MARGARINE, AT ROOM TEMPERATURE
- 2 TBSP COCOA POWDER
- 150 G/5 OZ DARK MUSCOVADO SUGAR

- 2 EGGS, SIZE 3, BEATEN
- 50 G/2 OZ SELF-RAISING FLOUR
- 50 G/2 OZ SHELLED WALNUTS, ROUGHLY CHOPPED

1 Grease and line an 18cm/7inch square cake tin. Set the oven to 180°C/350°F/Gas 4.

2 Melt 50g/2oz of the margarine and stir in the cocoa, then set aside to cool slightly.

3 Cream the remaining margarine with the sugar until light and fluffy, then gradually beat in the eggs. Fold in the flour, walnuts and the cocoa mixture.

4 Spread the mixture in the tin and smooth the surface level. Bake for 35–45 minutes until firm to the touch in the centre. Leave to cool in the tin, then turn out, remove the lining paper and cut into twelve squares.

TO FREEZE: *Wrap in foil. Keeps for 3 months.*

Illustrated opposite page 48

BLACK FOREST KIRSCHTORTE

Morello cherries, Kirsch, chocolate and cream provide a combination that makes this one of the most popular cakes ever. It is so irresistible I often serve it as a dinner party pudding, and it can be prepared well ahead of time.

- 5 EGGS, SIZE 2
- 175 G/6 OZ CASTER SUGAR
- 50 G/2 OZ PLAIN FLOUR
- 50 G/2 OZ COCOA POWDER
- 75 G/3 OZ BUTTER, MELTED AND COOLED
- **FILLING:**
- 1 × 425 G/15 OZ TIN MORELLO CHERRIES

- 5–6 TBSP KIRSCH
- 1 TBSP ARROWROOT
- 600 ML/1 PINT WHIPPING OR DOUBLE CREAM
- **DECORATION:**
- 225 G/8 OZ PLAIN CHOCOLATE
- 15–20 FRESH BLACK CHERRIES, IF AVAILABLE

1 Grease, base-line and flour two 20cm/8inch round sandwich tins. Set the oven to 180°C/350°F/Gas 4.

2 Put the eggs and sugar in a large heatproof bowl and set over a pan of hot water. Whisk until the mixture is very thick and pale and firm enough to leave a ribbon trail when the whisk is lifted. (You will need to whisk for about 8 minutes.) Remove from the hot water and continue whisking until the mixture is almost tripled in bulk, about 10 minutes.

3 Sift the flour and cocoa together into the whisked mixture, and fold in very gently. When the flour is almost incorporated, slowly pour in the melted butter in a thin stream, folding gently. Try not to be heavy-handed at this stage or the finished cake will be flat and heavy.

4 Divide the mixture between the tins and spread evenly. Bake for 25–30 minutes or until springy to the touch in the centre, and slightly shrunken away from the sides of the tins. Leave to cool in the tins, then turn out on to a wire rack and peel away the lining paper. When cold, cut each cake in half horizontally using a thin sharp knife.

5 To make the filling, drain the syrup from the cherries into a bowl and mix in the Kirsch. Blend half the syrup mixture with the arrowroot in a saucepan and boil until thickened, stirring constantly. Cool, then stir in the drained cherries. Sprinkle the remaining syrup over the four sponge layers.

6 Whip the cream until it forms soft peaks, then set half aside. Sandwich two layers together with one-third of the remaining cream and place on a serving plate. Spread another one-third on top, then spread over the cherries. Sandwich the remaining two layers with the remaining third of cream and place on top, so that the cherries are sandwiched in the centre layer.

Continued overleaf

7 Half fill a piping bag fitted with a star nozzle with some of the reserved cream, and spread the rest over the top and sides of the cake. Pipe the cream in two rings on top of the cake, then refrigerate.

8 Make chocolate curls (see page 184) with the plain chocolate, and press on to the sides of the cake. Place the fresh cherries between the two rings of piped cream. (If fresh cherries are not in season, decorate the top with extra chocolate curls.)

TO FREEZE: *Place in a rigid container, without the fresh cherries. Keeps for 3 months.*

Illustrated opposite page 48

*D*EVIL'S FOOD CAKE

This American cake is ideal for birthdays, covered in chocolate fudge icing (see page 168) or white seven-minute frosting (see page 166). Store it in an airtight tin for up to a week.

- 175 G/6 OZ PLAIN FLOUR
- 1 TSP BAKING POWDER
- ½ TSP BICARBONATE OF SODA
- 50 G/2 OZ COCOA POWDER
- 100 G/4 OZ BUTTER, AT ROOM TEMPERATURE

- 225 G/8 OZ DARK MUSCOVADO SUGAR
- 2 EGGS, SIZE 3
- 4 TBSP SOURED CREAM OR PLAIN YOGURT
- FILLING AND TOPPING (SEE STEP 5)

1 Grease and base-line two 20cm/8inch round sandwich tins. Set the oven to 190°C/375°F/Gas 5.

2 Sift the flour, baking powder and soda into a bowl. Mix the cocoa with 6 tbsp (90 ml) boiling water to make a smooth paste.

3 Cream the butter and sugar together until light and fluffy. Beat in the eggs, the soured cream or yogurt and the cocoa mixture, then fold in the sifted flour.

4 Divide the mixture evenly between the tins and level the tops. Bake for 30–35 minutes in the centre of the oven, until firm to the touch, cool in the tins for 3 minutes, then turn out on to wire racks to cool. Remove the lining paper from the cakes while still hot.

5 Sandwich the cakes together with chocolate fudge icing or seven-minute frosting, and spread over the top and sides as well.

TO FREEZE: *Wrap unfilled cake in foil. Keeps for 3 months.*

Illustrated opposite page 160

$\mathcal{D}$ECADENT CHOCOLATE ROULADE

This roulade makes a wonderful treat for tea or a dinner party pudding. It is always moist and delicious, and can easily be made the day before. Roulades have a tendency to crack, but I feel this improves their appearance – in life, nothing is perfect!

- 1 TBSP INSTANT COFFEE GRANULES
- 100 G/4 OZ PLAIN CHOCOLATE
- 4 EGGS, SIZE 2, SEPARATED
- 100 G/4 OZ CASTER SUGAR
- CASTER OR ICING SUGAR, TO DREDGE

- **FILLING:**
- 300 ML/½ PINT DOUBLE CREAM
- 1 TBSP GRAND MARNIER OR OTHER ORANGE LIQUEUR

1 Grease and line a 28 × 33cm/11 × 13inch Swiss roll tin with non-stick silicone paper (see lining a Swiss roll tin, page 32). Set the oven to 180°C/350°F/Gas 4.

2 Make the coffee into a smooth paste with 1 tbsp water. Melt the chocolate gently in a heatproof bowl set over warm water or in the microwave oven, then leave to cool slightly.

3 Whisk the egg yolks and sugar together in a bowl over hot water, using an electric beater, until thick and pale. Remove from heat, then stir in the cooled coffee and chocolate. Whisk the egg whites until stiff. Fold 2 tbsp into the chocolate mixture to loosen it, then fold in the remaining whites carefully, trying to keep the mixture as light as possible.

4 Spread the mixture in the tin and bake in the centre of the oven for about 15 minutes. The top of the cake will be crusty, but underneath it will be very moist. Place the tin on a wire rack, cover with a clean, damp tea towel, and leave overnight. This will make the crust soften.

5 Sprinkle a large sheet of greaseproof paper with caster or sifted icing sugar. Remove the tea towel, then turn out the cake on to the sugared paper. Peel off the lining paper and trim the crusty edges of the cake.

6 Whip the cream until stiff, then fold in the orange liqueur. Spread over the cake, then roll up carefully, using the paper to help you lift and roll. Place on a serving dish and dust with more sugar. You may find the roulade cracks on the surface, but this is quite normal. Decorate with chocolate curls or leaves (see page 184) if you want to cover any bad cracks.

Not suitable for freezing.

Illustrated opposite page 160

$\mathscr{D}$ELICIOUSLY MOIST
BIRTHDAY CAKE

This dark, moist chocolate cake is really easy to make and keeps well. I often use it as a base for birthday cakes as it can be made a few days ahead, which gives plenty of time to concentrate on the decoration.

- 75 G/3 OZ COCOA POWDER
- 175 G/6 OZ BUTTER, AT ROOM TEMPERATURE
- 275 G/10 OZ CASTER SUGAR
- 3 EGGS, SIZE 3, BEATEN
- 275 G/10 OZ PLAIN FLOUR
- 1 ½ TSP BICARBONATE OF SODA
- ½ TSP BAKING POWDER
- FILLING AND TOPPING (SEE STEP 6)

1 Dissolve the cocoa in 350 ml/12 fl oz boiling water, then leave until cold – this will take about 25 minutes.

2 Grease and line a 20cm/8inch round deep cake tin. Set the oven to 180°C/350°F/ Gas 4.

3 Cream the butter and sugar together until light and fluffy, then gradually beat in the eggs, adding a teaspoon of flour with each addition, to keep the mixture smooth.

4 Sift the remaining flour, the bicarbonate of soda and baking powder together into the creamed mixture. Fold in with the cocoa mixture until smooth.

5 Pour the mixture into the tin. Bake for about 1 hour or until firm to the touch. Leave to cool in the tin for 5 minutes, then turn out on to a wire rack to cool completely.

6 Sandwich the cake together with raspberry or apricot jam, or cream flavoured with liqueur. Cover with cream and chocolate curls (see page 184) or fondant icing (see page 164).

TO FREEZE: *Wrap undecorated cake in foil or freezer bag. Keeps for up to 2 months.*

$\mathcal{S}$QUIDGY CHOCOLATE FUDGE LAYER

This really is one of the richest of cakes — chocolate cake with a rich chocolate ganache filling. Sheer heaven! I'm informed that chocolate eaten in the morning is not quite as fattening as that eaten later in the day, so a slice for morning coffee is perfectly O.K.

- 250 G/9 OZ PLAIN CHOCOLATE
- 1 TBSP INSTANT COFFEE POWDER
- 2 TBSP BRANDY
- 4 EGGS, SIZE 3
- 1 TSP VANILLA ESSENCE
- 50 G/2 OZ SOFT LIGHT BROWN SUGAR
- 1 TBSP CORNFLOUR
- 25 G/1 OZ COCOA POWDER
- COCOA POWDER, TO DREDGE
- **CHOCOLATE GANACHE:**
- 150 ML/¼ PINT DOUBLE CREAM
- 100 G/4 OZ PLAIN OR MILK CHOCOLATE

1 Lightly oil a 900g/2lb loaf tin and line the base and sides with non-stick silicone paper. Set the oven to 180°C/350°F/Gas 4.

2 Break the chocolate into pieces and put in a heatproof bowl. Add the coffee powder, brandy and 2 tbsp water. Place over a pan of warm water, or in the microwave oven, and heat gently until melted. Stir together, then leave to cool.

3 Whisk the eggs, vanilla essence, sugar and cornflour together until very thick. Fold in the cooled chocolate mixture. Sift in the cocoa powder and fold in.

4 Pour the mixture into the prepared tin and bake for 1 hour to 1 hour 10 minutes or until a skewer inserted into the middle comes out clean. Leave to cool in the tin for 10 minutes, then turn out on to a wire rack to cool completely. The cake keeps well, and becomes softer after 1 day, so keep it overnight, if possible, before cutting it into layers.

5 To make the ganache filling, place the cream in a small saucepan and bring to the boil. Remove from the heat and add the chocolate, broken into pieces. Stir until completely melted, then return to the heat and bring back to the boil. Pour into a bowl and cool. If made ahead of time, keep in the refrigerator until needed, then soften at room temperature for about 1 hour before use.

6 To assemble the cake, cut carefully into three layers lengthways and sandwich back together with the ganache filling, spread or piped. Sift over cocoa powder and decorate with chocolate leaves (see page 184), if liked.

TO FREEZE: *Freeze unfilled cake in a rigid container, as it is delicate. Keeps for 3 months.*

*R*ICH CHOCOLATE AND ALMOND LAYER CAKE

A wickedly luxurious chocolate cake sandwiched together with almond cream and coated in a glossy layer of chocolate.

- 100 G/4 OZ PLAIN CHOCOLATE
- 4 EGGS, SIZE 3, SEPARATED
- FEW DROPS ALMOND ESSENCE
- 175 G/6 OZ BUTTER, AT ROOM TEMPERATURE
- 175 G/6 OZ DARK MUSCOVADO SUGAR
- 175 G/6 OZ SELF-RAISING FLOUR
- 25 G/1 OZ GROUND ALMONDS
- 25 G/1 OZ COCOA POWDER
- 3–4 TBSP MILK

- **FILLING:**
- 150 ML/¼ PINT DOUBLE OR WHIPPING CREAM
- 3–4 TBSP AMARETTO OR OTHER ALMOND LIQUEUR
- **TOPPING:**
- 175 G/6 OZ PLAIN CHOCOLATE
- 150 ML/¼ PINT DOUBLE CREAM
- 50 G/2 OZ PLAIN CHOCOLATE, MADE INTO CURLS (SEE PAGE 184)
- 8 WHOLE, SKINNED ALMONDS
- 1 TBSP COCOA POWDER

1 Set the oven to 180°C/350°F/Gas 4. Grease and base-line a 20cm/8inch round loose-based or spring-clip cake tin.

2 Break up the chocolate into pieces and put into a heatproof bowl with 4 tbsp boiling water. Melt over a pan of warm water until smooth. Remove from the heat and beat in the egg yolks and almond essence.

3 Cream the butter and sugar together until light and fluffy, then beat in the chocolate mixture. Sift the flour, almonds and cocoa together, then fold into the creamed mixture with the milk. Whisk the egg whites until they form soft peaks. Fold 2 tbsp into the mixture to loosen it, then fold in the remaining egg whites gently.

4 Spoon the mixture into the prepared tin. Bake in the centre of the oven for 50–60 minutes or until firm to the touch in the centre. Leave to cool in the tin, then turn out and peel away the lining paper. Slice the cake into three layers horizontally using a long sharp knife.

5 To make the filling, whip the cream with the liqueur until stiff. Use to sandwich the cake layers together.

6 To make the topping, break the chocolate into pieces and melt gently in a heatproof bowl over a pan of warm water. Stir in the cream, then quickly spread over the top and sides of the cake, to give a smooth finish. Press the chocolate curls round the side of the cake whilst still wet.

7 Dip the almonds in any leftover chocolate mixture to coat them. Leave to dry, then roll the nuts in the cocoa powder. Press the almonds into the top of the cake to decorate.

TO FREEZE: *Wrap filled cake in foil. Keeps for 3 months. Decorate after thawing.*

Illustrated opposite page 160

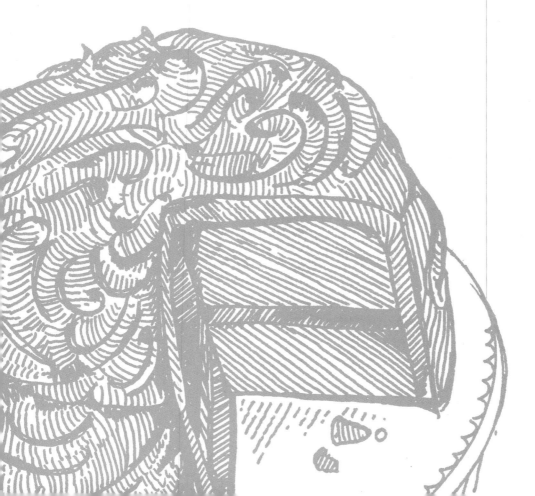

*Spoon alternative cake colours
around ring mould*

*When cooked, loosen edges
and turn out*

RIGHT (from top to
bottom): Black Forest
Kirschtorte (see page
41); Austrian
Chocolate and Orange
Ring Cake (see above);
Brownies (see page 40).

$\mathcal{A}$USTRIAN CHOCOLATE AND ORANGE RING CAKE

*This moist ring cake combines the flavours of chocolate and orange
which complement each other deliciously. For extra luxury, sprinkle
the cake with an orange liqueur before covering.*

- 50 G/2 OZ PLAIN CHOCOLATE
- 225 G/8 OZ UNSALTED BUTTER, AT ROOM TEMPERATURE
- 225 G/8 OZ SOFT BROWN SUGAR
- 4 EGGS, SIZE 2
- 225 G/8 OZ PLAIN FLOUR
- 2 TSP BAKING POWDER
- PINCH SALT
- 50 G/2 OZ GROUND ALMONDS

- FINELY GRATED ZEST ½ ORANGE
- 2 TBSP FRESH ORANGE JUICE
- **CHOCOLATE ICING AND DECORATION:**
- 175 G/6 OZ PLAIN CHOCOLATE
- 100 G/4 OZ UNSALTED BUTTER
- 50 G/2 OZ MILK CHOCOLATE

1 Set the oven to 180°C/350°F/Gas 4. Lightly butter a 1.7 litre/3 pint ring mould.

2 Break up the chocolate and melt in a small heatproof bowl set over a pan of warm water, or in the microwave oven. Add 1 tbsp water and stir, then remove from the heat to cool.

3 Cream the butter and sugar together until light and fluffy. Beat in the eggs one at a time, adding a little flour with each to prevent curdling.

4 Sift the remaining flour, the baking powder, salt and almonds together, then sift again into the creamed mixture. Stir in the orange zest and juice.

5 Place half the mixture in a separate bowl and stir in the cooled melted chocolate. Place large spoonfuls of each mixture alternately in the ring mould. Smooth the top level, then draw a knife through the mixture, turning the mould clockwise at the same time to swirl the two mixtures together. Level the top again.

6 Bake for 50 minutes to 1 hour or until a warmed skewer inserted into the deepest part comes out clean. Leave in the tin to cool for 3 minutes then turn out on a wire rack to cool.

7 To make the chocolate icing, break the plain chocolate into a heafproof bowl and add 2 tbsp water and the butter. Set over a pan of warm water, or in the microwave oven, and melt, stirring occasionally. Pour the icing over the cold cake and quickly spread it evenly over the sides. Leave to set for 1 hour.

8 To decorate, melt the milk chocolate, place in a small paper piping bag (see page 182) and snip a small hole in the end. Drizzle the chocolate over the cake in a zig-zag pattern and leave to set.

TO FREEZE: *Wrap undecorated cake in foil. Keeps for 2 months. Ice after thawing.*

Illustrated opposite

Chocolate Mincemeat Cake

Make this cake around Christmas time. It's based on a jar of mincemeat, but you can vary the fruit and nuts, and so on, according to whatever is in the store-cupboard. It makes a good last-minute Christmas or New Year party cake, and will keep well for up to 2 weeks.

- 100 G/4 OZ BUTTER, AT ROOM TEMPERATURE
- 100 G/4 OZ DARK MUSCOVADO SUGAR
- 3 EGGS, SIZE 3, BEATEN
- 225 G/8 OZ WHOLEMEAL SELF-RAISING FLOUR
- 1 TSP MIXED SPICE
- 1 × 400 G/14 OZ JAR MINCEMEAT
- 75 G/3 OZ RAISINS
- 50 G/2 OZ GLACÉ CHERRIES, RINSED, DRIED AND HALVED
- 100 G/4 OZ PLAIN CHOCOLATE, COARSELY GRATED
- 50 G/2 OZ SHELLED PECAN NUTS OR WALNUTS, ROUGHLY CHOPPED (OPTIONAL)
- TOPPING (OPTIONAL, SEE STEP 5)

1 Set the oven to 160°C/325°F/Gas 3. Grease and line a 20cm/8inch round deep cake tin or an 18cm/7inch square tin.

2 Cream the butter and sugar together until light and fluffy, then beat in the eggs gradually, adding a little flour with each addition.

3 Sift the remaining flour and spice into the bowl, add the bran from the sieve and fold in with all the remaining ingredients. Spoon into the prepared tin, make a slight hollow in the centre to allow for even rising, and spread the sides level.

4 Bake in the centre of the oven for just under 2 hours. Test with a skewer: if it comes out clean, the cake is done. Leave to cool in the tin.

5 If liked, cover with a thin layer of almond paste (see page 160) and royal or fondant icing (see page 162 or 164); alternatively brush the surface with honey and sprinkle with demerara sugar.

TO FREEZE: *Wrap undecorated cake tightly in foil. Keeps for 3 months.*

Illustrated opposite page 96

LEFT (from top to bottom): Spicy Date and Rum Cake (see page 63); Sachertorte (see page 39); Honey Cake (see page 60).

CHOCOLATE YULE LOG
(BÛCHE DE NOËL)

SERVES 10

In France, the Bûche de Noël, *or Christmas log, is traditionally eaten as the main festive cake. In Britain, we tend to serve it for family teas and gatherings together with a classic rich fruit Christmas cake – oh, we are greedy!*

- 90 G/3½ OZ SELF-RAISING FLOUR
- 2 TBSP COCOA POWDER
- PINCH SALT
- 4 EGGS, SIZE 3

- 100 G/4 OZ CASTER SUGAR
- FILLING AND TOPPING (SEE STEP 6)
- ICING SUGAR, TO DREDGE

1 Set the oven to 220°C/425°F/Gas 7. Oil and line a 23 × 33cm/9 × 13inch Swiss roll tin with oiled greaseproof paper.

2 Sift together the flour, cocoa and salt.

3 Place the eggs and sugar in a large heatproof bowl and set over a pan of hot water. Whisk until thick, remove from the hot water and continue whisking until the mixture is very thick and pale and firm enough to leave a ribbon trail when the whisk is lifted. Fold in half the flour mixture. Fold in the remaining flour with 1 tbsp hot water.

4 Pour the mixture into the prepared tin and spread evenly. Bake for about 10 minutes or until firm to the touch.

5 Have ready a dampened tea towel spread out flat and a large sheet of greaseproof paper on top of it, dusted with caster sugar. Turn out the sponge on to the paper, peel away the lining paper and trim the crusty edges quickly with a sharp knife. Loosely roll up the sponge, rolling the sugared paper inside. Leave the cake to cool, keeping it in a nice rounded shape.

6 To decorate, cover and fill with chocolate buttercream (see page 170) or crème au beurre (see page 167). Mark on lines with a fork to resemble wood, sprinkle with icing sugar, and decorate with holly or Christmas novelties.

TO FREEZE: *Wrap in foil or in a rigid container. Keeps for 3 months. Fill and ice after thawing.*

Illustrated opposite page 16

CARIBBEAN CAROB CAKE

I've included this delicious carob cake for those poor unfortunates who cannot eat chocolate – a fate worse than death as far as I'm concerned! The combination of pineapple and carob makes the cake taste very chocolatey, and you'll fool your guests into thinking it's the real thing.

- 2 TBSP CAROB POWDER
- 225 G/8 OZ SOFT VEGETABLE MARGARINE, AT ROOM TEMPERATURE
- 225 G/8 OZ SOFT LIGHT BROWN SUGAR
- 4 EGGS, SIZE 3
- 1 TSP VANILLA ESSENCE
- 225 G/8 OZ SELF-RAISING FLOUR

- 50 G/2 OZ CAROB BAR, TO DECORATE
- **FILLING:**
- 100 G/4 OZ FULL-FAT SOFT CHEESE
- 450 G/1 LB FROMAGE FRAIS
- 1 TBSP CASTER SUGAR
- 1 × 425 G/15 OZ TIN CRUSHED PINEAPPLE, WELL DRAINED

1 Grease and base-line a 22cm/8½–9inch round deep cake tin. Set the oven to 180°C/350°F/Gas 4.

2 Mix the carob powder with 4 tbsp cold water. Cream the margarine and sugar together until light and fluffy, then gradually whisk in the carob mixture, the eggs and vanilla essence. Gently fold in the flour.

3 Spread the mixture in the tin, and make a slight hollow in the centre. Bake for about 1 hour or until a skewer inserted in the middle comes out clean, with no mixture sticking to it.

4 Leave in the tin until almost cold, then turn out and peel away the lining paper. Cut the cake horizontally into three layers.

5 To make the filling, soften the cheese in a bowl, then beat in the fromage frais and sugar. Mix in the crushed pineapple.

6 Use one-third of the filling to sandwich the cake layers together. Spread the remaining filling over the top and sides of the cake. Coarsely grate the carob bar and sprinkle over the top and sides of the cake. Refrigerate until needed.

TO FREEZE: *Wrap undecorated cake in foil. Keeps for up to 2 months.*

$\mathscr{S}$PICY CAKES

CHAPTER THREE

From the time of the ancient Greeks and Romans, spices have been highly prized, and used in baking. The opening of trade routes in the Middle Ages brought spices like ginger, cloves, and cinnamon to Europe, which featured in the recipes of the rich. Sweet spice cakes were eaten as a luxury, and many of the cakes we know today, particularly continental ones, have their origins in these times. Spices were also thought to be highly medicinal, and cakes like gingerbread were taken as part of a 'cure'.

Today, spices are cheap, plentiful and easily available. They can provide a wealth of smooth, warm and mellow flavours to cakes and breads. Baking would be very dull indeed without the existence of cinnamon, nutmeg and all the wonderful spices that add those extra flavours and aromas we all love. No longer do you have to be rich or royal to enjoy the privilege of spices, so make the most of the extensive ranges sold in the shops today.

SPICY CAKES

KEEPING SPICES

Most of the seeds, bark and roots that we buy as spices are dried. They have a fairly long shelf life, but will not keep well indefinitely so follow these tips for storing them:

☞ Spices gradually lose their aroma, and some are past their best in three months, so buy your spices in small quantities, only when you need them.

☞ A pretty spice rack looks very nice in a kitchen, but remember the spices in it are deteriorating quickly.

☞ Both light and heat affect the flavour, so if you do use clear glass jars keep them stored away in a drawer cupboard, out of the light.

☞ Small tins with tightly fitting lids are ideal containers preferable to glass if you can find them.

☞ If your kitchen is hot and steamy or you have an Aga, or oven that is constantly burning, then find a cooler place for your spices.

☞ Don't tip spices straight from the jar into hot or steamy mixtures. The steam will go into the jar, causing the spices to get damp and quickly deteriorate.

☞ Whole spices can be freshly ground in a small electric mill or pestle and mortar. They have a much stronger flavour and aroma than the ground ones, so use them more sparingly.

☞ Nutmeg can be ground freshly into cake mixtures by grating the whole spice on a very fine grater. The flavour will be far superior than that of the dried, ground variety, but do remember the extra strength it has and cut down the amount used in the recipe.

☞ If you do use freshly ground spices in recipes, cut down the amount stated in the recipe by half.

$\mathcal{P}$ASSION CAKE

Passion or carrot cakes have been national favourites in the USA for years, and Mrs Beeton was fond of using carrots in jams and puddings. Luckily, the carrot has made a comeback with the 'healthy eating' trend. I love carrot cake with its spicy, mellow flavour and moist texture. It is popular at children's parties, too.

- 275 G/10 OZ PLAIN FLOUR
- PINCH SALT
- 1 TSP BICARBONATE OF SODA
- 2 TSP BAKING POWDER
- 2 TSP GROUND CINNAMON
- 175 G/6 OZ SOFT BROWN SUGAR
- 50 G/2 OZ SHELLED WALNUTS, CHOPPED
- 3 EGGS, SIZE 3

- 2 RIPE BANANAS, MASHED
- 150 G/5 OZ CARROTS, FINELY GRATED
- 175 ML/6 FL OZ VEGETABLE, CORN OR SUNFLOWER OIL
- SOFT CHEESE ICING (SEE PAGE 167)
- DECORATION (SEE STEP 4)

1 Grease and base-line a 22cm/8½inch loose-based or spring-clip cake tin. Set the oven to 180°C/350°F/Gas 4.

2 Sift the flour, salt, bicarbonate of soda, baking powder and cinnamon into a bowl and add the sugar and nuts. Add the eggs and bananas and beat well, then mix in the carrots and oil.

3 Spoon the mixture into the tin. Bake for 50 minutes to 1 hour or until firm to the touch in the centre. Leave to cool in the tin.

4 Turn out the cake and cover the top with soft cheese icing. Sprinkle with chopped walnuts, or use whole ones and place in a circle on top; alternatively make tiny carrots from coloured almond paste (see page 160), and place in a circle on top.

TO FREEZE: *Freeze with or without cheese icing, wrapped in foil. Keeps for 3 months un-iced, 6 weeks iced.*

Illustrated opposite page 64

Cinnamon-Crusted

CHEESECAKE

Not all cheesecakes have to be made with double cream and full-fat soft cheese. This recipe is my favourite, given to me by an Austrian chef, and is light and feathery. My guests usually ask for seconds!

- 75 G/3 OZ BUTTER
- 1½ TSP GROUND CINNAMON
- 225 G/8 OZ CAKE CRUMBS, FINELY GRATED
- ICING SUGAR, TO DREDGE
- FRESH FRUIT, TO DECORATE
- **FILLING:**
- 6 EGGS, SIZE 3, SEPARATED
- 225 G/8 OZ CASTER SUGAR

- FINELY GRATED ZEST AND JUICE 1 LEMON
- 450 G/1 LB LOW-FAT SOFT CHEESE OR CURD CHEESE
- 225 ML/8 FL OZ PLAIN SET YOGURT
- 2 TBSP PLAIN FLOUR
- 1 TBSP BRANDY, RUM OR SHERRY

1 Line the base and sides of a 23cm/9inch loose-based or spring-clip cake tin with a sheet of foil, shiny side towards you. Lightly grease the foil. Set the oven to 180°C/350°F/Gas 4.

2 Melt the butter in a pan over a low heat or in the microwave oven. Stir the cinnamon into the cake crumbs, then mix into the melted butter. Press the crumb mixture over the base and up the sides of the tin.

3 Whisk the egg yolks with the sugar until light and fluffy, then stir in the lemon zest and juice, cheese, yogurt, flour and alcohol. Whisk the egg whites until stiff and fold into the cheese mixture.

4 Pour the filling into the crumb crust. Bake for 1 hour, then turn off the heat. Leave the cake in the cooling oven for another hour, but check it doesn't get too brown. Cool the cheesecake in the tin, then refrigerate in the tin until needed.

5 To serve, remove the sides of the tin and carefully peel away the foil. Dust the top with sifted icing sugar and decorate with fresh fruit – redcurrants, raspberries or strawberries, and kiwi fruit look pretty.

Not suitable for freezing.

ORKNEY GINGERBREAD

This is a good-keeping cake for the cake tin, and it improves with a few days' storage. It is eaten in Scotland spread with butter and sometimes served with cheese or apples. Don't be put off by the very wet texture before baking; the mixture is supposed to be like this. This is a quickly made cake, and easy enough for children who want to lend a hand.

- 150 G/5 OZ PLAIN FLOUR
- PINCH SALT
- 1 TSP GROUND GINGER
- 1 TSP GROUND CINNAMON
- 2 TSP BAKING POWDER
- 150 G/5 OZ PORRIDGE OATS
- 175 G/6 OZ DARK MUSCOVADO SUGAR

- 6 TBSP DARK TREACLE
- 100 G/4 OZ BUTTER OR BLOCK MARGARINE
- 1 EGG, SIZE 3, BEATEN
- 300 ML/½ PINT MILK
- 100 G/4 OZ RAISINS
- 50 G/2 OZ SLIVERED ALMONDS

1 Set the oven to 180°C/350°F/Gas 4. Grease and then line a 20cm/8inch round deep cake tin.

2 Sift the flour, salt, spices and baking powder into a large bowl and stir in the oats and sugar.

3 Gently heat the treacle and fat together in a saucepan or the microwave oven until the fat has melted. Stir into the flour mixture with the egg and milk. Add the raisins and nuts and mix well. The mixture will have a very wet consistency.

4 Pour into the cake tin. Bake in the centre of the oven for 1¼–1½ hours or until firm to the touch in the centre. Leave to cool in the tin, then turn out and peel off the lining paper. Store in an airtight tin until required.

TO FREEZE: *Wrap in foil. Keeps for 2 months.*

ℋONEY CAKE

The ancient Greeks and Romans believed that honey would give
them a longer and healthier life, and they liked to eat baked small
cakes made with honey instead of sugar. This modern version will
be just as popular today.

- 300 ML/½ PINT CLEAR HONEY
- 75 G/3 OZ BUTTER
- 350 G/12 OZ WHOLEMEAL FLOUR
- 2 TSP MIXED SPICE
- 1 TSP BICARBONATE OF SODA
- 50 G/2 OZ CHOPPED CANDIED
  MIXED PEEL

- 3 EGGS, SIZE 3
- 3 TBSP MILK
- FINELY GRATED ZEST
  1 LEMON
- 50 G/2 OZ FLAKED ALMONDS

1 Set the oven to 170°C/325°F/Gas 3. Grease and line a 20cm/8inch square cake tin or 18cm/7inch round deep cake tin.

2 Spoon out 4 tbsp honey and reserve. Pour the rest of the honey into a saucepan, add the butter and heat until melted, keeping the heat low.

3 Sift the flour, spice and soda into a bowl and add any remaining bran left in the sieve. Stir in the mixed peel. Beat the eggs, milk and zest together, then add to the dry mixture with the cooled honey. Beat together until well combined, then pour into the cake tin.

4 Sprinkle over the almonds. Bake for about 1¼ hours or until firm and a skewer inserted in the middle comes out clean.

5 Leave to cool in the tin for 5 minutes, then turn out on to a wire rack. Prick the top of the cake with a skewer and brush over the reserved honey while the cake is still warm.

TO FREEZE: *Wrap tightly in foil. Keeps for 2 months.*

Illustrated opposite page 49

APFELKUCHEN

This rich, moist cake has a shortbread-like quality. Serve it hot as a pudding, or cold as a cake.

- 300 G/11 OZ SELF-RAISING FLOUR
- 200 G/7 OZ CASTER SUGAR
- 225 G/8 OZ BUTTER, AT ROOM TEMPERATURE
- 1 EGG, SIZE 2
- 450 G/1LB COOKING APPLES, PEELED, CORED AND SLICED
- 50 G/2 OZ SULTANAS
- 1 TBSP CLEAR HONEY
- 1½ TSP GROUND CINNAMON
- 100 G/4 OZ FLAKED ALMONDS
- ICING SUGAR, TO DREDGE

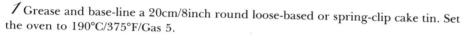

1 Grease and base-line a 20cm/8inch round loose-based or spring-clip cake tin. Set the oven to 190°C/375°F/Gas 5.

2 Place the flour and sugar in a bowl and rub in the butter until the mixture resembles fine breadcrumbs. Stir in the egg and knead lightly to make a smooth dough. Divide in half and press half into the tin to line the base, levelling as much as possible. Bake for 15–20 minutes until golden.

3 Meanwhile, place the apples, sultanas, honey, cinnamon and 2 tbsp water in a saucepan. Cover and cook for 5–6 minutes. Cool, then spoon on to the cooked pastry base.

4 Roll out the remaining dough to 1cm/½inch thick. Cut out a round the size of the tin. Scatter 25g/1oz almonds on top of the apple mixture, then press the dough round on top. Sprinkle over the remaining almonds.

5 Bake for a further 30 minutes or until the pastry top is firm. Leave to cool in the tin, then turn out and sprinkle with sifted icing sugar to serve.

TO FREEZE: *Wrap in foil. Keeps for 6 months.*

RICH GINGER CAKE

A truly delicious, sticky cake that improves with keeping. Wrap it in greaseproof paper, then keep in a tin for 2–3 days. Beware of prying hands!

- 100 G/4 OZ BUTTER OR BLOCK MARGARINE, AT ROOM TEMPERATURE
- 100 G/4 OZ SOFT BROWN SUGAR
- 2 EGGS, SIZE 3
- 1 TBSP GOLDEN SYRUP
- 1 TBSP DARK TREACLE
- 225 G/8 OZ PLAIN FLOUR
- ½ TSP GROUND GINGER
- ½ TSP BAKING POWDER
- 100 G/4 OZ PRESERVED STEM GINGER, CHOPPED
- **DECORATION** (OPTIONAL):
- 150 ML/¼ PINT DOUBLE CREAM, WHIPPED
- 10–12 BRANDY SNAPS

1 Set the oven to 190°C/375°F/Gas 5. Grease and line an 18cm/7inch round deep cake tin.

2 Cream the fat and sugar together until light and fluffy. Beat in the eggs one at a time, followed by the syrup and treacle.

3 Sift in the flour, ground ginger and baking powder, then fold in gently with the preserved ginger. Spoon into the tin and smooth level.

4 Bake for about 1 hour or until firm in the centre. Leave to cool in the tin for 5 minutes, then turn out on to a wire rack to cool completely.

5 To decorate, pipe cream into the brandy snaps and spread the remaining cream over the top of the cake. Arrange the brandy snaps on the cream in a circle like the spokes of a wheel.

TO FREEZE: *Wrap undecorated cake in foil. Keeps for 3 months.*

$\mathscr{S}$PICY DATE AND RUM CAKE

The flavours of dark rum, dates and spices blend together to make this a favourite for the cake tin. It will keep for 3 weeks.

- 225 G/8 OZ BUTTER, AT ROOM TEMPERATURE
- 175 G/6 OZ SOFT LIGHT BROWN SUGAR
- 3 TBSP DARK TREACLE
- 4 EGGS, SIZE 3, BEATEN
- 350 G/12 OZ WHOLEMEAL SELF-RAISING FLOUR
- 2 TSP GROUND NUTMEG
- 2 TSP GROUND CINNAMON
- 2 TSP GROUND GINGER
- 50 G/2 OZ FLAKED ALMONDS
- 225 G/8 OZ STONED DATES, ROUGHLY CHOPPED
- 350 G/12 OZ MIXED DRIED FRUIT
- 3 TBSP DARK RUM
- TOPPING (SEE STEP 4)

1 Set the oven to 150°C/300°F/Gas 2. Grease and line a 20cm/8inch square cake tin or a 23cm/9inch round deep cake tin, using a double layer of greaseproof paper.

2 Cream the butter and sugar together until light and fluffy, then beat in the treacle. Beat in the eggs gradually, adding a spoonful of flour with each one. Sift the remaining flour and the spices into the mixture, adding any bran left in the sieve, and fold in with the almonds, dates, fruit and rum.

3 Spoon into the tin and smooth level. Bake for about 2 hours or until firm to the touch in the centre. Leave to cool in the tin for 10 minutes, then turn out on to a wire rack to cool completely.

4 Sprinkle over more dark rum for extra flavour if liked. Spread with apricot glaze (see page 169) and sprinkle with demerara sugar, or cover with almond paste (see page 160) and ice with fondant or royal icing (see page 164 or 162).

TO FREEZE: *Wrap undecorated in foil. Keeps for 4 months.*

Illustrated opposite page 49

SCANDINAVIAN SPICED APPLE CAKE

The flavours of apples and warm spices have always complemented each other. They blend well together in this unusual, moist cake.

- 100 G/4 OZ BUTTER, AT ROOM TEMPERATURE
- 225 G/8 OZ DARK MUSCOVADO SUGAR
- 2 EGGS, SIZE 3, BEATEN
- 225 G/8 OZ WHOLEMEAL SELF-RAISING FLOUR
- ¼ TSP SALT
- 1 TSP GROUND CINNAMON
- ¼ TSP GROUND CLOVES
- 1 TSP VANILLA ESSENCE
- 275 G/10 OZ COOKING APPLES, PEELED, CORED AND COARSELY GRATED
- **TOPPING:**
- 1 TBSP CLEAR HONEY
- 1–2 TBSP TOASTED FLAKED ALMONDS

1 Set the oven to 180°C/350°F/Gas 4. Grease and line a 20cm/8inch round deep cake tin or a 18cm/7inch square cake tin.

2 Cream the butter and sugar together until light and fluffy, then beat in the eggs one at a time. Sift the flour, salt and spices into the creamed mixture, add the bran from the sieve and fold in with the vanilla essence and apples.

3 Spread the mixture in the prepared tin and level the top. Bake for about 1¼ hours or until lightly browned and the sides of the cake are beginning to shrink away from the tin.

4 Leave to cool in the tin for 5 minutes, then turn out on to a wire rack to cool completely.

5 Brush the top of the cake with the honey, then arrange the nuts over. Eat within 2–3 days, sliced and buttered.

Not suitable for freezing.

Illustrated opposite

RIGHT (from top to bottom): Apricot, Caraway and Brandy Ring (see page 68); Passion Cake (see page 57); Scandinavian Spiced Apple Cake (see above).

$\mathcal{G}$INGERBREAD HOUSE

'Crack, crack, crunch,
who is nibbling at my house?'
(Hansel and Gretel, Grimm's Fairy Tales).

*The witch won't get you if you eat this gingerbread house,
but it does deserve to be on display for a few days at Christmas first,
as a charming centrepiece.*

- 3 TBSP GOLDEN SYRUP OR HONEY
- 175 G/6 OZ BUTTER, AT ROOM TEMPERATURE
- 175 G/6 OZ MUSCOVADO SUGAR
- 3 EGG YOLKS, SIZE 3
- 700 G/1 ½ LB PLAIN FLOUR
- 1 ½ TSP BICARBONATE OF SODA
- 2 TSP GROUND GINGER
- 1 TSP MIXED SPICE
- 1 TBSP COCOA POWDER
- 9–10 TBSP MILK
- **DECORATION:**
- 900 G/2 LB ROYAL ICING (SEE PAGE 162)

1 Oil 4 baking sheets. Set the oven to 180°C/350°F/Gas 4. Copy the templates, seen below, out on to card and cut out.

2 Melt the golden syrup or honey in a small pan or in the microwave oven. Cream the butter and sugar together until light and fluffy, then beat in the egg yolks one at a time. Sift in the flour, soda, spices and cocoa and fold in with a spoon. Add the syrup or honey and enough milk to make a soft but not sticky dough. Knead until smooth.

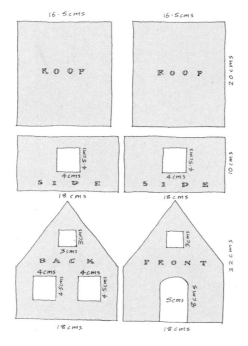

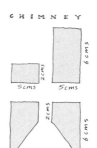

Templates for gingerbread house

Continued overleaf

LEFT: Gingerbread House (see above).

3 Roll out the dough between two sheets of non-stick paper on a floured surface to about 5mm /¼inch thick. Cut out the pieces using the templates: (1 front of house with windows, 1 back of house, 2 roof panels, 2 sides of house with windows, 1 door, 12 window shutters, 1 door and 4 chimney pieces). Lift them carefully on to the baking sheets (use a fish slice to help).

4 Bake for 15 minutes. Allow to cool on the sheets for the windows to set. Check the shapes against the templates and if necessary trim them to shape whilst still warm. Leave on a wire rack until firm enough to handle – 4–5 hours.

5 To assemble the house, fill a greaseproof paper piping bag (see page 182) with royal icing. Snip the end and pipe along the base and side edges of the frame. Fix in position on a 30cm/12inch square cake board. Support with a cardboard food pack or tin until dry. When the walls are set and firm, fix on the two roof panels, and hold in place until firm. Stick the chimney together and position in place with icing. Attach the lintel over the door, and set the door in position, slightly ajar. Stick the shutters to the lower windows. Leave the house to dry out until firm before decorating.

6 Pipe on roof tiles with royal icing, dripping it over the sides for a snow effect. Pipe on royal icing round the windows.

Not suitable for freezing.

Illustrated opposite page 65

Cut out dough pieces using templates

Assemble sides of house first

Decorate house with piped royal icing

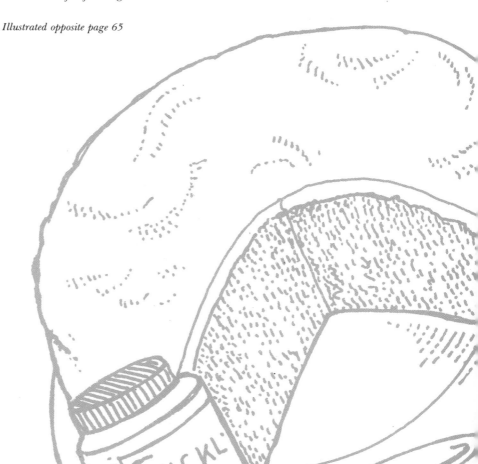

Nuremberg Nut Cake

This lovely cake is a collection of all of my favourite things – nuts, chocolate, spices and honey. It is so rich I often cut it into small squares and serve it as a petits fours cake with coffee.

- 100 G/4 OZ SHELLED HAZELNUTS OR PECAN NUTS
- 100 G/4 OZ WHOLE SKINNED ALMONDS
- 100 G/4 OZ CHOPPED CANDIED MIXED PEEL
- 100 G/4 OZ GLACÉ CHERRIES, HALVED
- 100 G/4 OZ SULTANAS OR RAISINS
- 50 G/2 OZ PLAIN FLOUR
- 40 G/1 ½ OZ COCOA POWDER
- 1 TSP GROUND CINNAMON
- ¼ TSP GROUND CLOVES
- ¼ TSP GROUND GINGER
- PINCH GROUND CARDAMOM (OPTIONAL)
- 75 G/3 OZ MUSCOVADO SUGAR
- 100 G/4 OZ CLEAR HONEY
- ICING SUGAR, TO DREDGE

1 Set the oven to 180°C/350°F/Gas 4. Line a 20cm/8inch round deep cake tin or an 18cm/7inch square tin with non-stick silicone paper, or rice paper if you have it.

2 Mix the whole nuts, peel, cherries and sultanas in a bowl. Sift in the flour, cocoa and spices and stir well.

3 Warm the sugar and honey together in a saucepan until the grains of sugar have dissolved. Stir into the fruit and nut mixture.

4 Pour into the lined tin and spread level. Bake for 30 minutes or until firm. Leave to cool in the tin, then turn out and store in an airtight tin or wrapped in foil for 3 days before eating. Dredge heavily with sifted icing sugar before serving.

TO FREEZE: *Wrap tightly in foil. Keeps for 4 months.*

Apricot, Caraway and Brandy Ring

*A Polish friend makes this cake every Christmas, and I must admit
it makes a light contrast to all the richer cakes around.*

- 225 G/8 OZ NO-NEED-TO-SOAK DRIED APRICOTS, ROUGHLY CHOPPED
- 100 G/4 OZ SULTANAS
- 4 TBSP RUM OR BRANDY
- 150 ML/¼ PINT FRESH ORANGE JUICE
- 175 G/6 OZ SELF-RAISING FLOUR
- 1 TSP BAKING POWDER
- 175 G/6 OZ BUTTER, AT ROOM TEMPERATURE
- 5 TBSP CLEAR HONEY
- 4 EGGS, SIZE 3, SEPARATED
- 1 TSP CARAWAY SEEDS
- TOPPING (OPTIONAL, SEE STEP 5)

1 Place the apricot and sultanas in a saucepan with the rum or brandy and the orange juice. Bring to the boil, stirring all the time, then remove from the heat and leave to cool and soak for 2–3 hours.

2 Set the oven to 180°C/350°F/Gas 4. Grease a 1.2 litre/2 pint ring mould.

3 Sift the flour and baking powder together. Beat the butter and honey together until light and fluffy. Beat in the egg yolks, adding a little flour to prevent curdling, then gently fold in the cooled apricot mixture, the remaining flour and the caraway seeds. Whisk the egg whites until they form soft peaks, then fold into the mixture as gently as possible.

4 Spoon into the mould and spread the top level. Bake for about 1¼ hours or until a skewer inserted into the deepest part comes out clean. Leave to cool in the mould for 10 minutes, then turn out on to a wire rack to cool completely. For an even boozier cake, sprinkle with more rum or brandy whilst still warm.

5 Serve plain, or paint with apricot glaze (see page 169) and sprinkle with golden granulated sugar, or decorate with glacé and crystallized fruits. Or drizzle glacé icing (see page 166) over the top and sides and top with a ring of chopped dried apricots.

TO FREEZE: *Wrap undecorated cake in foil. Keeps for 4 months.*

Illustrated opposite page 64

$\mathcal{G}$INGERBREAD

*This gingerbread is made by the melting method, and is an easy cake
for children to bake.*

- 350 G/12 OZ SELF-RAISING FLOUR
- PINCH SALT
- 2 TSP GROUND GINGER
- 2 TSP GROUND CINNAMON
- 175 G/6 OZ BUTTER OR BLOCK MARGARINE
- 2 ROUNDED TBSP GOLDEN SYRUP
- 2 ROUNDED TBSP DARK TREACLE

- 175 G/6 OZ DARK MUSCOVADO SUGAR
- 2 EGGS, SIZE 3
- 150 ML/¼ PINT MILK
- **CINNAMON GLACÉ ICING** (OPTIONAL):
- 225 G/8 OZ ICING SUGAR
- ¼ TSP GROUND CINNAMON
- FRESHLY SQUEEZED ORANGE JUICE, TO MIX

1 Set the oven to 180°C/350°F/Gas 4. Grease and line a 20cm/8inch square cake tin.

2 Sift the flour, salt and spices into a bowl. Place the fat, syrup, treacle and sugar in a saucepan, or in the microwave oven, and heat until the fat melts. Stir together, then cool slightly.

3 Pour the melted mixture into the flour, then beat in the eggs and milk. Pour into the prepared tin. Bake for about 1¼ hours or until firm in the centre. Leave to cool in the tin, then turn out and store for 1–2 days before eating. The longer the cake is kept, the stickier it becomes.

4 If liked, cover with cinnamon glacé icing: sift the icing sugar with the ground cinnamon. Blend to a coating consistency with freshly squeezed orange juice.

TO FREEZE: *Wrap in foil. Keeps for 3 months.*

LITTLE CAKES

CHAPTER FOUR

LITTLE CAKES

Morning coffee or afternoon tea parties are excellent ways to entertain friends and neighbours, and don't involve a lot of expense. A simple way to celebrate a birthday or christening is to make a good selection of small cakes and sandwiches, which is so much easier than a large scale buffet.

Little cakes can look stunning arranged on a stylish cloth with the best china. You can bake some of them well ahead of time and freeze them, decorating on the day, and mix in a few freshly made ones. A good selection of meringues, slices, fancies and scones will tempt even the strongest willed, and you will actually have far more time to chat with your guests, when you don't have to worry about cooking hot food. I think we should all make an effort to resurrect the tea party as it is really one of the most civilized and relaxing ways to entertain.

LITTLE CAKES

Roll madeleines into jam
then grated coconut

Top with halved cherries
and angelica leaves

ℰNGLISH MADELEINES

MAKES 12

These are a classic feature of the English tea table.

- 1 QUANTITY EASY CUPCAKES MIXTURE (SEE PAGE 82)
- 6 TBSP RASPBERRY JAM
- JUICE ½ LEMON

- 50 G/2 OZ DESICCATED COCONUT
- 6 GLACÉ CHERRIES, HALVED

1 Set the oven to 190°C/375°F/Gas 5. Grease 12 dariole moulds well and line the base of each with a small disc of greaseproof paper.

2 Divide the cupcakes mixture among the moulds. Bake for 15–20 minutes. Cool in the moulds for a few minutes, then turn out on to a wire rack to cool. When cold, trim the bases so that the cakes stand up straight.

3 Heat the jam and lemon juice in a small pan, or the microwave oven, until the jam melts. Pour through a sieve to remove the pips.

4 Hold each cake on a fork, and brush with the warm jam mixture. Place the coconut on a plate and roll each madeleine in it to cover top and sides evenly. Place each cake in a paper case, and decorate each with a halved cherry.

TO FREEZE: *Pack undecorated cakes in a rigid container. Keeps for 3 months.*

Illustrated opposite page 80

FRENCH MADELEINES

Marcel Proust ate madeleines with lime blossom tea as a child, when visiting his aunt on Sunday mornings. Ever since he wrote about these dainty little cakes in Remembrance of Things Past, *they have had a mystique which makes them very special, if not slightly formal. Madeleines will keep for up to a week in an airtight tin.*

- 50 G/2 OZ UNSALTED BUTTER
  - 2 EGGS, SIZE 3

- 50 G/2 OZ CASTER SUGAR, STORED WITH A VANILLA POD
  - 50 G/2 OZ PLAIN FLOUR

1 Set the oven to 200°C/400°F/Gas 6. Lightly grease two sheets of scalloped madeleine moulds with melted butter. Dust with flour, then tap away any excess.

2 Melt the butter, then remove from heat and allow to cool. Place the eggs and sugar in a heatproof bowl set over a pan of hot water and whisk until the mixture is very thick and pale and firm enough to leave a ribbon trail when the whisk is lifted. Remove from the heat and continue whisking for 2 minutes.

3 Sift the flour over the surface and fold in very gently with a metal spoon. Fold in the lukewarm butter. Fill each of the moulds three-quarters full and level them. Bake for about 10–14 minutes until firm and pale golden. Cool in the tins for 1 minute, then turn out on to a wire rack and leave to cool completely.

TO FREEZE: *Layer in a rigid container, interleaved with freezer tissue. Keeps for 3 months.*

Illustrated opposite page 80

*Fill moulds
three-quarters full*

$\mathcal{N}$APOLEONS

MAKES 12

Definitely very fancy work for a special occasion, but the pastry layers and cream can both be prepared well in advance and assembled on the day.

- 225 G/8 OZ PUFF PASTRY, PREFERABLY LAYERED SHEET TYPE
- **ALMOND CREAM FILLING:**
  - 110 G/4 OZ SACHET POWDERED GELATINE
  - 450 ML/¾ PINT MILK
  - 25 G/1 OZ CORNFLOUR
  - 50 G/2 OZ CASTER SUGAR, STORED WITH A VANILLA POD
  - 2 EGGS, SIZE 3, BEATEN

- 1 TSP ALMOND ESSENCE
- 150 ML/¼ PINT WHIPPING CREAM
- **DECORATION:**
  - 75 G/3 OZ PLAIN CHOCOLATE
  - 350 G/12 OZ ICING SUGAR, SIFTED
  - 2 TBSP GOLDEN SYRUP
  - ¼ TSP VANILLA ESSENCE
  - 1 TSP WHITE VEGETABLE FAT

1 Make the filling first. Sprinkle the gelatine over 4 tbsp of the milk and leave to soften. Blend the cornflour and sugar to a smooth paste with 2 tbsp milk in a saucepan, then blend in the rest of the milk. Bring to the boil, stirring constantly, and cook for 1 minute until thick. Remove from the heat and quickly beat in the eggs. Heat gently so that the eggs thicken the custard, then remove from the heat again and stir in the gelatine and essence. Stir until the gelatine is completely dissolved, then leave to cool and begin to set.

2 Cut the pastry into four quarters, or use four separate thin sheets if possible. Roll each piece to a rectangle 20 × 25cm/8 × 10inches, and place each piece on a wetted baking sheet. Chill for 30 minutes.

3 Set the oven to 200°C/400°F/Gas 6. Prick the pastry all over with a fork and bake two sheets at a time for 15–20 minutes until well risen and golden. Place on wire racks to cool.

4 Whip the cream until it forms soft peaks, and gently fold into the setting custard mixture. Chill until firm.

5 Trim all the pastry layers to the same size using a sharp knife. Choose the best and flattest layer for the top.

6 To make the decoration, melt the chocolate in a small heatproof bowl set over a pan of warm water or in the microwave oven. Put aside. Place the icing sugar, syrup, 2 tbsp water, the vanilla essence and fat in a heatproof bowl over a pan of hot water and heat gently, stirring, until the mixture is smooth and shiny and coats the back of the spoon. Do not allow to boil. If the icing is too thick add a little more water.

7 Place the melted chocolate in a paper piping bag (see page 182) and snip off the tip. Pour the icing directly from the bowl over the top pastry layer and spread even. Pipe strips of melted chocolate, 2.5cm/1inch apart, lengthways down the icing. Feather by pulling a skewer through the chocolate at 1cm/½inch intervals, crossways. Leave the icing and chocolate to set.

8 When the almond cream filling is firm, spread one-third over a plain pastry layer. Place on a serving plate and set another plain pastry layer on top. Layer with the remaining filling and pastry, finishing with the iced layer on top. Chill for 30 minutes, during which time the pastry will sink a little.

9 To serve, cut down the centre lengthways with a very sharp knife, then cut each half crossways into six thin fingers.

Not suitable for freezing.

Illustrated opposite page 128

Cut sponge into small shapes

*Pour over boiled fondant icing
and stand on a rack to set*

*Decorate with fondant
flowers, cherries and nuts*

*F*ONDANT FANCIES

MAKES ABOUT 12

*Fancies are made from one layer of sponge. Use patterned cutters
for interesting shapes.*

- 100 G/4 OZ SELF-RAISING
  FLOUR
- PINCH SALT
- 25 G/1 OZ CORNFLOUR
- 100 G/4 OZ BUTTER OR
  BLOCK MARGARINE,
  AT ROOM TEMPERATURE
- 100 G/4 OZ CASTER SUGAR

- FINELY GRATED ZEST 1/2 LEMON
- 2 EGGS, SIZE 2, BEATEN
- 1–2 TBSP MILK
- **TO FINISH:**
- APRICOT JAM, SIEVED
- BOILED FONDANT ICING
  (SEE PAGE 164)

1 Set the oven to 190°C/375°F/Gas 5. Grease and line a 28 × 18cm/11 × 7inch baking tin.

2 Sift the flour, salt and cornflour together. Cream the fat, sugar and zest together until light and fluffy. Gradually beat in the eggs, adding a little flour with each addition. Fold in the remaining flour with a large metal spoon and add enough milk to give a smooth consistency.

3 Spoon into the tin and spread level. Bake in the centre of the oven for about 20 minutes or until firm and golden. Cool in the tin for 3 minutes then turn out on to a wire rack to cool.

4 Cut into 12 squares, or other shapes using small cutters. Brush each square with sieved apricot jam and pour over boiled fondant icing. Decorate with crystallized flowers, fondant icing flowers (see pages 179–81) or shapes, or halved glacé cherries, walnuts and angelica. Serve in paper cases.

TO FREEZE: *Wrap undecorated, uncut slab cake in foil. Keeps for 3 months.*

Illustrated opposite page 80

SCOTTISH SHORTBREAD

Being married to a Scot, I always make plenty of shortbread, especially for New Year's Eve. This recipe makes enough for two rounds, so you can give one to a friend as a New Year's present, with a piece of coal and a wee dram, of course. The shortbread will keep well in an airtight tin for up to 2 weeks.

- 275 G/10 OZ PLAIN FLOUR
- 50 G/2 OZ RICE FLOUR
- PINCH SALT
- 75 G/3 OZ CASTER SUGAR

- 250 G/9 OZ BUTTER, AT ROOM TEMPERATURE
- CASTER SUGAR, TO DREDGE

Mark into eight wedges and flute edges

1 Set the oven to 160°C/325°F/Gas 3. Grease two baking sheets.

2 Sift the flours and salt into a bowl and stir in the caster sugar. Add the butter cut into small pieces and rub into the dry ingredients until the mixture resembles crumbs. You will then find that it can be kneaded into a soft dough, using no liquid.

3 Knead until a smooth ball is formed. Cut it in half and roll out each piecce into a 20cm/8inch round. Mark into eight wedges, and flute the edges like pastry, then prick with a fork.

4 Place a round on each baking sheet. Bake for about 35–40 minutes or until pale golden. Leave to cool completely on the sheets, as the warm shortbread is very soft to handle.

5 Dust with caster sugar, and tie up with red ribbons.

TO FREEZE: *Wrap in foil. Keeps for 2 months.*

Illustrated opposite page 97

*Pipe ovals and '2' shapes
of choux pastry*

*Split ovals when baked,
then cut tops into halves*

*Assemble swans, securing
pieces with cream*

CHOUX PASTRY SWANS

MAKES 8

*These choux pastry swans are fun to make for tea,
or for a surprise dinner party pudding.*

- CHOUX PASTRY:
- 100 G/4 OZ STRONG PLAIN FLOUR
- 2 TSP CASTER SUGAR
- PINCH SALT
- 75 G/3 OZ BUTTER

- 225 ML/8 FL OZ WATER
- 3 EGGS, SIZE 3
- **TO FINISH:**
- 300 ML/½ PINT DOUBLE OR WHIPPING CREAM
- ICING SUGAR, TO DREDGE

1 Set the oven to 200°C/400°F/Gas 6. Grease two baking sheets, then dust lightly with flour. Using your finger, trace eight figure '2's about 7.5cm/3inches high and eight oval shapes 7.5cm/3inches long on the baking sheets.

2 Sift the flour, sugar and salt on to a stiff piece of paper (you need to do this in order to add the flour all at once). Place the butter in a heavy-based saucepan with the water and heat until the butter melts, then bring to the boil. Shoot in the flour all at once and beat the mixture well with a wooden spoon until it leaves the sides of the pan and forms a ball. Take off the heat and cool for a minute, then beat in the eggs, using an electric mixer if possible. Beat until the mixture is smooth and glossy.

3 Spoon the choux pastry into a piping bag fitted with a 1cm/½inch plain nozzle. Pipe carefully on to the '2' shapes and into the ovals. Bake for about 15 minutes or until well risen and crisp, then make a small hole in each oval to allow the steam to escape. Return to the oven for another 3 minutes to dry out the pastry. Cool on wire racks.

4 To finish, whip the cream until stiff, adding a little liqueur or sugar to sweeten if liked. Cut each oval in half horizontally, then cut the top half in half lengthways to form two wings. Place some cream in the bottom half of each and press a '2' into this for the swan's neck. Press the two halves into the cream at an angle to form the wings. Lightly dust the wings with sifted icing sugar. Serve immediately, as the cream will start to soften the pastry if left too long.

Not suitable for freezing.

Illustrated opposite

RIGHT (from top to bottom): Choux Pastry Swans (see above); English Madeleines (see page 74); French Madeleines (see page 75); Fondant Fancies (see page 78).

$\mathcal{V}$IENNESE WHIRLS

MAKES 10–12

These little cakes are easy to make and are a good contrast to the richer items on the tea table.

- 175 G/6 OZ BUTTER OR
  BLOCK MARGARINE,
  AT ROOM TEMPERATURE
- 175 G/6 OZ PLAIN FLOUR
- 75 G/3 OZ CASTER SUGAR

- FEW DROPS VANILLA ESSENCE
- ICING SUGAR, TO DREDGE
- **TO FINISH:**
- 2–3 TBSP SIEVED RASPBERRY
  JAM

1 Set the oven to 180°C/350°F/Gas 4. Place twelve paper baking cases in a deep-hole bun tray.

2 Beat the fat until very soft and fluffy, then sift in the flour and beat in gradually. Beat in the sugar and vanilla essence. Spoon into a large piping bag fitted with a medium star nozzle.

3 Pipe into a rosette in each paper case. Bake in the centre of the oven for about 20 minutes or until light golden in colour. Leave to cool, in the paper cases, on a wire rack.

4 Dust with sifted icing sugar when cold, and fill the centre of each with a spot of raspberry jam.

TO FREEZE: *Freeze unbaked mixture in paper cases in a rigid container. Keeps for 6 weeks. Thaw at room temperature and bake as above.*

Illustrated opposite

LEFT (from top to bottom): Bakewell Tart Tray Bake (see page 88); Paradise Slices (see page 86); Viennese Whirls (see above); Chocolate Dipped Golden Meringues (see page 84).

Easy Cupcakes

There are endless decorating possibilities with these simple little cakes. Enlist the help of children for some new ideas.

- 100 G/4 OZ BUTTER OR BLOCK MARGARINE, AT ROOM TEMPERATURE
- 100 G/4 OZ CASTER SUGAR
- 2 EGGS, SIZE 3, BEATEN
- 150 G/5 OZ SELF-RAISING FLOUR
- FEW DROPS VANILLA ESSENCE
- 1–2 TBSP MILK
- TOPPING (SEE STEP 4)

1 Set the oven to 190°C/375°F/Gas 5. Arrange 18–20 paper baking cases in deep-hole bun trays.

2 Cream the fat and sugar together until light and fluffy, then beat in the eggs a little at a time, adding a teaspoon of flour with each addition. Gently fold in the remaining flour. Add the vanilla essence to the milk and fold in enough to give a soft consistency.

3 Spoon the mixture into the paper cases, filling them about two-thirds full. Bake for about 15 minutes or until well risen, firm and golden. Cool, in the paper cases, on a wire rack.

4 Decorate with glacé icing (see page 166), or with simple buttercream (see page 170), made using 75g/3oz unsalted butter and 175g/6oz icing sugar. If liked, divide the buttercream into portions and colour each differently, then use a piping bag with a small star nozzle to pipe patterns and shapes on top of each cupcake. Make butterfly wings by cutting away the centre top of each cake and cutting this in half. Position as 'wings', securing with a little buttercream, and pipe buttercream down the centre for the butterfly body.

TO FREEZE: *Freeze undecorated in rigid polythene boxes. Keeps for 2 months.*

Illustrated opposite page 17

$\mathcal{M}$ACAROONS

MAKES 20–24

A great Scottish favourite, home-made macaroons are hard to beat.
Make them larger for tea-time, or tiny as after-dinner petits fours.

- 100 G/4 OZ GROUND ALMONDS
- 175 G/6 OZ CASTER SUGAR
- 2 EGG WHITES, SIZE 3
- FEW DROPS ALMOND ESSENCE

- EGG WHITE TO GLAZE
- CASTER SUGAR, TO SPRINKLE
- 20–24 ALMOND HALVES

1 Set the oven to 180°C/350°F/Gas 4. Line two baking sheets with rice paper.

2 Mix the almonds and sugar together in a bowl. Whisk the egg whites with the almond essence in another bowl until stiff. Gradually beat in the almonds and sugar until the mixture forms a fairly stiff paste. Spoon into a large piping bag fitted with a 1cm/½inch nozzle.

3 Pipe out 20–24 small rounds, spaced well apart, on the rice paper. Brush each one lightly with egg white and sprinkle very lightly with caster sugar. Press a halved almond into each.

4 Bake for 15 minutes or until just beginning to colour. Cool on the sheets until firm, then pull the rice paper apart to separate the cakes.

Not suitable for freezing.

Illustrated opposite page 96

CHOCOLATE DIPPED GOLDEN MERINGUES

MAKES 12

These add style to the tea table, and make a good contrast when mixed into a selection of cakes. The meringues can be made well ahead of time, and stored in an airtight tin.

- 75 G/3 OZ GOLDEN CASTER OR SOFT LIGHT BROWN SUGAR
- 75 G/3 OZ CASTER SUGAR
- 3 EGG WHITES, SIZE 3
- PINCH CREAM OF TARTAR
- **FILLING:**
- 225 G/8 OZ PLAIN CHOCOLATE

- 150 ML/¼ PINT DOUBLE OR WHIPPING CREAM
- 1 PASSION FRUIT, OR 1 TBSP SPIRIT OR LIQUEUR SUCH AS BRANDY, GRAND MARNIER OR TIA MARIA

1 Set the oven to 110°C/225°F/Gas ¼. Line two baking sheets with some non-stick silicone paper.

2 Sift the sugars together. Place the egg whites in a completely grease-free bowl and whisk with the cream of tartar until they are stiff and standing in peaks. Whisk in the sugars, a tablespoon at a time, making sure the meringue is stiff before adding the next addition.

3 Place the meringue in a piping bag fitted with a small plain nozzle. Pipe out 24 small rounds on to the non-stick paper. Bake for about 1½ hours or until crisp and dry, reversing the trays in the oven halfway through the cooking. Leave to cool on the paper, then peel off the meringues and store in an airtight tin until needed.

4 To finish, break up the chocolate and melt very gently in a heatproof bowl set over a pan of warm water or in the microwave oven. Paint the flat underside of each meringue lightly with a layer of melted chocolate and leave to dry.

5 Whip the cream until stiff. Halve the passion fruit and scoop out the flesh into a sieve. Press the passion fruit juice through the sieve over the cream bowl, leaving the pips in the sieve. Fold the juice (or liqueur) into the cream, then use to sandwich pairs of meringues together, chocolate sides in. Place in paper cases to serve.

Not suitable for freezing.

Illustrated opposite page 81

$\mathscr{R}$UNNING A STALL
FOR CHARITY

If you have a reputation for good home baking you may well find yourself 'volunteered' to run a cake stall for a local charity. This really can be fun and very rewarding if you have a good military plan of attack. The following tactics will help you on your way.

☞ Make lots of different bakes in small batches as a variety of cakes always looks more attractive, and gives more choice. Bake and freeze over a few weeks, or ask two or three friends to make one batch each to help.

☞ Cost out all recipes before you bake. Try to keep the prices as low as possible, then people will buy two or three items.

☞ Start collecting chocolate boxes and attractive packaging well in advance. Package everything invitingly with doilies and ribbons; for fragile items, cover boxes with wrapping paper and top with cellophane.

☞ Label clearly so that people know what they are buying, including price, storage, and freezing instructions (but only if the cakes are fresh).

☞ Have plenty of paper and carrier bags for purchases to be taken away in.

☞ Start with plenty of change in your cash box, as lack of it can hinder sales.

☞ Make your stall and helpers as attractive as possible. Wear spotlessly clean matching aprons if possible to give a professional image.

The cakes on the following pages are good for selling at charity events as they can be made up in bulk and cut up on the day of the fête. Try two or three varieties.

$\mathscr{C}$HINESE CHEWS

MAKES 16 SLICES

Not as chewy as the name suggests, but sticky and delicious.

- 225 G/8 OZ STONED DATES, CHOPPED
- 100 G/4 OZ WALNUT PIECES, CHOPPED
- 200 G/7 OZ DARK MUSCOVADO SUGAR

- 75 G/3 OZ PLAIN FLOUR
- 1 TSP BAKING POWDER
- 3 EGGS, SIZE 3, BEATEN

1 Set the oven to 180°C/350°F/Gas 4. Grease and line an 18 × 28cm/7 × 11inch tin.

2 Mix all the ingredients together, then pour into the tin and spread evenly. Bake just above the centre of the oven for about 25 minutes. Leave to cool in the tin, and mark into squares or fingers whilst still warm. Cut when cold.

TO FREEZE: *Wrap in foil. Keeps for 2 months.*

*T*REACLE SCONES

MAKES 12

*These are a Scottish favourite for tea-time. Just a wee bit different
from plain scones, these are delicious split and buttered.*

- 225 G/8 OZ PLAIN FLOUR
- ½ TSP BICARBONATE OF SODA
- 1 TSP CREAM OF TARTAR
- ½ TSP SALT
- ½ TSP GROUND CINNAMON

- ½ TSP MIXED SPICE
- 25 G/1 OZ BUTTER
- 25 G/1 OZ CASTER SUGAR
- 1 TBSP TREACLE
- 150 ML/¼ PT MILK, TO MIX

1 Set the oven to 230°C/450°F/Gas 8. Grease a baking sheet.

2 Sift the dry ingredients into a bowl and rub in the butter until the mixture resembles fine crumbs. Stir in the sugar. Dilute the treacle with a little milk, then add to the mixture and mix to a light dough, adding more milk as necessary.

3 Turn out on to a floured surface and knead lightly until smooth. Roll out to about 2cm/¾inch thick and cut into rounds using a 5cm/2inch floured cutter, cutting as close to each other as possible. Re-roll the trimmings and make more rounds.

4 Place on the baking sheet. Bake for about 10 minutes or until well risen. Serve hot or cold, split and buttered.

TO FREEZE: *Wrap in freezer bags or store in rigid container. Keeps for up to 6 months.*

*P*ARADISE SLICES

MAKES 16 SLICES

*These are lovely old-fashioned cakes, with a homely quality. Keep
some handy in the cake tin, or freezer.*

- 225 G/8 OZ SHORTCRUST PASTRY
- 100 G/4 OZ SOFT TUB
  MARGARINE
- 100 G/4 OZ CASTER SUGAR
- 2 EGGS, SIZE 3
- 50 G/2 OZ GROUND ALMONDS
- 50 G/2 OZ SELF-RAISING FLOUR

- 3–4 TBSP JAM OR MARMALADE
- 25 G/1 OZ SULTANAS
- 25 G/1 OZ CURRANTS
- 25 G/1 OZ GLACÉ CHERRIES,
  RINSED, DRIED AND QUARTERED
- ICING SUGAR, TO DREDGE

1 Set the oven to 200°C/400°F/Gas 6. Grease an 18 × 28cm/7 × 11inch tin.

2 Roll out the pastry and use to line the tin. Cover with greaseproof paper and weigh down with baking beans. Bake blind for 15 minutes or until the pastry is light golden. Remove the paper and beans. Turn the oven down to 180°C/350°F/Gas 4.

3 Beat the margarine, sugar, eggs, almonds and flour together quickly until smooth. Spread the jam in the pastry case, then sprinkle over the dried fruit and cherries evenly. Spread the sponge mixture over the top.

4 Bake for about 20 minutes or until the sponge is firm in the centre. Leave to cool in the tin. Dredge with sifted icing or caster sugar when cold and cut into slices.

TO FREEZE: *Freeze in baking tin, covered with foil. Keeps for 2 months.*

Illustrated opposite page 81

$\mathscr{B}$ AKLAVA

MAKES 20

Filo or strudel pastry is now available from supermarkets, so it is easy to make this rich Middle Eastern delicacy.

- 225 G/8 OZ CHOPPED MIXED NUTS OR WALNUTS
- 50 G/2 OZ CASTER SUGAR
- ½ TSP GROUND CINNAMON
- 450 G/1 LB FILO PASTRY

- 175 G/6 OZ BUTTER, MELTED
- 175 G/6 OZ CLEAR HONEY
- 50 G/2 OZ SHELLED PISTACHIO NUTS, FINELY CHOPPED (OPTIONAL)

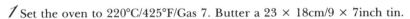

1 Set the oven to 220°C/425°F/Gas 7. Butter a 23 × 18cm/9 × 7inch tin.

2 Chop or process the nuts until fairly fine, then mix with the sugar and spice.

3 Cut the sheets of pastry to measure 25cm/10inches square. Fit one square into the tin, then brush with melted butter. Repeat with five more buttered layers of pastry, then sprinkle over 50g/2oz of the nut mixture.

4 Repeat the last stage four more times to give five layers of nut mixture. Top with the remaining pastry, then trim the pastry edges. Using a very sharp knife, mark the pastry into 20 squares.

5 Bake for 10 minutes, then lower the oven temperature to 180°C/350°F/Gas 4 and bake for about 15 minutes longer or until golden.

6 Heat the honey in a small pan or in the microwave until melted, then pour over the cooked pastry. Leave to cool in the tin for 2–3 hours, then cut through the squares again. Sprinkle the top with chopped pistachio nuts to decorate.

Not suitable for freezing.

Illustrated opposite page 17

$\mathscr{B}$ AKEWELL TART
TRAY BAKE

MAKES 16 SLICES

*This is a good recipe to bake up for bazaars, as the almonds keep the
filling moist, and you can make the bakewell tart the day before,
or freeze it well in advance.*

PASTRY:
- 75 G/3 OZ BLOCK MARGARINE
- 175 G/6 OZ PLAIN FLOUR
- ICING SUGAR, TO DREDGE
- **TOPPING:**
- 3–4 TBSP SEEDLESS RASPBERRY JAM
- 150 G/5 OZ SOFT TUB MARGARINE
- 75 G/3 OZ CASTER SUGAR

- 2 EGGS, SIZE 2, BEATEN
- 1/4 TSP ALMOND ESSENCE
- 100 G/4 OZ GROUND ALMONDS
- 50 G/2 OZ SELF-RAISING FLOUR
- 2 TBSP MILK
- 50 G/2 OZ FLAKED ALMONDS
- **TO FINISH:**
- ICING SUGAR, TO DREDGE, OR GLACÉ ICING (PAGE 166)

1 Set the oven to 200°C/400°F/Gas 6. Grease an 18 × 28cm/7 × 11inch shallow baking tin or roasting tray.

2 To make the pastry, rub the margarine into the flour until it resembles fine crumbs, then stir in enough cold water to bind to a soft dough. Knead lightly, then roll out and use to line the baking tin. Prick lightly all over with a fork. Spread with the raspberry jam, and chill while making the topping.

3 Place all the remaining topping ingredients, except the flaked almonds, in a bowl and quickly beat together until smooth. Spread over the jam and level the top. Sprinkle with the flaked almonds.

4 Bake just above the centre of the oven until golden and springy to the touch in the centre. Leave to cool in the tin, then turn out and dredge heavily with sifted icing sugar. Alternatively, drizzle over glacé icing. Cut into 16 slices.

VARIATIONS: *Use 4 tbsp mincemeat or marmalade instead of traditional raspberry jam.*

TO FREEZE: *Wrap in freezer bags. Keeps for 3 months.*

Illustrated opposite page 81

Mocha Nut Squares

MAKES 18

These are easy to bake for sale or bazaars. Make them in bulk in a large tin, spread over the icing, and simply cut into squares — couldn't be easier.

- 175 G/6 OZ SOFT TUB MARGARINE
- 50 G/2 OZ SHELLED WALNUTS, CHOPPED
- 175 G/6 OZ SOFT LIGHT BROWN SUGAR
- 3 EGGS, SIZE 3, BEATEN
- 1 TBSP COFFEE ESSENCE, OR 1 TBSP INSTANT COFFEE DISSOLVED IN 1 TBSP BOILING WATER

- 175 G/6 OZ SELF-RAISING FLOUR
- 1 ½ TSP BAKING POWDER
- **MOCHA ICING:**
- 225 G/8 OZ ICING SUGAR
- 75 G/3 OZ SOFT TUB MARGARINE
- 1 TBSP COCOA POWDER
- 2 TSP INSTANT COFFEE POWDER
- 1 TBSP MILK

1 Grease and base-line a 30 × 22 × 5cm/12 × 8 × 2inch tin. Set the oven to 180°C/350°F/Gas 4.

2 Place the margarine, walnuts, sugar, eggs and coffee essence in a bowl. Sift in the flour and baking powder and quickly beat together until smooth.

3 Spread in the tin and smooth level. Bake for 35 minutes or until the sides begin to shrink away from the tin and the centre is springy. Leave to cool in the tin for 10 minutes, then turn out on to a wire rack and peel away the lining paper.

4 To make the icing, sift the icing sugar into a bowl and add the margarine. Blend the cocoa and coffee with 1 tbsp boiling water. Cool a little, then stir in to the sugar with the milk. Beat until smooth.

5 Spread the icing over the top of the cold cake and, if liked, sprinkle with chopped walnuts. Cut into 3 lengthways, then cut into 18 squares.

TO FREEZE: *Wrap un-iced cake in foil. Keeps for 3 months.*

Illustrated opposite page 17

$\mathcal{R}$ ICH AND LIGHT FRUIT CAKES

CHAPTER FIVE

*F*ruits have been dried from very early times, and in Arab cuisine formed part of the staple winter diet. Little cakes stuffed with rich fruit fillings were, and still are, made in this part of the world. In Europe, the first fruit cakes were simple bread doughs enriched with spice and dried fruits, and the cakes we bake today have evolved from these.

Rich fruit cakes were often symbols of prosperity and fertility in the past and are still the traditional centrepieces for all kinds of family celebrations like weddings, christenings and Christmas.

As well as the beautifully decorated centrepieces for grand occasions, fruit cakes can be perfect to bake and keep in the tin for tea. Sliced and buttered there is nothing that can beat a piece of tasty fruit cake with a cup of tea to revive flagging spirits and help you through the day.

RICH AND
LIGHT FRUIT
CAKES

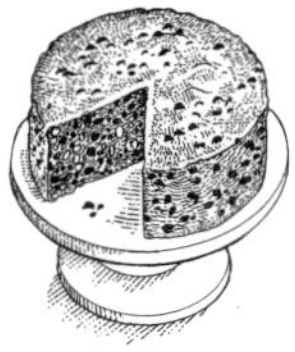

FRUIT CAKE INGREDIENTS

BUTTER

Most rich fruit cakes are made by creaming the butter, and this is a vital stage, which must be done thoroughly to give a light fluffy mixture; air gives the cake its structure. Large amounts of butter are more easily beaten in a free-standing table-top mixer, as hand-held mixers can become overheated with the strain. Alternatively, you can beat by hand – try small batches if the mix is large or you will soon become tired. Use salted butter in rich cakes, for a good flavour. When I trained at Westminster College, we had to beat the very yellow salted New Zealand butter by hand until it turned pale. Although this was hard work, I've not found a better basis for a cake yet.

SUGAR

Moist dark brown sugar is essential for rich cakes. Muscovado and molasses are relatively unrefined raw sugars which give wonderful flavour and colour, and are well worth using. If brown sugar from your store-cupboard has dried and gone hard, place it in a bowl, cover with a damp cloth or slices of bread, and leave overnight.

DRIED FRUIT

Most vine fruits such as currants, sultanas and raisins are sold ready cleaned and washed, but it is still advisable to pick them over, as stalks, stems and small stones can escape the factory cleaning, especially in the cheaper brands. You really do get what you pay for with dried fruits, so don't skimp at this stage.

Plump up weighed-out fruit before mixing – steep it in warm water for 15–30 minutes, then spread out on a tea towel or kitchen paper to soak up excess liquid, or steep in sherry, rum or brandy for 3–5 days prior to baking, stirring daily. West Indian cooks soak their fruit in dark rum, brandy, port and cherry brandy for months in sealed jars, which gives the most delicious flavour ever!

TINS

Cake tins for rich, heavy cakes need to be deep, firm and of good quality. All sorts of shapes and sizes like hearts, hexagons, ovals and petals can now be bought or hired. To find the capacity of a shaped tin, fill a 20cm/8inch round tin with water to the baking level. Pour into the shaped tin, noting the amount, and adapt from the chart (see page 97) accordingly.

Make sure that all tins, especially square ones, have sharp corners, not curved ones, as these are difficult to cover with marzipan. Some very old tins can measure smaller in size and newer ones can actually be larger by 5mm/¼inch, so bear this in mind when timing the baking.

DEPTH TEST

If you are making a tiered cake, make sure that all the tins are filled to exactly the same depth. Check by inserting a skewer marked with the exact level into each tin; you can then even them out if they are not the same. When baking a three-tiered cake, you can cook two or three tiers in the same oven, but rotate their shelf positions halfway through the baking time, moving the largest cake to the highest position. Opening the door for such a short period will not do any harm. When baking more than one cake at a time the total cooking time will be a little longer. Do not be tempted to raise the temperature to speed things up or a tough outer crust will form.

95

*Press a hollow into centre
of cake mixture*

RIGHT (from top to
bottom): Chocolate
Mincemeat Cake (page
49); Sultana and
Lemon Loaves (page
107); Macaroons (see
page 83).

OPPOSITE PAGE 97
(from top to bottom:
Simnel Cake (see page
102); Guinness Cake (see
page 100); Scottish
Shortbread (see page 79).

R ICH FRUIT CAKE

*This cake is suitable for a Christmas, wedding or formal
celebration. It is moist and fruity and gets better with keeping, so do
try to make it well ahead of time. For the larger cakes on the chart it
might be easier to make up the mixture the day before, as they do
need long slow cooking. The mixture will not be harmed from being
left overnight. Just put it in the tins, cover with a sheet of paper,
and leave in a cool place until needed.*

1 Set the oven to 150°C/300°F/Gas 2. Grease and line the tin(s), using a treble thickness of greaseproof paper. Tie a double thickness of newspaper or brown paper round the outside of the tin to help protect the sides of the cake from forming a hard crust.

2 Place the butter and sugar in a warmed mixing bowl and cream until very light and fluffy. This can be quite hard work, especially if it is a very large cake, but it is vital to cream the mixture well, to provide a structure for the rest of the ingredients.

3 Add the eggs in small batches, beating well between each addition. Add a teaspoon of flour if the mixture begins to curdle. Sift in the flour and spice, then sprinkle over the dried fruit and peel. Fold the mixture together (use your hand for this if you have lots of mixture – it is much easier).

4 Add the cherries, nuts, treacle and brandy and mix well, making sure all the fruit is combined and that there are no patches of flour in the mixture.

5 Turn the mixture into the tin and make a hollow in the centre, to prevent the cake from peaking when it rises. Stand the tin on a double sheet of newspaper or brown paper. Bake for 1 hour, then turn down the oven temperature to 140°C/275°F/Gas 1 for the remaining time. To test the cake, insert a warmed skewer into the centre. If it comes out clean, the cake is cooked; if any sticky mixture adheres to it, bake the cake a little longer.

6 When cooked, leave the cake in the tin to cool. Turn it out, leaving on the lining paper. Prick the top with a fine skewer and paint brandy or rum over the cold cake. (Repeat this process 2 or 3 times during storage for a really rich cake.) Overwrap the cake in sheets of greaseproof paper and tape tightly and neatly. Overwrap the greaseproof paper with doubled foil and tape tightly to make an airtight parcel. Place on a really level surface, or a baking sheet, and store in a cool dry place for 2–3 months.

TO FREEZE: *Rich fruit cakes improve with freezing, which tends to blend and mellow the flavours more quickly. Apart from freezing cut pieces, this is the only real reason for freezing as a rich fruit cake will keep well in a tin for a number of years. Freeze the cake wrapped as above. Keeps for 4 months. Leave plenty of time for thawing, especially for a larger cake.*

Illustrated opposite page 16

$\mathcal{R}$ICH FRUIT CAKES

Round tin	15cm/6inch	18cm/7inch	20cm/8inch	23cm/9inch	25cm/10inch	28cm/11inch	30cm/12inch	
Square tin	12cm/5inch	15cm/6inch	18cm/7inch	20cm/8inch	23cm/9inch	25cm/10inch	28cm/11inch	30cm/12inch
Brown sugar	150g/5oz	175g/6oz	275g/10oz	350g/12oz	500g/1lb2oz	600g/1lb5oz	800g/1¾lb	950g/2lb2oz
Butter	150g/5oz	175g/6oz	275g/10oz	350g/12oz	500g/1lb2oz	600g/1lb5oz	800g/1¾lb	950g/2lb2oz
Eggs, size 3	2–2½	3	5	6	9	11	14	16
Plain flour	175g/6oz	225g/8oz	350g/12oz	450g/1lb	600g/1lb5oz	700g/1½lb	800g/1¾lb	1kg/2lb6oz
Mixed spice	¼ tsp	½ tsp	1 tsp	1 tsp	1½ tsp	2 tsp	2½ tsp	3 tsp
Currants	200g/7oz	275g/10oz	400g/14oz	450g/1lb	550g/1¼lb	800g/1¾lb	975g/2lb5oz	1.2kg/2lb11oz
Sultanas	200g/7oz	275g/10oz	400g/14oz	450g/1lb	550g/1¼lb	800g/1¾lb	975g/2lb5oz	1.2kg/2lb11oz
Raisins	50g/2oz	75g/3oz	100g/4oz	225g/8oz	275g/10oz	350g/12oz	400g/14oz	450g/1lb
Chopped candied peel	50g/2oz	75g/3oz	100g/4oz	175g/6oz	225g/8oz	250g/9oz	275g/10oz	350g/12oz
Glacé cherries	25g/1oz	50g/2oz	50g/2oz	75g/3oz	100g/4oz	175g/6oz	225g/8oz	275g/10oz
Flaked almonds	25g/1oz	50g/2oz	50g/2oz	100g/4oz	100g/4oz	175g/6oz	225g/8oz	275g/10oz
Dark treacle	1 tbsp	1 tbsp	1½ tbsp	2 tbsp	3 tbsp	3½ tbsp	4 tbsp	5 tbsp
Rum or brandy	1 tbsp	1 tbsp	1½ tbsp	2 tbsp	2½ tbsp	3 tbsp	3½ tbsp	4 tbsp
Cooking time	2½ hours	3 hours	5 hours	6–6½ hours	7 hours	7½ hours	8 hours	8½ hours

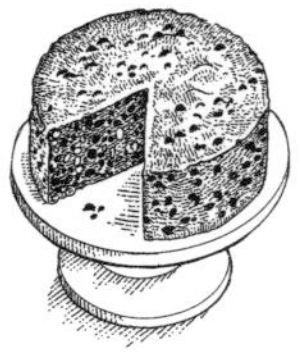

$\mathcal{D}$UNDEE CAKE

*This lighter fruit cake is a favourite of mine. I make it for fêtes, for
guessing the weight, and as a present for friends. It looks lovely
wrapped in cellophane with a tartan ribbon tied round it.*

- 100 G/4 OZ SULTANAS
- 100 G/4 OZ CURRANTS
- 100 G/4 OZ RAISINS
- 50 G/2 OZ CHOPPED CANDIED MIXED PEEL
- 75 G/3 OZ GLACÉ CHERRIES, RINSED, DRIED AND CHOPPED
- 75 G/3 OZ GROUND ALMONDS
- 225 G/8 OZ BUTTER, AT ROOM TEMPERATURE

- 225 G/8 OZ SOFT LIGHT BROWN SUGAR
- FINELY GRATED ZEST 1 LEMON
- 3 EGGS, SIZE 3, BEATEN
- 250 G/9 OZ PLAIN FLOUR
- 1 TSP BAKING POWDER
- 1 TBSP SHERRY OR WATER
- 50 G/2 OZ SHELLED ALMONDS, SKINNED

1 Set the oven to 160°C/325°F/Gas 3. Grease and line an 18cm/7inch round deep
cake tin.

2 Mix the dried fruits, peel and cherries in a bowl with the ground almonds, tossing
to coat the fruit. Cream the butter, sugar and zest together until light and fluffy, then
beat in the eggs gradually. Beat in a teaspoon of flour with each addition of egg to
prevent the mixture from curdling.

3 Sift the remaining flour and the baking powder together into the dried fruit
mixture. Stir together, then add to the creamed mixture a little at a time, mixing in
well. Add the sherry or water. Spoon the mixture into the tin and make a slight
hollow in the centre, then spread the sides level. Arrange the almonds neatly over the
surface in radiating circles.

4 Bake in the centre of the oven for 2½–3 hours or until a skewer inserted in the
centre comes out clean, with no mixture sticking to it.

5 Leave to cool in the tin for 10 minutes, then turn out on to a wire rack to cool
completely. If liked, decorate with whole almonds, placed in a circle on top. Store in
an airtight tin; the flavour will mature and be better after a week.

TO FREEZE: *Wrap whole cake or slices in foil. Keeps for up to 4 months.*

Illustrated opposite page 144

TWELFTH NIGHT CAKE

*The twelfth night after Christmas marks the end of the celebrations
and is the time for taking down the decorations. It was originally a
night for games, feasting and masques in medieval times, and the
Lord of Misrule, appointed at the beginning of Christmas, held his
final court on that day. The French still keep the medieval custom of
baking a cake containing a dried bean. The person who gets the
slice with the bean is King or Queen for the evening, and is crowned
with a paper crown. He or she is all-powerful and can demand
favours and forfeits from the guests, so make sure you know where
the bean is hidden in the cake!*

- 175 G/6 OZ BUTTER, AT ROOM TEMPERATURE, OR SOFT TUB MARGARINE
- 175 G/6 OZ CASTER SUGAR
- 175 G/6 OZ PLAIN FLOUR
- 1½ TSP BAKING POWDER
- 75 G/3 OZ GROUND ALMONDS
- 6 TBSP EVAPORATED MILK
- 3 EGG WHITES, SIZE 3
- 50 G/2 OZ CRYSTALLIZED GINGER, CHOPPED
- 100 G/4 OZ GLACÉ PINEAPPLE, CHOPPED
- 75 G/3 OZ CHOPPED CANDIED MIXED PEEL
- 75 G/3 OZ GLACÉ CHERRIES, RINSED, DRIED AND HALVED
- 75 G/3 OZ FLAKED ALMONDS
- DRIED BEAN (BROAD, KIDNEY OR HARICOT)
- TOPPING (SEE STEP 4)

1 Set the oven to 160°C/325°F/Gas 3. Grease and line a 20cm/8inch round deep cake tin.

2 Cream the fat and sugar together until light and fluffy. Sift in the flour, baking powder and ground almonds, add the evaporated milk and fold together. Whisk the egg whites until stiff, then fold into the mixture with the fruits and nuts. Press the bean into the mixture.

3 Spoon the mixture into the tin and level the top. Bake for about 1½ hours or until firm to the touch in the centre. Leave to cool in the tin for 5 minutes, then turn out on to a wire rack to cool completely.

4 Decorate the top with a fluted round of almond paste (see page 160), or brush the top of the cake with 3 tbsp sieved apricot jam and press over 100g/4oz crystallized fruits in a pattern.

Not suitable for freezing.

Illustrated opposite page 16

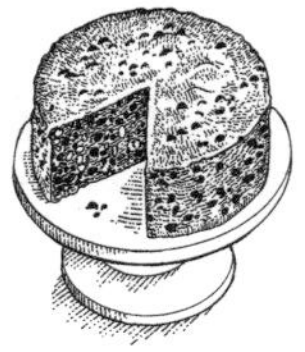

GUINNESS CAKE

*Start preparations the day before, as you need to soak the fruit
overnight for this moist fruit cake. Keep it for a week in an airtight
tin for perfect flavour and texture.*

- 175 G/6 OZ RAISINS
- 175 G/6 OZ SULTANAS
- 8 TBSP GUINNESS OR STOUT
- 175 G/6 OZ BUTTER,
  AT ROOM TEMPERATURE
- 175 G/6 OZ DARK MUSCOVADO
  SUGAR

- 3 EGGS, SIZE 3, BEATEN
- 225 G/8 OZ PLAIN FLOUR
- 2 TSP MIXED SPICE
- 75 G/3 OZ CHOPPED CANDIED
  MIXED PEEL
- 75 G/3 OZ CHOPPED MIXED
  NUTS

1 Place the dried fruit in a large bowl, pour over the Guinness and leave to soak for
12 hours, or overnight.

2 Grease and line an 18cm/7inch round cake tin. Set the oven to 170°C/325°F/Gas 3.

3 Cream the butter and sugar together until light and fluffy. Add the eggs
gradually, adding a little flour with each addition. Sift the remaining flour with the
spice, and fold into the mixture with the soaked fruit and liquid, the peel and nuts.
The mixture should be soft and drop easily from a spoon. If it is a little dry, add 1
tbsp milk or water.

4 Spoon the mixture into the tin and spread level. Bake in the centre of the oven for
about 1½ hours or until a skewer inserted into the centre of the cake comes out clean.

5 Leave to cool in the tin for 10 minutes, then turn out on to a wire rack and cool
completely. Peel away the lining paper and store in an airtight tin for a week before
eating, to improve the flavour. Serve sliced and buttered.

TO FREEZE: *Wrap in foil. Keeps for 4 months.*

Illustrated opposite page 97

$\mathscr{B}$LACK BUN

Black bun is an unusual pastry-wrapped cake made in Scotland for the Christmas and New Year celebrations. Scottish children go 'guising' where they soot their faces and sing New Year's songs in exchange for 'hogmanays' — drinks, or gifts of food like black bun.

- 350 G/12 OZ SHORTCRUST PASTRY
- 225 G/8 OZ PLAIN FLOUR
- 1 TSP GROUND CINNAMON
- 1 TSP GROUND GINGER
- 1 TSP GROUND ALLSPICE
- ¼ TSP FRESHLY MILLED BLACK PEPPER
- 1 TSP CREAM OF TARTAR

- 1 TSP BICARBONATE OF SODA
- 900 G/2LB MIXED DRIED FRUIT
- 100 G/4 OZ FLAKED ALMONDS
- 100 G/4 OZ DARK MUSCOVADO OR MOLASSES SUGAR
- 1 EGG, SIZE 3, BEATEN
- 150 ML/¼ PINT WHISKY OR BRANDY
- 3 TBSP MILK
- BEATEN EGG, TO GLAZE

1 Set the oven to 180°C/350°F/Gas 4. Grease and base-line a 20cm/8inch loose-based or spring-clip round cake tin.

2 Divide the pastry into two pieces, two-thirds and one-third. Roll out the larger piece thinly into a round about 35cm/14inches in diameter. Use to line the cake tin, gently pressing it on to the bottom and sides of the tin, trying not to pleat it as this will spoil the appearance of the outside of the cake. Leave the pastry hanging over the sides of the tin. Cover with a tea towel and set aside.

3 Sift the flour, spices, cream of tartar and soda into a bowl. Mix in the dried fruit, almonds and sugar. Add the egg, whisky or brandy and milk and stir until combined and moist. Pack into the pastry case and smooth level. Fold the overhanging pastry edges over the filling.

4 Roll out the remaining pastry to a round to fit the top of the tin. Moisten the pastry edges in the tin, place the round on top and press together. Pinch the edges together in a fluted pattern to seal. Make six or seven large holes in the pastry lid with a skewer, then prick over the top with a fork, making an even pattern. Brush liberally with beaten egg.

5 Bake in the centre of the oven for about 2½ hours or until a warmed metal skewer inserted in the middle comes out clean. If the top begins to brown too quickly, cover with a sheet of brown paper or a sheet of greaseproof paper and several sheets of newspaper.

6 Leave to cool in the tin, then store for 4 weeks to allow the filling to mellow.

TO FREEZE: *Freezing speeds up the mellowing process of the filling, as it does for all fruit cakes. Store in a rigid container. Keeps for up to 4 months.*

Illustrated opposite page 144

$\mathcal{S}$IMNEL CAKE

*Traditionally, Simnel cake was made for Mothering Sunday. Girls
working in service were allowed to use up the leftover dried fruits
from the Christmas celebrations to make this cake as a present for
their mothers. Live-in servants quite often did not see their parents
for long periods of time, and these cakes, decorated with bunches of
wild spring flowers, must have been a very welcome gift. Nowadays,
Simnel cakes are often made for Easter, decorated with eleven balls
of almond paste to represent all of the apostles except for Judas.*

- 225 G/8 OZ PLAIN FLOUR
- 1 TSP BAKING POWDER
- 2 TSP MIXED SPICE
- PINCH SALT
- 175 G/6 OZ BUTTER,
AT ROOM TEMPERATURE
- 175 G/6 OZ SOFT BROWN SUGAR
- 3 EGGS, SIZE 2
- 100 G/4 OZ RAISINS
- 175 G/6 OZ CURRANTS
- 100 G/4 OZ SULTANAS

- 50 G/2 OZ CHOPPED CANDIED
MIXED PEEL
- 50 G/2 OZ GLACÉ CHERRIES,
RINSED, DRIED AND HALVED
- 2 TBSP MILK
- FINELY GRATED ZEST
1 ORANGE AND ½ LEMON
- 450 G/1LB ALMOND PASTE
(SEE PAGE 160)
- 2 TBSP APRICOT GLAZE
(SEE PAGE 169)

1 Set the oven to 160°C/325°F/Gas 3. Grease and line an 18cm/7inch round deep
cake tin.

2 Sift together the flour, baking powder, spice and salt. Cream the butter and sugar
together until light and fluffy. Beat the eggs into the mixture one at a time, adding a
little flour with each addition. Add the fruits and peel to the remaining flour and toss
lightly to coat, then fold into the creamed mixture with the milk and grated zests. Stir
well together.

$\mathcal{3}$ Roll out one-third of the almond paste to a round the same size as the cake tin. Spoon half the cake mixture into the tin, place the almond paste round on top and cover with the remainder of the cake mixture. Smooth level. Bake for about 2 hours or until the centre of the cake is firm. Leave to cool in the tin, then turn out on to a wire rack and remove the lining paper.

$\mathcal{4}$ When the cake is cold, brush the top with the apricot glaze. Roll out just over half the remaining almond paste to a round to fit the top of the cake. Place on the cake. Mark a criss-cross pattern in the middle, then flute up the edges of the paste like pastry. Roll the rest of the almond paste into eleven balls. Dab each with apricot jam and stick to the top, arranging in a ring. Add sugar or fresh flowers, and tie a nice bright ribbon round the outside.

NOTE: *The 18cm/7inch tin makes a deep cake. If you wish to make a shallower one, use a 20cm/8inch tin, and bake about 15 minutes less.*

TO FREEZE: *Wrap whole cake or pieces in foil. Keeps for 3 months.*

Illustrated opposite page 97

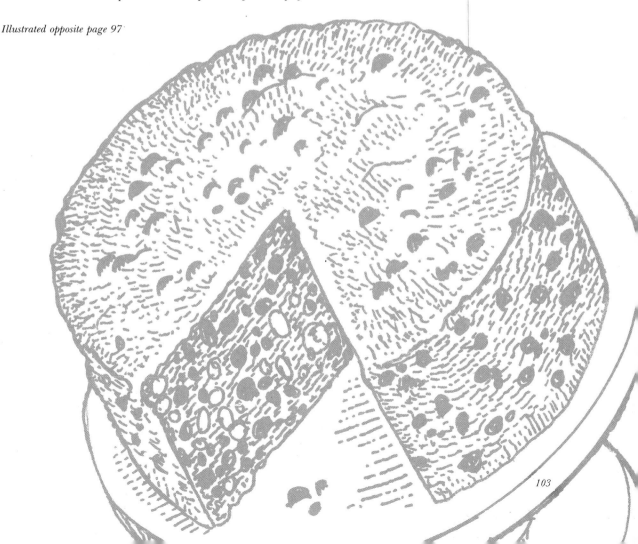

WHISKY FRUIT CAKE

This is a really moist fruit cake made by the old-fashioned method of simmering the fruit in liquid before mixing, which really plumps it up. You can replace the whisky with dark rum, brandy or sherry, but as mine is a Scottish household, we've usually the odd 'wee dram' around. This is a good cake for keeping in the cake tin for 2–3 weeks.

- 175 G/6 OZ STONED DATES, CHOPPED
- 175 G/6 OZ NO-NEED-TO-SOAK DRIED APRICOTS, CHOPPED
- 225 G/8 OZ RAISINS OR SULTANAS
- 100 G/4 OZ CHOPPED CANDIED MIXED PEEL
- 50 G/2 OZ GLACÉ CHERRIES, HALVED
- 150 G/5 OZ BUTTER

- 150 ML/¼ PINT MILK
- 5 TBSP GOLDEN SYRUP
- 3 TBSP WHISKY
- 225 G/8 OZ PLAIN WHOLEMEAL FLOUR
- 1 TSP MIXED SPICE
- 2 EGGS, SIZE 3
- ½ TSP BICARBONATE OF SODA
- DEMERARA SUGAR, TO DECORATE

1 Set the oven to 150°C/300°F/Gas 2. Grease and line a 20cm/8inch round deep cake tin.

2 Place the dried fruits, peel and cherries in a heavy-based saucepan with the butter, milk and syrup and heat gently until the butter has melted. Simmer for about 5 minutes, stirring regularly, then pour the mixture into a bowl. Leave it to cool for 30 minutes (this is important as the cake will not rise if the mixture is still warm when the soda is added). Stir in the whisky as the mixture cools.

3 Sift the flour and mixed spice together, then add any bran remaining in the sieve. When the fruit mixture is cold, beat in the eggs and soda, then stir in the flour. Spoon into the tin and make a small hollow in the centre.

4 Bake in the centre of the oven for about 1¾ hours or until the cake is firm to the touch in the centre. Sprinkle with demerara sugar whilst still hot, then leave to cool in the tin. Remove the lining paper and store in an airtight tin until needed.

TO FREEZE: *Wrap tightly in foil. Keeps for up to 6 months.*

$\mathcal{V}$INEGAR CAKE

This is an eggless cake that I make for a friend who has an allergy to eggs. You can't taste the vinegar, but it does give the cake a lovely tartness, which combines beautifully with a slice of cheese.

- 225 G/8 OZ BUTTER
- 450 G/1LB PLAIN FLOUR
- 450 G/1LB MIXED DRIED FRUIT
- 225 G/8 OZ DARK MUSCOVADO SUGAR
- 1 TSP BICARBONATE OF SODA
- 300 ML/½ PINT MILK
- 3 TBSP CIDER OR MALT VINEGAR

1 Set the oven to 200°C/400°F/Gas 6. Grease and line a 20cm/8inch square or 23cm/9inch round deep cake tin.

2 Rub the butter into the flour until the mixture resembles fine crumbs, then stir in the fruit and sugar. Sprinkle the bicarbonate of soda over the milk, then add the vinegar, which will make the mixture foam and froth. Add to the dry mix in the bowl and stir quickly together.

3 Spoon into the prepared tin and level the top. Bake for 20 minutes, then reduce the heat to 170°C/325°F/Gas 3 and continue baking for about 1½ hours or until firm to the touch. If the top starts to become too brown, cover with screwed-up dampened greaseproof paper. Leave to cool in the tin.

TO FREEZE: *Wrap in foil. Keeps for 3 months.*

Tie brown paper around tin
to protect sides of cake

A skewer will come out clean
when cake is cooked

ℬUTTERSCOTCH
FRUIT CAKE

This is my favourite light fruit cake, which makes an excellent base
for all sorts of celebration cakes. It keeps well for about 4 weeks,
and has a delicious butterscotchy flavour.

- 1 TBSP BLACK TREACLE
- 225 G/8 OZ BUTTER,
  AT ROOM TEMPERATURE
- 225 G/8 OZ SOFT LIGHT
  BROWN SUGAR
- ½ TSP ALMOND ESSENCE
- ½ TSP VANILLA ESSENCE
- 2 TBSP ORANGE MARMALADE

- 4 EGGS, SIZE 3, SEPARATED
- 275 G/10 OZ PLAIN FLOUR
- ½ TSP GROUND NUTMEG
- 400 G/14 OZ DRIED
  MIXED FRUIT
- 4 TBSP DARK RUM
- TOPPING (OPTIONAL,
  SEE STEP 5)

1 Set the oven to 170°C/325°F/Gas 3. Grease and line a 20cm/8inch square or 23cm/9inch round deep cake tin.

2 Cream together the treacle, butter and sugar until light and fluffy, then beat in the essences and marmalade. Gradually add the egg yolks, beating well. Sift in the flour and nutmeg, then sprinkle over the fruit and stir into the mixture.

3 Whisk the egg whites until they form soft peaks. Gently fold a little egg white into the mixture to loosen it, then fold in the remainder, with 3 tbsp rum.

4 Spoon into the tin and smooth level. Bake in the centre of the oven for about 2½ hours or until a skewer inserted in the centre comes out clean. Leave to cool in the tin for 15 minutes, then turn out on to a wire rack to cool completely. Peel away the lining paper.

5 Sprinkle with 1 tbsp rum, or more if you are feeling generous, and store in an airtight tin for 1 week. Eat plain, or decorate with almond paste (see page 160) and royal or fondant icing (see page 162 or 164).

TO FREEZE: *Wrap in foil. Keeps for 2–3 months.*

Sultana and Lemon Loaves

I make these easy teabreads for slicing and buttering at bazaars and fêtes. You can make them in batches of two and freeze or store them in airtight tins for up to 2 weeks. This is a great standby when your friends volunteer you to 'do the teas'.

- 450 G/1 LB SULTANAS
- 225 G/8 OZ DEMERARA SUGAR
- 300 ML/½ PINT WARM TEA, STRAINED
- 1 EGG, SIZE 3
- 2 TBSP LEMON OR LIME MARMALADE
- 225 G/8 OZ PLAIN FLOUR
- 225 G/8 OZ PLAIN WHOLEMEAL FLOUR
- 4 TSP BAKING POWDER

1 Place the sultanas, sugar and tea in a bowl and leave to soak overnight.

2 Set the oven to 170°C/325°F/Gas 3. Grease and base-line two 450g/1lb loaf tins.

3 Beat the egg and marmalade into the sultanas and liquid. Sift in the flours and baking powder, adding any bran left in the sieve. Mix together well. If dry, add 1–2 tbsp milk. Divide between the two tins and spread the tops level.

4 Bake in the centre of the oven for about 1½ hours or until the cakes are firm to the touch in the centre. Cool in the tins for 5 minutes, then turn out on to wire racks to cool completely. Serve sliced and buttered.

VARIATIONS: *Replace the sultanas with mixed dried fruit or raisins and the lemon marmalade with orange marmalade. For a malt loaf, replace the marmalade with malt extract.*

TO FREEZE: *Wrap in foil and pack in freezer bags. Keeps for up to 4 months.*

Illustrated opposite page 96

GEORGE WASHINGTON
CAKE

*The recipe for this cake was taken over to the USA from England in
the eighteenth century.*

- 350 G/12 OZ UNSALTED BUTTER
  OR BLOCK MARGARINE, AT
  ROOM TEMPERATURE
- 350 G/12 OZ CASTER SUGAR
- 4 EGGS, SIZE 3, SEPARATED
- 450 G/1LB PLAIN FLOUR
- 1 TBSP BAKING POWDER
- 1 TSP GROUND MACE
- 1 TSP GROUND CINNAMON
- ½ TSP SALT
- 300 ML/½ PINT MILK
- 100 G/4 OZ RAISINS
- 50 G/2 OZ CURRANTS
- FINELY GRATED ZEST
  1 LARGE LEMON
- FILLING AND TOPPING
  (SEE STEP 5)

1 Set the oven to 170°C/325°F/Gas 3. Grease and double-line a 23cm/9inch round or
20cm/8inch square deep cake tin.

2 Cream the fat and sugar together until light and fluffy, then beat in the egg yolks,
adding a teaspoon of flour to help the mixture combine.

3 Sift the remaining flour, the baking powder, spices and salt together and fold
alternately into the creamed mixture with the milk. Stir in the dried fruit and zest.
Whisk the egg whites until they form soft peaks and fold in as lightly as possible.

4 Spoon into the tin. Bake for about 1½ hours or until a warmed skewer inserted in
the centre comes out cleanly. Leave to cool in the tin for 10 minutes, then turn out on
to a wire rack to cool completely.

5 Cut the cake in half horizontally and sandwich together with simple buttercream
(see page 170). Spread the top with thin glacé icing (see page 166) or royal icing (see
page 162) and let it dribble down the sides unevenly.

TO FREEZE: *Wrap in non-stick silicone paper, then foil. Keeps for 3 months.*

*W*HAT WENT WRONG?

☞ THE FRUIT SINKS:

Dried fruits are heavy and if the mixture is too wet, the weighty fruits will drop to the bottom, so keep the mixture stiff enough to support the fruit. Rinse off any syrup from glacé cherries, dry them well and toss in flour, as syrupy cherries will sink. Wet fruit will also sink, so if you wash or soak it before use, pat it dry with a tea towel or kitchen paper before adding to the mixture.

☞ A HARD CRUST FORMS:

A crust will form if the oven is too hot, or if the cake is baked for too long or too near the top of the oven. A fruit cake baked for several hours must be protected by several layers of brown paper or newspaper wrapped around the tin to prevent a crust from forming.

☞ THE TOP SINKS IN THE MIDDLE:

Too much raising agent can cause this, as can overbeating after adding the eggs. Use of too small a tin, too cool an oven, underbaking, or slamming the door during baking can also cause this to happen.

☞ THE TOP CRACKS OR PEAKS:

This can be caused by too hot an oven, too dry a mixture, or using a shelf too near the top of the oven.

☞ THE CAKE SLOPES TO ONE SIDE:

This can be caused by not thoroughly preheating the oven, not positioning the cake centrally, or the shelf or oven itself not being level.

☞ THE COOKED CAKE HAS MOULD AFTER STORAGE:

Patches of mould can occur if the cake is stored in humid, wet, warm or steamy conditions, and usually occurs on an undercooked cake. Plastic storage boxes encourage mould, and should never be used to store fruit cakes for long periods, as they keep in moisture. Always use airtight tins or layers of foil for storage.

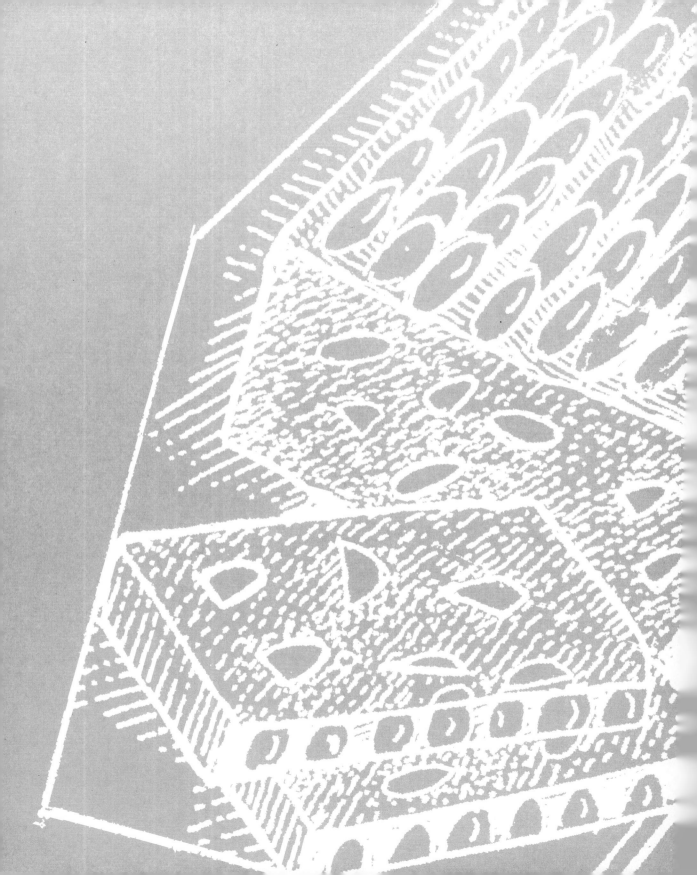

$\mathcal{N}$ UTTY CAKES

CHAPTER SIX

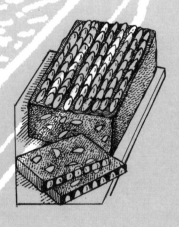

Cakes baked with nuts are truly delicious, moist and tender. Continental cakes and gâteaux are absolutely loaded with nuts of every description, and really make the most of these delectable morsels. Ground nuts impart a moist texture, and as they have a high fat content, they also enrich a cake.

When buying nuts, choose shops that have a rapid turnover of stock. Since nuts have such a high fat content, they can go rancid very quickly, which gives them an awful, bitter flavour. Do not buy nuts in bulk, as they do not have a long shelf life at home; only buy them when you need them. If you do have some left to store, keep them in a jar in a cool place for up to 4 months. Whole or shelled nuts can be frozen in polythene bags, but do label them clearly with the date, and don't keep them for longer than 12 months, or 3 months if toasted.

RIGHT (from top to bottom): Hazelnut Meringue Torte with Raspberry Cream Filling (see page 115); Frosted English Walnut Layer (see page 121); Almond, Grand Marnier and Strawberry Gâteau (see page 124).

NUTTY CAKES

LEFT (from top to bottom): Coffee and Walnut Gâteau (see page 117); Nutty Orange Kugelhupf (see page 122); Crunchy Topped Coconut Cake with Apricots (see page 120).

$\mathcal{U}$SING NUTS FOR BAKING

ALMONDS

Almonds can be bought blanched, flaked, slivered, chopped or ground, or you can buy the whole almonds and prepare them at home for real freshness.

Shelled almonds still have their skins on. To remove these, blanch the nuts in boiling water for a few minutes; the nuts will then slip easily out of the skins. It is easier to chop, split or grind blanched nuts while they are still warm.

To grind almonds, place them in a food processor and work until fine. Take care not to over-process as the natural oils from the nuts will be released, and they will be difficult to handle. Chop or process in small batches to make the job easier.

Pour boiling water over almonds to blanch

BRAZIL NUTS

These rich nuts have a wonderful flavour, and are more often sold in the shell. To crack them easily, place in the freezer for a few hours (this is particularly helpful if you have lots to shell). Brazils can be used whole or chopped, or you can slice them lengthways with a knife or peeler and toast them. Use as an outer coating for a gâteau instead of flaked almonds.

HAZELNUTS

Hazelnuts are sold whole, shelled in their skins, chopped or ground. Most cake recipes used toasted hazelnuts because toasting brings out their flavour. To toast, spread whole nuts on a baking sheet and place under a hot grill for a few minutes, shaking the sheet occasionally. To remove the feathery skins, rub the hot nuts in a tea towel and the skins will flake away. To grind the nuts, work them in a food processor in small amounts, taking care not to over-process as this makes them oily.

Remove nuts after a few minutes

PISTACHIO NUTS

These sweet aromatic little nuts have a dark brown skin, but a wonderful bright green kernel, which makes them ideal for decoration. To remove the outer skins, blanch the nuts in boiling water for 1 minute, then slip them out of their skins while still warm. Use them whole or chopped.

Slip the nuts out of their skins

WALNUTS

Walnuts are very oily and will turn rancid quickly, so should not be stored in bulk. Whole nuts will wither inside the shell if not eaten quickly. The larger the nuts, the more expensive and better quality they are. They can be bought in halves or pieces, and these are ideal for chopping or grinding. Chop them quickly in a food processor to prevent them releasing too much oil, or snip a small amount with kitchen scissors.

HAZELNUT MERINGUE TORTE WITH RASPBERRY CREAM FILLING

The meringue bases can be made well ahead of time and stored for 1–2 days before spreading with chocolate and sandwiching together with cream and raspberries.

- 150 G/5 OZ CHOPPED, TOASTED HAZELNUTS
- 5 EGG WHITES, SIZE 3
- 275 G/10 OZ CASTER SUGAR, STORED WITH A VANILLA POD
- 1 TSP LEMON JUICE
- 225 G/8 OZ PLAIN CHOCOLATE
- **FILLING:**
- 300 ML/½ PINT DOUBLE OR WHIPPING CREAM
- 225 G/8 OZ RASPBERRIES

1 Set the oven to 190°C/375°F/Gas 5. Grease and line two 20cm/8inch sandwich tins.

2 Place the nuts in a food processor, grinder or blender and grind them finely. Whisk the egg whites until they form stiff peaks, then add half the sugar, a tablespoon at a time, whisking after each addition. Stir the nuts and remaining sugar together, then fold them gently into the egg whites with the lemon juice, using a metal spoon.

3 Divide the meringue evenly between the tins and spread level. Bake in the centre of the oven for about 35 minutes. Leave to cool completely in the tins, then loosen the sides with a knife, turn out and peel away the lining paper.

4 Break the chocolate into pieces and melt gently in a heatproof bowl set over a pan of warm water, or in the microwave oven. Paint the underside of each meringue layer with a thin coat of chocolate, then leave to dry and set.

5 To make the filling, whip the cream until stiff, then fold in the raspberries. Place one meringue layer on a plate, chocolate side up, then spread with the cream and place the other meringue layer on top, chocolate side down. If liked, dredge with sifted icing sugar and decorate with any leftover raspberries. If you have a little melted chocolate left, place it in a paper piping bag (see page 182), cut a small hole in the tip and drizzle thin lines of chocolate across the top of the torte. Chill for 30 minutes before serving, to firm the cream.

Not suitable for freezing.

Illustrated opposite page 112

GÂTEAU SANS RIVAL

This cake contains no flour, but lots of almonds. It makes a very special party cake.

- 100 G/4 OZ GROUND ALMONDS
- 150 G/5 OZ CASTER SUGAR
- 4 EGG WHITES, SIZE 3
- DOUBLE QUANTITY PRALINE (SEE PAGE 171), FINELY CRUSHED
- **FILLING:**
- 4 EGG YOLKS, SIZE 3
- 200 ML/7 FL OZ WHIPPING CREAM, WHIPPED

- 75 G/3 OZ CASTER SUGAR
- 50 G/2 OZ BUTTER
- **DECORATION:**
- 225 G/8 OZ ALMOND PASTE (SEE PAGE 160)
- 50 G/2 OZ FLAKED ALMONDS, LIGHTLY TOASTED

1 Set the oven to 200°C/400°F/Gas 6. Line three baking sheets with non-stick silicone paper, and mark a 20cm/8inch square on each.

2 Mix the ground almonds with the sugar. Whisk the egg whites until stiff, then gradually fold in the almond mixture, keeping the mixture as light as possible. Divide the mixture between the three baking sheets, spreading it inside the squares, and level with a palette knife. Bake for 12–15 minutes or until firm.

3 Leave the meringue layers to cool on the baking sheets until firm enough to handle, then peel away the paper.

4 To make the filling, place all the ingredients in a saucepan and cook gently, stirring, until the mixture thickens. Do not allow to boil at any time. Pour into a bowl to cool. When cold, add the crushed praline.

5 Sandwich the meringue layers together with praline cream, then trim any edges straight with a sharp knife. Spread the remaining filling thinly over the top and round the sides of the gâteau.

6 Colour the almond paste if liked, then roll it out into a thin strip long enough to go round the sides of the cake and wide enough to cover the layers. Press into place. Re-roll the trimmings and cut into flowers or other shapes such as hearts.

7 Sprinkle the top of the gâteau with the flaked almonds, then decorate with the almond paste shapes.

Not suitable for freezing.

$\mathcal{C}$OFFEE AND WALNUT GÂTEAU

This cake makes an ideal large birthday or celebration cake, and can be covered in fondant icing (see page 164) and decorated to suit the occasion.

- 350 G/12 OZ UNSALTED BUTTER, AT ROOM TEMPERATURE
- 350 G/12 OZ SOFT LIGHT BROWN SUGAR
- 6 EGGS, SIZE 3, BEATEN
- 350 G/12 OZ SELF-RAISING FLOUR
- 1 TSP BAKING POWDER
- 1 TBSP INSTANT COFFEE GRANULES
- 100 G/4 OZ SHELLED WALNUTS, CHOPPED

- **TOPPING:**
- CRÈME AU BEURRE (SEE PAGE 167), MADE WITH 225 G/8 OZ CASTER SUGAR, 4 EGG YOLKS, SIZE 3, AND 275 G/10 OZ UNSALTED BUTTER
- **DECORATION:**
- 100 G/4 OZ WALNUT HALVES
- 4 TBSP MAPLE SYRUP

1 Set the oven to 180°C/350°F/Gas 4. Grease and base-line a round 23cm/9inch loose-based or spring-clip cake tin.

2 Cream the butter and sugar together until light and fluffy, then gradually beat in the eggs, adding a little of the self-raising flour with each addition to prevent the mixture from curdling.

3 Sift the remaining flour and baking powder together and fold into the creamed mixture. Dissolve the coffee in 2 tbsp boiling water and cool slightly, then add to the mixture with the walnuts.

4 Spoon the mixture into the tin. Bake in the centre of the oven for 1 hour 10 minutes or until well risen and firm to the touch in the centre. Leave to cool in the tin for 5 minutes, then turn out on to a wire rack and peel away the lining paper. Cool completely.

5 Cut the cake in half horizontally, then sandwich the layers together with one-quarter of the crème au beurre. Spread the remainder over the top and sides of the cake and smooth with a palette knife. Decorate the top with the walnut halves, placed in rings, then drizzle the maple syrup over, letting it trickle down the sides.

TO FREEZE: *Open-freeze filled and iced cake, without the nuts and syrup, in a rigid container. Keeps for 2 months.*

Illustrated opposite page 113

Banana and Nut Teabread

This is a really quick bake and a perfect way of using up those mushy old bananas left in the fruit bowl.

- 200 G/7 OZ SELF-RAISING FLOUR
- PINCH SALT
- ¼ TSP BICARBONATE OF SODA
- 75 G/3 OZ SOFT TUB MARGARINE
- 100 G/4 OZ SOFT LIGHT BROWN SUGAR
- 1 EGG, SIZE 2, BEATEN

- 100 G/4 OZ RAISINS OR CHOPPED DATES
- 75 G/3 OZ SHELLED WALNUTS, CHOPPED
- 2 LARGE VERY RIPE BANANAS, WELL MASHED
- 1–2 TBSP GOLDEN SYRUP

1 Set the oven to 180°C/350°F/Gas 4. Grease and line a 450g/1lb loaf tin.

2 Sift the flour, salt and soda into a bowl. Add all the other ingredients, except the golden syrup, and beat well together. Add 1–2 tbsp milk if the mixture is too dry.

3 Spoon into the prepared tin. Bake in the centre of the oven for about 1 hour or until firm in the middle and just shrinking away from the tin. Leave to cool in the tin for 10 minutes, then turn out on to a wire rack.

4 Brush the top of the loaf with the golden syrup while still warm, to give a sticky glaze. Serve warm or cold, sliced and buttered.

VARIATION: *Omit the walnuts and add 50g/2oz rinsed, chopped glacé cherries.*

TO FREEZE: *Wrap whole loaf or slices in a freezer bag. Keeps for 3 months.*

Moist Almond Gâteau

The ground almonds and spirit in this cake make it beautifully moist. It can be baked a few days ahead, and decorated with caramel-dipped almonds or fondant icing for a special occasion.

- 100 G/4 OZ UNSALTED BUTTER, AT ROOM TEMPERATURE
- 100 G/4 OZ CASTER SUGAR
- 2 EGGS, SIZE 3, BEATEN
- 100 G/4 OZ SELF-RAISING FLOUR

- 75 G/3 OZ GROUND ALMONDS
- 2–3 TBSP KIRSCH, MARSALA OR WATER
- TOPPING (SEE STEP 4)

1 Set the oven to 180°C/350°F/Gas 4. Grease and line a 20cm/8inch round deep cake tin or a 450g/1lb loaf tin.

2 Cream the butter and sugar together until pale and fluffy, then gradually beat in the eggs, adding a little flour with each addition. Stir the almonds and remaining flour together, then gradually fold into the creamed mixture with the Kirsch, Marsala or water, to give a soft consistency.

3 Spoon into the tin and spread level. If using the loaf tin, make a hollow in the middle. Bake the round cake for about 50 minutes or until firm, or the loaf for 1–1¼ hours. Leave to cool in the tin, then store in an airtight tin.

4 Decorate with caramel-dipped almonds (see page 171), arranged into flowers, or with fondant icing (see page 164).

TO FREEZE: *Wrap undecorated cake in foil. Keeps for 2 months.*

Halva Cake for Easter

This cake is made in Cyprus for the Easter celebrations. It is very moist and refreshing and keeps well. It is ideal for an informal Easter buffet party.

- 175 G/6 OZ BUTTER, AT ROOM TEMPERATURE
- 175 G/6 OZ CASTER SUGAR
- 4 EGGS, SIZE 3
- 175 G/6 OZ SEMOLINA
- 1 TSP GROUND CINNAMON
- 50 G/2 OZ GROUND ALMONDS

- 50 G/2 OZ FLAKED ALMONDS
- **SYRUP:**
- 225 G/8 OZ CASTER SUGAR
- 600 ML/1 PINT WATER
- 1 TBSP LEMON JUICE
- 1 CINNAMON STICK

1 Set the oven to 190°C/375°F/Gas 5. Grease and line an 18cm/7inch round deep cake tin.

2 Cream the butter and sugar together until light and fluffy. Beat in the eggs one at a time, then beat in the semolina and cinnamon. Fold in the ground almonds and half the flaked almonds, reserving the rest for the top.

3 Turn the mixture into the tin. Bake for 40 minutes or until a skewer inserted in the middle comes out clean.

4 Make the syrup while the cake is baking: place all the ingredients in a large pan and heat gently until every grain of sugar has dissolved. Boil rapidly for 15 minutes until a syrup is formed, then remove the cinnamon stick.

5 Pour the syrup over the warm cake in the tin and leave to cool completely, in the tin. When cold, sprinkle over the remaining almonds.

TO FREEZE: *Wrap cake in foil and seal. Keeps for 2 months.*

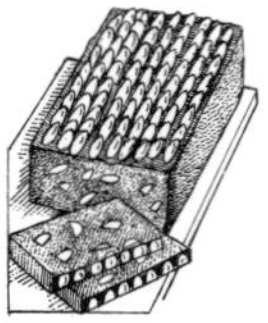

CRUNCHY TOPPED
COCONUT CAKE
WITH APRICOTS

This crunchy topped coconut cake is delicious served just warm with cream or yogurt, or cold on its own.

- **CRUNCHY TOPPING:**
- 25 G/1 OZ BUTTER OR BLOCK MARGARINE
- 40 G/1½ OZ PLAIN FLOUR
- 50 G/2 OZ DEMERARA SUGAR
- 25 G/1 OZ DESICCATED COCONUT
- **CAKE:**
- 175 G/6 OZ BUTTER OR BLOCK MARGARINE, AT ROOM TEMPERATURE

- 175 G/6 OZ CASTER SUGAR
- 3 EGGS, SIZE 3, BEATEN
- 175 G/6 OZ SELF-RAISING FLOUR
- 6 FRESH APRICOTS, PEELED, STONED AND CHOPPED OR 1 × 225 G/8 OZ TIN APRICOTS, DRAINED AND CHOPPED
- 75 G/3 OZ DESICCATED COCONUT

1 Set the oven to 160°C/325°F/Gas 3. Grease and base-line a 20cm/8inch round loose-based or spring-clip cake tin.

2 Make the topping by rubbing the fat into the flour until it resembles fine crumbs, then stirring in the remaining ingredients.

3 To make the cake, cream the fat with the sugar until light and fluffy. Beat in the eggs gradually, adding a little flour with each addition to prevent curdling. Fold in the remaining flour, the apricots and coconut.

4 Turn the mixture into the prepared tin and smooth the top level. Sprinkle the topping in an even layer over the cake mixture. Bake in the centre of the oven for about 1¼ hours or until the middle of the cake is firm. Leave to cool in the tin for 10 minutes, then remove the sides of the tin and cool the cake completely on a wire rack.

Not suitable for freezing.

Illustrated opposite page 113

FROSTED ENGLISH WALNUT LAYER

I still remember being taken out to tea at the local Fuller's Tea Shop as a child. The pièce de résistance was their famous frosted walnut cake. They were so irresistible we usually bought one to take home in a box. This obviously accounts for a life-long addiction to cakes!

- 225 G/8 OZ SELF-RAISING FLOUR
  - 1 TSP BAKING POWDER
  - 225 G/8 OZ BUTTER OR BLOCK MARGARINE, AT ROOM TEMPERATURE
  - 225 G/8 OZ SOFT LIGHT BROWN SUGAR
  - 4 EGGS, SIZE 2, BEATEN
- 75 G/3 OZ SHELLED WALNUTS, FINELY CHOPPED
  - 1 TBSP BLACK TREACLE
  - 1 QUANTITY SEVEN-MINUTE FROSTING (SEE PAGE 166)
  - 8 WALNUT HALVES, TO DECORATE

1 Grease and base-line three 20cm/8inch sandwich tins. Set the oven to 170°C/325°F/Gas 3.

2 Sift the flour and baking powder together. Cream the fat and sugar together until light and fluffy, then beat in the eggs gradually, adding a little flour with each addition. Fold in the remaining flour with the chopped walnuts and black treacle.

3 Divide the mixture among the three tins and level the tops. Bake as centrally in the oven as possible for about 30 minutes or until springy to the touch in the centre. Leave to cool in the tins for 5 minutes, then turn out on to wire racks and cool completely.

4 Sandwich the cakes together thinly with frosting, then cover the top and sides, flicking and swirling the frosting with a palette knife. Decorate with the walnut halves in a ring, and leave on the serving place to allow the frosting to set.

TO FREEZE: *Wrap unfilled layers in freezer bags. Keeps for 3 months.*

Illustrated opposite page 112

Nutty Orange
KUGELHUPF

The kugelhupf or gugelhupf mould is round and deep with fluted or patterned sides and a chimney in the middle. The mould comes from Southern Germany and Austria, and bakes wonderful cakes because the heat is distributed so evenly in the centre. Traditionally, yeasted mixtures were baked in these moulds, but light sponge and fruit cakes work just as well.

- 225 G/8 OZ BUTTER OR BLOCK MARGARINE, AT ROOM TEMPERATURE
- 225 G/8 OZ SOFT LIGHT BROWN SUGAR
- 3 EGGS, SIZE 3
- 225 G/8 OZ SELF-RAISING FLOUR
- FINELY GRATED ZEST 1 ORANGE
- 50 G/2 OZ CHOPPED CANDIED MIXED PEEL
- 50 G/2 OZ CHOPPED MIXED NUTS
- **SYRUP:**
- 3 TBSP CLEAR HONEY
- 4 TBSP FRESH ORANGE JUICE
- **DECORATION:**
- 100 G/4 OZ ICING SUGAR
- 1 TBSP ORANGE JUICE
- 2 TBSP CHOPPED MIXED NUTS

1 Brush a 1.75 litre/3 pint kugelhupf mould with melted lard. Set the oven to 190°C/375°F/Gas 5.

2 Cream the fat and sugar together until light and fluffy, then beat in the eggs, one at a time, adding a little flour with each to prevent curdling. Fold in the remaining flour, the zest, peel and nuts, with 1 tbsp of cold water.

3 Spoon into the prepared mould and smooth the top level. Bake in the centre of the oven for about 1 hour or until firm to the touch and golden. Leave to cool in the mould for 2 minutes, then turn out on to a wire rack to cool completely.

4 When cold, place the honey and orange juice in a saucepan or microwave bowl and heat gently to melt the honey. Brush over the cake, and leave to cool.

5 To decorate, sift the icing sugar into a bowl and stir in the orange juice until well blended. Drizzle this glacé icing over the top and down the sides of the cake, then sprinkle the chopped nuts in a ring round the top. Alternatively, just dust the kugelhupf with sifted icing sugar to give a pretty snow-capped effect.

TO FREEZE: *Wrap undecorated cake in foil. Keeps for 2 months.*

Illustrated opposite page 113

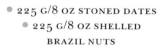
ITALIAN FRUIT AND NUT FESTIVE RING

This cake contains very little flour, and the fruit and nuts are almost stuck to each other. It is a lovely cake to have in the tin around Christmas time, and looks very pretty with its glazed fruit top.

- 225 G/8 OZ STONED DATES
- 225 G/8 OZ SHELLED BRAZIL NUTS
- 100 G/4 OZ GLACÉ CHERRIES
- 50 G/2 OZ DARK MUSCOVADO SUGAR
- 50 G/2 OZ PLAIN FLOUR
- ½ TSP MIXED SPICE
- ¼ TSP BAKING POWDER
- 50 G/2 OZ CHOPPED CANDIED MIXED PEEL
- 2 TBSP DARK RUM OR SHERRY
- 1 EGG, SIZE 2, BEATEN
- ½ TSP VANILLA ESSENCE
- TOPPING (SEE STEP 4)

1 Grease and line an 18cm/7inch ring mould or a 450g/1lb loaf tin. Set the oven to 150°C/300°F/Gas 2.

2 Chop the dates, nuts and cherries roughly into large pieces and put in a bowl. Add the sugar, and sift in the flour, spice and baking powder. Stir to mix. Place the peel and rum or sherry in a small pan and heat gently to soften the peel. Cool slightly, then add to the bowl with the egg and vanilla essence. Mix together well.

3 Spoon into the mould or tin and press down level. Bake for 1¼–1½ hours, covering with foil if the cake starts to overbrown. Cool in the tin for 5 minutes, then turn out on to a wire rack to cool completely.

4 When cold, brush with apricot glaze (see page 169) or honey, and decorate with candied peel, fruit and nuts, plus a red ribbon bow.

TO FREEZE: *Wrap undecorated cake in foil. Keeps for 6 months.*

ALMOND, GRAND MARNIER AND STRAWBERRY GÂTEAU

This larger cake makes a good centrepiece for a family christening or party. You can easily make the cake base ahead of time, then decorate with lots of luscious strawberries just before serving.

- 175 G/6 OZ BUTTER, AT ROOM TEMPERATURE
- 175 G/6 OZ CASTER SUGAR
- FINELY GRATED ZEST 1 ORANGE
- 3 EGGS, SIZE 2, BEATEN
- 175 G/6 OZ SELF-RAISING FLOUR
- 2 TBSP ORANGE JUICE
- 50 G/2 OZ GROUND ALMONDS

- **FILLING AND DECORATION:**
- 4 TBSP GRAND MARNIER OR OTHER ORANGE LIQUEUR
- 275 G/10 OZ FRESH STRAWBERRIES
- 300 ML/½ PINT DOUBLE CREAM, WHIPPED
- 100 G/4 OZ FLAKED ALMONDS
- ICING SUGAR

1 Set the oven to 170°C/325°F/Gas 3. Grease and line a 20cm/8inch round deep cake tin.

2 Cream the butter, sugar and zest together until very light and fluffy. Beat in the eggs, a little at a time, adding a teaspoon of flour if necessary to prevent the mixture from curdling. Fold in the orange juice, then sift in the remaining flour with the ground almonds. Fold lightly together until a soft consistency is reached.

3 Spoon into the tin. Bake in the centre of the oven for about 1¼ hours or until the sides are slightly shrunken away from the tin and the top is springy. Cool in the tin for 3 minutes, then turn out on to a wire rack and peel away the lining paper. Leave to cool completely.

4 Cut the cold cake in half horizontally, and sprinkle each half with 1 tbsp Grand Marnier. Keep aside 10–12 strawberries for decoration; hull and slice the rest and place on a plate. Sprinkle over the remaining liqueur and leave to soak for 2 hours.

5 To assemble the cake, divide the cream in half. Fold the sliced strawberries and their liquid into one half, and spread this on to the bottom cake layer. Set the other layer on top. Place neatly on a plate, then spread the remaining cream over the top and sides of the cake, smoothing with a palette knife.

6 Press the flaked almonds on to the sides of the cake thickly to cover. Cut thick strips of greaseproof paper and place diagonally across the top of the cake. Sift icing sugar over the top, then remove the paper strips, leaving a diagonal pattern. Halve the reserved strawberries, leaving the green tops attached, and arrange on the cake in diagonal lines, between the icing sugar. Chill until ready to serve.

TO FREEZE: *Wrap unsplit, undecorated cake in foil. Keeps for 3 months.*

Illustrated opposite page 112

$\mathcal{G}$RATED CHOCOLATE
AND HAZELNUT GÂTEAU

This cake has a combination of flavours: when you first bite into it,
it tastes of hazelnuts, then the secondary flavour of grated chocolate
comes through. A wonderful experience!

- 200 G/7 OZ UNSALTED BUTTER, AT ROOM TEMPERATURE
- 175 G/6 OZ SOFT LIGHT BROWN SUGAR
- 3 EGGS, SIZE 3, SEPARATED
- 75 G/3 OZ SELF-RAISING FLOUR
- 75 G/3 OZ SKINNED HAZELNUTS, FINELY GROUND
- 100 G/4 OZ PLAIN CHOCOLATE, FINELY GRATED
- PINCH SALT
- 1 TBSP BRANDY (OPTIONAL)
- **CHOCOLATE GANACHE:**
- 150 ML/¼ PINT DOUBLE CREAM
- 100 G/4 OZ PLAIN CHOCOLATE, BROKEN INTO PIECES

1 Set the oven to 170°C/325°F/Gas 3. Grease and line a 900g/2lb loaf tin.

2 Cream the butter and sugar together until light and fluffy. Beat in the egg yolks one by one, then gently fold in the flour. Stir in the ground hazelnuts and grated chocolate.

3 Whisk the egg whites with the salt until they form floppy peaks. Fold a little into the mixture to loosen it, then fold in the remaining egg white gently.

4 Turn into the tin. Bake in the centre of the oven for 1¼ hours, then cool in the tin for 5 minutes. Turn out on to a wire rack to cool and peel away the lining paper. Sprinkle over the brandy if used.

5 To make the ganache filling, put the cream in a small saucepan and bring to the boil. Remove from the heat, add the chocolate and stir until melted. Pour into a bowl and leave to cool for 30 minutes, then whisk the mixture for 4–5 minutes with an electric mixer until it becomes very pale and fluffy. Chill for 15 minutes.

6 Split the cake into three horizontally and sandwich the layers together with ganache. Pipe rosettes of ganache on top or dredge with sifted icing sugar and decorate with fresh fruit such as cherries and strawberries.

TO FREEZE: *Wrap unfilled cake in foil. Keeps for 6 months.*

Illustrated opposite page 128

$\mathscr{M}$ ICROWAVE BAKING

CHAPTER SEVEN

MICROWAVE
BAKING

A new method of cooking – by microwave – has brought many advantages with it. Foods can be cooked in a matter of minutes, including many cakes. If you need to bake a cake in a hurry, then the microwave oven really does come into its own, although you do miss out on all those lovely aromas that normally fill the kitchen. When you have no space left in your conventional oven, then use the microwave for a quick bake – this is especially useful to help busy mothers survive children's party catering or comes to the rescue when those 'unexpected guests' turn up.

There are new and simple rules to be observed when using this source of power, so you will not be able to use your favourite baking recipes without adapting them first. The ones on the following pages have been specially created just for the microwave oven.

RIGHT (from top to bottom): Grated Chocolate and Hazelnut Gâteau (see page 125); Napoleons (see page 76); Angel Cake (see page 27), with Seven-minute Frosting (see page 166) and a raspberry coulis.

MICROWAVE
BAKING

LEFT (from top to bottom): Cherry Cake (see page 133); Rich Fruit Ring Cake (see page 134); Sticky Gingercake (see page 132).

Shield corners with
foil squares

Test cake while surface
is still wet

A ring-shaped cake dish is best

$\mathcal{B}$AKING MICROWAVE CAKES

Microwave-baked cakes rise well, but their texture and flavour are slightly different from cakes baked conventionally. As this is essentially a moist form of cooking, there is no dry heat to bake a brown crust on the outside; therefore, the cakes may be pale, and will need decorating. Here are a few points that need to be followed:

☞ When trying a new recipe, use a deeper container than you think necessary. Cakes can rise up very high, before falling back and setting. Also, only half fill dishes.

☞ Circular containers with rounded corners and straight sides are best for cakes. Pyrex soufflé dishes or casseroles can double up as cake tins. Avoid square containers with sharp corners, as the corners tend to over-cook. If you do use them, shield the corners with small pieces of foil.

☞ A ring-shaped cake dish is ideal for micro-bakes as the centres of most cakes are slower to cook, and this eliminates the problem. If you don't have a ring-shaped dish, stand an upturned microproof tumbler inside a large round dish.

☞ Lightly grease dishes and line them with non-stick silicone paper, but do not dredge with flour, as it will form a soggy crust on the cooked cake.

☞ Cakes look more appetizing if made with wholemeal flour, dark brown sugar, treacle or syrup to give colour.

☞ Cakes with a really high proportion of sugar will dry easily, so don't use these or meringue-type recipes. Make sure that all sugar is well rubbed or creamed in, as lumps of sugar will burn easily.

☞ To convert your favourite recipe for micro-baking you will need to add extra liquid in the form of water, milk, egg or fruit juice. Add about 1 tbsp liquid per egg for sponges and light cakes. Dried fruit in fruit cakes will dry up if not softened first. Microwave it in fruit juice or water for 3 minutes on High (100% power) to soften it first, then leave to cool and plump up. Add the liquid from the fruit and enough extra liquid to give a really soft dropping consistency to the mixture.

☞ Place the cake dish on an upturned soup plate, saucer or trivet. The microwaves need to reach the cake from all angles to cook it evenly.

☞ The top of a cake may look sticky and uncooked, but don't over-cook it. Putting it back in the oven will result in a dry cake which stales quickly.

☞ Do not turn cakes out immediately when cooked. They need 15 minutes standing time to continue to cook and settle down as they cool. Heavy mixtures like fruit cakes need a longer standing time.

☞ Turn cakes out on to a wire rack lined with non-stick silicone paper, otherwise as the cake dries and solidifies it will stick to the rack. If there are any uncooked spots on the cake, don't put it back into the container, but slide it into the oven on the paper and finish cooking in short bursts.

☞ Do not cover cakes with microwave-safe cling film, as you do in much microwave cooking. The steam needs to escape from cakes.

☞ Test the cake when the surface is still wet. Scratch the surface and lift with the point of a knife. Although the top is wet, the area underneath should be cooked. The cake will finish setting and drying as it cools.

☞ Cook sponge batters on High (100% power). The lower power settings pulsate and cause the cake to rise and fall repeatedly, which knocks out the air. Cook rich fruit cakes on Defrost (30% power) to give gentle slow cooking.

☞ Packet cake mixes cook well in the microwave. Add 2–3 extra tbsp liquid or as the packet instructs.

Gently ease cake off wire rack

*Turn cake on to
non-stick paper*

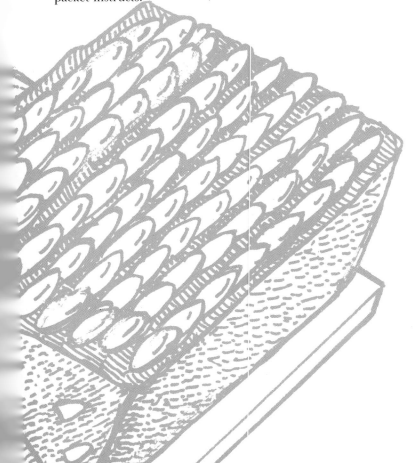

Moist Chocolate Cake

- 100 G/4 OZ GOLDEN SYRUP
- 100 G/4 OZ DARK MUSCOVADO SUGAR
- 100 G/4 OZ SOFT TUB MARGARINE
- 175 G/6 OZ SELF-RAISING FLOUR
- 50 G/2 OZ COCOA POWDER
- 150 ML/¼ PINT MILK
- 1 EGG, SIZE 3, BEATEN
- 1 TSP FINELY GRATED ORANGE ZEST (OPTIONAL)
- 225 G/8 OZ PLAIN CHOCOLATE

1 Butter a 20cm/8inch microwave-proof ring mould. Place the syrup, sugar and margarine in a microwave-proof bowl and cook on High (100% power) for 2 minutes, to melt. Leave to cool for 10 minutes.

2 Sift the flour and cocoa powder into the bowl, then beat in the milk, egg and zest if used. Spoon into the mould and set on an upturned plate. Cook for 5 minutes on High (100% power), then leave to stand for 10 minutes before turning out.

3 When the cake is cold, break up the chocolate and melt it in a microwave-proof bowl in the microwave oven. Spread over the cake and leave to cool and set. Alternatively cover the cake with quick fudge icing (see opposite).

Sticky Gingercake

- 75 G/3 OZ SOFT TUB MARGARINE
- 175 G/6 OZ BLACK TREACLE
- 50 G/2 OZ SOFT DARK BROWN SUGAR
- 2 TBSP GINGER PRESERVE
- 7 TBSP MILK
- ½ TSP BICARBONATE OF SODA
- 75 G/3 OZ SELF-RAISING FLOUR
- 75 G/3 OZ PLAIN FLOUR
- 2 TSP GROUND GINGER
- 1 EGG, SIZE 2, BEATEN
- DEMERARA SUGAR, TO DREDGE

1 Grease and base-line an 18cm/7inch round microwave-proof cake dish.

2 Place the margarine, treacle, sugar and ginger preserve in a microwave-proof bowl and cook on High (100% power) for 1 minute to melt. Warm the milk in a separate bowl on High (100% power) for 30 seconds, then stir in the bicarbonate of soda.

3 Sift the flours and ginger together into a bowl, add the melted mixture, milk and egg and beat together.

4 Spoon into the prepared dish and set on an upturned plate. Cook on High (100% power) for 8 minutes, turning the dish halfway through the cooking. Leave to stand for 5 minutes, then turn out. Dredge with demerara sugar and cool completely.

Illustrated opposite page 129

CHERRY CAKE

- 100 G/4 OZ BUTTER,
AT ROOM TEMPERATURE
- 225 G/8 OZ CASTER SUGAR
- 2 EGGS, SIZE 3, BEATEN
- 200 G/7 OZ SELF-RAISING FLOUR
- 25 G/1 OZ GROUND ALMONDS
- 5 TBSP EVAPORATED MILK

- 75 G/3 OZ GLACÉ CHERRIES,
RINSED, DRIED AND QUARTERED
- **DECORATION:**
- 100 G/4 OZ ICING SUGAR,
SIFTED
- GLACÉ CHERRIES

1 Grease and base-line an 18cm/7inch round cake dish or 900g/2lb microwave-proof loaf tin.

2 Cream the butter and sugar together until light and fluffy, then beat in the eggs gradually. Sift in the flour and almonds, then fold in with the milk and 5 tbsp water. Fold in the quartered cherries gently.

3 Spoon into the prepared dish and set on an upturned plate. Cook on High (100% power) for 8 minutes. Leave to stand for 10 minutes before turning out.

4 To make the icing, beat the sugar and 1 tbsp water together. Drizzle over the cold cake, letting it trickle down the sides. Decorate with glacé cherries.

Illustrated opposite page 129

QUICK FUDGE ICING

- 50 G/2 OZ BUTTER
- 200 G/7 OZ ICING SUGAR,
SIFTED

- 25 G/1 OZ COCOA POWDER,
SIFTED
- 1 TBSP MILK OR CREAM

1 Place all the ingredients plus 1 tbsp boiling water in a microwave-proof bowl and cook on High (100% power) for 10 seconds. Beat well and cook for a further 10–15 seconds. Beat quickly until really smooth. Cool, then beat or whisk again and spread evenly over the moist chocolate cake.

RICH FRUIT RING CAKE

- 150 G/6 OZ BUTTER, AT ROOM TEMPERATURE
- 150 G/6 OZ MOLASSES OR DARK MUSCOVADO SUGAR
- 4 EGGS, SIZE 3, BEATEN
- 2 TBSP BLACK TREACLE
- 2 TBSP DARK RUM
- 1 TBSP GRAVY BROWNING
- 100 G/4 OZ PLAIN WHOLEMEAL FLOUR
- 100 G/4 OZ SELF-RAISING FLOUR
- 1 TBSP MIXED SPICE
- 50 G/2 OZ FINELY GRATED CARROT
- 400 G/14 OZ MIXED DRIED FRUIT, PRE-SOAKED OR PLUMPED
- 100 G/4 OZ GLACÉ CHERRIES, RINSED, DRIED AND HALVED
- 50 G/2 OZ FLAKED ALMONDS OR CHOPPED WALNUTS
- 2 TBSP MILK

1 Grease a 2.5litre/4pint microwave-proof ring mould and dust with caster sugar.

2 Cream the butter and sugar together until light and fluffy, then gradually beat in the eggs, treacle, rum and gravy browning, adding a little flour with each addition to prevent curdling. Sift the remaining flours and spice into the mixture, add the bran from the sieve, then stir in with the carrot, dried fruit, cherries, nuts and milk.

3 Spoon the mixture into the greased ring mould and tap to remove any air pockets. Set the mould on an upturned plate and cook on Low or Defrost (30% power) for 35–40 minutes, turning the cake 2–3 times during cooking. The cake is done when a skewer inserted into the deepest part comes out clean. The surface may still appear sticky. Leave to stand for 25 minutes, then turn out on to a wire rack to cool completely. If liked, decorate with crystallized fruits. Store in an airtight tin for 1 week before cutting.

Illustrated opposite page 129

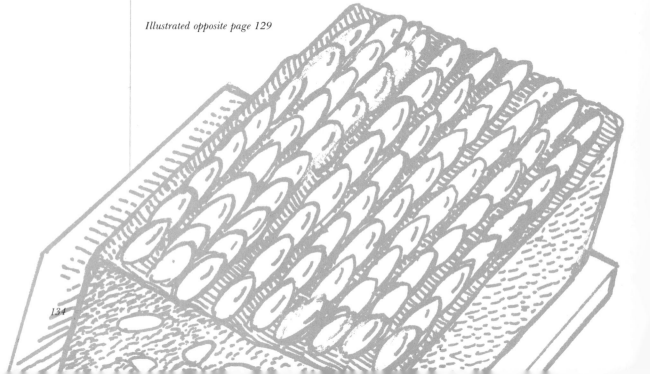

QUEEN CAKES

- 100 G/4 OZ SOFT TUB
MARGARINE
- 100 G/4 OZ CASTER OR SOFT
LIGHT BROWN SUGAR
- 2 EGGS, SIZE 3, BEATEN
- 100 G/4 OZ SELF-RAISING FLOUR
- 50 G/2 OZ CURRANTS
- ½ TSP FINELY GRATED
LEMON ZEST
- 2–3 TBSP MILK
- TOPPING (SEE STEP 4)

1 Arrange six doubled paper cases in a microwave-proof bun tray.

2 Place all the ingredients in a large bowl and beat together until smooth and the mixture has a soft dropping consistency.

3 Half fill the paper cases. Cook, in batches, on High (100% power) for 1 minute or until risen but still slightly moist on the surface. Place on a wire rack to cool.

4 As the cakes are so pale, cover with glacé icing (see page 166) or quick fudge icing (see page 133).

VARIATIONS: *Omit the currants and replace with 50g/2oz of the following: sultanas, finely chopped dates, chocolate chips, chopped glacé cherries or angelica.*

BANANA AND WALNUT CAKE

This is a quickly made moist cake that keeps well in a tin.

- 175 G/6 OZ SOFT DARK
BROWN SUGAR
- 175 G/6 OZ SOFT TUB
MARGARINE
- 3 EGGS
- 175 G/6 OZ WHOLEWHEAT
SELF-RAISING FLOUR
- 2 MEDIUM BANANAS
- 60 ML/4 TBSP EVAPORATED MILK
- 100 G/4 OZ WALNUTS, CHOPPED

1 Grease and base line a 23cm(9in) round dish.

2 Put the sugar, margarine, eggs and flour into a bowl and mix lightly. Mash the bananas with the evaporated milk, and beat into the mixture with half the walnuts.

3 Pour into the dish and spread level. Cook on High for 4 minutes, then sprinkle over the remaining walnuts. Cook for a further 4–5 minutes or until the centre is cooked.

4 Leave to stand for 5 minutes before turning out, then slice when cold.

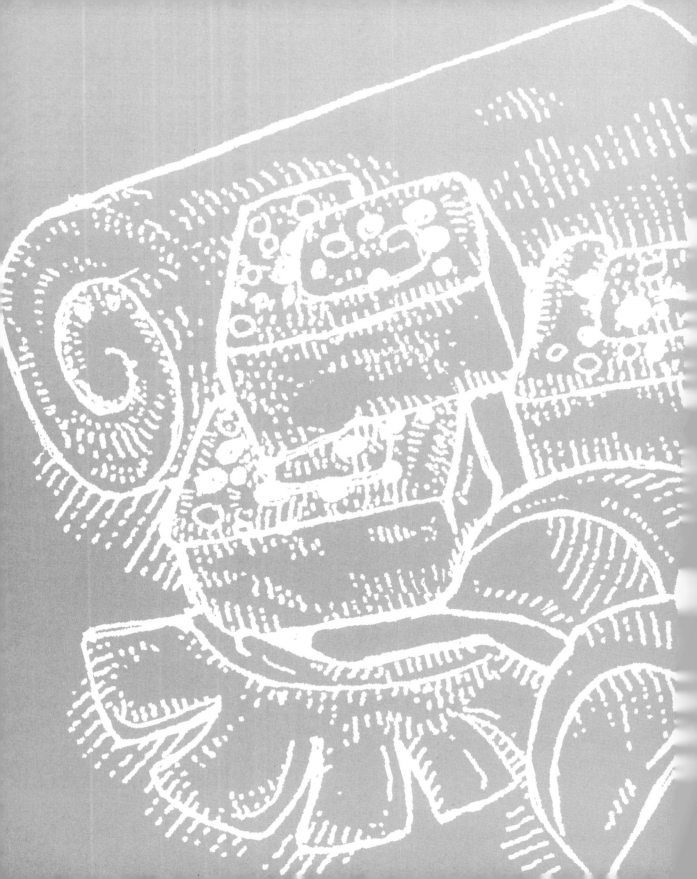

YEAST BAKING

CHAPTER EIGHT

aking with yeast is a true pleasure, and one of the most rewarding pastimes ever. Kneading a large piece of dough until it is smooth must also be one of the most natural ways of relaxing and relieving stress.

Enriched doughs go way back into history, and were the first type of risen cake. They are the most delicious of cakes, moist, rich and delectable. In many parts of the world they double up as breakfast, but you can really eat cakes at any time of day or night.

There is still something rather magical about watching dough rise, shaping it and then filling the house with that unmistakable aroma that only yeast bakes produce. It is well worth all the extra time and effort that is involved, so try a few of the following recipes, I'm sure you'll soon be hooked.

$\mathscr{B}$AKING WITH YEAST

Knead yeast dough well until
smooth and elastic

☞ Fresh yeast is preferable to dried, if you can find it. It can be difficult to obtain – try bakers or health food shops, or buy some in bulk and freeze it in small portions. It should be creamy in colour, cool to the touch and easy to break. It will keep for 4–5 days stored in a polythene bag in the refrigerator, and can be frozen for up to 6 months.

☞ Dried yeast is more convenient as it is readily available in supermarkets. Keep it no longer than 6 months.

☞ Easy-blend yeast is a quick-acting dried yeast, with added improvers which activate the yeast more quickly. It is stirred directly into the dry ingredients, not reconstituted with water. It will keep for up to 6 months in a cool place.

☞ Strong plain flour is needed for yeast baking because it develops quickly into an elastic dough and gives better results than ordinary flours.

☞ Sugar is the food that yeast needs in order to grow. Sometimes sugar is added to dried yeast to get it working.

☞ Fat is used in yeast baking to enrich doughs, delay staling, and improve the quality of the cake.

☞ Liquid for mixing a dough must be at blood heat. If it is any warmer, it can kill off the yeast, and the dough will not rise at all. To test for blood heat, dab a few drops of the liquid on your wrist. If it feels warm, the liquid is too hot.

PREPARING THE YEAST LIQUID

Fresh yeast should be creamed with some of the liquid from the recipe. Dried yeast needs reconstituting: put about 150ml/¼ pint of the measured liquid into a jug, stir in the sugar and sprinkle over the dried yeast. Leave this in a warm place until frothy, about 15 minutes. Dried yeast works more slowly than fresh so allow a little extra time for rising.

KNEADING

Kneading strengthens and develops the gluten in the dough, so that you get a good rise. Use only enough flour on the work surface to prevent the dough from sticking. Knead by folding the dough towards you, then pushing down and away from you with the heels of your hands. Give a quarter turn, fold and push away, developing a rocking motion. Knead for about 10 minutes or until the dough feels firm and elastic and is no longer sticky.

USING A MIXER OR PROCESSOR

A table-top electric mixer with a dough hook attachment is ideal for kneading dough. (Smaller mixers cannot cope with the power needed to handle dough.) Food processors fitted with a plastic blunt blade can knead small amounts of dough, but it is still advisable to knead by hand a little afterwards to get a really smooth dough.

Danish pastry shapes:

Tivolis

Chocolate pinwheels

Cockscombs

Windmills

141

STOLLEN

In Germany, Christmas Eve is a day of feasting and real
celebration and the 25th is a quieter family celebration. Stollen
fruit bread first became popular in Dresden, but now it is made all
over Germany for the Christmas season. Make extra for friends and
wrap the bread in red ribbons to contrast with the white sugar.

- **YEAST BATTER:**
- 2 TSP YEAST AND
½ TSP CASTER SUGAR,
OR 15 G/½ OZ FRESH YEAST
- 6 TBSP MILK, AT BLOOD HEAT
- 50 G/2 OZ STRONG PLAIN
  WHITE FLOUR
- **DOUGH:**
- 175 G/6 OZ STRONG PLAIN
  WHITE FLOUR
- ½ TSP SALT
- 25 G/1 OZ CASTER SUGAR

- 25 G/1 OZ BUTTER
- 1 EGG, SIZE 3, BEATEN
- 25 G/1 OZ FLAKED ALMONDS
- GRATED ZEST 1 LEMON
- 50 G/2 OZ CURRANTS
- 50 G/2 OZ SULTANAS
- 25 G/1 OZ CHOPPED CANDIED
  MIXED PEEL
- 25 G/1 OZ BUTTER, MELTED
- 50 G/2 OZ GLACÉ CHERRIES,
  RINSED, DRIED AND HALVED
- ICING SUGAR, TO DREDGE

1 To make the yeast batter, stir the dried yeast and sugar into the milk and leave for 5 minutes, or blend the fresh yeast into the milk. Mix in the flour and leave in a warm place until frothy; this should take about 20 minutes.

2 Sift the flour and salt into a bowl and stir in the sugar, then rub in the butter until it resembles fine crumbs. Make a well in the middle, add the egg and the yeast batter and mix to a soft dough. Turn on to a floured surface and knead until smooth. Return to the bowl, cover with oiled polythene and leave to rise until doubled in size, about 1 hour.

3 Grease a baking sheet. Place the dough on the floured surface and knead lightly to knock out the air. Press the almonds, zest, currants, sultanas and peel into the dough and knead until well mixed in.

4 Roll out the dough to a round 25cm/10inches in diameter. Brush the surface with the melted butter, then spread the cherries in a strip across the centre. Fold the dough over into three to cover the cherries. Place on the baking sheet, brush with melted butter and cover with the oiled polythene again. Leave to prove until light and puffy, about 30 minutes.

5 Set the oven to 200°C/400°F/Gas 6. Bake towards the top of the oven for about 35 minutes, until golden, then cool on a wire rack. Dredge heavily with icing sugar when cold. Serve sliced and buttered.

VARIATION: *Omit the cherries and add 75g/3oz of almond paste (see page 160), rolled into a sausage shape. Place along the centre of the dough, fold over and bake as above.*

TO FREEZE: *Wrap in foil. Keeps for 5 months.*

Illustrated opposite page 144

PANETTONE

Panettone is an Italian cake made in Milan. It is usually sold, in festive boxes, in delicatessens around Christmas. Make your own version for a fraction of the cost of a bought one – it is a nice light alternative to all the rich foods of the festive season.

- 350 G/12 OZ STRONG PLAIN WHITE FLOUR
- ¼ TSP GROUND NUTMEG
- 20 G/¾ OZ FRESH YEAST
- 225 ML/8 FL OZ MILK, AT BLOOD HEAT
- 150 G/5 OZ BUTTER, AT ROOM TEMPERATURE
- 2 EGG YOLKS, SIZE 3

- 50 G/2 OZ SOFT BROWN SUGAR
- 100 G/4 OZ CHOPPED CANDIED MIXED PEEL
- 75 G/3 OZ SULTANAS
- FINELY GRATED ZEST ½ LEMON
- BEATEN EGG YOLK OR MILK, TO GLAZE
- ICING SUGAR, TO DREDGE

1 Grease an 18cm/7inch round deep cake tin and line with a double band of greased greaseproof paper to come 10cm/4inches higher than the rim of the tin. Secure the join with a paper clip. Or grease a deep kugelhupf mould.

2 Sift the flour and nutmeg into a large bowl and make a well in the centre. Blend the yeast with the milk until dissolved, then pour into the flour. Gradually draw in the flour from the sides and mix together well to make a soft dough. Cover the bowl with a clean cloth and leave to rise in a warm place until the dough is doubled in size, about 1 hour.

3 Turn out the dough on to a floured surface or into a table-top electric mixer with a dough hook. Knead to knock out the air, until the dough is smooth, then gradually mix in the butter in pieces followed by the egg yolks. Gently mix in the sugar, peel, sultanas and zest until well combined.

4 Cover with a cloth and leave to rise for 45 minutes or until doubled in size. Place the dough in the tin, and leave to rise again until it reaches halfway up the paper lining or fills the kugelhupf mould and looks puffy.

5 Set the oven to 200°C/400°F/Gas 6. Cut a cross right through the dough. Brush the surface with beaten egg yolk or milk and bake for 20 minutes, then turn down the oven temperature to 180°C/350°F/Gas 4 and bake for a further 30–40 minutes or until a skewer inserted in the centre comes out clean.

6 Leave the cake to cool in the tin for 10 minutes, then turn out on to a wire rack to cool completely. Dust with sifted icing sugar when cold. Eat within 5 days.

TO FREEZE: *Wrap in foil. Keeps for 2 months.*

RIGHT (from top to bottom): Black Bun (see page 101); Dundee Cake (see page 98); Stollen (see page 142).

DANISH PASTRIES

MAKES 8 OF EACH VARIETY

- 550 G/1 ¼ LB STRONG
  PLAIN WHITE FLOUR
- ½ TSP SALT
- 275 G/10 OZ BUTTER
- 1 7 G SACHET EASY-BLEND
  DRIED YEAST
- 75 G/3 OZ CASTER SUGAR
- 175ML/6FLOZ WATER,
  AT BLOOD HEAT

- 2 EGGS, SIZE 3, BEATEN
- 1 EGG WHITE, TO GLAZE
- **DECORATION:**
- GLACÉ ICING, MADE WITH
  175 G/6 OZ ICING SUGAR AND
  1 TSP LEMON JUICE
  (SEE PAGE 166)
- GLACÉ CHERRIES OR
  FLAKED ALMONDS

1 Sift the flour and salt into a large bowl. Cut 50g/2oz butter into small pieces and rub into the flour until it resembles crumbs. Stir in the yeast and sugar, then mix in the water and eggs to make a soft dough.

2 Turn on to a lightly floured surface and knead for 5 minutes or until smooth and elastic. Place the dough in an oiled polythene bag and chill in the refrigerator for 15 minutes. Cut the remaining butter into sixteen slices and chill these on a plate.

3 Cut the dough in half, and roll out each half into a rectangle 38 × 20cm/15 × 8inches. Arrange four slices of chilled butter evenly in the centre of each rectangle.

4 Fold one-third of each dough rectangle over to the centre to cover the butter slices, and press down lightly to seal. Put four more slices on top of the folded dough, then fold over the remaining plain third to cover. Press the edges to seal.

5 Give each piece of dough a half turn and roll out to a strip 40 × 15cm/16 × 6 inches. Fold the ends to meet in the centre, then fold over in half again. Cover both pieces with oiled polythene, and chill in the refrigerator for 30 minutes.

6 Repeat the last step twice more, chilling for at least 2 hours, then divide each piece of dough in half and roll out as needed (see the options given on page 146).

7 Place the shaped pastries on a baking sheet and leave to rise for 20–30 minutes.

8 Set the oven to 200°C/400°F/Gas 6. Glaze the pastries with egg white, then bake for 10 minutes. Reduce the oven temperature to 180°C/350°F/Gas 4 and bake for a further 15 minutes. Leave to cool on the baking sheets.

9 When the pastries are cold, decorate them with glacé icing and glacé cherries or flaked almonds.

TO FREEZE: *Wrap dough in freezer bag or foil. Thaw overnight in refrigerator or for 6 hours at room temperature, then shape, fill and bake as required. Keeps for 1 month.*

Illustrated opposite

LEFT (from top to bottom): Chelsea Buns (see page 152); Danish Pastries (see above); Hot Cross Buns (see page 148).

WINDMILLS

Mix 6 tbsp ground almonds with 2 tbsp lemon curd. Roll out one-quarter of the dough into a rectangle 15 × 30cm/6 × 12 inches. Cut into eight 7.5cm/3inch squares. Make diagonal cuts from each corner to within 1cm/½inch of the centre. Place a knob of filling in the centre of each square. Starting clockwise, fold each left-hand top corner to the centre and press to seal. Decorate each baked pastry with a halved glacé cherry.

TIVOLIS

Mix 50g/2oz butter, at room temperature, 1 tbsp demerara sugar, 2 tsp ground cinnamon and 100g/4oz no-need-to-soak dried apricots, chopped. Roll out one-quarter of the dough into a rectangle 15 × 30cm/6 × 12inches. Cut into eight 7.5cm/3inch squares. Spread a little filling diagonally over each square from corner to corner. Half turn the square so it is diamond-shaped. Make a small slit in the near corner of the dough. Fold edge A over filling to the centre. Lift the top corner B to centre and push it through the slit piece to seal.

CHOCOLATE PINWHEELS

Melt 100g/4oz plain chocolate with 1 tbsp coffee essence, then stir in 2 tbsp chopped toasted hazelnuts. Roll out one-quarter of the dough to a 30cm/12inch square. Cut into eight strips each 30 × 4.5cm/12 × 1½inches. Spread a little filling along each and roll up the two long ends towards the middle. Press together to seal then turn on to one side and flatten out with the palm of your hand. Decorate baked pastries with flaked almonds.

COCKSCOMBS

Peel, core and slice 1 large Cox's apple and cook to a pulp with 1 tsp lemon juice and a knob of butter. Stir in 25g/1oz sultanas and 1 tsp mixed spice, cook for 1 minute longer and leave to cool. Roll out one-quarter of the dough into a rectangle 15 × 30cm/6 × 12inches. Cut into eight 7.5cm/3inch squares. Spread the apple filling over half of each square to within 1cm/½inch of the edges. Fold over in half and slit the folded edge in three places. Curve round slightly to open out. Decorate the baked pastries with flaked almonds.

$\mathscr{B}$ATH BUNS

MAKES 12

*These buns were prescribed by an eighteenth-century physician,
Dr Oliver, who sent his patients to Bath to take the waters.
The buns were so rich and delicious that the patients often ate
more than was good for them, and were then put on to Dr Oliver's
regime of slimming yet nourishing Bath Oliver Biscuits. I think
I prefer the buns.*

- 675 G/1 ½ LB STRONG PLAIN WHITE FLOUR
- 1 TSP SALT
- 75 G/3 OZ BUTTER
- 75 G/3 OZ CASTER SUGAR
- 1 7G SACHET EASY-BLEND DRIED YEAST
- 2 EGGS, SIZE 3
- 150 ML/¼ PINT PLAIN YOGURT

- 300 ML/½ PINT WATER, AT BLOOD HEAT
- 175 G/6 OZ DRIED MIXED FRUIT
- MILK, TO GLAZE
- 25 G/1 OZ SUGAR NIBS, LUMP SUGAR OR PRESERVING SUGAR
- 2 TBSP GOLDEN SYRUP

1 Sift the flour and salt into a bowl and rub in the butter until the mixture resembles fine crumbs. Stir in the caster sugar and yeast. Beat the eggs, yogurt and water together, then pour into the dry mixture. Mix to a sticky dough and knead for 5 minutes or until smooth.

2 Replace the dough in the bowl and cover with oiled polythene. Leave in a warm place to rise for about 1 hour or until the dough is doubled in size.

3 Grease one large or two small baking sheets. Turn out the dough on to a floured surface and knead to knock out the air, until the dough is smooth and elastic again. Knead in the dried fruit. Cut into twelve equal pieces and roll each into a round. Place well apart on the baking sheet and cover with oiled polythene. Leave to rise for 30 minutes until doubled in size.

4 Set the oven to 190°C/375°F/Gas 5. Brush the tops of the buns with milk and sprinkle over the sugar nibs. Bake for 35 minutes or until firm and brown. Leave on the sheet to cool, then brush with golden syrup for a sticky glaze.

5 Pull the buns apart and serve split and buttered.

TO FREEZE: *Wrap in freezer bags, removing all air. Keeps for 3 months.*

*H*OT CROSS BUNS

These sweet and sticky buns are a traditional treat for Good Friday,
served split and spread with plenty of butter.

- 450 G/1 LB STRONG PLAIN
  WHITE FLOUR
- PINCH SALT
- 50 G/2 OZ BUTTER
- 1 7 G SACHET EASY-BLEND
  DRIED YEAST
- 50 G/2 OZ DARK
  MUSCOVADO SUGAR
- 2 TSP MIXED SPICE
- 100 G/4 OZ CURRANTS

- 50 G/2 OZ CHOPPED CANDIED
  MIXED PEEL
- 150 ML/¼ PINT MILK,
  AT BLOOD HEAT
- 1 EGG, SIZE 3, BEATEN
- **GLAZE:**
- 40 G/1 ½ OZ CASTER SUGAR
- 4 TBSP MILK
- **CROSSES:**
- 2 TBSP STRONG WHITE FLOUR
  OR SHORTCRUST PASTRY SCRAPS

1 Sift the flour and salt into a bowl and rub in the butter until it resembles fine crumbs. Stir in the yeast, sugar, mixed spice, fruit and peel.

2 Make a well in the centre and pour in the milk, 6 tbsp lukewarm water and the beaten egg. Mix thoroughly into a dough.

3 Turn on to a lightly floured surface and knead for about 10 minutes or until smooth and very elastic. Alternatively, knead the dough in a food processor with a plastic blade for 30 seconds, or in a table-top mixer with a dough hook for 2–3 minutes.

4 Oil two baking sheets. Divide the dough into thirteen pieces and shape each piece into a smooth round. Place on the baking sheets, spaced well apart. Cover loosely with oiled polythene and leave in a warm place to rise until doubled in size. This should take 1 hour.

5 Set the oven to 200°C/400°F/Gas 6. Mix 2 tsp of the caster sugar and 2 tbsp of milk together for the first glaze. Remove the oiled polythene and gently brush the buns with the glaze.

6 To make the crosses, mix the flour with 2 tbsp water to make a smooth paste. Place in a greaseproof paper piping bag (see page 182) and snip a small hole in the end. Pipe a cross on each bun. Alternatively, roll out shortcrust pastry scraps, cut into thin strips and place on the buns in the shape of a cross.

7 Bake the buns for 20 minutes or until dark golden and hollow sounding when tapped on the base.

8 Gently heat the remaining sugar with the rest of the milk until dissolved, then boil for 3 minutes. Place the buns on a wire rack and brush with the glaze while still warm. Leave to cool completely.

TO FREEZE: *Freeze unglazed buns in a rigid container. Keeps for 5 months. Thaw at room temperature and refresh in a warm oven.*

ALTERNATIVELY: *Freeze the unrisen, unbaked buns on their baking sheets. Keeps for up to 3 months. Thaw at room temperature for 3–4 hours and allow time for rising.*

Illustrated opposite page 145

*Fold dough into thirds,
roll and repeat*

*Roll out filled dough to fit tin,
and mark diagonally*

ᴸARDY CAKE

*Lardy cake is rich and sticky, and definitely not for dieters. Serve
it upside-down, to show the delicious toffee-like layer which
forms underneath.*

- 1 TSP DRIED YEAST AND
  ½ TSP CASTER SUGAR, OR
  7 G/¼ OZ FRESH YEAST
- 150ML/¼ PINT MIXED MILK
  AND WATER, AT BLOOD HEAT
- 225 G/8 OZ STRONG PLAIN
  WHITE FLOUR
- ½ TSP SALT
- 25 G/1 OZ LARD

- **FILLING:**
- 100 G/4 OZ LARD
- 100 G/4 OZ SOFT LIGHT
  BROWN SUGAR
- 175 G/6 OZ MIXED
  DRIED FRUIT
- 1 TSP MIXED SPICE

1 Stir the dried yeast and sugar into the liquid and leave for 15 minutes until frothy,
or blend the fresh yeast into the liquid. Sift the flour and salt into a bowl and rub in
the lard. Add the yeast liquid and mix to a soft dough.

2 Turn on to a floured surface and knead until smooth and elastic. Return to the
bowl, cover with oiled polythene and leave the dough to rise until doubled in size,
about 1¼ hours.

3 Turn out the risen dough and knock out the air. Roll out to an oblong 1cm/½inch
thick. Place one-third of the lard in small dots over the top two-thirds of the dough
and sprinkle with one-third of the sugar, fruit and spice. Fold the uncovered dough
up and the top third down over it. Give the dough a quarter turn, then roll out to an
oblong again. Repeat the rolling and folding twice more, using up the remaining
filling ingredients.

4 Grease a 20 × 25cm/8 × 10inch roasting tin. Roll out the dough to fit the tin, then
cover and leave to prove until light and puffy, about 1 hour.

5 Set the oven to 220°C/425°F/Gas 7. Bake for about 40 minutes or until golden
brown. Leave to cool in the tin, to let the cake absorb the fat as it cools. Serve
upside-down, sliced.

TO FREEZE: *Wrap in freezer bags or foil. Keeps for 3 months.*

CORNISH SAFFRON CAKE

- ½ TSP SAFFRON STRANDS
- 4 TSP DRIED YEAST AND ¼ TSP CASTER SUGAR, OR 25 G/1 OZ FRESH YEAST
- 150ML/¼ PINT MILK, AT BLOOD HEAT
- 450 G/1 LB STRONG PLAIN WHITE FLOUR

- 1 TSP SALT
- 100 G/4 OZ BUTTER
- FINELY GRATED ZEST ½ LEMON
- 25 G/1 OZ SOFT BROWN SUGAR
- 175 G/6 OZ CURRANTS OR MIXED DRIED FRUIT

1 Place the saffron in a bowl and pour over 150ml/¼ pint boiling water. Leave to infuse and cool for about 2 hours. Grease a 20cm/8inch round deep cake tin.

2 Stir the dried yeast and sugar into the milk and leave for 15 minutes until frothy, or blend the fresh yeast into the milk.

3 Sift the flour and salt into a bowl and rub in the butter until it resembles fine crumbs. Stir in the lemon zest and sugar. Strain in the saffron infusion and add the yeast liquid. Beat well, with a table-top electric mixer if possible, then mix in the fruit. Place the dough in the tin and leave to rise in a warm place until the dough is puffy and reaches the top of the tin.

4 Set the oven to 200°C/400°F/Gas 6. Bake for 30 minutes, then turn down the oven temperature to 180°C/350°F/Gas 4 and bake for a further 20–30 minutes or until golden on top and hollow-sounding when tapped on the base.

5 Turn out to cool on a wire rack, and serve sliced and buttered.

TO FREEZE: *Wrap in foil. Keeps for 3 months.*

*Sprinkle filling over dough,
and roll up*

*Cut along length into
nine slices*

CHELSEA BUNS

*King George the Third and Queen Charlotte used to travel to
the Old Chelsea Bun House and eat these buns in public on
Sunday afternoons.*

- **YEAST BATTER:**
- 2 TSP DRIED YEAST AND
  1 TSP CASTER SUGAR,
  OR 15 G/½ OZ FRESH YEAST
- 5 TBSP MILK, AT BLOOD HEAT
- 50 G/2 OZ STRONG PLAIN
  WHITE FLOUR
- **DOUGH:**
- 175 G/6 OZ STRONG PLAIN
  WHITE FLOUR
- ½ TSP SALT
- 25 G/1 OZ CASTER SUGAR

- 25 G/1 OZ BUTTER
- 1 EGG, BEATEN
- **FILLING:**
- 15 G/½ OZ BUTTER, MELTED
- 100 G/4 OZ MIXED DRIED FRUIT
- 25 G/1 OZ CHOPPED CANDIED
  MIXED PEEL
- 1 TSP GROUND CINNAMON
- 50 G/2 OZ DARK MUSCOVADO
  SUGAR
- GOLDEN SYRUP, TO GLAZE

1 To make the yeast batter, stir the dried yeast and sugar into the milk and leave for 5 minutes, or blend the fresh yeast into the milk. Stir in the flour and leave in a warm place for about 20 minutes until frothy.

2 For the dough, mix the flour, salt and sugar together in a bowl. Rub in the butter, then mix in the egg and yeast batter to make a soft dough. Place on a well-floured surface and knead until smooth and no longer sticky. Return to the bowl, cover with oiled polythene and leave to rise in a warm place until doubled in size. This should take about 1 hour. Grease a 18–20cm/7–8inch square tin.

3 Place the risen dough on the floured surface and knead to knock out the air. Roll out into a rectangle 30 × 23cm/12 × 9inches. Brush the surface of the dough with the melted butter. Mix the fruit, peel, cinnamon and sugar together and sprinkle over the butter. Roll up from a long side and cut across into 9 equal slices. Place the slices, cut side down, close together in the tin. Cover and leave to prove until doubled in size, about 40 minutes.

4 Set the oven to 220°C/425°F/Gas 7. Remove the polythene and bake for 20–25 minutes until golden brown. Turn out on to a wire rack to cool, then brush with golden syrup to give a sticky glaze. Pull the buns apart to serve.

TO FREEZE: *Wrap in freezer bags. Keeps for 3 months.*

Illustrated opposite page 145

BABAS WITH RUM AND HONEY SYRUP

MAKES 12

- **YEAST BATTER:**
- 2 TSP DRIED YEAST AND
  1 TSP CASTER SUGAR,
  OR 15 G/½ OZ FRESH YEAST
- 5 TBSP MILK, AT BLOOD HEAT
- 25 G/1 OZ STRONG PLAIN
  WHITE FLOUR
- **DOUGH:**
- 150 G/5 OZ STRONG PLAIN
  WHITE FLOUR
- LARGE PINCH SALT
- 1 TBSP CASTER SUGAR

- 75 G/3 OZ BUTTER
- 3 EGGS, SIZE 3, BEATEN
- 75 G/3 OZ CURRANTS
- FINELY GRATED ZEST
  ½ LEMON
- **RUM AND HONEY SYRUP:**
- 8 TBSP CLEAR HONEY
- RUM TO TASTE
- **TO FINISH:**
- APRICOT GLAZE (SEE PAGE 169)
- 300 ML/½ PINT DOUBLE OR
  WHIPPING CREAM, WHIPPED

1 To make the yeast batter, stir the dried yeast and sugar into the milk and leave for 5 minutes, or blend the fresh yeast with the milk. Mix in the flour and leave in a warm place until frothy, about 20 minutes.

2 Lightly grease twelve 9cm/3½inch ring or baba moulds, or use flan tins or dariole moulds.

3 Sift the flour, salt and sugar into a bowl. Rub in the butter, then add the eggs, currants, zest and yeast batter. Beat well with a wooden spoon for 3–4 minutes.

4 Half fill the prepared moulds with the dough. Cover and leave to rise for about 25 minutes, until the tins are two-thirds full.

5 Set the oven to 200°C/400°F/Gas 6. Bake for 10–15 minutes until golden brown. Cool in the moulds for a few minutes.

6 Make the syrup while the babas are baking: warm all the syrup ingredients together with 8 tbsp water. Spoon the syrup over each cake while they are still warm. Leave to cool, in the moulds, on a wire rack.

7 Brush each cake with apricot glaze when cold and pipe on a whirl of cream.

TO FREEZE: *Wrap baked unsoaked babas in foil. Keeps for 1 month. Thaw, soak in syrup and decorate.*

*S*AVARIN

Make up the baba dough (see page 153), omitting the currants. Grease a 20cm/8inch ring mould or kugelhupf mould and spoon in the dough. Cover and leave to rise until the mixture almost reaches the top of the tin, about 30–40 minutes.

Bake at 200°C/400°F/Gas 6 for 20–30 minutes or until golden brown and springy to the touch. Leave to cool in the tin for 5 minutes, then turn out on to a wire rack placed over a tray and prick with a fine skewer. Paint with the rum and honey syrup, or substitute Kirsch for the rum. When cold, brush with apricot glaze, and decorate with large pieces of glacé fruit or fill the centre with fresh fruit. Freeze as for babas.

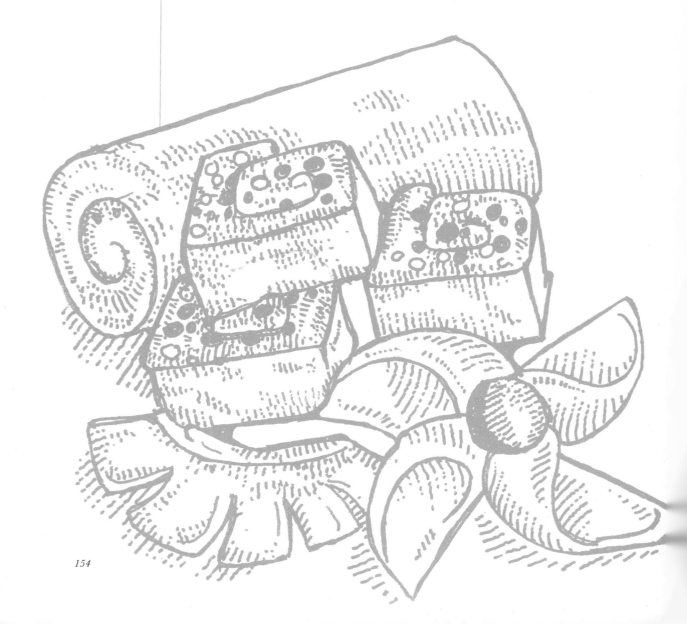

WHAT WENT WRONG?

Baking with yeast can be more complicated than ordinary baking. If you have encountered problems with baking with yeast, the following tips may be of help:

☞ **THE DOUGH COLLAPSES WHEN IT IS PUT IN THE OVEN:**
This happens when the dough has been left to prove for too long.

☞ **THE CAKE HAS A COARSE, OPEN TEXTURE:**
This can be caused by adding too much liquid, baking in too cool an oven, or over-proving.

☞ **THE CAKE HAS LARGE HOLES IN IT:**
This happens when the dough is not knocked back properly, causing large air bubbles to remain in it.

☞ **THERE IS A SOUR, YEASTY SMELL TO THE CAKE:**
This happens when too much yeast is used, and is also caused by over-proving.

☞ **THE CAKE HAS A CLOSE, HEAVY TEXTURE AND DID NOT RISE SUFFICIENTLY:**
This will happen when too much salt is added, or the wrong flour is used, i.e., ordinary soft flour, not strong flour. It can also happen when the dough has not been kneaded or proved sufficiently, or if the yeast has actually been killed off by rising in too hot a place.

☞ **THE CAKE STALES QUICKLY AND BECOMES CRUMBLY:**
Again this can be caused by the addition of too much yeast, so measure it out carefully. Use of soft flour can also cause this, as can rising too quickly in too warm a place, or not rising enough.

$\mathcal{I}$CINGS AND FILLINGS

CHAPTER NINE

The plainest of cakes can be made that little bit more special with a quick and simple icing or filling. The more elaborate the decoration, however, the more eye-catching and appealing the cake appears.

Almond paste, royal and fondant icings can all be used to create impressive effects for special occasion cakes, and with skill and practice you really can produce amazing results. Those sticky items of pâtisserie that we often see in continental cake shops are often covered in sophisticated coatings, such as crème au beurre or praline. These delicious toppings are not so difficult to make, and can be produced easily at home with a little extra care to help simple cakes look expensive.

If you need to whip up a children's party cake quickly, it is very easy to make a plain buttercream and cover it in minutes. Add a few sweets and novelties and the cake's complete. Once you have tried the chocolate fudge icing or seven-minute frosting, you will realize it doesn't take long to decorate a cake, and you'll be the most popular person around. Life just wouldn't be the same without the occasional gooey piece of cake, would it?

ICINGS
AND FILLINGS

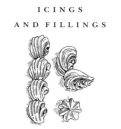

ALMOND PASTE

MAKES 450G/1LB

Almond paste is used to cover cakes that are going to be finished with royal icing or fondant icing. The layer of almond paste seals in the cake underneath, keeping it moist, and provides a good flat surface to decorate. Any minor disasters such as broken or tilting cakes can be rectified or repaired with almond paste, before decorating. You can also use almond paste for making decorative tops as in Simnel cake (see page 102), or for modelling animals, flowers and shapes. Colour it only with paste food colours, as liquid food colouring will alter the consistency, especially if used in large amounts.

There are some excellent ready-made brands of almond paste on the market, and some of these will actually work out cheaper to use if you are covering a large cake. Home-made almond paste has a wonderful texture and flavour of its own, and, of course, contains no additives like colourings or preservatives. The ready-made white almond paste now on sale is a good alternative, however, and sometimes works out to be more economical. Only buy the yellow type for decorative purposes as this can show through icings or cause staining. Staining of royal icing, in particular, can occur if the almond paste has not been allowed to dry out sufficiently or home-made paste has been over-kneaded, bringing out the oil from the almonds.

The almonds given in the chart show how much almond paste is needed to cover cakes of different sizes. Store made-up or opened packs of almond paste, wrapped tightly in polythene, for up to 3 weeks in the refrigerator, or keep scraps, useful for patching, or modelling, in a polythene bag in the freezer. Always roll out the almond paste on a surface dusted with icing or caster sugar; never be tempted to use cornflour, as this will ferment underneath the cake. See page 176 for how to cover a cake with almond paste.

- 100 G/4 OZ ICING SUGAR
- 100 G/4 OZ CASTER SUGAR (PREFERABLY STORED WITH A VANILLA POD)
- 225 G/8 OZ GROUND ALMONDS

- 1 EGG, SIZE 3
- 1 TSP LEMON JUICE
- 1 TBSP BRANDY OR SHERRY
- 1 DROP VANILLA ESSENCE

1 Sift the sugars and almonds into a bowl. Whisk the remaining ingredients together, then mix into the dry mixture. Knead well until the paste is smooth.

2 Wrap in cling film and keep in a cool place until needed. The paste can be made 2–3 days before use, but after that it will start to dry out and be difficult to handle.

NOTE: *To make a white almond paste, use 2 egg whites instead of 1 whole egg.*

RIGHT (from top to bottom): Devil's Food Cake (see page 42); Rich Chocolate and Almond Layer Cake (see page 46); Decadent Chocolate Roulade (see page 43).

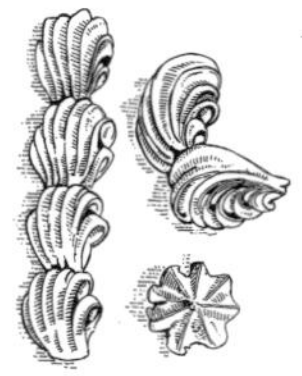

QUANTITY GUIDE FOR ALMOND PASTE

TO COVER TOP AND SIDES OF A CAKE

Round Tin	Square Tin	Almond Paste
15cm/6inches	12.5cm/5inches	350g/12oz
18cm/7inches	15cm/6inches	450g/1lb
20cm/8inches	18cm/7inches	675g/1½lb
23cm/9inches	20cm/8inches	800g/1¾lb
25cm/10inches	23cm/9inches	900g/2lb
28cm/11inches	25cm/10inches	1kg/2¼lb
30cm/12inches	28cm/11inches	1.1kg/2½lb
33cm/13inches	30cm/12inches	1.4kg/3lb
35cm/14inches	33cm/13inches	1.6kg/3½lb

BOILED ALMOND PASTE

MAKES 450G/1LB

This type of almond paste can be iced over almost immediately, and needs less time to dry out. This is useful if you ever have to ice a cake in a real hurry, or are worried about eating uncooked eggs, which bind the paste. You will need a sugar thermometer to ensure accurate results.

- 225 G/8 OZ GRANULATED SUGAR
- PINCH CREAM OF TARTAR
- 175 G/6 OZ GROUND ALMONDS

- 1 EGG WHITE, SIZE 3
- 75 G/3 OZ ICING SUGAR, SIFTED

1 Place the granulated sugar and 5 tbsp water in a heavy-based saucepan and dissolve over a low heat. When every grain has dissolved, bring to boiling point, add the cream of tartar and boil to 116°C/240°F.

Continued overleaf

LEFT: Child's 'Number' Cake (see page 186).

2 Remove from the heat and stir rapidly until the syrup begins to turn cloudy. Add the ground almonds. Whisk the egg white lightly and add to the mixture. Return to a low heat and cook for 2 minutes, stirring constantly.

3 Pour on to a marble slab or clean heatproof surface. Work in the icing sugar using a palette knife, lifting the edges of the mixture and bringing it into the centre. When the mixture is cool enough to handle, knead it well. If the paste is too sticky, add a little more icing sugar. Wrap in foil until needed.

ROYAL ICING

Royal icing is simply a paste made from icing sugar and egg whites.
Glycerine can be added during mixing to soften it for covering
cakes, and lemon juice added to harden it for detailed piping work
or for the first coating of a wedding cake that has to support heavy
tiers. Adding a tiny dot of blue colouring will make the icing look
whiter, but don't overdo this as it can easily turn to grey.

CONSISTENCY

The problem most cooks have with royal icing is that of using the wrong consistency. For example, if you make the icing for piping too stiff it will be difficult to work with and you will end up with an aching arm. Make the basic recipe thicker or thinner according to the use you are putting it to.

Cover the cake with two or more thin coats of icing, each progressively thinner than the last. For the first coat, the icing should stand up in peaks when the spoon is pulled away. Do not add glycerine to the icing to cover the base of a wedding cake, as this is the layer that will take most weight.

Make icing for piping of a firmer consistency, with added lemon juice, particularly for trellis work. Icing for run-out work should be very thin. It is a good idea to beat all icing to the consistency of thick cream, then add more sugar gradually until you are happy with the feel of the icing.

Under-beating is the reason for the jaw-breaking royal icing we've all eaten on Christmas cakes. Well-beaten icing is also easier to handle as well. See page 177 for how to cover a cake with royal icing.

SUGAR

Always sift the icing sugar before mixing. It is extremely frustrating if you find a lump of unsifted sugar blocking a nozzle and halting the flow of icing. Old sugar, or sugar that has become damp, can be lumpy and gritty, so sift this two or three times. Always use a nylon sieve, as specks of metal can come away from metal sieves and fleck the icing.

Egg whites used for royal icing must be perfectly fresh, and untainted by odours from strong foods stored in the refrigerator. When separating eggs, take care not to let any yolk get into the whites. If this happens, use the egg for cooking and start again, otherwise the icing will have a yellow tinge and heavy consistency. Be sure to remove all specks of membrane too. Dried egg whites give excellent results for icing and can be stored for long periods in the cupboard; they are simply reconstituted with water according to the packet instructions.

$\mathcal{Q}$UANTITY GUIDE FOR ROYAL ICING

TO COVER TOP AND SIDES OF A CAKE

Round Cake	Square Cake	Royal Icing
(weight of sugar)		
15cm/6inches	12.5cm/5inches	450g/1lb
18cm/7inches	15cm/6inches	550g/1¼lb
20cm/8inches	18cm/7inches	700g/1½lb
23cm/9inches	20cm/8inches	900g/2lb
25cm/10inches	23cm/9inches	1kg/2¼lb
28cm/11inches	25cm/10inches	1.1kg/2½lb
30cm/12inches	28cm/11inches	1.4kg/3lb
33cm/13inches	30cm/12inches	1.6kg/3½lb
35cm/14inches	33cm/13inches	1.8kg/4lb

$\mathscr{F}$ONDANT ICING

MAKES 675G / 1 ½LB

*Fondant or sugar paste icing is something of a newcomer to cake
decoration. It was developed in hot, humid countries, where royal
icing just refused to set. Its popularity has really grown as it can be
used so quickly and easily; just roll it out like pastry and smooth it
over the cake. It is a wonderful medium for modelling frills, flowers
and small animals, too.*

*Fondant can be made at home or purchased ready-made. The
home-made variety contains liquid glucose, which is available in
tubs from chemists' shops. See page 179 for how to cover a cake with
fondant icing.*

- 675 G/1 ½LB ICING SUGAR, SIFTED
- 2 EGG WHITES, SIZE 3
- 2 TBSP LIQUID GLUCOSE
- 1 TSP GLYCERINE
- FEW DROPS ROSEWATER (OPTIONAL)

1 Sift the icing sugar into a large, grease-free, dry bowl and make a well in the centre. Add the remaining ingredients to the well and gradually blend into the sugar with the fingertips.

2 Knead together until smooth, then roll up the paste into a ball. The paste should be smooth and easy to roll. If sticky, knead in a little more sugar until manageable. Keep in a thick polythene bag until needed.

$\mathscr{B}$OILED FONDANT ICING

COVERS 12–16 FANCIES OR A 20 CM (8") ROUND CAKE

*This fondant is poured over cakes, particularly small ones
like fancies.*

- 450 G/1 LB GRANULATED SUGAR
- 1 TBSP LIQUID GLUCOSE

1 Place 150ml/¼ pint water and the sugar in a heavy-based saucepan and gently heat until the sugar has completely dissolved. Bring to the boil slowly, then add the liquid glucose.

2 Boil until the syrup reaches 115°C/240°F on a sugar thermometer. Remove from the heat and when the liquid stops bubbling, pour it into two heatproof bowls. Leave to cool until a skin forms.

$\mathcal{3}$ Beat one half with a wooden spoon until the liquid becomes thick and white and turns into a solid mass. Place on a clean surface and knead with your fingers until smooth. Repeat with the other half of the mixture.

$\mathcal{4}$ Break the fondant into large lumps and smooth into balls. Store in an airtight container until needed. The icing will keep for 2 months in the refrigerator.

$\mathcal{5}$ To use, take four pieces at a time for small cakes and place in a heatproof bowl set over a pan of hot water. Heat gently until a thick, coating consistency is reached. If too thick, thin down with a little hot water. Beat in colourings.

$\mathcal{6}$ Pour over apricot-glazed or almond-pasted cakes. Smooth on with a palette knife, covering any gaps immediately, then leave to set.

$\mathcal{Q}$UANTITY GUIDE FOR FONDANT ICING

TO COVER TOP AND SIDES OF A CAKE

Round Cake	Square Cake	Fondant Icing
15cm/6inches	12.5cm/5inches	350g/12oz
18cm/7inches	15cm/6inches	450g/1lb
20cm/8inches	18cm/7inches	675g/1½lb
23cm/9inches	20cm/8inches	800g/1¾lb
25cm/10inches	23cm/9inches	900g/2lb
28cm/11inches	25cm/10inches	1kg/2¼lb
30cm/12inches	28cm/11inches	1.1kg/2½lb
33cm/13inches	30cm/12inches	1.4kg/3lb
35cm/14inches	33cm/13inches	1.6kg/3½lb

$\mathscr{S}$EVEN-MINUTE FROSTING

COVERS A 20 CM (8") ROUND CAKE

- 1 EGG WHITE, SIZE 2
- 175 G/6 OZ CASTER SUGAR
- PINCH SALT
- PINCH CREAM OF TARTAR

1 Place all the ingredients with 2 tbsp water in a large grease-free heatproof bowl and whisk until foamy. Set the bowl over a saucepan of boiling water and whisk until the mixture forms soft peaks – this should take about 7 minutes.

2 Use to cover the cake immediately, smoothing and swirling on with a palette knife. The frosting will set as it cools.

VARIATIONS:
LEMON: *Beat in 1 tsp lemon juice before the frosting thickens.*
BUTTERSCOTCH: *Substitute demerara sugar for white sugar.*
COFFEE: *Beat in 1 tsp liquid coffee essence before the frosting thickens.*

$\mathscr{G}$LACÉ ICING

COVERS 12 CUP CAKES OR TOP OF A 20 CM (8") ROUND CAKE

- 100 G/4 OZ ICING SUGAR
- LIQUID FOOD COLOURING (OPTIONAL)

1 Sift the icing sugar into a bowl and gradually mix in 1 tbsp hot water until the icing is smooth. It should be thick enough to coat the back of the spoon. Mix in colouring if used.

VARIATIONS:
CITRUS: *Replace the water with orange or lemon juice.*
ROSE: *Replace the water with rosewater.*
MOCHA: *Dissolve 1 tsp instant coffee powder in 1 tsp water. Sift 1 tsp cocoa powder with the icing sugar and mix together with the coffee, adding extra water if too thick.*
FEATHERING: *Keep a little icing separate and colour it, then place in a small piping bag. Cover the cake with plain icing and pipe parallel lines or circles of coloured icing at 2.5cm/1inch intervals. Draw a skewer through the piped lines at equal intervals in alternate directions.*

CRÈME AU BEURRE
(RICH BUTTERCREAM)

COVERS A 20CM (8") ROUND CAKE

To make this successfully you will need a sugar thermometer.

- 75 G/3 OZ CASTER SUGAR
- 2 EGG YOLKS, SIZE 3, BEATEN

- 150 G/5 OZ UNSALTED BUTTER

1 Place the sugar and 4 tbsp water in a heavy-based saucepan. Heat gently until the sugar has completely dissolved, then boil rapidly for 3–5 minutes until a temperature of 108°C/220°F is reached.

2 Pour the syrup slowly on to the yolks in a thin stream and whisk until the mixture is thick and cold.

3 Beat the butter in a separate bowl until very soft, then gradually beat in the egg yolk mixture until thick and glossy. Do not refrigerate the buttercream, but store in a cool place until needed.

VARIATIONS:
CHOCOLATE: *Gently melt 50g/2oz plain chocolate in a heatproof bowl set over warm water or in the microwave oven, then beat into the finished buttercream.*
FRUIT: *Crush 100g/4oz fresh raspberries, strawberries or apricots and beat well into the finished buttercream.*
CITRUS: *Add the finely grated zest of 1 orange, lemon or lime to the finished buttercream.*
NUT: *Stir 2 tbsp chopped nuts into the finished buttercream.*
COFFEE: *Dissolve 1 tbsp instant coffee powder in 2 tbsp boiling water and beat into the finished buttercream.*

SOFT CHEESE ICING

- 100 G/4 OZ FULL-FAT
  SOFT CHEESE
- 75 G/3 OZ ICING SUGAR, SIFTED

- FINELY GRATED ZEST 1 LEMON
- 2 TBSP LEMON JUICE

1 Place the cheese in a bowl with the sugar, zest and juice. Beat with a wooden spoon until soft and creamy.

Chocolate Fudge Icing

COVERS A 20 CM (8") ROUND CAKE

- 100 G/4 OZ PLAIN CHOCOLATE
- 50 G/2 OZ BUTTER
- 1 EGG, SIZE 3, BEATEN
- 175 G/6 OZ ICING SUGAR, SIFTED

1 Break up the chocolate and place in a heatproof bowl with the butter. Set over a saucepan of warm water and melt gently, stirring occasionally. Beat in the egg.

2 Remove from the heat, then beat in the icing sugar until the mixture is smooth. For a smooth finish, cover the cake with warm icing; for a thicker finish, leave the icing to cool before spreading on the cake.

Italian Meringue

COVERS A 20 CM (8") ROUND CAKE

- 100 G/4 OZ CASTER SUGAR
- 2 EGG WHITES, SIZE 3

1 Heat the sugar and 6 tbsp water in a heavy-based saucepan until the sugar has completely dissolved. Bring to the boil without stirring and boil until the mixture reaches 120°C/248°F on a sugar thermometer (hard ball stage). During boiling, wash down any sugar crystals on the side of the saucepan with a pastry brush dipped in cold water.

2 Whisk the egg whites until stiff. Pour the sugar syrup slowly on to the whites, whisking at high speed, and whisk until the mixture cools. It should be stiff and glossy. Swirl over the cake with a palette knife.

Soured Cream Chocolate Icing

COVERS A 20 CM (8") ROUND CAKE

- 225 G/8 OZ PLAIN CHOCOLATE
- 300 ML/½ PINT SOURED CREAM

1 Break up the chocolate and melt very gently in a heatproof bowl set over a pan of warm water or in the microwave oven. Stir the soured cream into the melted chocolate and mix together quickly.

2 Place the cake on a wire rack set over a tray to catch the drips, then pour the icing over quickly, scooping up the drips and patching any uncovered areas. Leave to cool completely and set.

QUICK CHOCOLATE ICING

COVERS AND FILLS A 20CM (8") ROUND CAKE

- 225 G/8 OZ SOFT TUB
  MARGARINE
- 4 TBSP GOLDEN SYRUP
- 8 TBSP COCOA POWDER, SIFTED

1 Place all the ingredients in a saucepan and heat gently until melted and smooth.

2 Cool the icing quickly by standing the pan in a bowl of iced water. Stir until the icing thickens, then pour immediately over the cake to cover. Leave to set.

CRÈME PÂTISSIÈRE

MAKES 300ML / ½ PINT

- 2 EGGS, SIZE 3
- 50 G/2 OZ CASTER SUGAR,
  (PREFERABLY STORED WITH
  A VANILLA POD)
- 2 TBSP PLAIN FLOUR
- 2 TBSP CORNFLOUR
- 300 ML/½ PINT FULL-FAT
  MILK
- VANILLA ESSENCE
  (IF NECESSARY)

1 Whisk the eggs and sugar together until the mixture is pale and thick. Sift the flour and cornflour into a bowl and stir in a little milk to form a paste. Whisk into the egg mixture.

2 Heat the remaining milk until almost boiling, then pour on to the egg mixture, stirring well all the time. Return to the saucepan and stir over a low heat until boiling. Add a few drops of vanilla essence (if you are not using vanilla-flavoured sugar) and cook over a low heat, stirring constantly, until thick and smooth. Pour into a bowl and cover with dampened greaseproof paper to prevent a skin forming on the surface. Leave to cool before using.

APRICOT GLAZE

- 50 G/2 OZ APRICOT JAM

1 Place the jam and 1 tbsp water in a saucepan and heat gently to melt the jam. Bring to the boil, then simmer for 1 minute. Pass through a metal sieve. Use warm, or store in a lidded container in the refrigerator, and heat to use.

VARIATION:
REDCURRANT GLAZE: *Use redcurrant jelly instead of apricot jam and add ½ tsp lemon juice.*

AMERICAN BUTTERCREAM

FILLS AND COVERS A 20CM (8") ROUND CAKE

- 2 EGG WHITES
- 100 G/4 OZ ICING SUGAR, SIFTED

- 100 G/4 OZ UNSALTED BUTTER, AT ROOM TEMPERATURE

1 Place the egg whites in a clean, grease-free heatproof bowl. Sift in the icing sugar and set the bowl over a saucepan of hot but not boiling water.

2 Whisk until the mixture thickens and leaves a ribbon trail when the whisk is lifted. Remove the bowl from the saucepan and whisk until the mixture is cool and stands up in peaks.

3 Beat the butter until light and fluffy, then add the meringue mixture, a little at a time, beating well. Use immediately.

VARIATIONS:
CHOCOLATE: *Add 50g/2oz melted plain chocolate.*
CITRUS: *Add 1 tsp finely grated orange, lime or lemon zest and 1 tbsp juice.*

SIMPLE BUTTERCREAM

COVERS TOP AND SIDES OF A 20CM (8") CAKE

- 100 G/4 OZ UNSALTED BUTTER, AT ROOM TEMPERATURE
- 225 G/8 OZ ICING SUGAR, SIFTED

- FEW DROPS VANILLA ESSENCE OR OTHER FLAVOURING
- FOOD COLOURING (OPTIONAL)
- 1–2 TBSP WARM MILK

1 Cream the butter until very soft, using an electric mixer if possible. Beat in the sugar, a little at a time, to avoid clouds of dust. Beat in the flavourings and colouring if used, then the milk to give a good spreading consistency.

2 Use immediately or keep stored in the refrigerator or freezer until needed.

VARIATIONS:
CHOCOLATE: *Add 25g/1oz melted plain chocolate, or 2 tbsp cocoa powder dissolved in 2 tsp boiling water. Cool, then beat into basic buttercream.*
MOCHA: *Dissolve 1 tsp cocoa powder in 1 tbsp strong black coffee and add in place of the milk.*
CITRUS: *Omit the vanilla essence; replace the milk with fresh orange or lemon juice and add the finely grated zest of 1/2 an orange or lemon.*
LUXURY: *Replace the milk with Grand Marnier or other orange liqueur or with rum, brandy, sweet sherry, or Madeira.*

QUICK ROYAL FROSTING

COVERS A 20CM (8") ROUND CAKE

- 2 EGG WHITES,
  SIZE 3 EGGS

- 400 G/14 OZ ICING SUGAR,
  SIFTED

1 Whisk the egg whites lightly, then gradually whisk in the icing sugar until the frosting is soft and glossy. Spread on to the cake with a palette knife.

PRALINE

- 75 G/3 OZ CASTER SUGAR

- 50 G/2 OZ SHELLED ALMONDS,
  BLANCHED AND SKINNED

1 Oil a baking sheet. Place the sugar and 4 tbsp water in a heavy-based saucepan. Heat gently until the sugar has completely dissolved, then increase the heat until it begins to turn golden.

2 Add the nuts and quickly swirl round in the pan. Pour on to the baking sheet, spread out and leave to cool and harden.

3 Place the praline in a food processor and grind roughly, or put in a strong polythene bag and crush with a rolling pin.

PRALINE CREAM

Whip 300ml/½ pint double cream, then fold in the praline. Use to fill or decorate cakes. Alternatively, cover the cake with cream and press praline on to the sides of cake for a neat finish. Or place strips of greaseproof paper across the top of the cake and sprinkle praline across to make a stripy pattern.

CARAMEL-DIPPED ALMONDS

Whole almonds can be half or completely dipped in the caramel above and left to set separately on an oiled baking sheet. Dip them using tongs or tweezers, being careful not to get any of the boiling caramel near your hands. The French use these almonds a lot, arranged in daisy shapes on their tiered wedding cakes.

CAKE DECORATING

CHAPRER TEN

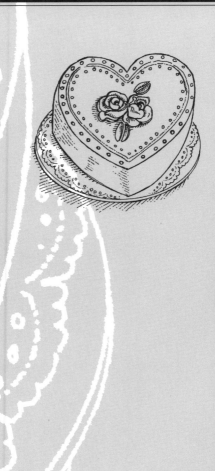

*E*ver since nuts and sugar came to us through the trade routes, cakes have been decorated. The era of grand pâtisserie and decoration began in France with Anton Careme. He used ground sugar in the most innovative ways, based on sculpture and architecture, and his highly elaborate designs paved the way for the cake designs we know today.

Cake decoration or sugarcraft, as it is known, has now become a widespread hobby, with many amateur local guilds producing highly skilled decorated cakes for competitions and exhibitions. The ability to produce a lavishly decorated cake for a wedding or just a simple one for tea is highly prized, and comes only by developing skills with lots of practice. This does give a great sense of achievement, so I hope you will follow some of the guidelines on the next few pages and have as much fun decorating cakes as I do.

CAKE
DECORATION

Place cakes over rolled paste

to cut exact top

Cut a long strip and wrap

round cake sides

For straight sides, cut four

separate strips

RIGHT (from top to
bottom): Coconut and
Mandarin Pudding (see
page 235); Apple and
Orange Surprise Crunch
(see page 198); Maple
Syrup and Grapefruit
Pancakes (see page 250).

*A*LMOND PASTE

To achieve a perfect finish on a decorated cake, you need a really good base to work on. Almond paste is used to seal in the cake, protecting the icing from crumbs and moisture, and also gives you the opportunity to rectify faults such as slopes, bumps or a broken cake, before you ice the cake.

Place the covered cake on a cake board 5–8cm/2–3 inches larger than the cake, to give a balanced finish and protect the sides of the cake. See pages 160–1 for recipes and quantity guide.

COVERING A CAKE WITH ALMOND PASTE

Use this method for round, square and all types of shaped cakes.

1 Remove any paper wrappings and place the cake on a flat surface. Roll with a rolling pin to flatten the surface slightly, or trim level if necessary. Brush the top of the cake with apricot glaze (see page 169).

2 Sprinkle a flat clean surface with sifted icing or caster sugar. Knead two-thirds of the measured almond paste into a ball and roll it out to 5mm/¼ inch thickness, the same shape as the top of the cake.

3 Turn the cake, glazed side down, on to the paste. Trim away the excess paste to within 1cm/½inch of the cake sides, then fold this up, pressing it to the sides to give an even edge to the top.

4 Turn the cake right way up and place on a cake board. Brush the sides with more apricot glaze. Knead the almond paste trimmings into the remaining almond paste, making sure not to include any crumbs or spots of jam. Patch any holes or gaps in the sides with small scraps of almond paste.

5 Measure a piece of string that will wrap all the way around a round cake or that is the length of one side of a square cake. Roll out the remaining paste into a strip (or four strips for a square cake), the length of the piece of string and wide enough to cover the sides.

6 Loosely roll up the paste strip into a coil. Press one end on to the cake and then unroll the paste round it, pressing it on as you go.

7 Press top and side joins together and smooth out with a palette knife. Leave the almond paste to dry out for at least 24 hours in a cool dry place, or ideally 1 week if you are planning to use royal icing. This drying is vital, as the oils from the almond paste can seep into royal icing if it is not sufficiently dried out first.

$\mathcal{R}$OYAL ICING

Royal icing is used to cover and form beautiful decorations, particularly on wedding cakes. This firm icing keeps particularly well and forms a strong seal which also preserves the flavour and texture of the cake inside. To produce these results, it is essential to make good royal icing of the right texture. (See recipe and quantity guide on pages 162–3.)

COVERING A CAKE WITH ROYAL ICING

Cover a cake with royal icing in stages – cover the top first and leave to dry out for 24 hours, then trim away any rough edges and cover the sides. Give yourself plenty of time if it is a large, tiered wedding cake. Before you start, check that the surface is level, and trim away any bumps. This is much easier to do at this stage, and it will prevent a tilting cake. Don't use royal icing until the almond paste is completely dry. Prepare the royal icing and keep the bowl covered with a damp cloth at all times; this prevents a hard skin from forming, which will break into hard lumps if stirred in.

Work royal icing over top and sides of cake

TO COVER THE TOP

1 Place the cake on its board on a flat rigid surface. Place half the measured icing on top of the cake, then work it over the top using a palette knife in a spreading movement. Spread the icing until all the almond paste is covered.

2 Stand directly in front of the cake and take a steel icing ruler that is longer than the diameter of the cake. Hold the ruler at an angle of·45° and, with a firm movement, pull the ruler over the icing across the cake, towards you. Sweep the ruler back in the opposite direction, still at an angle, and continue until the top is completely smooth. Be careful not to press down too hard or the icing will become too thin.

3 Scoop away any excess icing from the sides with a palette knife to give a clean, neat edge. Leave to dry out for 24 hours.

Pull a steel ruler across to smooth top

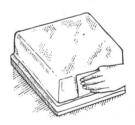

Smooth sides with an icing scraper

LEFT (from top to bottom): Light Apple Pudding (see page 225); Chocolate Truffle Loaf (see page 313); Greengage and Almond Shuttles (see page 277).

1 This is easier to do on a turntable. If you don't have an icing turntable, stand the cake on a large-based, upturned bowl.

2 For square cakes: cover the two opposite sides first, using a small palette knife. With a plastic icing scraper, pull the icing towards you to straighten and flatten it. Trim the edges straight and leave to dry out for 24 hours, then cover the other two sides in the same way.

3 For round cakes: place the cake on a turntable and smooth the icing on the sides with a palette knife. Position your left arm as far round the cake as possible, holding the edge of the board. Hold a plastic icing scraper upright in the right hand and rotate the cake slowly in an anti-clockwise movement. Sweep the scraper round in one movement and pull it away at the point where you started. Leave to dry out. Any thin lines can be smoothed down with fine sandpaper when the icing is dry.

4 Store the cake in a cool dry place. If the storage area is too warm the oil from the almond paste may sweat into the icing, and too damp a place will not allow the icing to dry out.

THE SECOND COAT

After 24 hours, take a critical look at the outline and sides. With a sharp knife, pare away any bumps and make the surface level with fine sandpaper. Apply a second thin coat of icing and leave to dry out for 48 hours.

THE FINAL COAT

Repeat the trimming and sandpapering processes. Take a little royal icing and gently press it into any holes or gaps with a clean fingertip. Make a batch of thin icing and leave it to stand for 24 hours to allow any air bubbles to escape to the surface. Cover the cake carefully with the final coat of icing and leave to dry out, then decorate with piped decorations.

$\mathcal{F}$ONDANT ICING

Fondant paste can be rolled out and smoothed over a cake in a matter of minutes. It is also a versatile icing and can be moulded into thin dainty frills or flowers or modelled into practically any shape. (See recipe and quantity guide on pages 164–5.)

COVERING A CAKE WITH FONDANT ICING

1 Brush the marzipanned cake with sherry or boiled water so the fondant will stick.

2 Roll out the fondant icing to 5mm/¼inch thickness on a surface lightly dusted with icing sugar. Move the rolled fondant continually to prevent it from sticking. Measure the cake's circumference and sides and roll the fondant 2–5cm/1–2inches larger, to cover the whole cake.

3 Lift the fondant carefully on to the cake, holding it with both hands flat until it is in a central position, covering the whole cake.

4 Dust your hands with icing sugar and smooth the icing into position. Treat it like fabric and flute out the bottom edges, but do not pleat them as this will leave a line.

5 Very gently smooth down in one direction to remove air bubbles under the icing. Press the fondant on, and trim the edges with a sharp knife. Roll any scraps into a ball and keep tightly wrapped in a thick polythene bag.

6 If any air bubbles remain on top of the cake, prick them with a pin and smooth over. Use the flat of your hand (don't wear rings or these will leave ridges in the icing) or a special icing smoother to flatten and smooth the top, using a circular movement.

7 The cake can be decorated with a royal icing piped border, and piped or fondant decorations straightaway. Crimped patterns can be marked on to the cake, but do these immediately, before the fondant dries and becomes less pliable.

Roll icing out slightly larger than cake

Smooth icing gently around the sides

Smooth baseline with edge of a knife

$\mathcal{F}$ONDANT FLOWERS

Roses

Roses can be made in different size and are much simpler to make than they appear.

1 Take a small coloured piece of fondant about the size of a pea. Roll it into a ball, then pull one end to a point to make a tear-drop shape. Take another pea-sized piece and flatten it out thinly to make an oval-shaped petal. If you are not sure of the shape, look at a real rose petal. Wrap the petal right round the tear-drop bud.

2 Continue to make petals, keeping the edges as thin as possible, and wrap these around the bud. As you position each petal, pinch it into the base and flute out the edges to give a natural effect.

3 Continue to add petals until the rose is the right size, then very carefully pull away the thick base, and smooth the end. Place in an old egg box lined with crumpled foil to dry out for 48 hours, in a cool dry place.

*Fondant briar rose: roll icing
and cut into petals*

*Flute edges of each petal
with a tool*

*Secure petals together at base
with royal icing*

Briar roses

Briar roses take longer to make, as each petal is made and dried before being assembled into a flower. These are my favourite flowers. They double up as pretty dog roses, blushed with pink petals for summer wedding cakes, or you can leave them pure white with yellow centres, for Christmas roses.

1 Roll the fondant out thinly on a surface dusted with cornflour, then cut out into petals, using a cutter, or by hand with a sharp knife.

2 Place a petal in the palm of your hand and press out the edges about two-thirds of the way round with your finger or a plastic tool, thus causing the edges to flute up and make the centre round and dipped. Place the petal on a piece of crumpled foil to support the shape and dry it out. Dry for 48 hours.

3 To assemble, pipe a small dot of royal icing on to the base of each petal, then arrange in a circle in a bun tray lined with foil. Pipe yellow dots in the centre and attach florist's stamens, if liked. Dry for 24 hours, then attach to the cake.

Daisies

1 Roll a small ball of white fondant into a tear-drop shape, then flatten out the bulbous end until thin, and pinch the long end into a stalk shape.

2 Using a small pair of clean scissors, snip tiny petals all round. Use the scissor tips to make indentations in the middle for the stamens.

3 Fluff out the petals, then leave to dry on crumpled foil for 24 hours. Using edible food colouring, paint the outer tips of the petals a very faint pink and dab the centres with a little yellow.

Carnations

1 Roll out a small ball of fondant on a surface lightly dusted with cornflour. Cut out a small round with a small fluted pastry cutter. Make 5mm/¼inch deep cuts round the outer edge, then make smaller slashes between the deep cuts. This gives the jagged edge.

2 Roll a wooden cocktail stick backwards and forwards around each curve until the edge flutes and frills up. Continue with the next curve until all the edge is frilled.

3 Carefully fold the round in half, then in half again. Make four petals like this. Pinch three together in a bunch, then wrap the fourth one round the outside to enclose them. Fluff out the edges with the tip of a cocktail stick, then leave in an egg box lined with foil to dry out for 48 hours.

Blossom

1 Roll a small ball of white fondant into a cone shape, then hollow this out over the top of a clean ball point pen top, or similar shape.

2 Cut five tiny petals with nail scissors, then flatten and pinch each petal together with your fingers.

3 Pipe a yellow dot in the centre or attach florist's stamens. Dry out for 24 hours, then use arranged in small bunches.

Leaves

1 On a surface lightly sprinkled with cornflour, thinly roll out some green-coloured fondant. Cut out oval shapes with a cutter or sharp knife.

2 With the point of a sharp knife, mark on the central and side veins, then twist the end of each leaf. Leave to dry out on foil for 24 hours.

*Fondant daisy: make a
hollow cone from a ball*

*Snip all around the cone
nearly to the base*

*Bend the strips back,
and thread through a wired
fondant core*

*Fondant rose: wrap a petal
shape around a teardrop bud*

*Pinch base of each petal
on to base of bud*

*Continue to wrap petals
around bud*

*Pull away the excess base,
and smooth*

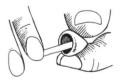

*Fondant blossom: hollow out
a small cone, then snip round
and pinch into points*

*Thread through a
florist's stamen*

Making a paper piping bag:

*Curl one corner into the
middle of the triangle*

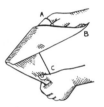

*Pull the bottom corner round
to make a cone*

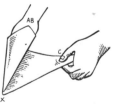

*Pull to tighten and make
a sharp point*

*Wrap corner round and fold
over top to secure*

$\mathscr{P}$IPING

Royal icing, buttercream and crème au beurre can all be piped on to cakes to decorate them. The art of piping requires a steady hand, and lots of practice. Ordinary buttercream can be used for practising on a clean table-top or cake boards.

Most decoration can be achieved with simple nozzles fitted into non-stick silicone paper or greaseproof paper bags, so just invest in a few basic ones. A plain writing nozzle and small and large star nozzles will get you started.

The icing used for piping must be smooth and completely free of lumps, or these will block the nozzle. It must be soft enough to force through the nozzle, but firm enough to hold its shape.

Making a paper piping bag
There are many plastic piping bags on the market with nozzles and connecting bolts. These are useful if you have a lot of piping to do with the same colour, but I prefer to make small paper piping bags for each colour. These are also easier to handle as you can get a good grip on them, using the strength of your palm to force out the icing, and not your arm muscles. If you do lots of icing over a few hours, your arm will start to ache if you are not comfortable, so don't grapple with large over-filled bags.

Always use the strongest paper you can buy. Non-stick silicone paper is stronger than greaseproof; if only greaseproof is available, then use it double thickness. There is nothing more infuriating than a bag which splits halfway through its use.

1 Cut out a 25cm/10inch square, then cut in half diagonally to make a triangle.

2 Keeping the longest edge in front of you, take a corner point and curl it into the middle (A). Curl the other corner to the middle and wrap round to form a cone with a sharp point (B).

3 Secure the top by folding the top edge over twice.

Filling a paper piping bag
Half fill the bag only. If you add more icing the bag will split or burst and you will end up in a mess! Fold the top edge down until the bag is sealed and firm, then fold over again to seal it. Hold the bag across the palm of one hand, place your thumb over the top, then grasp the fingers round the bag. Apply even pressure to force the icing out of the bag.

Stars

Fit a star nozzle into the bag. Hold the bag upright above the surface of the cake and squeeze out the icing. When the star appears, stop pressing and lift the bag away.

Shells

Use a star or special shell nozzle. Hold the bag at a 45° angle, just touching the cake. Press out the icing until a rounded shape forms. Release the pressure and gently pull the nozzle away, pulling the tail downwards on to the cake. Make the next shell 5mm/¼inch away from the first. Press out the icing; as it makes the rounded shape it should meet the tail of the preceeding shell.

Scrolls

Use a star nozzle. Hold the bag at a 90° angle to the cake. Press out the icing to make a shell shape, but twist the nozzle in a circular shape like the tail of an 'S'. Pull the bag away to make a tail, then pipe the next scroll to meet this tail.

Dots

Use a plain nozzle or snip a small hole in the end of the paper bag. Place the tip of the nozzle on the surface and hold the bag upright. Squeeze the bag gently, at the same time lifting it away. Only slight pressure is required. Move the nozzle away, using no pressure, or you will get a 'tail'. Larger dots can be made by moving the nozzle in a small circle.

Straight lines

Place the tip of the nozzle where the line is to begin. Press the bag and as the icing starts to come out, lift it away from the surface. Guide the bag in the direction of the line. Before the end of the line stop squeezing and lower the nozzle down on to the surface to finish.

Writing

Use a small plain nozzle. Follow the technique above, guiding the string of icing into place. Practise on a plate first, to ensure that all the letters will fit in. Draw the letters on greaseproof paper and prick them through to the cake with a pin as a guide for total precision.

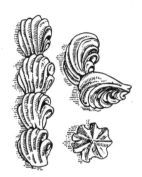

Piped stars and shells

Piped lettering

Making chocolate caraque

Pour melted chocolate over a work surface

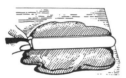

Spread out with a palette knife

Scrape chocolate curls with a potato peeler

Scrape off long curls with a sharp knife

CHOCOLATE
DECORATIONS

Chocolate curls, *caraque* and leaves can add that final touch to a cake. They are easy to make, but give yourself plenty of time to allow the chocolate to cool and set.

Chocolate curls
Using a potato peeler, scrape off curls from a block of chocolate. This will work better if the chocolate is at room temperature as the curls come away easily in one piece.

Chocolate caraque

1 Melt the chocolate gently in a heatproof bowl set over a pan of warm water. Spread it out on a marble slab or clean cool work surface, spreading from side to side with a palette knife to make a large flat pool. Leave to cool and set.

2 When set, scrape off large curls using a large sharp knife held at both ends, pulling it slowly towards you over the chocolate. Refrigerate curls until needed.

Chocolate leaves
Wash and dry rose leaves, then brush the back of the leaf with a thin layer of melted chocolate. Drape over the handle of a wooden spoon to dry, then carefully peel away the leaves when the chocolate is set.

184

ƒUGAR-FROSTED FLOWERS, FRUITS AND LEAVES

Frosted flowers and fruits add an attractive finish to a cake and are simple to make. They keep well for up to 2 weeks in an airtight container between layers of tissue. Some flowers will keep longer than this, but fruits will not.

FRUIT, FLOWERS OR LEAVES OF CHOICE (SEE BELOW)

- **1 EGG WHITE**
- **CASTER SUGAR**

1 Make sure the fruit, flowers or leaves are clean and completely dry. Place the egg white in a small bowl and whisk with 2 tsp water until lightly frothy.

2 Dip or paint the flower with the egg white, until evenly coated, then sprinkle or roll in caster sugar. Leave to dry on non-stick silicone paper that has been lightly dusted with caster sugar.

3 Use to decorate large or small cakes, when the icing is still wet.

Brush flowers or fruits with whisked egg white

FLOWERS: *Choose flowers with a few petals only, or divide large flowers like roses into separate petals. Small flowers like primroses and violets are ideal, but never use narcissi, as these contain a poison.*

FRUITS: *Small fruits and currants work best; choose red or black currants, grapes, cherries or segmented mandarin oranges.*

LEAVES: *These should be small, and the leaves of herbs like mint, bay or rosemary look particularly pretty.*

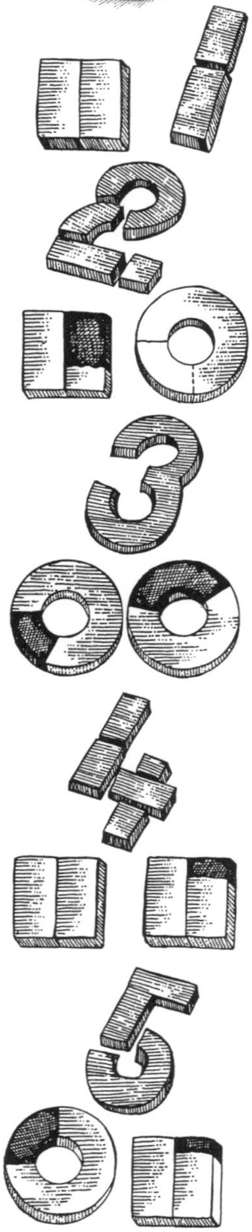

'ANY NUMBER' OF CAKES

*I've often been asked to make cakes in the shape of a number,
especially for children's birthday parties. These can present
problems as the tins are very expensive to buy or hire, and you really
don't know how much mixture they will hold or how long the cakes
will take to bake. I always take the easy way, and stick to a tried and
trusted recipe, baked in an 18cm/7inch square tin or a 23cm/9inch
flat-based ring tin. There is a bit of chopping and sticking back
together involved, but I find this method produces good results, with
very little waste. If there are any spare pieces over, freeze them away
for making trifles, or chocolate truffles.*

NUMBER 1

Bake a square cake. Simply cut down the centre, position on a board and stick the two short ends together with jam.

NUMBER 2

Bake one square cake and one ring cake. Cut as shown in the diagram. Remove the curved cut third from the ring, and turn it round in the opposite direction to make a question mark shape. Cut a long oblong and a short square from the square cake and position them along the base. Seal all the joins with jam.

NUMBER 3

Bake two ring cakes and cut as shown in the diagram. Place the one with the largest section cut out at the base and the other one adjoining it. Seal the join with jam.

NUMBER 4

Bake two square cakes, and cut down the centre as shown. Remove a small section from one block as shown on the diagram, then position the oblongs on a board, sealing all the joins with jam.

NUMBER 5

Bake one square cake and one ring cake, and cut as shown. Position the two oblongs to form a right angle, then stick the curved base piece in place.

NUMBER 6 AND NUMBER 9

Bake one square cake and one ring cake, and cut as shown. Position and stick the two oblongs together, then place the curved piece at the base, and stick with jam. For Number 9, simply use the same cakes but position upside-down.

NUMBER 7

Bake two square cakes and cut as shown. Stick the two sets of oblongs together at a slanting angle, and secure with jam.

NUMBER 8

Bake two ring cakes and trim the tops as shown. Position and join the two rings together on a board.

NUMBER 0

Bake one square cake and one ring cake. Cut the ring in half and cut two oblongs as shown. Position and stick the two semi-circles at either end of the oblongs.

TIN TIP

If you don't own a ring tin, then use a 23cm/9inch round deep cake tin and place a 7.5cm/3inch wide empty fruit or baked bean tin in the centre. Grease and line the outside of the fruit or bean tin, then fill with weights or baking beans, to prevent it moving around during baking.

Illustrated opposite page 161

*Create numerals with cut
sponge lengths as shown*

HOT BAKED PUDDINGS

Until the seventeenth century puddings were usually savoury, although they might contain dried fruits and spices and were sometimes served with sugar and almonds. As sugar became more widely available and fruit production improved, so sweet versions of puddings evolved and were specially created. In Britain, the royal seal of approval for puddings was given by 'the pudding-eating monarch', George I, who loved hearty, substantial sweet puddings. In fact, the British as a nation had a reputation for being pudding eaters, which was not usually meant as a term of flattery. (Even then, 'dessert' had other connotations. Derived from the French desservir, *meaning to clear the table, it was a selection of elaborate sweet dishes, fresh fruits, ices, fancy cakes and pastries and conserves.) But the culinary world would be much poorer without our beloved crumbles, charlottes, rice puddings, sponge puddings, bread and butter puddings — the list is long and richly varied.*

Whisk the egg yolks and sugar
together in a bowl placed over
a saucepan of hot water until
the mixture is very thick
and airy

$\mathcal{S}$ECRETS OF SUCCESS

☞ Unless a recipe specifies to the contrary, most puddings are best if they are baked as soon as they are prepared.

☞ To reduce the amount of work you have to do just before a meal, weigh out all the ingredients, do any preliminary preparation such as chopping nuts, lay out equipment and prepare baking containers in advance.

☞ Preheat the oven in plenty of time.

☞ Have ingredients and containers at room temperature, unless a recipe specifies to the contrary.

☞ To ensure puddings made by the creaming method are light, the butter and sugar must be beaten until they are light and fluffy, then eggs at room temperature gradually beaten in. Lastly, gently fold in the flour and any other ingredients using a large, cold metal spoon.

☞ If using a rotary whisk to whisk whole eggs or egg yolks with sugar to make a whisked sponge, place the bowl containing the eggs over a saucepan of hot, not boiling, water making sure the underside of the bowl is above the level of the water. If using an electric hand-held whisk, there is no need to place the bowl over a saucepan of hot water.

☞ Whisked egg whites help to lighten mixtures, but they must be folded into the mixture very carefully. Plain whisked whites are particularly fragile, so they are often whisked with some of the sugar from the recipe to make them firmer (see notes on making meringues on page 307).

☞ The heavier the main mixture, the more difficult it is to fold in egg whites, and for most puddings it is a good idea to fold in about a quarter of the whisked whites to lighten it, then fold in the rest in batches.

☞ Serve the pudding on hot or warm plates.

RIGHT (from top to bottom): Jaqui's Bread and Butter Pudding (see page 224); Omelette Norvégienne (see page 206); Apricot Pandowdy (see page 219).

$\mathcal{R}$HUBARB CHARLOTTE BETTY

SERVES 4–6

*The difference between a fruit charlotte and a betty, both very
popular traditional British puddings, is that a charlotte has a
jacket of sliced bread and a betty has a lighter jacket of
breadcrumbs. In a betty, breadcrumbs are also layered with the
filling, which makes it more solid; spices may also be added.
This recipe combines the breadcrumb jacket of a betty with the
fruit-only filling of a charlotte. For extra flavour and crunch,
I add sesame seeds.*

- 3 REINETTE OR COX'S ORANGE PIPPIN APPLES
- 450 G/1 LB RHUBARB, CUT INTO APPROXIMATELY 2.5 CM/1 IN LENGTHS
- 55 ML/2 FL OZ TANGERINE OR ORANGE JUICE
- 70 G/2½ OZ LIGHT MUSCOVADO SUGAR
- 55 G/2 OZ DARK MUSCOVADO SUGAR
- ½ TSP CHINESE FIVE SPICE POWDER
- PINCH OF GROUND CLOVES
- PINCH OF FRESHLY GROUND NUTMEG
- 150 G/5 OZ FRESH BREADCRUMBS
- 3 TBSP SESAME SEEDS, LIGHTLY TOASTED
- 85 G/3 OZ UNSALTED BUTTER, MELTED
- **TO SERVE:**
- CUSTARD (SEE PAGE 353) OR VANILLA DAIRY ICE CREAM

1 Set the oven to 180°C/350°F/Gas 4. Butter an 850 ml/1½ pint baking dish.

2 Peel, core and slice the apples, then mix with the rhubarb and tangerine or orange juice.

3 Stir the sugars and spices together. Mix 2 tablespoonfuls with the breadcrumbs, seasame seeds and butter, then press half evenly into the sides and base of the dish. Stir the remaining sugar mixture into the fruit, then spoon into the dish. Cover with the remaining breadcrumb mixture, cover loosely and bake for 20 minutes. Uncover and bake for 25 minutes until the fruit is tender and the top browned. Serve warm with Custard or vanilla dairy ice cream.

LEFT (from top to
bottom): Charlie's Apple
Dappy (see page 227); Hot
Orange Cake (see page
208); Glazed Nectarine
Slices (see page 207).

$\mathscr{P}$EAR AND
BLACKCURRANT CRUMBLE

SERVES 4-6

*Crumbles are so easy to make that it is very difficult to make a bad
one, and everyone I know loves them. It was very difficult to choose
just one crumble recipe, because there are so many for toppings and
fruit mixtures, as well as innumerable permutations – and I like
them all, to the same degree! Friends were not much help; whatever
I suggested was greeted by 'Oh yes, use that one'. So I wrote a list
and stuck a pin in.*

- 700 G/1 ½ LB PEARS
- 300 G/10 OZ BLACKCURRANTS,
  FRESH OR FROZEN, THAWED
- ABOUT 2 TBSP VANILLA SUGAR
- 115 G/4 OZ PLAIN FLOUR
- 85 G/3 OZ DEMERARA SUGAR

- 115 G/4 OZ UNSALTED
  BUTTER, DICED
- 115 G/4 OZ GROUND ALMONDS
- 2–3 TBSP SLIVERED ALMONDS
- **TO SERVE:**
- CUSTARD (SEE PAGE 353)

1 Set the oven to 180°C/350°F/Gas 4.

2 Peel, core and slice the pears and place in a 20–22.5 cm/8–9 inch shallow baking
dish with the blackcurrants. Sprinkle over the vanilla sugar, according to the
sweetness of the fruit and your taste.

3 Sift the flour into a mixing bowl, stir in the demerara sugar, add the butter and
toss to coat in flour, then rub in until the mixture resembles breadcrumbs. Stir in the
ground almonds.

4 Scatter evenly over the fruit, sprinkle over the slivered almonds, then press down
lightly. Bake for about 40 minutes until the top is brown and the fruit cooked. Serve
with Custard.

CARIBBEAN
UPSIDE-DOWN PUDDING

SERVES 6

Lime, coconut and papaya are obvious flavours to bring together;
add demerara sugar, and you have a pudding that evokes images of
hot sunshine, balmy breezes, golden beaches, laughter and calypsos.
If you can get knobbly Thai kaffir limes, use the rinds, but not the
juice, as they have a really fragrant lime flavour.

Use a spoon to scoop the seeds
from the halved papaya

- 2 PAPAYAS
- GRATED RIND AND JUICE OF 2 LIMES
- 85 G/3 OZ CASTER SUGAR
- 150 G/5 OZ DEMERARA SUGAR
- 115 G/4 OZ UNSALTED BUTTER
- 2 EGGS, SIZE 2, BEATEN
- 115 G/4 OZ PLAIN FLOUR
- 1½ TSP BAKING POWDER
- 25 G/1 OZ DESICCATED COCONUT

- **COCONUT SAUCE:**
- 300 ML/10 FL OZ DOUBLE CREAM
- 2 TBSP CASTER SUGAR, PREFERABLY VANILLA-FLAVOURED
- 55 G/2 OZ CREAMED COCONUT, CHOPPED
- 4 TBSP MILK
- **DECORATION:**
- LIGHTLY TOASTED FLAKED COCONUT

1 To make the sauce, pour the cream into a bowl. In a small saucepan, gently heat the sugar and coconut in the milk until the coconut and sugar have dissolved. Stir into the cream, then cover and place in the refrigerator to chill well.

2 Peel the papayas, cut in half and discard the seeds. Slice the papayas and place in a shallow dish. Sprinkle over the lime juice and leave for 2–3 hours.

3 Set the oven to 180°C/350°F/Gas 4. Well butter the base of a 24–25 cm/9½–10 inch fluted flan dish at least 4 cm/1½ inches deep, and butter the sides.

4 Drain the lime juice from the papaya slices into a bowl. Stir in the caster sugar and reserve for spooning over the baked pudding.

5 Arrange the papaya slices in the dish and sprinkle over 2 tablespoons of the demerara sugar.

6 Beat together the butter and the remaining demerara sugar until light and fluffy, then gradually beat in the eggs. Stir in the flour, baking powder, lime rind and coconut. Carefully spoon over the papaya slices and bake for about 50 minutes until a knife inserted in the centre comes out clean.

7 Prick the top of the pudding all over with a fine skewer or needle, stir the sweetened lime juice and spoon evenly over. Leave for a few minutes, then invert onto a warm plate. Sprinkle over flaked coconut to decorate and serve with the cold sauce.

$\mathscr{A}$ PLUM PUDDING

SERVES 4

*Not the traditional British 'plum pudding', that is,
Christmas Pudding, this simple, dare I say foolproof, recipe
contains fresh plums beneath a light, moist and tender
topping that is a cross between a custard and a sponge.*

- 550 G/1¼ LB RIPE PLUMS, HALVED AND STONED
- APPROXIMATELY 150 G/5 OZ VANILLA CASTER SUGAR
- 115 G/4 OZ GROUND ALMONDS
- 115 G/4 OZ UNSALTED BUTTER, MELTED AND COOLED
- 2 EGGS, SIZE 3, BEATEN
- 3 TBSP AMARETTO OR FEW DROPS ALMOND ESSENCE AND 2 TBSP SWEET SHERRY
- 150 ML/5 FL OZ MILK
- 25 G/1 OZ FLAKED ALMONDS
- ICING SUGAR, FOR DUSTING (OPTIONAL)

1 Set the oven to 180°C/350°F/Gas 4. Well butter the base of a 21.5 cm/8½ inch shallow baking dish, and butter the sides.

2 Place the plums in the dish and sprinkle with 1–2 tablespoons of the vanilla caster sugar, according to the sweetness of the plums and your taste.

3 Stir together the ground almonds, 115 g/4 oz sugar, the butter, eggs, amaretto or almond essence and sherry, and milk.

4 Spoon the almond mixture over the plums and sprinkle over the flaked almonds. Bake for 45–50 minutes until lightly set. Serve the pudding warm, dusted with icing sugar, if liked.

Illustrated opposite page 208

$\mathscr{P}$RUNES BAKED IN A RICH CUSTARD

SERVES 4

This regal and easy-to-make pudding — a far cry from watery
prunes swimming in a tasteless liquid served with a watery custard,
which is a very distant, lowly cousin — has that special something
that makes it irresistible, especially to me.

- 225 G/8 OZ LARGE, PLUMP PRUNES, SOAKED OVERNIGHT JUST COVERED BY WATER
- 5 TBSP ARMAGNAC, BRANDY OR WHISKY
- 225 G/8 OZ FULL-FAT SOFT CHEESE
- 85 ML/3 FL OZ DOUBLE OR WHIPPING CREAM
- 115 G/4 OZ VANILLA CASTER SUGAR
- FEW DROPS ALMOND ESSENCE
- FINELY GRATED RIND OF 1 LEMON
- 2 EGGS, SIZE 2, BEATEN
- 2 TBSP PLAIN FLOUR
- ICING SUGAR, FOR DUSTING

1 Cook the prunes in their soaking liquor until just tender. Drain the prunes from the liquid, cut them into halves and discard the stones. Place the prunes in a bowl, pour over the Armagnac, brandy or whisky, cover and leave for 2–3 hours.

2 Set the oven to 180°C/350°F/Gas 4. Butter a 675 ml/1¼ pint shallow, round baking dish.

3 Beat together the cheese, cream, sugar, almond essence and lemon rind until smooth, then mix in the eggs. Stir in the flour.

4 Drain the liquid from the prunes into the cheese mixture and stir in. Place the fruit in a single layer on the base of the dish and cover with the mixture. Bake for 30–35 minutes until lightly set in the centre.

5 Allow the pudding to cool for at least 30 minutes before serving lukewarm dusted with icing sugar.

VARIATION:
To make prunes in a rich, fluffy custard, divide the soaked prunes between 4 large individual ramekin dishes. Separate the eggs. Mix the yolks with the cheese, cream, sugar, almond essence and lemon rind. Whisk the egg whites and fold into the mixture (omit the flour). Divide between the dishes and bake for about 18 minutes.

*A*PPLE AND ORANGE
SURPRISE CRUNCH

`SERVES 4`

*The surprise is the creamy layer between the crunchy oat topping
and the piquant fruit base, all of which add up to a pudding
that is interesting and tasty to eat. The creamy layer can be
enriched by beating in about 55 g/2 oz full-fat soft cheese.*

- 550 G/1 ¼ LB COOKING APPLES
- 1 ORANGE, PEELED, SLICED
- 1 TBSP FINELY CHOPPED FRESH GINGER
- 2–3 TBSP VANILLA CASTER SUGAR
- 2 TBSP WATER

- 2 EGGS, SIZE 2
- 300 ML/10 FL OZ CREAMY MILK
- 40 G/1 ½ OZ UNSALTED BUTTER, DICED
- 40 G/1 ½ OZ DARK MUSCOVADO SUGAR
- 70 G/2 ½ OZ ROLLED OATS

1 Set the oven to 180°C/350°F/Gas 4. Butter an approximately 22.5 cm/9 inch ovenproof dish.

2 Peel, core and slice the apples. Reserve a few slices and put the rest in the dish. Gently stir in the orange slices, finely chopped ginger and 1–2 tbsp of the vanilla caster sugar, to taste.

3 Place the reserved apple slices in a small saucepan with the water and poach gently until just tender. Remove with a slotted spoon and reserve.

4 Meanwhile, stir together the eggs and 1 tablespoon of the vanilla caster sugar in a medium-sized bowl. Bring the milk to the boil, stir into the egg mixture, then pour back into the saucepan and cook over a low heat, stirring constantly, until thickened; do not allow to boil. Pour over the fruit.

5 Gently heat the butter and muscovado sugar, stirring, until melted, then stir in the oats. Scatter over the custard and bake for about 35 minutes until the apple is tender and the topping brown and crisp.

6 Place the poached apple slices on top and serve hot.

Illustrated opposite page 177

Walnut and Date Pudding

SERVES 4

When you've had a bad day and everything seems to have gone wrong, or when simply feeling a little low, there's nothing like a pudding that's stood the test of time, like this one, to calm you down, buck you up and put things back into perspective.

- 175 G/6 OZ STONED DATES, COARSELY CHOPPED
- 115 ML/4 FL OZ BOILING WATER
- 2 EGGS, SEPARATED
- 55 G/2 OZ LIGHT MUSCOVADO SUGAR
- 85 G/3 OZ UNSALTED BUTTER, DICED

- 2 TBSP MAPLE SYRUP OR GOLDEN SYRUP
- 175 G/6 OZ PLAIN FLOUR
- 1½ TSP BAKING POWDER
- FEW DROPS VANILLA ESSENCE
- 85 G/3 OZ WALNUTS, ROUGHLY CHOPPED

1 Set the oven to 180°C/350°F/Gas 4. Butter a 1.2 litre/2 pint ovenproof dish. Put the dates in a bowl, pour over the boiling water, stir and leave to cool.

2 In a medium-sized bowl, whisk the egg yolks with the sugar until thick and fluffy. In a small saucepan, gently warm together the butter and syrup until the butter has melted. Allow it to cool slightly if very warm. Using a large metal spoon, gently fold the flour and baking powder into the egg yolk mixture with the syrup mixture, vanilla essence, walnuts and dates and their soaking liquid. In a clean, dry bowl, whisk the egg whites until stiff but not dry, then, using a large metal spoon, gently fold into the date mixture.

3 Pour into the dish and bake for about 1 hour until the pudding is springy to the touch in the centre.

IN THE STYLE OF
QUEEN OF PUDDINGS

*I admit to being slightly devious when naming this recipe,
as I wanted to attract both the many people who like
Queen of Puddings and those who are less enamoured.
Members of both camps who have tried this recipe have all
become fans of it. The changes are subtle: I use an enriched bread,
such as brioche; a little single cream in place of some of the milk;
plenty of lemon, but not too much; and a very good, high-fruit
content raspberry jam, often labelled as a 'conserve', which I boost
with puréed raspberries for a fresher flavour or with
eau-de-vie de framboise.*

- 425 ML/15 FL OZ MILK
- 150 ML/5 FL OZ SINGLE CREAM
- 40 G/1½ OZ UNSALTED BUTTER
- 115 G/4 OZ BRIOCHE CRUMBS
- 3 EGGS, SEPARATED
- GRATED RIND OF 1 LARGE LEMON
- 55 G/2 OZ CASTER SUGAR,
  PLUS 1 TSP

- 2–4 TBSP GOOD QUALITY
  RASPBERRY JAM, WARMED
- 2–4 TBSP RASPBERRY PURÉE
  OR FEW DROPS *EAU-DE-VIE DE
  FRAMBOISE* OR FRAMBOISE
  LIQUEUR (OPTIONAL)

1 Bring the milk, cream and butter to simmering point, remove from the heat and stir in the brioche crumbs, egg yolks, lemon rind and half the sugar. Leave the mixture to stand for 30 minutes.

2 Set the oven to 170°C/325°F/Gas 3. Butter a 850 ml/1½ pint ovenproof dish.

3 Pour the crumb mixture into the dish and bake for about 45 minutes until lightly set in the centre.

4 If 'boosting' the raspberry jam, mix it with the raspberry purée or the eau-de-vie or liqueur.

5 Spread the jam over the pudding.

6 Whisk the egg whites until soft peaks form, then gradually whisk in the remaining sugar, whisking well after each addition, until the mixture is stiff and shiny. Pile onto the pudding, sprinkle over the teaspoon of sugar, and return to the oven for about 15 minutes until crisp and brown on top. Serve warm.

VARIATIONS:

If you want to go further and make a richer pudding, replace more of the milk with cream. Flavourings can be chopped candied peel, ground almonds or hazelnuts, desiccated coconut, rose water or orange flower water (omit the lemon rind), melted chocolate or cocoa powder (omit the lemon rind). Orange rind can be used instead of lemon rind, with orange segments in place of the jam. The breadcrumbs can be changed to plain cake crumbs, or the bread mixture can be poured over a fruit base.

$\mathcal{M}$AGIC LIME PUDDING

SERVES 4

This is a new, more tangily fragrant version of the popular 'classic' lemon pudding that separates as if by magic during baking into a light, spongy layer floating on a sauce.

- 55 G/2 OZ UNSALTED BUTTER
- 115 G/4 OZ CASTER SUGAR
- FINELY GRATED RIND AND JUICE OF 3 LARGISH LIMES

- 2 EGGS, SEPARATED
- 55 G/2 OZ SELF-RAISING FLOUR
- 150 ML/5 FL OZ MILK

1 Set the oven to 180°C/350°F/Gas 4. Butter an 850 ml/1½ pint ovenproof dish.

2 Beat the butter, sugar and lime rind together until well softened (because there is more sugar than butter, the mixture will not become light and fluffy). Gradually beat in the egg yolks. Lightly fold in the flour alternately with the milk and lime juice. Whisk the egg whites until stiff but not dry, then, using a large metal spoon, gently fold into the butter mixture (don't worry if it looks a little curdled at this stage – it's quite normal). Pour into the dish and bake for 40–45 minutes until golden and the sponge is just set.

Illustrated opposite page 224

ℛICE 'GÂTEAU'

Rice pudding has many different faces, ranging from the school meals version, which should be served hot but is invariably tepid, to extravagant, refined, moulded creations of French 'haute cuisine', which are served cold. The presentation of this version is quite unlike any other – served hot, it is 'moulded' so that it can be turned out like a cake and has a consistency somewhere between that of a soufflé and a light sponge, with a fairly soft, creamy centre and a crisp outside. It has a certain elegance, yet it is still 'homely', hence the name – to call it 'Rice Cake' would not convey the right impression. Coconut milk (see page 262) and almond milk (see page 339) produce very interesting variations. If time allows, soak the rice in the milk for a couple of hours.

- 550 ML/1 PINT CREAMY MILK OR MILK AND SINGLE CREAM, MIXED
- 100 G/3½ OZ PUDDING RICE
- 70 G/2½ OZ VANILLA SUGAR
- 40 G/1½ OZ UNSALTED BUTTER
- FINELY GRATED RIND OF 1 LEMON
- 40 G/1½ OZ BRIOCHE, CHOLLA OR OTHER GOOD BREADCRUMBS
- SPRINKLING ICING SUGAR
- 3 EGGS, SEPARATED
- FEW DROPS ROSE WATER
- **TO SERVE:**
- CHERRY COMPOTE (SEE PAGE 223), PLUM AND RASPBERRY COMPOTE (SEE PAGE 261), APRICOT SAUCE (SEE PAGE 359) OR LIGHTLY SWEETENED, SIEVED RASPBERRIES

1 Put the milk and rice into a heavy-based saucepan and bring to just below simmering point. Stir in the sugar and butter and simmer gently, stirring occasionally, for about 30 minutes until the rice is swollen and creamy. Stir in the lemon rind and leave to cool slightly.

2 Set the oven to 140°C/275°F/Gas 1. Well butter an 850 ml/1½ pint soufflé dish. Mix the breadcrumbs with a little icing sugar, then press evenly into the sides and base so there are no gaps.

3 Beat the egg yolks and rose water into the rice.

4 In a clean, dry bowl, whisk the egg whites until stiff but not dry, then, using a large metal spoon, gently fold into the rice mixture in three batches. Gently pour into the dish, taking care not to dislodge the crumb coating. Bake for 1 hour 20 minutes until just firm to the touch in the centre and the top is crisp and golden. Serve from the dish or turn out onto a warm plate and serve with Cherry Compote, Plum and Raspberry Compote, Apricot Sauce or lightly sweetened, sieved raspberries.

CHRISTMAS PUDDING
SOUFFLÉ

SERVES 4

*I like Christmas pudding and will eat it all year round (I find it
difficult to resist puddings sold post-Christmas at reduced prices),
providing the pudding is a good one. During the course of my
researches to find good puddings, despite exercising my experience
of the subject, which enables me to reject the really bad ones,
I end up with some that I feel would benefit from a little 'doctoring'
– and this is what I do with them.*

- 225 G/8 OZ CHRISTMAS
  PUDDING, CRUMBLED
- 3 TBSP RUM, WHISKY OR BRANDY
- 2 TBSP DOUBLE OR WHIPPING
  CREAM OR MILK
- 4 EGGS, SIZE 2, SEPARATED
- 1 EXTRA EGG WHITE, SIZE 2
- 25–55 G/1–2 OZ VANILLA
  CASTER SUGAR, DEPENDING ON
  THE SWEETNESS OF THE PUDDING

- **TO SERVE:**
- CREAM, VANILLA DAIRY ICE
  CREAM, ICED MASCARPONE (SEE
  PAGE 254) OR SABAYON SAUCE
  (SEE PAGE 357)

1 If you have an hour or so before you need to start to make the pudding, put the
Christmas pudding into a shallow dish, sprinkle over the rum, whisky or brandy and
leave to soak.

2 Set the oven to 200°C/400°F/Gas 6. Butter 4 individual soufflé or ramekin dishes.

3 Put the Christmas pudding into a mixing bowl, add the cream or milk, egg yolks,
and rum, whisky or brandy if the pudding has not been soaked in it, and beat
together to remove large lumps but so the mixture is a little nobbly.

4 In a clean, dry bowl, whisk the egg whites until soft peaks form, then gradually
whisk in the sugar, whisking well after each addition, until the mixture is stiff and
shiny. Using a large metal spoon, gently fold about a quarter into the Christmas
pudding mixture to loosen it, then lightly fold in the remainder.

5 Fill the dishes to their rim, then run a spoon, knife or fork handle between the
pudding and the dish so the mixture will rise upwards rather than flow over the
sides. Bake for about 25–30 minutes until well risen, and lightly set. To serve, make a
small hole in the top and pour or spoon in cream, vanilla dairy ice cream, Iced
Mascarpone or Sabayon Sauce.

Spoon the meringue over the
custard and swirl into peaks

$\mathscr{P}$EACH MERINGUE
PUDDING

SERVES 6

*My grandmother's speciality was a pineapple pudding and, as she
grew older and cooked less, she would make it, or suggest making it,
for any occasion that was not part of normal daily life. A simple
dessert, it consisted of canned pineapple, a cornflour custard
enriched with egg yolks and flavoured with vanilla essence, and a
meringue topping. Peach Meringue Pudding belongs to the same
family, but the fruit is fresh, the custard is thickened only with egg
yolks and a vanilla pod replaces the essence. I know Grandmother
would have approved.*

- 425 ML/15 FL OZ MILK, OR A MIXTURE OF MILK AND CREAM
- 1 VANILLA POD
- 3 EGGS, SEPARATED
- 2 EGG YOLKS
- 125 G/4½ OZ VANILLA CASTER SUGAR
- 20 G/¾ OZ UNSALTED BUTTER
- 1½ TBSP LIGHT MUSCOVADO SUGAR
- 4 PEACHES
- APPROXIMATELY 2 TBSP LEMON JUICE
- 1 TBSP KIRSCH (OPTIONAL)
- 2–3 TBSP FLAKED ALMONDS

1 In a heavy-based saucepan, gently heat the milk with the vanilla pod to just on simmering point. Remove from the heat, cover and leave for 20 minutes.

2 In a medium-sized bowl, beat the egg yolks with about 1 tablespoon of the vanilla caster sugar. Bring the milk to the boil, then stir into the egg yolk mixture. Return to the saucepan and heat very gently, stirring with a wooden spoon, until thickened; do not allow to boil. Remove the vanilla pod.

3 Set the oven to 190°C/375°F/Gas 5. Spread the butter over the base of a wide 1.2–1.5 litre/2–2½ pint ovenproof dish and sprinkle with the light muscovado sugar.

4 If the peaches are very ripe, the skin should easily peel off. If it clings stubbornly to the fruit, place the peaches in a bowl, cover with boiling water, leave for about 20 seconds, then drain off the water – the skin should then come away without any problem. Thickly slice the peaches and discard the stones. Place the peach slices in a frying pan, cover with cold water and bring to simmering point. Poach gently for 5–10 minutes until tender. Drain and place in the dish. Sprinkle over the lemon juice and the kirsch, if using.

5 In a clean, dry bowl, whisk the egg whites until soft peaks form, then gradually whisk in the remaining sugar, whisking well after each addition, until the mixture is stiff and shiny. Spoon over the custard. Scatter over the flaked almonds and bake for 12–15 minutes until brown and crisp on top. Serve warm.

$\mathscr{A}$PPLE AND
BLACKBERRY FLAPJACK

SERVES 6

*The chewy, oaty flapjack jacket packed with seasonal apples
and blackberries provides compensation for the colder days and
longer nights of autumn.*

- 550 G/1 ¼ LB COOKING APPLES
- 25 G/1 OZ CASTER OR
  GRANULATED SUGAR
- 550 G/1 ¼ LB BLACKBERRIES
- 40 G/1 ½ OZ DARK
  MUSCOVADO SUGAR
- 150 G/5 OZ UNSALTED BUTTER,
  DICED
- 4 TBSP GOLDEN SYRUP

- 200 G/7 OZ ROLLED OATS
- 40 G/1 ½ OZ SUNFLOWER SEEDS
- 1 ¼ TSP GROUND CINNAMON
- **DECORATION:**
- POACHED APPLE RINGS, OR
  BLACKBERRIES AND ICING SUGAR
- **TO SERVE:**
- CUSTARD (SEE PAGE 353)

1 Set the oven to 190°C/375°F/Gas 5. Butter a 20 cm/8 inch springform cake tin, line
with greaseproof paper, then butter the paper.

2 Peel, core and slice the apples, then very gently simmer with the caster or
granulated sugar in a covered saucepan until soft. Stir in the blackberries and leave to
cool slightly.

3 Gently heat the dark muscovado sugar, butter and golden syrup, stirring
occasionally, until the sugar has dissolved and the butter melted. Stir in the oats,
sunflower seeds and cinnamon. Use three-quarters to line the cake tin, taking the
mixture to about 2.5 cm/1 inch from the rim. Pour in the apple and blackberries,
then cover with the remaining oat mixture, pressing it down lightly. Bake for about
35 minutes.

4 Allow to cool for 10 minutes before loosening the edges and removing the
pudding from the tin. Decorate with poached apple rings, or blackberries and icing
sugar. Serve warm with Custard.

$\mathcal{O}$MELETTE NORVÉGIENNE

SERVES 4-6

*Omelette Norvégienne is less well known than baked Alaska,
but it is very similar and, I think, much better. The addition of
whisked yolks to the egg whites gives them body without requiring
the same amount of sugar as the meringue for a baked Alaska,
and makes a more rounded and successful dish. The ice cream must
be really hard before starting. Other fruits can, of course,
be used in place of the blackcurrants.*

- 225 G/8 OZ BLACKCURRANTS, FRESH OR FROZEN, THAWED
- 2 TBSP WATER
- 2 TBSP CASTER SUGAR
- 2 TBSP WHITE RUM
- 3 EGGS, SEPARATED

- 1 × 17.5 CM/7 INCH OBLONG SPONGE CAKE
- 550 ML/1 PINT HOME-MADE OR VANILLA DAIRY ICE CREAM
- CASTER SUGAR, FOR SPRINKLING

1 Set the oven to 220°C/425°F/Gas 7.

2 Gently heat the blackcurrants with the water and half the sugar in a fairly small, covered saucepan, shaking the pan occasionally, until the fruit juices just begin to run. Add the white rum, then leave uncovered until cold.

3 Whisk the egg yolks and remaining sugar together until thick and creamy. In a clean, dry bowl, and using a clean whisk, whisk the egg whites until stiff but not dry. Using a large metal spoon, gently fold the egg whites into the yolks.

4 Place the sponge on a large ovenproof serving plate. Spoon over the blackcurrants and juices then place the ice cream on top, trimming to fit, if necessary. Quickly cover the ice cream and cake completely with the egg mixture. Sprinkle with caster sugar and bake for 3 minutes until the top is golden. Serve at once.

Illustrated opposite page 192

$\mathscr{G}$LAZED NECTARINE
SLICES

SERVES 2–4

*The butter and sugar melt and bathe the nectarines and brioche
in a spicy, butterscotch glaze. In place of the whole seeds,
you could use about half a teaspoon of Chinese five spice powder,
which is sold by a major British food company and
is available in supermarkets.*

- 2 RIPE BUT FIRM NECTARINES
- 2–4 SLICES OF BRIOCHE, OR
OTHER GOOD, FIRM BREAD SUCH AS
CHOLLA OR VIENNA, DEPENDING
ON SIZE, CRUSTS REMOVED
- APPROXIMATELY 55 G/2 OZ
UNSALTED BUTTER
- ½ TSP CORIANDER SEEDS
- ½ TSP SZECHUAN PEPPERCORNS
- ⅓ CINNAMON STICK

- APPROXIMATELY 55 G/2 OZ
LIGHT MUSCOVADO SUGAR
- APPROXIMATELY 3 TBSP FLAKED
ALMONDS (OPTIONAL)
- **TO SERVE:**
- ORANGE BUTTER SAUCE (SEE
PAGE 358), ICED MASCARPONE
(SEE PAGE 254), SABAYON SAUCE
(SEE PAGE 357), CREAM, VANILLA
DAIRY ICE CREAM OR
STRAINED GREEK YOGURT

1 Set the oven to 180°C/350°F/Gas 4. Butter a shallow baking sheet.

2 Place the nectarines in a bowl, pour over boiling water and leave for about 30 seconds. Remove the nectarines from the water, then peel off the skins and cut each nectarine in half and remove the stone.

3 Cut the slices of bread in half if they are large. Generously butter one side of each slice of bread.

4 Crush the spices together very finely. Mix with the sugar and sprinkle some over the buttered side of the bread.

5 Place a nectarine half, cut-side down, on the buttered and sugared side of each piece of bread and cut deep slashes in the fruit. Insert slivers of butter in the slashes, scatter over the almonds, if using, and sprinkle generously with the remainder of the sugar and spice mixture. Lay the slices on the baking sheet and bake for about 15 minutes until the bread is crisp and browned at the edges, the fruit softened and coated in sauce. Serve warm with Orange Butter Sauce, Iced Mascarpone, Sabayon Sauce, cream, vanilla dairy ice cream or strained Greek yogurt.

Illustrated opposite page 193

*Holding the orange over a
bowl, cut down between the
flesh and the membrane to
remove the segments*

ℋOT ORANGE CAKE

SERVES 6

*The tangy soured cream filling melts deliciously into the hot cake,
so it should be served quickly. The syrup is really meant to be
optional as the pudding is sufficiently good without it, but I always
seem to be able to find the few seconds needed to make it —
and on occasions (not just special ones!) I add some Cointreau.
Around Christmas, tangerines or satsumas can be substituted
for the oranges.*

- 115 G/4 OZ UNSALTED BUTTER
- 115 G/4 OZ CASTER SUGAR
- 2 LARGE EGGS, SEPARATED
- 115 G/4 OZ SELF-RAISING FLOUR
- JUICE AND FINELY GRATED RIND OF 3 SMALL ORANGES
- 225 ML/8 FL OZ SOURED CREAM
- FRESH ORANGE SEGMENTS WITH ALL THE PITH AND SKIN REMOVED

- ICING SUGAR, FOR SIFTING (OPTIONAL)
- **SYRUP (OPTIONAL):**
- 5 TBSP ORANGE JUICE
- 1 TBSP COINTREAU (OPTIONAL)
- 7–8 TBSP ICING SUGAR

1 Set the oven to 180°C/350°F/Gas 4. Butter a 20 cm/8 inch springform or non-stick cake tin.

2 Beat together the butter and 85 g/3 oz of sugar until light and fluffy. Beat in the egg yolks, then stir in half the flour and the juice and rind of 1 orange.

3 In a clean, dry bowl, whisk the egg whites until soft peaks form, then gradually whisk in the remaining sugar. Using a large metal spoon, gently fold into the orange mixture with the remaining flour. Spoon into the tin and bake for 20–30 minutes until golden and springy to the touch.

4 Meanwhile, lightly beat the soured cream with the remaining orange juice and finely grated rind.

5 To make the syrup, if using, gently warm the orange juice, Cointreau, if using, and icing sugar in a small saucepan just before the cake is cooked.

6 Remove the cake from the oven, leave for 2 minutes, then turn out and cut in half horizontally using a bread knife. Quickly prick the top of the cake all over, then brush with the syrup, if used, and spread the soured cream over the bottom half, then cover with the top half. Top with orange segments, sift icing sugar over if the syrup has not been used and serve while the cake is still very warm.

RIGHT (from top to
bottom): Plum Pudding
(see page 196); Mother's
Mincemeat Pudding (see
page 214); Hot Brownie
Soufflé with Ice Cream
Sauce (see page 222).

Illustrated opposite page 193

FRANGIPANE CUSTARD

SERVES 4-6

Luxurious to eat, yet simplicity itself to make,
this is an all-round popular pudding.

- 85 G/3 OZ BLANCHED
  ALMONDS, GROUND
- 85 G/3 OZ UNSALTED BUTTER,
  MELTED AND COOLED
- 425 ML/15 FL OZ SINGLE CREAM
- 85 G/3 OZ VANILLA CASTER
  SUGAR
- 4 EGGS, SIZE 2, BEATEN
- FINELY GRATED RIND AND
  JUICE OF 1/2 LEMON

- FEW DROPS VANILLA ESSENCE
- 3 TBSP AMARETTO
- **TO SERVE:**
- FRESH RASPBERRIES, SLICED
  STRAWBERRIES SPRINKLED WITH
  SUGAR, COLD CHERRY COMPOTE
  (SEE PAGE 223) OR COLD PLUM
  AND RASPBERRY COMPOTE
  (SEE PAGE 261)

1 Set the oven to 180°C/350°F/Gas 4. Butter an approximately 22.5 cm/9 inch shallow baking dish.

2 Stir together all the ingredients. Pour into the dish and bake for about 30–35 minutes until *very* lightly set in the centre. Serve warm with fresh raspberries, sliced strawberries sprinkled with just a little sugar to draw out their juices, cold Cherry Compote or cold Plum Compote.

LEFT (from top to bottom): Baked Apples with a Middle Eastern Flavour (see page 215); Cherry Casket (see page 223).

Lining the base of a tin:

*Place the tin on greaseproof
paper and draw its outline
on the paper*

Butter the tin

Fit the paper into the tin

Succulent, Smooth
APPLE CAKE

SERVES 6–8

*Unlike most apple cakes, which contain pieces of apple either
folded into or placed on the top or bottom of a creamed or rubbed in
cake mixture, this moist and tasty cake contains a fresh-tasting
apple purée, which is simply stirred in to nearly all the remaining
ingredients, leaving just the whisking of egg whites to be done.*

- 450 G/1 LB BRAMLEY APPLES
- 1 TBSP WATER
- STRIP ORANGE OR LEMON PEEL
- 175 G/6 OZ LIGHT MUSCOVADO SUGAR
- 2 EGGS, SEPARATED
- 150 ML/5 FL OZ SUNFLOWER OR LIGHT OLIVE OIL
- 225 G/8 OZ SELF-RAISING FLOUR
- 1½ TSP GROUND CINNAMON
- 1½ TSP GROUND GINGER
- 85 G/3 OZ PLUMP RAISINS
- **TO SERVE:**
- ORANGE BUTTER SAUCE (SEE PAGE 358), FLUFFY ORANGE SAUCE (SEE PAGE 356), SABAYON SAUCE (SEE PAGE 357), CUSTARD (SEE PAGE 353) OR ORANGE CUSTARD (SEE PAGE 354)

1 Peel, core and chop the apples, then cook gently in a covered saucepan with the water, citrus peel and 25 g/1 oz of the sugar, shaking the pan occasionally, until the apples are soft.

2 Set the oven to 180°C/350°F/Gas 4. Butter and flour a 20 cm/8 inch cake tin and line the base with non-stick silicone paper.

3 Discard the citrus peel from the apple, then purée the apples with 70 g/2½ oz of the sugar, the egg yolks and oil. Sift together the flour and spices, then lightly mix into the apple mixture with the raisins.

4 In a clean, dry bowl, whisk the egg whites until soft peaks form, then gradually whisk in the remaining sugar, whisking well after each addition, until the mixture is stiff and shiny. Using a large metal spoon, gently fold into the apple mixture. Transfer to the tin and bake for 35–40 minutes until golden and springy to the touch in the centre. Serve with Orange Butter Sauce, Fluffy Orange Sauce, Sabayon Sauce, Custard or Orange Custard.

Illustrated opposite page 321

$\mathscr{B}$LACKBERRY MERINGUE
SHORTBREAD CAKE

SERVES 8

*The blackberries, sitting on a melt-in-the-mouth shortbread base
and covered by a billowy meringue that is crisp outside but soft
inside, are deliciously warm and just yielding their juice, so neither
their texture nor their taste are spoilt by cooking. A subtle
flavouring of rose water will enhance the flavour of the
blackberries, adding a special flavour and fragrance that is both
slightly exotic and very traditionally English.*

- 450 G/1 LB BLACKBERRIES
- 40 G/1½ OZ CASTER SUGAR
- **SHORTBREAD CAKE:**
- 175 G/6 OZ UNSALTED
  BUTTER, SOFTENED
- 115 G/4 OZ CASTER SUGAR
- 4 EGG YOLKS, SIZE 2

- 85 G/3 OZ ALMONDS, GROUND
- 250 G/9 OZ SELF-RAISING FLOUR
- **MERINGUE:**
- 4 EGG WHITES, SIZE 2
- 115 G/4 OZ CASTER SUGAR
- ROSE WATER, TO TASTE

1 Set the oven to 190°C/375°F/Gas 5. Butter a 25 cm/10 inch loose-based flan tin.

2 To make the cake, beat the butter with the sugar until pale and creamy, then gradually beat in the egg yolks. Using a large metal spoon, gently fold in the ground almonds and the flour. Spread evenly in the tin, then bake for about 30 minutes until a light fawn colour and just firm to the touch in the centre.

3 Gently mix together the blackberries and sugar, then place in an even layer on the cake, leaving a 1.25 cm/½ inch border all the way round.

4 To make the meringue, in a large, clean, dry bowl, whisk the egg whites until soft peaks form, then gradually whisk in the sugar, whisking well after each addition, until the mixture is stiff and shiny. Whisk in rose water to taste with the last of the sugar. Spoon over the blackberries and the border around the edge of the cake to seal in the fruit. Use the back of a spoon to swirl the top of the meringue into soft peaks. Turn the oven temperature up to 220°C/425°F/Gas 7 and bake for 5–10 minutes until the meringue is just firm and the peaks lightly browned.

Illustrated opposite page 224

ℳOCHA PUDDING WITH FUDGE-MUD SAUCE

*A wonderfully rich, chocolatey, fudgy variation on the theme of
a spongy pudding sitting on a self-made sauce.*

- 115 G/4 OZ LIGHT MUSCOVADO SUGAR
- 115 G/4 OZ SELF-RAISING FLOUR
- ½ TSP BAKING POWDER
- 1 TBSP COCOA POWDER
- 55 G/2 OZ UNSALTED BUTTER, DICED
- APPROXIMATELY 1½ TBSP INSTANT COFFEE GRANULES

- 150 ML/5 FL OZ MILK
- 1 TSP VANILLA ESSENCE
- **SAUCE:**
- 225 G/8 OZ DEMERARA SUGAR
- 5 TBSP COCOA POWDER
- 425 ML/15 FL OZ MILK

1 Set the oven to 180°C/350°F/Gas 4. Butter a deep 1.5 litre/2½ pint ovenproof dish.

2 Stir together the sugar, flour, baking powder and cocoa powder. Gently heat the butter and coffee granules in the milk until the butter has melted, then gradually beat into the dry ingredients and add the vanilla essence. Pour into the dish.

3 To make the sauce, mix together the sugar and cocoa powder, then scatter evenly over the top of the pudding mixture. Pour over the milk. Bake for about 1 hour until the sponge is set throughout.

HAZELNUT AND BERRY SHORTCAKE

SERVES 6

*This pudding, which has a soft hazelnutty centre surrounding
moist fruit, is equally good made using either raspberries,
loganberries or blackberries. The apple can be added raw, as in the
recipe, so that it still has some texture at the end of the baking,
or it can first be gently cooked in a covered saucepan, shaking the
pan occasionally, until softened, then left to cool. For flavourings,
I like to include orange flower water either with the fruit or the
hazelnut mixture, or I mix ground cinnamon with the caster sugar
sprinkled over the baked shortcake.*

- 150 G/5 OZ UNSALTED
  BUTTER, DICED
- 150 G/5 OZ VANILLA SUGAR
- 1 EGG, BEATEN
- 150 G/5 OZ HAZELNUTS, GROUND
- 150 G/5 OZ SELF-RAISING FLOUR
- 175 G/6 OZ EATING APPLES,
  SUCH AS COX'S ORANGE PIPPINS
  OR REINETTES

- 300 G/10 OZ FRESH BERRIES
- CASTER SUGAR, FOR SPRINKLING
- **TO SERVE:**
- DOUBLE CREAM OR STRAINED
  GREEK YOGURT

1 Set the oven to 180°C/350°F/Gas 4. Butter a 22.5 cm/8½ inch loose-based deep
flan tin.

2 Beat together the butter, sugar and egg until well mixed. Stir in the hazelnuts and
flour. Spread half in the base of the flan tin, using a fork to flatten lightly.

3 Peel, core and finely chop the apples. Mix with the berries, then place in an even
layer on the hazelnut mixture. Dot over the remaining hazelnut mixture so that the
fruit is almost covered.

4 Place on a baking sheet and bake for about 1 hour, covering lightly when well
browned. The cake should feel *just* firm, with a springy texture. Remove from the
oven, but leave in the tin for about 1 hour. Sprinkle over caster sugar and serve warm
with double cream or strained Greek yogurt.

MOTHER'S
MINCEMEAT PUDDING

SERVES 4

Like many other people, my mother always buys and makes far too much food at Christmas. Mince pies, and the ingredients for making yet more mince pies, is a particular foible. Consequently, there is always a supply of mincemeat left in the larder, which is transformed very effectively into this delicious, tasty pudding. If you have good, moist, home-made mincemeat, the apple and brandy should not be needed.

- 1 BRAMLEY APPLE (OPTIONAL)
- 225 G/8 OZ MINCEMEAT
- FINELY GRATED RIND OF 1 ORANGE
- 2–3 TBSP BRANDY (OPTIONAL)
- 85 G/3 OZ UNSALTED BUTTER

- 70 G/2½ OZ DARK MUSCOVADO SUGAR
- 2 EGGS, BEATEN
- 115 G/4 OZ SELF-RAISING FLOUR
- **TO SERVE:**
- CUSTARD (SEE PAGE 353) OR VANILLA DAIRY ICE CREAM

1 Set the oven to 160°C/325°F/Gas 3. Butter an approximately 20 cm/8 inch round, shallow baking dish.

2 Peel, core and grate the apple, if using. Mix with the mincemeat, orange rind and brandy, if using.

3 Beat together the butter and sugar until light and fluffy, then gradually beat in the eggs, beating well after each addition. Using a large metal spoon, lightly fold in the flour, then the mincemeat mixture. Spoon into the dish and bake for 10 minutes.

4 Lower the oven temperature to 150°C/300°F/Gas 2 and bake for a further 40–45 minutes until set in the centre. Serve hot with Custard or vanilla dairy ice cream.

Illustrated opposite page 208

BAKED APPLES WITH A MIDDLE EASTERN FLAVOUR

SERVES 6

*The special yet simple combination of ingredients in the filling,
together with the honey-sweetened, fragrant, buttery citrus basting
juices, give an exotic, luxurious air to an everyday pudding
that is hard to resist.*

- 6 LARGE EATING APPLES
- 40 G/1½ OZ DRIED FIGS, FINELY CHOPPED
- 40 G/1½ OZ STONED, NO-NEED-TO-SOAK PRUNES, FINELY CHOPPED
- 40 G/1½ OZ WALNUTS, CHOPPED
- 2 TBSP FINELY CHOPPED STEM GINGER
- 1 TSP FINELY GRATED LEMON RIND

- 1 TBSP APRICOT PRESERVE
- ¼ TSP FRESHLY GROUND CINNAMON
- 25 G/1 OZ UNSALTED BUTTER
- 115 G/4 OZ CLEAR HONEY
- 85 ML/3 FL OZ ORANGE JUICE
- 1 TBSP LEMON JUICE
- FINELY CRUSHED SEEDS FROM 3 CARDAMOM PODS

1 Set the oven to 180°C/350°F/Gas 4.

2 Core the apples and slightly enlarge the cavities. Score a fine line around the circumference of each apple. Place in a shallow baking dish they just fit.

3 In a bowl, beat together the figs, prunes, walnuts, ginger, lemon rind, apricot preserve and cinnamon until well combined. Pack the mixture into the cavities in the apples.

4 In a small saucepan, gently heat the butter, honey, orange juice, lemon juice and cardamom seeds, stirring with a wooden spoon, until the butter has melted and the mixture is smooth. Pour over the apples and bake for about 45 minutes, basting every 10 minutes or so with the cooking juices, until the apples are soft. Serve with the cooking juices spooned over.

Illustrated opposite page 209

Butter a kugelhopf mould or fancy ring cake mould

To turn out the pudding, place a warm plate over the top of the mould, hold the mould and plate firmly together, then invert them

Carefully lift away the mould

HAZELNUT PRALINE
SOUFFLÉ PUDDING

SERVES 4–6

This is an extremely moreish but quite light and not-too-sweet pudding. I first made it using hazelnut biscuits, but I thought the addition of small pieces of chocolate speckled through it might be an improvement. The nearest biscuits I could find contained chocolate chips, and they worked very well. You could, of course, buy hazelnut biscuits and chop some chocolate yourself.

- 100 G/3½ OZ UNSALTED BUTTER, SOFTENED
- 4 EGGS, SEPARATED
- 125 ML/4½ FL OZ MILK
- 25 G/1 OZ HAZELNUTS, ROASTED, SKINNED AND GROUND
- 125 G/4½ OZ HAZELNUT AND CHOCOLATE CHIP BISCUITS, CRUSHED

- 25 G/1 OZ SELF-RAISING FLOUR
- **PRALINE:**
- 125 G/4½ OZ CASTER SUGAR
- 100 G/3½ OZ HAZELNUTS, SKINNED
- **TO SERVE:**
- CUSTARD (SEE PAGE 353) OR VANILLA DAIRY ICE CREAM

1 To make the praline, in a small heavy-based saucepan, gently heat 100 g/3½ oz of the sugar and the skinned nuts without stirring, until the sugar melts. Increase the heat and cook until the mixture turns a rich brown colour, tossing the pan occasionally to prevent the nuts sticking. Tip quickly into a thin layer on a baking tray and leave until cold. Crush using a rolling pin and either continue crushing with the rolling pin to make a coarse powder, or use a food processor.

2 Set the oven to 190°C/375°F/Gas 5. Butter a 1.5 litre/2½ pint kugelhopf mould or fancy cake ring mould and place in a baking tin.

3 Beat the butter with the praline until pale and creamy, then whisk in the egg yolks, followed by the milk. Using a large metal spoon, lightly fold in the ground hazelnuts, biscuits and flour.

4 In a clean, dry bowl, whisk the egg whites until soft peaks form, then gradually whisk in the remaining sugar, whisking well after each addition, until the mixture is stiff and shiny. Using a large metal spoon, gently fold into the hazelnut mixture, then spoon into the mould and cover the top loosely with greaseproof paper. Surround the mould with boiling water. Cook the pudding for 50 minutes to 1 hour until just set in the centre.

5 Remove the mould from the baking tin, leave to stand for a few minutes, then turn onto a warmed plate and cover the mould with a damp cloth. Leave for 5 minutes, then remove the mould from the pudding. Serve warm with a little cold Custard or vanilla dairy ice cream.

CRUNCHY
MARMALADE PUDDING

SERVES 6-8

*This pudding combines several features that make it interesting
and enjoyable to eat – a nutty-crunchy top, a sweet tang and
appetite-tickling spices. One day when I had a bottle of Guinness
open, I substituted it for the milk and was sufficiently pleased
with the result that, if I am in the mood for drinking the rest of
the bottle, I will open one specifically to make the pudding.*

*Use a pestle in a mortar to
crush cinnamon and cloves*

- 4 CLOVES OR A PINCH OF GROUND CLOVES
- 2.5 CM/1 INCH CINNAMON STICK OR 1 TSP GROUND CINNAMON
- 150 G/5 OZ DARK, THICK-CUT MARMALADE, SUCH AS OXFORD, CHOPPED
- 125 G/4½ OZ UNSALTED BUTTER, DICED
- 7 TBSP GOLDEN SYRUP
- 2 EGGS, SIZE 3, BEATEN
- 225 G/8 OZ SELF-RAISING FLOUR
- 1 TSP BAKING POWDER
- ¾ TSP FRESHLY GRATED NUTMEG
- APPROXIMATELY 70 ML/ 2½ FL OZ MILK OR GUINNESS
- 40 G/1½ OZ CORNFLAKES, FINELY CRUSHED
- 40 G/1½ OZ WALNUT HALVES, FINELY CHOPPED
- **TO SERVE:**
- CUSTARD (SEE PAGE 353)

1 Use a pestle and mortar to finely crush the cloves and cinnamon.

2 Set the oven to 180°C/350°F/Gas 4. Butter a 20 cm/8 inch square cake tin and spread 2 tablespoons of the marmalade over the base.

3 Beat the butter with 4½ tablespoons of the syrup until well mixed, then gradually beat in the eggs, keeping the mixture smooth. Stir in half the remaining marmalade.

4 Sift together the flour, baking powder and nutmeg (and cloves and cinnamon if using ready ground ones), then fold into the syrup mixture with the finely crushed cinnamon and cloves. Add sufficient milk or Guinness to make a fairly stiff consistency. Spoon into the dish.

5 Mix the cornflakes and walnuts with the remaining syrup and marmalade, then spread evenly over the pudding. Bake for about 45 minutes until a skewer inserted in the centre comes out clean. Serve hot with plenty of Custard.

PECAN WHISKY PUDDING

SERVES 6

Opinions vary about the sauce for this pudding. Some say that the sweet richness of the sauce complements the opulent nuts, moist raisins and delicate crumb and flavour of the pudding. Others think that it detracts from the pudding's merits, and prefer vanilla dairy ice cream or Iced Mascarpone (see page 254), perhaps laced with a little whisky. The only debate about the pudding itself is how soon will it be served again!

- 125 G/4½ OZ PLUMP RAISINS
- 70 ML/2½ FL OZ WHISKY
- 70 G/2½ OZ UNSALTED BUTTER, DICED
- 85 G/3 OZ LIGHT MUSCOVADO SUGAR
- 2 EGGS, SEPARATED
- 160 G/5¼ OZ PLAIN FLOUR
- 1½ TSP BAKING POWDER
- ½ TSP FRESHLY GRATED NUTMEG

- 150 G/5 OZ PECAN HALVES
- **SAUCE (OPTIONAL):**
- 115 G/4 OZ LIGHT MUSCOVADO SUGAR
- 115 G/4 OZ UNSALTED BUTTER, CHOPPED
- 150 ML/5 FL OZ WHIPPING CREAM
- 1 TSP VANILLA ESSENCE

1 Leave the raisins to soak in the whisky for several hours.

2 Set the oven to 170°C/325°F/Gas 3. Butter and lightly flour a 15 cm/6 inch round baking dish or cake tin.

3 Beat the butter and 100 g/3½ oz of the sugar until light and fluffy, then beat in the egg yolks.

4 Sift together the flour, baking powder and nutmeg. Using a large metal spoon, gently fold into the butter mixture with the nuts and raisins and whisky.

5 In a clean, dry bowl, whisk the egg whites until soft peaks form, then gradually whisk in the remaining sugar. Gently fold half into the egg mixture, then gently fold in the remainder. Spoon into the dish or tin and bake for about 50 minutes until a fine skewer inserted into the centre comes out clean.

6 To make the sauce, if using, gently heat all the ingredients together in a small, heavy-based saucepan, stirring with a wooden spoon, until evenly blended. Remove from the heat and whisk for 1 minute.

7 Leave the cake to cool in the tin or dish for a few minutes, then turn onto a warm plate. Trickle the sauce over. Serve warm.

Illustrated opposite page 224

$\mathcal{A}$PRICOT PANDOWDY

SERVES 4–6

A pandowdy is an American name for a type of upside-down pudding. The recipe for this version was given to me – after I had eaten two helpings of the pudding – by a friend who has an American aunt who had given it to her.

- 350 G/12 OZ FRESH APRICOTS, HALVED AND STONED
- 85 G/3 OZ SUGAR
- 150 ML/5 FL OZ WATER
- 4 TBSP MAPLE SYRUP
- 55 G/2 OZ UNSALTED BUTTER
- SQUEEZE OF LEMON JUICE
- 55 G/2 OZ PECAN OR WALNUT HALVES
- **TOPPING:**
- 200 G/7 OZ SELF-RAISING FLOUR
- 2 TSP BAKING POWDER
- 100 G/3½ OZ VANILLA SUGAR
- FINELY GRATED RIND AND JUICE OF 1 LEMON
- 115 G/4 OZ UNSALTED BUTTER, DICED
- 115 ML/4 FL OZ BUTTERMILK OR MILK
- 2 EGGS
- **TO SERVE:**
- DOUBLE CREAM, CUSTARD (SEE PAGE 353) OR VANILLA DAIRY ICE CREAM

1 Butter the sides of a 22.5 cm/9 inch cake tin, preferably springform. Set the oven to 180°C/350°F/Gas 4.

2 Put the apricots, sugar and water into a wide saucepan. Heat gently until the sugar dissolves, then cook gently until the apricots are almost tender, about 5 minutes. Drain off and reserve the syrup.

3 Beat the maple syrup with the butter and a squeeze of lemon juice, then spread over the base of the cake tin. Arrange the apricot halves, cut side uppermost, on the base and fill the spaces between them with the pecan or walnut halves.

4 To make the topping, sift the flour and baking powder into a bowl and stir in the vanilla sugar and lemon rind. In a small saucepan, gently heat the butter in the buttermilk until the butter has melted. Remove from the heat, beat in the eggs, then slowly pour onto the flour mixture, stirring constantly to make a smooth batter. Spoon into the tin, taking care not to dislodge the fruit.

5 Bake for about 45 minutes, until a fine skewer inserted in the centre of the topping comes out clean.

6 Just before the pudding is cooked, boil the reserved apricot juice and the lemon juice until reduced by half. Quickly pierce the pudding several times with a fork and pour the very hot syrup over. Turn onto a warmed plate. Serve with cream, Custard or vanilla dairy ice cream.

Illustrated opposite page 192

Spread the cake with the
damsons, then roll up
from the short end

$\mathscr{D}$ AMSON ROLL

SERVES 4

The full, sharp flavour of damsons and the sweet, moist spiciness
of the roll are an excellent partnership, which is further enhanced
by serving with cool whipped cream or crème fraîche *or*
strained Greek yogurt.

SPICED ROLL:
- 115 G/4 OZ PLAIN FLOUR
- 1 TSP BICARBONATE OF SODA
- 1 TSP MIXED SPICE
- 1 TSP VERY FINELY CHOPPED FRESH ROOT GINGER
- 70 G/2 ½ OZ UNSALTED BUTTER, DICED
- 2 TBSP GOLDEN SYRUP

- 2 TBSP BLACK TREACLE
- 1 EGG, BEATEN
- 150 ML/5 FL OZ SWEET WHITE WINE OR WATER
- CASTER SUGAR, FOR SPRINKLING

FILLING:
- 900 G/2 LB DAMSONS, HALVED AND STONED
- 55 G/2 OZ SUGAR

1 Set the oven to 180°C/350°F/Gas 4. Butter a Swiss roll tin, then line the base with greaseproof paper and butter the paper.

2 To make the filling, gently cook the damsons with the sugar in a covered saucepan until the juices run. Using a slotted spoon, transfer the damsons to a non-metallic sieve and press them through. Leave to cool.

3 To make the spiced roll, stir the flour, bicarbonate of soda and spices together. Form a well in the centre.

4 Gently heat together the butter, syrup and treacle until evenly mixed. Stir in the egg and wine or water. Slowly pour into the well in the spiced flour, gradually drawing the flour into the liquid using a balloon whisk.

5 Beat until smooth, then pour into the tin and sprinkle with a fine layer of caster sugar. Bake for 12–15 minutes until springy to the touch.

6 Sprinkle a sheet of greaseproof paper with caster sugar. Turn the spiced roll onto the paper and carefully peel off the lining. Quickly spread the damsons over the cake. Starting at a narrow end, roll up like a Swiss roll and serve warm.

$\mathcal{P}$ARKIN PUDDING

A real winter pudding — lightly sticky and chewy, and slightly spicy,
which is offset by the contrasting texture and juicy fruitiness of the
pineapple. Use fresh pineapple if possible, otherwise use pineapple
canned in natural juice.

- 175 G/6 OZ UNSALTED BUTTER, DICED
- 115 G/4 OZ LIGHT MUSCOVADO SUGAR
- 85 G/3 OZ GOLDEN SYRUP
- 55 G/2 OZ BLACK TREACLE
- 85 ML/3 FL OZ SOURED CREAM
- 175 G/6 OZ PLAIN FLOUR
- 1½ TSP BICARBONATE OF SODA
- 175 G/6 OZ PORRIDGE OATS
- 2 TSP GRATED FRESH ROOT GINGER
- 350–400 G/12–14 OZ PREPARED FRESH, OR DRAINED, CANNED, PINEAPPLE SLICES OR RINGS
- **TO SERVE:**
- VANILLA DAIRY ICE CREAM OR STRAINED GREEK YOGURT

1 Set the oven to 160°C/325°F/Gas 3. Butter a 20 × 12.5 cm/8 × 5 inch oval baking dish, being particularly generous with the butter in the bottom of the dish.

2 Gently heat together the butter, half of the sugar, the syrup, treacle and soured cream, stirring occasionally, until the butter has melted and the sugar dissolved. Remove from the heat, then stir in the flour, bicarbonate of soda, oats and ginger.

3 Put an even layer of pineapple in the pie dish, sprinkle with the remaining sugar, then top with the parkin mixture. Bake for about 1 hour until dark brown and just set in the centre – I think this pudding is better if it is still nice and moist.

4 Run a knife around the edge of the pudding, leave for a couple of minutes, then turn the pudding onto a warmed plate and serve hot with vanilla dairy ice cream or strained Greek yogurt.

HOT BROWNIE SOUFFLÉ WITH ICE CREAM SAUCE

SERVES 4

very few children who do not love brownies, and few of
e taste when they grow up, so this pudding will appeal
and youngsters alike, especially accompanied by the
uce. When serving it to grown-ups, you could dissolve
.a 1 tablespoon of rum or a coffee or orange liqueur.

- 85 G/3 OZ UNSALTED BUTTER
- CASTER SUGAR, FOR SPRINKLING
- 85 G/3 OZ PLAIN CHOCOLATE, CHOPPED
- 100 G/3½ OZ LIGHT MUSCOVADO SUGAR
- 3 EGG YOLKS
- 2 TSP INSTANT COFFEE POWDER

- ¾ TSP VANILLA ESSENCE
- 40 G/1½ OZ SELF-RAISING FLOUR
- 4 EGG WHITES
- **ICE CREAM SAUCE:**
- 425 ML/15 FL OZ VANILLA DAIRY ICE CREAM
- 1½ TSP DARK RUM

1 Set the oven to 230°C/450°F/Gas 8. Butter a 1 litre/1¾ pint soufflé dish and sprinkle the inside lightly with caster sugar.

2 In a bowl, combine the butter and chocolate, place over a saucepan of hot water, and stir occasionally until smooth. Stir in half of the sugar, egg yolks, coffee, vanilla essence and flour. Remove the bowl from the saucepan.

3 In a clean, dry bowl, whisk the egg whites until soft peaks form, then gradually whisk in the remaining sugar until stiff.

4 Using a large metal spoon, gently fold a quarter of the whites into the chocolate mixture, then gently fold the chocolate into the remaining whites. Spoon into the dish, sprinkle a little caster sugar over the top and bake for 5 minutes.

5 Lower the oven temperature to 200°C/400°F/Gas 6 and bake for about 20 minutes until well risen (the centre will still be moist).

6 While the pudding is cooking, place the ice cream for the sauce in a bowl and leave at room temperature for 10 minutes. Beat in the rum, if using, until smooth.

7 Serve the pudding as soon as it is cooked, accompanied by the sauce.

Illustrated opposite page 208

CHERRY CASKET

SERVES 4-6

*As the name suggests, the filling is enclosed so that when the
pudding has been assembled it looks like a plain sponge.
Inside though, there is a flavourful cherry compote, which oozes
onto the plate when the restraining wall is cut.*

- 2 EGGS, SIZE 2, BEATEN
- 115 G/4 OZ VANILLA
  CASTER SUGAR
- 115 G/4 OZ SELF-RAISING FLOUR
- 115 G/4 OZ UNSALTED BUTTER,
  MELTED AND COOLED
- FEW DROPS ROSE WATER OR
  ALMOND ESSENCE (OPTIONAL)
- ICING SUGAR, FOR DUSTING
- **CHERRY COMPOTE:**
- 450 G/1 LB RIPE BLACK
  CHERRIES, STONED

- 40 G/1½ OZ UNSALTED BUTTER
- 2 TSP VANILLA CASTER SUGAR
- PINCH OF GROUND CINNAMON
- JUICE OF 1 ORANGE
- JUICE OF 1 LEMON
- 1–2 TBSP REDCURRANT JELLY
- 2 TBSP KIRSCH OR BRANDY
- **TO SERVE:**
- SABAYON SAUCE
  (SEE PAGE 357)

1 Set the oven to 190°C/375°F/Gas 5. Butter a 850–1.2 litre/1½–2 pint soufflé dish.

2 Whisk the eggs and sugar together until very thick and pale. Sift the flour over
the surface, then, using a large metal spoon, begin to gently fold in, at the same time
slowly pouring the butter around the insides of the bowl. Add rose water or almond
essence, if liked. Transfer to the dish and bake for about 40–45 minutes until lightly
browned and a skewer comes out clean when inserted in the centre.

3 To make the cherry compote, place the cherries in a heavy-based saucepan
together with the butter, sugar, cinnamon and orange and lemon juices and heat
gently, shaking the pan occasionally, for 5–10 minutes. Drain the cherries, catching
the juice. Return the juice to the pan and boil until syrupy. Lower the heat and stir in
the redcurrant jelly and kirsch or brandy. Return the cherries to the pan, taste and
adjust the sweetness by adding more redcurrant jelly or lemon juice. Cover and keep
warm over a very low heat (a diffuser mat might be necessary if using a gas hob).

4 Remove the sponge from the oven, leave for 2–3 minutes, then turn onto a wire
rack lined with a tea towel to protect the cake from being marked by the wires. Using
a long, sharp knife, cut a thin slice from the uppermost side of the sponge and
reserve. Using a large metal spoon, scoop out the centre of the cake to leave a shell
with walls approximately 2 cm/¾ inch thick.

5 Spoon the cherry mixture into the sponge then replace the slice. Sift icing sugar
over the top and serve immediately with the warm Sabayon Sauce.

Illustrated opposite page 209

JAQUI'S BREAD AND BUTTER PUDDING

SERVES 4–6

Jaqui, a friend of mine, is very fond of puddings, but her husband, Frank, adores them, or, more particularly, traditional puddings, including bread and butter pudding. This has recently become one of the most fashionable traditional puddings, and many variations have appeared. This one, which is given a refreshing lift by citrus juices and tangy marmalade, pleases Frank and everyone else to whom Jaqui has served it, including me, because it is slightly different without deviating too far from the original and becoming gimmicky.

- 100 G/3½ OZ UNSALTED BUTTER
- 8 THIN SLICES BREAD FROM A SMALL LOAF, 6 FROM A LARGE ONE
- 3½ TBSP BITTER MARMALADE
- FINELY GRATED RIND AND JUICE OF 2 ORANGES
- FINELY GRATED RIND AND JUICE OF 1 LEMON
- 85 G/3 OZ VANILLA CASTER SUGAR
- 425 ML/15 FL OZ MILK
- 3 EGGS, SIZE 3

1 Set the oven to 180°C/350°F/Gas 4. Butter a 1.2 litre/2 pint ovenproof dish.

2 Butter one side of each slice of bread and spread with marmalade. Cut off the crusts and cut each slice into triangles or fingers.

3 In a shallow dish, stir together the orange and lemon rinds and juices and 2 tablespoons of the sugar. Dip the bread in this mixture, then line the bottom and sides of the ovenproof dish with some of the bread. Reserve the remaining orange and lemon mixture and bread.

4 Heat the milk to boiling point in a heavy-based saucepan. In a medium-sized bowl, whisk together the eggs and remaining sugar, then slowly stir in the milk. Pour back into the saucepan and cook over a very low heat, stirring constantly with a wooden spoon until lightly thickened; do not allow to boil.

5 Pour into the dish. Arrange the remaining bread on top, pour over the remaining orange and lemon mixture and bake for about 30–40 minutes until softly set and creamy inside and crisp and golden on top.

VARIATION:
Much to his regret, Frank is unable to eat cream, so Jaqui uses only milk to make the custard, but for a richer pudding you could replace 150 ml/5 fl oz of the milk with the same amount of single, whipping or double cream.

RIGHT (from top to bottom): Blackberry Meringue Shortbread Cake (see page 211); Magic Lime Pudding (see page 201); Pecan Whisky Pudding (see page 218).

Illustrated opposite page 192

LIGHT APPLE PUDDING

SERVES 4

*This recipe started life as Eve's Pudding, or Temptation, a simple
creamed sponge mixture baked over apples (hence the name, or so
I read), but I have modified it a number of times until this light
version, deliciously flavoured with aromatic, sweet but sharp
guava, was reached. Guavas combine well with apples and really
do give the pudding a special quality, but if they are not available
the segments of 2 oranges and 2 tablespoons of demerara sugar,
or 55–85 g/2–3 oz dark, chunky marmalade can be substituted for
the guava and added to the apples after they have been cooked.*

- 1 GUAVA
- COOKING APPLES TO MAKE THE
  WEIGHT WITH THE GUAVA UP TO
  550–700 G/1 ¼–1 ½ LB
- 115 G/4 OZ UNSALTED BUTTER
- APPROXIMATELY 2 TBSP CLEAR
  HONEY OR SUGAR TO TASTE
  (OPTIONAL)

- 70 G/2 ½ OZ LIGHT MUSCOVADO
  SUGAR
- 2 EGGS, SIZE 2, SEPARATED
- 85 G/3 OZ FRESH BREADCRUMBS
- 25 G/1 OZ SELF-RAISING FLOUR

1 Set the oven to 180°C/350°F/Gas 4. Butter a 900 ml/2 pint ovenproof pie dish.

2 Halve the guava, then scoop out and discard the seeds. Core and slice the apples.
Heat 25 g/1 oz butter in a saucepan, add the apples, then scoop the flesh from the
guava into the pan and cook gently for about 5 minutes; the apple slices should not
break up. Remove from the heat and stir in the honey or sugar, if liked. Spoon into
the dish to make an even layer.

3 Beat the remaining butter and 55 g/2 oz of the light muscovado sugar together
until light and creamy. Gradually beat in the egg yolks.

4 Mix together the breadcrumbs and flour. In a clean bowl, whisk the egg whites
until stiff but not dry, then whisk in the remaining sugar. Using a large metal spoon,
gently fold one quarter of the egg whites into the creamed mixture. When just evenly
combined, add the remaining egg whites in three batches with the dry ingredients.

5 Spoon over the fruit, then bake for about 35 minutes until risen, just set in the
centre and golden.

VARIATION:
*Use 55 g/2 oz ground almonds or hazelnuts in place of the flour, or 115 g/4 oz in place of both
the flour and breadcrumbs, and sprinkle the top with flaked almonds if adding ground almonds.*

Illustrated opposite page 177

LEFT (from top to
bottom): Fragrant
Almond Sponge with
Apricot Cream (see page
239); Cumberland Rum
Pudding (see page 234);
Marmalade Duff (see
page 237).

225

*Q*UICK, GOOD PUD

SERVES 4

The friend who gave me this recipe said that it served one — herself!
A good testimonial to its irresistibility, yet it is very simple to make and
uses straightforward store-cupboard ingredients.

- 85 G/3 OZ UNSALTED BUTTER
- 70 G/2½ OZ LIGHT MUSCOVADO SUGAR
- 2 EGGS, SIZE 3, SEPARATED
- 85 G/3 OZ DRIED APRICOTS, CHOPPED, SOAKED OVERNIGHT AND DRAINED

- 55 G/2 OZ HAZELNUTS, CHOPPED
- 85 G/3 OZ PLAIN CAKE CRUMBS

1 Set the oven to 180°C/350°F/Gas 4. Butter an approximately 18 cm/7¼ inch deep round baking dish.

2 Beat the butter and sugar together until light and fluffy, then beat in the egg yolks one at a time.

3 In a clean, dry bowl, whisk the egg whites until stiff but not dry. Using a large metal spoon, fold into the egg yolk mixture in three batches, adding the apricots, hazelnuts and cake crumbs with the final batch.

4 Spoon into the dish and bake for 30 minutes until risen, golden brown and just set in the centre.

CHARLIE'S APPLE DAPPY

SERVES 6

*Charlie is a neighbour in the country with whom I trade in the
old-fashioned way — for example, in exchange for his runner beans,
which put the majority of haricots verts to shame, and armfuls of
colourful, fragrant sweet peas, all of which bring more than a hint
of the sights and smells of a country garden to a London flat,
I share with him what I cook. When prompted into telling me what
were his favourites he gave this pudding the highest score
of ten out of ten.*

- 225 G/8 OZ SELF-RAISING FLOUR
- 1 TSP BAKING POWDER
- 1 TSP MIXED SPICE
- 85 G/3 OZ UNSALTED
  BUTTER, DICED
- 115 ML/4 FL OZ MILK
- 225 G/8 OZ COOKING APPLES
- 85 G/3 OZ DRIED FIGS,
  FINELY CHOPPED
- 1 TBSP LIGHT MUSCOVADO
  SUGAR

- **SYRUP:**
- FINELY GRATED RIND AND JUICE
  OF 1 LEMON
- 85 G/3 OZ SUGAR
- 85 ML/3 FL OZ WATER
- 15 G/½ OZ UNSALTED BUTTER
- **TO SERVE:**
- CUSTARD (SEE PAGE 353)

*Using a large sharp knife,
cut the roll into slices*

*Pour the syrup evenly over
the slices in the baking dish*

1 Set the oven to 180°C/350°F/Gas 4. Butter a shallow ovenproof dish approximately 35 × 17.5 cm/14 × 7 inches.

2 Sift the flour, baking powder and mixed spice into a bowl. Toss in the butter, then rub in until the mixture resembles breadcrumbs. Slowly pour in the milk and quickly mix the ingredients to a soft but not sticky dough using a round-bladed knife.

3 Turn the dough onto a lightly floured surface, knead briefly then roll out to a 27.5 × 25 cm/13 × 10 inch rectangle.

4 Peel, core and grate the apples, toss with the figs, then spread over the dough, leaving a narrow border free around the edge. Roll up the dough like a Swiss roll. Using a large sharp knife, cut the roll into 12 slices and arrange in the dish, cut side uppermost.

5 To make the syrup, gently heat the lemon rind and juice, sugar and water in a small saucepan, stirring with a wooden spoon, until the sugar has dissolved. Bring to the boil, remove from the heat and add the butter. Pour over the slices, sprinkle with the muscovado sugar and bake for 30 minutes. Serve hot with Custard.

Illustrated opposite page 193

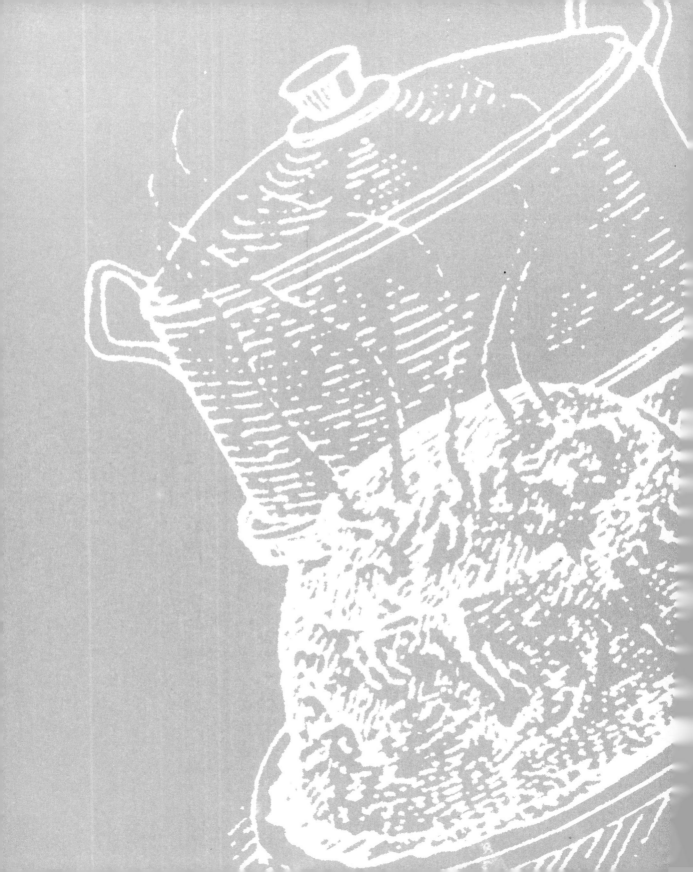

STEAMED PUDDINGS

arming, comforting and nostalgic, steamed puddings have a special place in any true pudding-lover's heart. Traditionally, they were served as filling food for hearty appetites in cold weather, but a well-made steamed pudding is not stodgy and heavy, sitting stubbornly in the stomach for what seems like an age afterwards. It can, in fact, be delicate and airy, such as the Light Lemon Pudding, but even the more substantial recipes, such as Marmalade Duff, are just that, more substantial, not leaden. This type of steamed pudding does not have to be reserved for the coldest of winter days and the sharpest of appetites; it can be equally enjoyed at other times — just serve smaller portions.

A steaming basket is useful for cooking steamed puddings, but it is not essential. You can improvise by placing a trivet or an upturned heatproof saucer or small dish in the bottom of a large saucepan and standing the pudding container on it.

*Cover the top of the basin
with a cloth pleated across the
centre, and tie securely in
place with string*

*Knot the corners of the cloth
over the basin. The knot can
be used as a handle to lift
the pudding*

$\mathcal{S}$TEAMING TECHNIQUES

☞ A heatproof basin is the most usual container in which to steam a pudding, but other containers, such as brioche or springform cake tins, or individual ramekin dishes, can also be used.

☞ Whether cooking the pudding in a steaming basket or directly in the saucepan, there should be at least a 2.5 cm/1 inch space between the sides of the container and the saucepan or steaming basket to allow steam to circulate.

☞ Fill the saucepan about three-quarters full with water and bring to the boil before starting to prepare the pudding mixture.

☞ Butter the basin or container, then, if possible, place a circle of buttered greaseproof paper in the bottom so that the pudding will turn out easily.

☞ Do not fill the container for the pudding more than two-thirds full with the pudding mixture to allow room for expansion.

☞ To prevent the top of the pudding becoming soggy, butter a piece of greaseproof paper, fold a pleat across the centre so that the pudding can rise, then place the paper over the top of the container. Cover with a piece of foil pleated in the same way, or a pudding cloth if using a basin with a lip. Secure the paper and foil or cloth by tying string under the lip of the basin. If using a container without a lip, fold the foil and paper under each other around the top of the basin or container. Form a string handle so you can lift the basin or container into and from the saucepan or steaming basket. Alternatively, make a sling from a double thickness of foil and place under the basin or container.

☞ If cooking the pudding in the saucepan rather than in a basket, the water should come about halfway up the sides of the container.

☞ Make sure the water is boiling before starting to cook the pudding, and that it continues to boil throughout the cooking. Keep an eye on the water level and top up with boiling water if necessary.

☞ Cover the top of the steamer or the saucepan with a tight-fitting lid.

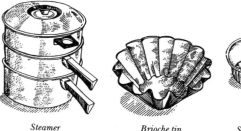

Steamer   *Brioche tin*   *Small heatproof dishes*

$\mathscr{C}$OOKING STEAMED PUDDINGS IN A PRESSURE COOKER

Using a pressure cooker can reduce the steaming time by about a third.

☞ The container for the pudding must be able to withstand the higher temperature inside a pressure cooker.

☞ There must be at least 850 ml/1½ pints of water in the cooker.

☞ Before bringing the cooker up to pressure, the pudding must be pre-steamed in boiling water in the pressure cooker with the lid closed but without the weights in place.

☞ Large puddings are usually steamed at LOW (5 lb) pressure, small and individual ones at HIGH (15 lb) pressure.

☞ Release the pressure slowly at the end of the cooking time, following the manufacturer's instructions.

$\mathcal{C}$UMBERLAND
RUM PUDDING

SERVES 6

*When the pudding is unmoulded, it looks innocuous and not
particularly interesting, but secreted in the centre is a wonderful,
fragrant moist filling that oozes out as the pudding is cut.*

- 175 G/6 OZ UNSALTED
  BUTTER, DICED
- 350 G/12 OZ PLAIN FLOUR
- 1 TSP BAKING POWDER
- 100 G/3½ OZ LIGHT
  MUSCOVADO SUGAR
- 1 EGG, BEATEN
- 4 TBSP MILK
- FEW DROPS VANILLA ESSENCE

- **FILLING:**
- 85 G/3 OZ PLUMP RAISINS
- 25 G/1 OZ CANDIED PEEL
- 2 TBSP RUM
- 55 G/2 OZ UNSALTED BUTTER,
  SOFTENED
- 70 G/2½ OZ LIGHT
  MUSCOVADO SUGAR
- ½ TSP GROUND CINNAMON

1 Leave the raisins and peel for the filling to soak in the rum for several hours.

2 Butter a 1.2 litre/2 pint pudding basin. Fill a large saucepan three-quarters full
with boiling water, place over a high heat and return to the boil.

3 Rub the butter into the flour and baking powder until the mixture resembles
breadcrumbs, then stir in the sugar, egg, milk and vanilla essence.

4 Place two-thirds of the mixture in the basin. With the back of a spoon, spread
evenly over the base and sides to within 5 cm/2 inches of the top.

5 Beat all the filling ingredients together until well blended. Spoon into the basin.
Cover with the remaining pudding mixture, cover the basin and steam (see page 232)
for about 1½–1¾ hours until the pudding feels springy to the touch.

6 Turn out onto a warmed serving plate.

Illustrated opposite page 225

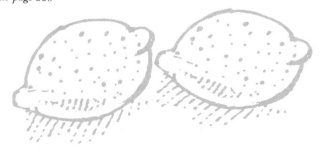

Coconut and Mandarin Pudding

SERVES 4–5

*With juicy pieces of mandarin speckled through a unique
light-textured and moist, not-too-sweet coconut mixture that is
given an extra fillip by an intriguing, subtle hint of aniseed,
this recipe never fails to win converts to puddings.*

- 85 G/3 OZ DESICCATED COCONUT
- 115 ML/4 FL OZ MILK
- 100 G/3½ OZ UNSALTED BUTTER, DICED
- 70 G/2½ OZ CASTER SUGAR
- 2 EGGS, SIZE 2, SEPARATED
- FEW DROPS VANILLA ESSENCE
- FINELY GRATED RIND OF 1 ORANGE
- 150 G/5 OZ PLAIN FLOUR
- 2 TSP BAKING POWDER
- ½ TSP ANISEEDS, FINELY CRUSHED
- 1 × 200 G/7 OZ CAN MANDARINS, WELL DRAINED AND ROUGHLY CHOPPED
- **TO SERVE:**
- ORANGE CUSTARD (SEE PAGE 354)

1 Fill a large saucepan three-quarters full with boiling water, place over a high heat and return to the boil. Butter a 1.2 litre/2 pint round baking dish.

2 In a medium-sized bowl, stir together the coconut and milk.

3 Beat the butter and sugar together until light and creamy, then gradually beat in the egg yolks and vanilla essence. Add the orange rind.

4 Sift the flour and baking powder together. In a clean, dry bowl, whisk the egg whites until stiff but not dry, then, using a large metal spoon, gently fold into the creamed mixture in batches alternating with the flour mixture and aniseeds. Lightly fold in the coconut and mandarins.

5 Transfer the mixture to the dish, cover the top of the dish and steam (see page 232) for about 2¾ hours until lightly set. Remove from the heat and serve with Orange Custard.

Illustrated opposite page 176

Making glazed lemon rind:

Pare strips of rind from the lemon, taking care not to include any white pith

Pile the strips on top of each other, then cut into fine shreds, using a large sharp knife

Add fine shreds of blanched citrus rind to a light sugar and water syrup.

*L*IGHT LEMON PUDDING

SERVES 4

One taste of this pudding with its fresh flavour and feather-light texture will quickly dispel the lie that steamed puddings are heavy and to be avoided at all costs. It takes someone with a lot of willpower to resist a second mouthful.

- 2 TBSP LEMON CURD
- 115 G/4 OZ UNSALTED BUTTER
- 115–150 G/4–5 OZ SUGAR
- 2 EGGS, SEPARATED
- 55 G/2 OZ SELF-RAISING FLOUR
- 55 G/2 OZ FRESH BREADCRUMBS
- JUICE AND FINELY GRATED RIND OF 2 LEMONS

- **LEMON SAUCE:**
- JUICE AND GRATED RIND OF 3 LARGE, JUICY LEMONS
- 1 ROUNDED TSP ARROWROOT
- APPROXIMATELY 85 G/3 OZ CASTER SUGAR
- 85 G/3 OZ UNSALTED BUTTER, DICED
- **DECORATION:**
- GLAZED LEMON RIND (SEE NOTE)

1 Butter a 850 ml/1½ pint pudding basin, then coat the base and inside with lemon curd, Prepare a steamer.

2 Beat together the butter and sugar until light and creamy, then gradually beat in the egg yolks. Using a large metal spoon, lightly fold in the flour, breadcrumbs and lemon juice and rind.

3 In a clean, dry bowl, whisk the egg whites until stiff but not dry, then gently fold into the lemon mixture using the metal spoon. Spoon into the basin, cover (see page 232) and steam for about 1½ hours.

4 To make the sauce, in a small bowl mix a little lemon juice with the arrowroot. Put the arrowroot mixture, the sugar and butter into a saucepan and heat, stirring, until smooth, thickened and clear. Adjust the sweetness, if necessary. Turn the pudding onto a warmed serving plate, pour over some of the sauce and sprinkle with glazed lemon rind.

N O T E : To make the glazed lemon rind, pare thin strips of lemon rind, taking care not to include any white pith. Cut into thin strips, then add to a small saucepan of boiling water, and boil for 2 minutes. Drain and refresh under cold running water. Gently heat 25 g/1 oz sugar in 2 tablespoons of water in the saucepan, then add the lemon strips and simmer for 8–10 minutes until transparent. Remove using a slotted spoon. The strips can be kept in an airtight container for 2 days.

MARMALADE DUFF

SERVES 6

*'Duff' signifies a steamed pudding containing suet, the thought of
which can make some people's hearts, or stomachs, sink, while other
people's eyes light up at the prospect of a good, hearty pudding.
This recipe will please both camps. Soft white breadcrumbs lighten
the 'duff' mixture and the chunky pieces of bitter marmalade
add a welcoming 'bite' and tang. For a final, wicked touch,
pour warmed orange juice and whisky over the pudding after
turning it out of the basin.*

- 115 G/4 OZ SELF-RAISING FLOUR
- 115 G/4 OZ SOFT WHITE
  BREADCRUMBS
- 25 G/1 OZ DEMERARA SUGAR
- 1 TSP MIXED SPICE
- 115 G/4 OZ SHREDDED SUET

- 175 G/6 OZ CHUNKY,
  DARK MARMALADE
- MILK OR ORANGE JUICE
  TO MIX
- **TO SERVE:**
- CUSTARD (SEE PAGE 353)

1 Butter a 1.2 litre/2 pint pudding basin. Fill a large saucepan three-quarters full
with boiling water, place over a high heat and return to the boil.

2 Sift together the flour, breadcrumbs, sugar, mixed spice and suet. Stir in the
marmalade and sufficient milk or orange juice to give a soft, dropping consistency.
Turn into the basin, cover the top of the basin and steam (see page 232) for 2½ hours
until the top feels springy to the touch.

3 Turn onto a warmed serving plate and serve with plenty of Custard.

Illustrated opposite page 225

Stem Ginger Pudding with an Orange Cap

SERVES 5-6

Although you might think that turning this pudding out would not make any difference to its enjoyment, the glistening orange cap looks so appetizing and appealing that the taste buds are stimulated and the overall eating experience enhanced.

- 3 TBSP GOLDEN SYRUP, WARMED
- 2 MEDIUM ORANGES
- 115 G/4 OZ UNSALTED BUTTER
- 85 G/3 OZ DEMERARA SUGAR
- 2 EGGS, BEATEN
- 175 G/6 OZ SELF-RAISING FLOUR
- 1 TSP BICARBONATE OF SODA

- 1½ TSP GROUND GINGER
- 6 PIECES PRESERVED STEM GINGER IN SYRUP, DRAINED AND CHOPPED
- 2 TBSP GINGER SYRUP
- MILK (OPTIONAL)
- **TO SERVE:**
- CUSTARD (SEE PAGE 353)

1 Butter a 1.5 litre/2½ pint pudding basin, add the syrup and tilt the basin to coat the sides. Cut each orange into 6 slices, put into a saucepan of cold water and boil for 3 minutes. Using a slotted spoon, transfer to absorbent kitchen paper to drain. Arrange on the bottom and around the sides of the basin. Fill a large saucepan three-quarters full with boiling water, place over a high heat and return to the boil.

2 Beat the butter and sugar together well, then gradually beat in the eggs, adding a tablespoon or so of the flour towards the end. Using a large metal spoon, lightly fold in the flour, bicarbonate of soda, ground ginger and stem ginger, then add the ginger syrup and sufficient milk to make a soft, dropping consistency, if necessary.

3 Spoon into the basin, taking care not to dislodge the orange slices. Cover the basin and steam (see page 232) for about 1½–1¾ hours until the pudding feels springy to the touch.

4 Turn out onto a warmed plate and serve with Custard.

FRAGRANT ALMOND SPONGE WITH APRICOT CREAM SAUCE

SERVES 6

The contrast of the cold tang of the sauce with the warm spice
of the pudding makes a deliciously enticing combination.

- 100 G/3½ OZ BLANCHED ALMONDS, GROUND
- 175 G/6 OZ UNSALTED BUTTER, SOFTENED
- 85 G/3 OZ VANILLA SUGAR
- 85 G/3 OZ LIGHT MUSCOVADO SUGAR
- SEEDS FROM 4 LARGE GREEN CARDAMOM PODS, CRUSHED
- 3 EGGS, BEATEN
- 100 G/3½ OZ SELF-RAISING FLOUR

- 55 G/2 OZ TOASTED FLAKED ALMONDS
- ICING SUGAR, FOR DUSTING (OPTIONAL)
- **SAUCE:**
- 225 G/8 OZ DRIED APRICOTS, SOAKED OVERNIGHT
- JUICE AND FINELY GRATED RIND OF 1 SMALL ORANGE
- 150 ML/5 FL OZ SOURED CREAM

1 Lightly butter six 150 ml/5 fl oz ramekin dishes, then sprinkle about half a teaspoon of gound almonds into each ramekin, saking the ramekin to coat the sides and base evenly. Half fill a large saucepan with water and bring to the boil.

2 Beat the butter, sugars and cardamom seeds together until very light and fluffy. Gradually beat in the eggs, beating well after each addition and adding a little of the flour towards the end. Fold in the remaining flour and ground almonds. Spoon into the ramekins. Cover loosely with buttered greaseproof paper, place in a steaming basket, cover and steam (see page 232) for about 40–45 minutes or until a skewer inserted into the centre comes out clean.

3 Meanwhile, make the sauce. Drain the apricots and reserve the soaking liquor. Purée the fruit with the orange rind and the juice made up to 150 ml/5 fl oz with the soaking liquor to give a thick pouring consistency. Add more of the liquor if necessary. Whisk in the soured cream then cover and chill.

4 Turn the ramekins out onto warm plates, spoon some of the sauce onto the centre of each pudding so that it runs down the sides and sprinkle with toasted flaked almonds and dust with icing sugar, if liked.

Illustrated opposite page 225

*C*HRISTMAS PUDDING

SERVES 6-8

I think a good Christmas pudding is amongst the best puddings in the world. But, of course, 'good' is the operative word. Too many people have been turned away from Christmas pudding by examples that were heavy and with too high a suet content, but nowadays the move towards better quality, lighter foods made from more 'pure' ingredients means that far superior versions are being made, both at home and commercially. Although the list of ingredients for Christmas pudding is long, the method is short and easy. I admit that the whole process does take a little time, though, as the fruit and pudding benefit from being allowed to soak and the cooking is lengthy, but does that matter? Other advantages of a home-made pudding is that you can make it months in advance so it has time to mature (manufacturers do not do this because it means a 'negative cash flow') and you can make an all-important wish when you stir the pudding.

- 400 G/14 OZ MIXED SULTANAS, CURRANTS AND LARGE, PLUMP RAISINS
- 115 G/4 OZ PRUNES, STONED AND CHOPPED
- 55 G/2 OZ MIXED PEEL, CHOPPED
- 55 G/2 OZ EACH ALMONDS, HAZELNUTS AND BRAZIL NUTS, FINELY CHOPPED
- 200 ML/7 FL OZ GUINNESS
- GRATED RIND AND JUICE OF 1 LEMON
- GRATED RIND AND JUICE OF 1 ORANGE
- 2 TBSP RUM OR BRANDY
- 115 G/4 OZ UNSALTED BUTTER
- 115 G/4 OZ DARK MUSCOVADO SUGAR

- 2 EGGS, BEATEN
- 85 G/3 OZ SELF-RAISING FLOUR
- 150 G/5 OZ FRESH WHITE BREADCRUMBS
- 1 TSP MIXED SPICE
- ¾ TSP GROUND CINNAMON
- ¾ TSP GROUND GINGER
- LARGE PINCH OF GRATED NUTMEG
- 1 DESSERT APPLE, GRATED (PEEL AND ALL)
- 85 G/3 OZ CARROT, GRATED
- 2 TBSP BLACK TREACLE
- **TO SERVE:**
- 4 TBSP BRANDY, TO FLAME
- **BRANDY BUTTER SAUCE** (SEE PAGE 358)

RIGHT (from top to bottom): Pear and Ginger Sauté with Iced Mascarpone (see page 254); Crema Fritta de Luxe (see page 251); Strawberry Soufflé Omelette (see page 255).

1 Put the dried fruits, prunes, mixed peel and nuts in a large bowl, pour over the Guinness, orange and lemon juices and brandy or rum, stir well, cover and leave in a cool place, not the refrigerator, overnight.

2 Beat the butter with the sugar until light and fluffy, then gradually beat in the eggs, beating well after each addition. Using a large metal spoon, fold in the flour, breadcrumbs, spices, grated apple and carrot, soaked fruits and nuts and the soaking liquor and black treacle. Cover the bowl and leave in a cool place, not the refrigerator, overnight.

3 Fill a large saucepan three-quarters full with water and bring to the boil. Butter a 1.5 litre/2½–2¾ pint pudding basin, then line the base with a double thickness of greaseproof paper and butter the paper. Spoon the pudding mixture into the basin, then cover with two circles of greaseproof paper and finally with foil tied securely in place with string. Steam (see page 232) for 8 hours; keep an eye on the level of water in the saucepan and top up as necessary.

4 Leave until cold, then cover with fresh foil and keep in a cold, dry place.

5 To reheat the pudding, steam again for 5 hours. To flame, warm the brandy in a small saucepan, pour over the pudding and set alight using a lighted taper. Carefully baste with the flaming brandy. Serve with Brandy Butter.

Illustrated opposite page 321

LEFT (from top to bottom): Dried Fruit Compote (see page 256); Austrian Pillows with Plum and Raspberry Compote (see page 261); Mangoes with Sticky Rice (see page 262).

$\mathcal{H}$ONEY AND
CINNAMON PUDDING

SERVES 4

*A pudding whose simplicity belies how good it is to eat, with its
combination of flavours that is always welcoming and appetizing,
and its top and sides bathed in honey.*

- 4 TBSP CLEAR HONEY,
  GENTLY WARMED
- 115 G/4 OZ UNSALTED BUTTER
- 55 G/2 OZ LIGHT
  MUSCOVADO SUGAR

- 2 EGGS, SIZE 2, BEATEN
- 115 G/4 OZ SELF-RAISING FLOUR
- GRATED RIND OF 1 LEMON
- ¾ TSP GROUND CINNAMON

1 Butter an 850 ml/1½ pint pudding basin, then add the honey and swirl the basin
around to coat the sides and base. Fill a large saucepan three-quarters full with water
and bring to the boil.

2 Using a wooden spoon, beat the butter and sugar together until light and creamy,
then gradually beat in the eggs. Using a large metal spoon, gently fold in the flour,
lemon rind and cinnamon. Transfer to the basin, cover the top of the basin and
steam (see page 232) for 1½ hours until a skewer inserted into the centre of the
pudding comes out clean.

3 Turn onto a warmed serving plate.

STICKY FIG PUDDING

SERVES 6

*The quintessential steamed pudding; this is manna
to all lovers of good food.*

- 150 G/5 OZ DRIED FIGS, CHOPPED
- 150 ML/5 FL OZ BOILING WATER
- 85 G/3 OZ UNSALTED BUTTER, CHOPPED
- 115 G/4 OZ LIGHT MUSCOVADO SUGAR
- 1 EGG, BEATEN
- 175 G/6 OZ PLAIN FLOUR
- 1 TSP BAKING POWDER
- ½ TSP BICARBONATE OF SODA

- **TOPPING:**
- 85 G/3 OZ UNSALTED BUTTER, DICED
- 175 G/6 OZ DARK MUSCOVADO SUGAR
- 3 TBSP DOUBLE CREAM (OPTIONAL)
- 2 TBSP DARK RUM
- **TO SERVE:**
- BRANDY BUTTER SAUCE OR ONE OF THE VARIATIONS (SEE PAGE 358) OR RUM-FLAVOURED CREAM OR BUTTER, OR VANILLA DAIRY ICE CREAM

1 Soak the figs in the boiling water for about 1 hour. Butter a 1.5 litre/2½ pint pudding basin. Fill a large saucepan three-quarters full with boiling water, place over a high heat and return to the boil.

2 Put the topping ingredients except the rum in a small saucepan, then heat gently, stirring occasionally, until the butter has melted and the sugar dissolved. Bring to the boil, then simmer for 3 minutes. Pour into the pudding basin.

3 Beat together the butter and sugar until light and fluffy. Gradually beat in the egg. Sift over the flour, baking powder and bicarbonate of soda, then fold in using a large metal spoon. Fold in the figs and soaking liquid.

4 Transfer to the basin, cover the top of the basin and steam (see page 232) for about 2 hours until the pudding is springy to the touch.

5 Turn the pudding onto a warmed serving plate to serve.

CARROT AND
SWEET POTATO PUDDING

SERVES 4

*Do try this recipe – it was an experiment that worked extremely well.
No one suspects that it is based on anything out-of-the-ordinary as
they gobble it up, and being made privy to its components usually
provides them with an excuse to ask for second helpings.
My reasoning behind the initial experiment was that while sweet
carrot cakes and puddings are quite widely well known and
popular, sweet potatoes often have an even sweeter taste than
carrots and taste good with sugar or honey and in Latin America
they are actually used for puddings – so why not combine sweet
potatoes and carrots? The two vegetables enhance each other,
so the result is better than if either was used alone.*

- 1 SWEET POTATO, ABOUT
  350 G/12 OZ
- 115 G/4 OZ GRATED CARROTS
- FINELY GRATED RIND AND JUICE
  OF 1 LARGE ORANGE
- 55 G/2 OZ UNSALTED BUTTER
- 55 G/2 OZ LIGHT
  MUSCOVADO SUGAR

- 55 G/2 OZ DARK
  MUSCOVADO SUGAR
- 3 EGGS, SEPARATED
- 85 G/3 OZ SELF-RAISING FLOUR
- 1 TSP BAKING POWDER
- **TO SERVE:**
- APRICOT SAUCE (SEE PAGE 359)
  OR FLUFFY ORANGE SAUCE
  (SEE PAGE 356)

1 Set the oven to 180°C/350°F/Gas 4. Prick the sweet potato all over and bake for
about 1¼ hours until tender. Peel off the skin, then purée or mash the flesh. Mix
with the carrots and the orange rind.

2 Butter a 1.5 litre/2½ pint pudding basin. Half fill a large saucepan with water and
bring to the boil.

3 Beat the butter with the sugars, then gradually beat in the egg yolks. Using a large
metal spoon, fold in the flour, baking powder and carrot mixture.

4 In a clean, dry bowl, whisk the egg whites until stiff but not dry. Using a large
metal spoon, gently fold into the carrot mixture, then spoon into the basin. Cover the
top of the basin and steam (see page 232) for about 1¾ hours until a skewer inserted
in the centre comes out clean. Serve with Apricot Sauce or Fluffy Orange Sauce.

$\mathcal{W}$HAT WENT WRONG?

☞ THE PUDDING IS HEAVY:
This is caused by insufficient raising agent, whether a chemical one such as baking powder, or air, being used, or the water going off the boil.

☞ THE PUDDING DOES NOT TURN OUT CLEANLY:
The pudding will not turn out cleanly if the container was not buttered, or was not buttered sufficiently.

☞ THE PUDDING IS NOT COOKED IN THE CENTRE:
The cooking time was insufficient or the water was not kept boiling throughout are the causes of this.

FRIED AND OTHER PUDDINGS

CHAPTER THIRTEEN

*F*ried puddings, whether a mouthwatering Strawberry Soufflé Omelette (see page 255), crisp Cinnamon Churros (see page 253), or Pear and Ginger Sauté (see page 254), are all cooked quickly and deserve to be eaten piping hot from the pan. This, I think, makes them very socuable puddings that inspire informality.

The remaining entries in this chapter do not fall conveniently into any other categories. I did not see why, however, this should be a reason for excluding some of my favourite recipes. Each dish is an individual, with its own particular method of preparation and cooking. When making the selections, I realized that they are all traditional recipes from various countries around the world, from England across Europe to Thailand. Consequently, they are cooked on the hob, ovens having only relatively recently been in general use in ordinary people's kitchens in the West and not yet having a place in kitchens in the East or even the Middle East.

FRIED
AND OTHER
PUDDINGS

Maple Syrup and Grapefruit Pancakes

SERVES 4

*One day when searching for something a little different for a
pudding, I tried this recipe although I was a little unsure about
how well it would be received. Silence followed serving, which
immediately told me that it had met with complete approval.
The pancakes are really a cross between conventional pancakes and
the thicker drop scones, or pikelets.*

BATTER:
- 115 G/4 OZ PLAIN FLOUR
- 1 TSP BAKING POWDER
- ½ TSP GROUND CINNAMON
- 1 TSP CASTER SUGAR
- 1 WHOLE EGG, SIZE 3, BEATEN
- 1 EGG YOLK
- 175 ML/6 FL OZ MILK

TOPPING:
- 3 GRAPEFRUIT
- 6 TBSP MAPLE SYRUP
- 15 G/½ OZ UNSALTED BUTTER,
  PLUS EXTRA FOR FRYING

TO SERVE:
- VANILLA DAIRY ICE CREAM

1 To make the batter, sift the flour with the baking powder, cinnamon and sugar
into a bowl. Form a well in the centre, add the egg and egg yolk and gradually pour in
the milk, drawing the dry ingredients into the liquids to make a smooth batter. Leave
to stand for 30 minutes.

2 To make the topping, remove the pith and peel from 2 of the grapefruit, then,
holding 1 grapefruit over a bowl (to catch any juice), use a small sharp knife to cut
down between the flesh and the skin of a segment and remove it. Repeat all the way
around the grapefruit, then prepare the other peeled grapefruit in the same way.
Squeeze the juice from the third grapefruit and pour into a small saucepan with any
juice that has collected in the bowl. Stir in the maple syrup and set to one side.

3 Heat a heavy frying pan, then add a small knob of butter. When it is hot, stir the
batter and pour a couple of tablespoonfuls into the pan, spreading the mixture out to
a circle approximately 9 cm/3½ inches in diameter. Repeat two or three times more,
but do not crowd the pan, and cook over a moderate heat until bubbles appear on the
surface, then turn over and cook for a further 2 minutes until lightly browned
underneath. Using a fish slice, transfer to a folded tea towel to keep warm while
cooking the remaining batter.

4 Bring the grapefruit juice and maple syrup to the boil, lower the heat and swirl in
the butter.

5 Serve the pancakes topped with grapefruit segments and spoon the sauce onto
the fruit. Serve with vanilla dairy ice cream.

Illustrated opposite page 176

CREMA FRITTA DE LUXE

SERVES 4–6

Two recipes, one Italian, Crema fritta *(also prepared in Spain and called* Lecha frite*), and one French, for cream cheese* beignets, *have been merged into one and further modifications made to give a luscious, soft, feather-light filling contained in a crisp coating. The custard mixture can be flavoured to taste with a liqueur, brandy, whisky, rum or orange flower water or rose water (do not use lemon cake crumbs if using a flower water).*

Coat shapes in beaten egg, then in crumbs

- 115 G/4 OZ RICOTTA CHEESE, SIEVED
- APPROXIMATELY 2 TBSP CASTER SUGAR
- 3 EGGS, SIZE 2, BEATEN
- FEW DROPS VANILLA ESSENCE
- 40 G/1½ OZ PLAIN FLOUR
- 200 ML/7 FL OZ WHIPPING CREAM
- 200 ML/7 FL OZ MILK
- 100 G/3½ OZ CAKE CRUMBS, PREFERABLY LEMON
- VEGETABLE OIL FOR DEEP FRYING
- **TO SERVE:**
- FRESH FRUIT SAUCE, SUCH AS FRESH APRICOT, NECTARINE, RASPBERRY OR BLACKCURRANT

1 Lightly flour a baking sheet.

2 In a bowl, beat the cheese with the sugar. Gradually beat in two of the eggs and the vanilla essence, then stir in the flour. Using a balloon whisk, gradually whisk in the cream and milk.

3 Pour into a heavy, preferably non-stick, saucepan and heat gently, stirring, until thickened; do not allow to boil.

4 Pour onto the baking sheet to make an even layer about 1.25 cm/½ inch thick, leave to cool completely, then cover and place in the refrigerator for at least 1 hour.

5 Cut the cold custard mixture into approximately 2.5 cm/1 inch squares, rectangles or diamonds. Dip in the remaining egg, then in the cake crumbs.

6 Half fill a deep-fat frying pan with vegetable oil and heat to 190°C/375°F. Add the coated shapes in batches and cook for about 1½ minutes until golden and crisp on the outside. Keep an eye on the temperature of the oil to make sure that it does not drop; the shapes must cook very quickly. Using a slotted spoon, transfer to absorbent kitchen paper, drain quickly and serve immediately accompanied by a fruit sauce.

Illustrated opposite page 240

CARIBBEAN BANANAS

SERVES 4

Orange, lime, allspice, rum and brown sugar all seem to have a natural affinity with bananas and each other, so it is not surprising that when they are all used together the result is a success.

- 4 FIRM BANANAS
- 40 G/1½ OZ UNSALTED BUTTER
- 1 TSP FINELY CRUSHED ALLSPICE BERRIES OR GROUND MIXED SPICE
- 2 TBSP DARK MUSCOVADO SUGAR
- GRATED RIND OF ½ ORANGE

- JUICE OF 1 LARGE ORANGE
- JUICE OF 1 LIME
- 3 TBSP RUM
- 1 TBSP COINTREAU OR OTHER ORANGE LIQUEUR

1 Peel the bananas and cut diagonally into thick slices.

2 Heat the butter in a frying pan, stir in the allspice or mixed spice, then the bananas and fry gently, turning occasionally, until the bananas have softened and are lightly browned. Transfer the bananas to a warmed serving dish.

3 Heat the sugar in the pan until dissolved and lightly caramelized, then stir in the orange rind and juice and the lime juice. Bubble for a few minutes until lightly thickened. Return the bananas to the pan and remove from the heat.

4 Heat the rum and liqueur in a ladle over a flame. Using a lighted taper, ignite the rum and liqueur, then carefully pour into the pan, returning it to the heat and shaking it to mix the ingredients. Serve immediately.

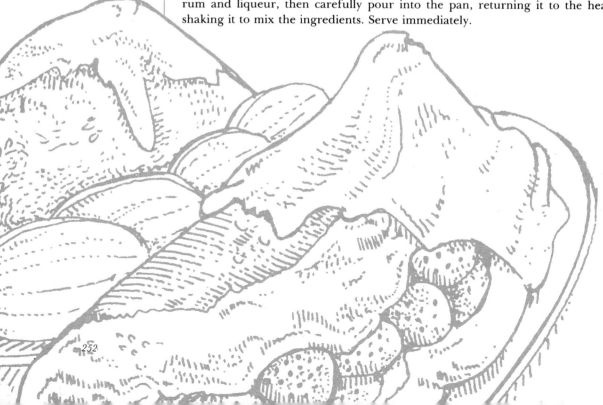

CINNAMON CHURROS

SERVES 4

In Spain, churros *are eaten, freshly made and piping hot,*
for breakfast, but they also make a very good pudding.
In place of the traditional large cups of rich chocolate that
accompany churros *and are just right for dunking them in,*
serve with Hot Chocolate Sauce.

- 100 G/3½ OZ SELF-RAISING
  FLOUR
- ¼ TSP GROUND CINNAMON
- 55 G/2 OZ UNSALTED
  BUTTER, DICED
- 185 ML/6½ FL OZ WATER
- 3–4 EGGS, SIZE 2, BEATEN
- VEGETABLE OIL FOR
  DEEP FRYING

- **TO FINISH:**
- MIXTURE OF VANILLA
  CASTER SUGAR AND ICING SUGAR,
  FOR DUSTING
- **TO SERVE:**
- HOT CHOCOLATE SAUCE
  (SEE PAGE 355)

Pipe lengths of dough into the
hot oil, cutting the dough off
at the required length, near
the nozzle

1 Sift the flour and cinnamon onto a plate and place beside the hob. Gently heat the butter in the water until the butter has melted, then quickly bring to the boil. Immediately remove from the heat and quickly add the flour mixture in one go and beat vigorously until smooth. Return to the heat for about 30 seconds, still beating. Remove from the heat and allow to cool slightly. Gradually beat in the eggs until the mixture is a smooth, thick, glossy paste.

2 Half fill a deep-fat frying pan with oil and heat to 190°C/375°F.

3 Spoon the egg mixture into a piping bag fitted with a 5 mm–1.25 cm/¼–½ inch plain nozzle and pipe lengths into the hot oil, forming them into rings, spirals or horseshoes; use a sharp knife to cut off the mixture at the required length and only cook about three at a time. Fry for about 3–4 minutes, turning once, until golden.

4 Using a slotted spoon, transfer the *churros* to absorbent kitchen paper to drain. Keep warm while frying the remaining mixture. Serve hot, dusted thickly with the sugar mixture, and with the Hot Chocolate Sauce in a jug.

$\mathscr{P}$EAR AND GINGER
SAUTÉ WITH
ICED MASCARPONE

*Recipes such as this, for puddings that can be made very quickly
and are a little out of the ordinary (and, of course, delicious),
are always useful to have. The pears with their ginger-spiked sauce
are very good as they are, but the smooth richness of the iced
mascarpone lifts the dish into a different class, melting deliciously
on the pears and into the sauce.*

- 4 FIRM BUT RIPE PEARS
- 55 G/2 OZ UNSALTED BUTTER
- ½ TSP GROUND GINGER
- 2 TBSP WALNUT HALVES,
  ROUGHLY CHOPPED
- 1 ½ TBSP SYRUP FROM THE JAR
  OF PRESERVED GINGER
- 2 TBSP DRY WHITE WINE,
  PREFERABLY MEDIUM-BODIED
  (OPTIONAL)

- 1 PIECE STEM GINGER, SLICED
- LEMON JUICE
- **ICED MASCARPONE:**
- 2 EGG YOLKS, SIZE 3
- 85 G/3 OZ ICING SUGAR
- 225 G/8 OZ MASCARPONE CHEESE
- FEW DROPS VANILLA ESSENCE

1 To make the iced mascarpone, beat the egg yolks with the icing sugar, then gradually whisk in the mascarpone. Flavour with a few drops of vanilla essence, then spoon into a freezer-proof container. Cover and freeze for at least 6 hours. Return to the refrigerator about 30 mintues before serving.

2 Peel the pears, core and cut each one into quarters.

3 Heat the butter in a frying pan, stir in the ginger, then add the pears and walnuts and cook gently for about 6–8 minutes until the pears are tender; turn them over carefully after about 3 minutes.

4 Stir in the syrup from the ginger jar and the wine, if liked, then allow to bubble until lightly syrupy. Stir in the stem ginger and add a little lemon juice, to 'lift'. Serve straight away with the Iced Mascarpone.

Illustrated opposite page 240

$\mathcal{S}$TRAWBERRY
SOUFFLÉ OMELETTE

SERVES 2

This is a delightful pudding. At first glance it may seem a little
complicated, but a closer inspection will reveal that it involves no
more than a series of simple, short steps and not all the ingredients
are essential (although certainly worth including if you can).
The purée and the strawberries can also be warmed.

- 225 G/8 OZ STRAWBERRIES
- FINELY GRATED RIND AND JUICE OF 1 ORANGE
- 2 TBSP CASTER SUGAR
- 4 EGGS, SIZE 3
- 150 ML/5 FL OZ MILK
- 1 ALMOND MACAROON, CRUSHED

- 1 TBSP WHIPPING CREAM
- 15 G/½ OZ UNSALTED BUTTER
- 1 TBSP FLAKED ALMONDS (OPTIONAL)
- ICING SUGAR FOR SPRINKLING (OPTIONAL)

1 Cut two-thirds of the strawberries into halves and sprinkle over the orange rind and half the juice. Cover and set aside.

2 Purée the remaining strawberries in a blender or food processor with the remaining orange juice and 1 tablespoon of sugar. Strain the purée through a non-metallic sieve; discard the seeds.

3 In a heatproof medium-sized bowl, placed over a saucepan of hot water, whisk 1 egg with 1½ teaspoons of sugar. Heat the milk to boiling point, then slowly whisk into the egg. Cook, stirring with a wooden spoon, until slightly thickened. Remove the bowl from the pan and leave the custard to cool, stirring occasionally.

4 Separate the remaining eggs. Whisk the yolks with the remaining sugar. In a separate clean, dry bowl, using a clean whisk, lightly fold the macaroon and cream into the egg yolks, then gently fold in the egg whites until just evenly combined.

5 Melt the butter in a 17.5 cm/7 inch omelette pan, add the flaked almonds, if using, fry until lightly browned, then add the egg mixture and cook over a moderate heat until browned underneath and almost set.

6 Slide the omelette onto a warmed serving plate, place the strawberry halves on one half of the omelette and fold it over. Spoon over the strawberry purée and pour the custard over the open edge. Sprinkle with a little icing sugar, if liked.

Illustrated opposite page 240

DRIED FRUIT COMPOTE

SERVES 6

*I never tire of dried fruit compote, which can be eaten at any time
of the day and night, not just as a pudding. The recipe is
enormously variable – apple juice is not necessary, but it really
enhances the fruity taste. Orange juice could also be used, in which
case I would omit the orange segments. Ginger wine is another
option, and all the spices can be changed, in quantity as well as
selection. Plenty of chopped fresh ginger stirred in with the oranges
is one of my favourite variations. A dried fruit compote is a very
useful pudding as it needs very little preparation or cooking.
In fact, it can be made without any cooking at all – simply leave
the fruits to soak in a covered bowl in the refrigerator for at least
2 days, stirring occasionally. Not only will it stay in good condition
(if given a chance!), but it will also improve over a number of days.*

- 700 G/1 ½ LB MIXED DRIED
FRUITS SUCH AS PEARS, APRICOTS
(PREFERABLY HUNZA), FIGS,
PEACHES, PRUNES AND
APPLE RINGS
- 1 LEMON
- 2 LARGE ORANGES
- SEEDS FROM 6 GREEN CARDAMOM
PODS, LIGHTLY CRUSHED
- 425 ML/15 FL OZ FRUITY
MEDIUM DRY WHITE WINE,
SUCH AS CHENIN BLANC

- 300 ML/10 FL OZ APPLE JUICE
- 1 CINNAMON STICK ABOUT
5 CM/2 IN LONG
- 4 STAR ANISE PODS (OPTIONAL)
- 4 CLOVES
- **TO SERVE:**
- CHILLED STRAINED
GREEK YOGURT

RIGHT (from top to
bottom): Black Forest
Puffs (see page 291);
Gâteau Pithiviers (see
page 292); King-Size Fig
Newton (see page 289).

1 Place all the dried fruits in a bowl. Using a potato peeler, pare a long strip of rind from the lemon and one of the oranges. Squeeze the juice from the lemon. Add the juice, citrus peels and spices to the bowl, pour over the wine, stir, cover and leave in a cool place over night.

2 Tip the contents of the bowl into a saucepan, add the apple juice and heat to simmering point, then simmer gently for about 25 minutes until the fruit is just tender – adjust the cooking to suit how soft you like the fruit to be and remember that the fruit will continue to soften as it cools. Leave to cool.

3 Just before serving, peel the orange and divide into segments, removing all the skin and pith, stir into the dried fruits. Serve with strained Greek yogurt.

Illustrated opposite page 241

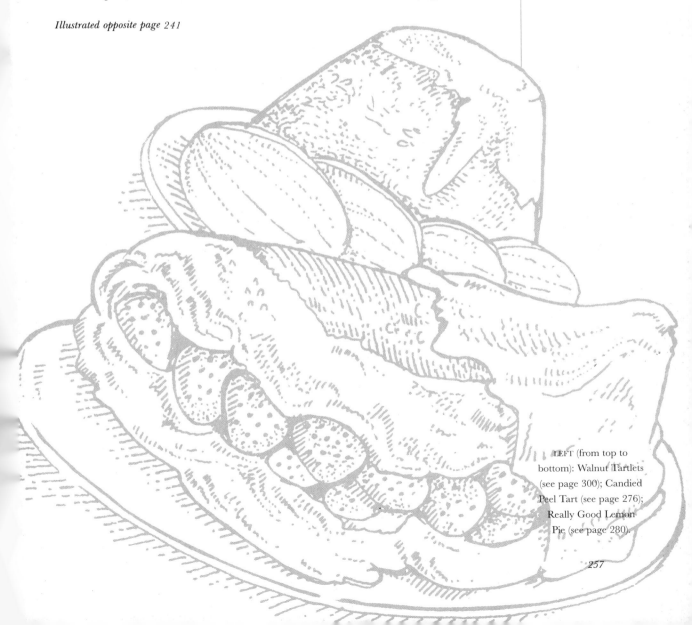

LEFT (from top to bottom): Walnut Tartlets (see page 300); Candied Peel Tart (see page 276); Really Good Lemon Pie (see page 280).

Traditional glazed, heatproof
earthenware fondue pot

*C*HOCOLATE FONDUE

SERVES 4

A sweet fondue is one of the most sociable ways to end a meal,
because everyone can relax and linger, selecting a morsel and
dipping it into the pot at their leisure. Although there must be quite
a few people who have a fondue set hidden away — at one time they
were a popular purchase or present — a fondue set is not vital.
The sauce can just as easily be kept warm in a heatproof bowl
placed over a table-top or plate-warming lamp, or small spirit
·stove. Fruit for dipping that is to be cut into chunks, such as
pineapple, should not be prepared until shortly before the fondue is
to be served, and fruits that discolour soon after cutting, such as
pears and bananas, should be brushed with lemon juice.

- 225 G/8 OZ PLAIN CHOCOLATE, CHOPPED
- 25 G/1 OZ UNSALTED BUTTER, DICED
- 150 ML/5 FL OZ DOUBLE CREAM
- 2 TBSP DARK RUM

- **FOR DIPPING:**
- FRUIT, SUCH AS PEARS, PINEAPPLE, BANANAS, CHERRIES OR STRAWBERRIES CUT INTO BITE-SIZED PIECES
- FIRM CAKE, SUCH AS MADEIRA, SPONGE OR CHOCOLATE, CUT INTO CHUNKS, FINGER-SHAPED BISCUITS, SUCH AS SPONGE FINGERS
- MARSHMALLOWS

1 Place the chocolate, butter and cream in a heatproof bowl that can also be used for serving and place over a saucepan of hot water. Leave until the chocolate and butter have melted and the mixture is smooth, stirring occasionally. Stir in the rum.

2 Place the bowl or dish over a fondue lamp or table heater and serve with fruit, cake or biscuits for dipping.

$\mathcal{F}$ RUMENTY

SERVES 6–8

*Frumenty dates from early medieval times. The rich served it
as an accompaniment to game and meat; while for the poor,
frumenty provided a complete meal. Later it became a dessert,
sweetened with honey and dried fruits, which also added texture to
this porridge-like dish. A more luxurious pudding, my version
contains cream and whisky, and is quite filling, so I advise serving
it in small bowls.
Whole-wheat grains are available from good wholefood stores.*

- 200 G/7 OZ WHOLE-WHEAT GRAINS
- 400 ML/14 FL OZ MILK
- 85 ML/3 FL OZ DOUBLE CREAM
- 175 G/6 OZ MIXED DRIED FRUITS, SUCH AS PEARS, PEACHES, APRICOTS AND FIGS, CHOPPED

- LONG STRIP OF LEMON RIND
- 3 TBSP WHISKY
- **TO SERVE:**
- HONEY, LEMON JUICE AND CREAM

1 Set the oven to 110°C/225°F/Gas ¼.

2 Put the wheat into a large casserole, pour over warm water to cover generously, then cover the casserole. Place in the oven for about 12 hours.

3 Drain the wheat through a colander, then tip into a saucepan. Stir in the milk, cream, dried fruit and lemon rind and bring slowly to the boil, stirring. Reduce the heat to very low and cook gently, stirring frequently, until nearly all the liquid has been absorbed (about 20–25 minutes).

4 Remove the lemon rind and stir in the whisky. Serve honey, lemon juice and cream separately.

RASPBERRY ZABAGLIONE

SERVES 4

A potent little pudding. The first time I made it I did not whisk any raspberries with the egg yolk mixture. The result was very pale and its impact seemed greater because it looked so innocuous. It is not only for appearance's sake, though, that the raspberries are whisked in – the zabaglione does taste better that way.

- 4 EGG YOLKS
- 4 TBSP *EAU-DE-VIE DE FRAMBOISE*
- APPROXIMATELY 115 G/4 OZ CASTER SUGAR

- 115 G/4 OZ FRESH RASPBERRIES
- **TO SERVE:**
- CRISP ALMOND BISCUITS

1 Put the egg yolks, eau-de-vie and sugar into a heatproof bowl, then place over a saucepan of hot water. Whisk the mixture until very thick and light; this will take about 10 minutes.

2 Stir in half the raspberries and a little more sugar, if liked, then divide the mixture between 4 glasses or individual serving dishes.

3 Place an equal number of raspberries on top of each zabaglione (they will fall through it) and serve immediately with crisp almond biscuits.

AUSTRIAN PILLOWS WITH PLUM AND RASPBERRY COMPOTE

SERVES 4–6

A cousin of Italian savoury gnocchi, Austrian pillows are soft, lightly sweetened balls served with a compote that really brings the pudding to life.

- APPROXIMATELY 1 TBSP VANILLA SUGAR
- JUICE AND FINELY GRATED RIND OF 1 LEMON
- 25 G/1 OZ UNSALTED BUTTER
- 300 G/10 OZ COTTAGE CHEESE, DRAINED AND SIEVED
- 2 EGGS
- 40 G/1½ OZ FINE SEMOLINA

- **PLUM AND RASPBERRY COMPOTE:**
- 350 G/12 OZ RIPE BUT FIRM PLUMS, HALVED AND STONED
- 150 ML/5 FL OZ MEDIUM-BODIED DRY WHITE WINE, SUCH AS VOUVRAY OR OTHER CHENIN BLANC
- 1 BAY LEAF
- APPROXIMATELY 1 TBSP REDCURRANT JELLY
- 225 G/8 OZ RASPBERRIES

1 Put the sugar and lemon juice into a bowl. In a small saucepan, melt 25 g/1 oz butter, then pour into the bowl and beat until frothy. Add the cottage cheese and eggs and beat until smooth. Stir in the semolina, then cover and leave in the refrigerator for 1 hour.

2 To make the compote, put the plums into a saucepan with the wine and bay leaf, then simmer very gently until the plums are just tender. Discard the bay leaf. Stir in the red currant jelly to taste and keep warm over a low heat.

3 Heat a large saucepan of salted water to simmering point. Using 2 wetted dessertspoons, form the mixture into small dumplings and lower into the water. Poach for about 10 minutes, or until they rise to the surface. Using a slotted spoon, transfer the dumplings to absorbent kitchen paper to drain briefly.

4 Remove the compote from the heat and stir in the raspberries. Serve warm with the pillows.

Illustrated opposite page 241

Slicing mangoes:

*Remove the mango skin using
a potato peeler*

*Slice through the flesh to the
stone in the centre*

Making coconut milk:

*Squeeze the cloth hard over
the bowl to extract as much
liquid as possible*

Mangoes with Sticky Rice

SERVES 4

*Thai food has been rapidly gaining in popularity, and Mangoes
with Sticky Rice is the most popular Thai pudding, which will come
as no surprise to anyone who has eaten it. Ripe mangoes are the
most marvellous of fruits, with a haunting, exotic fragrance,
texture and taste, and Thailand grows some of the best. Sticky rice
is available from Thai and other Oriental food stores.*

- 225 G/8 OZ STICKY RICE OR
  PUDDING RICE, SOAKED
  OVERNIGHT IN COLD WATER
- 225 ML/8 FL OZ COCONUT MILK
  (SEE NOTE)
- PINCH OF SALT
- 2–4 TBSP SUGAR, TO TASTE

- 2 LARGE RIPE MANGOES,
  PEELED AND HALVED
- 3 TBSP COCONUT CREAM
  (SEE NOTE)

1 Line a steaming basket with a double thickness of muslin. Half fill a saucepan with water and bring to the boil.

2 Drain and rinse the rice thoroughly and put it into the steaming basket. Cover the basket, place over the saucepan and steam over simmering water for 30 minutes.

3 Just before the rice is ready, in a large bowl, stir together the coconut milk, salt and sugar to taste until the sugar has dissolved. Stir in the warm rice, cover and leave for 30 minutes.

4 Thinly slice the mangoes by cutting lengthways through the flesh to the stone. Discard the stones. Spoon the rice into a mound in the centre of 4 warm serving plates and arrange the mango slices around, and decorate with fresh mint sprigs, if liked. Pour a little coconut cream over the rice and serve immediately.

NOTE: Coconut milk is not the liquid inside a coconut, but made from shredded coconut flesh that has been soaked in water. To make it, and the coconut cream for this recipe, pour 300 ml/10 fl oz boiling milk that has not been homogenized over 225 g/8 oz desiccated coconut. Leave until cooled, then pour into a blender or food processor, mix for 1 minute, then leave for 30 minutes. Tip into a sieve lined with muslin or fine cloth and squeeze the cloth hard to extract as much liquid as possible. Leave the liquid to stand and the cream will rise to the top.

Illustrated opposite page 241

$\mathscr{P}$LUM OR
STRAWBERRY KNÖDELN

SERVES 3-6

I have used part of the original Austrian name for this dish because the English translation is dumplings, but the unfortunate associations with solid suet pastry that this title has in Britain do a great disservice to the delicate covering of this recipe. The plums can have their stones replaced by marzipan, walnuts or almonds. Traditionally, the dumplings are rolled in breadcrumbs that have been fried in plenty of butter until crisp and golden then dusted with icing sugar. Crushed sweet biscuits can be used instead of breadcrumbs and the final icing sugar dusting omitted. I like crushed macaroons or amaretti biscuits, and finely grated plain chocolate or cocoa powder are very good with strawberries.

- 40 G/1 ½ OZ UNSALTED BUTTER
- 1 WHOLE EGG, SIZE 2, BEATEN
- 1 EGG YOLK, SIZE 3
- 350 G/12 OZ CREAM CHEESE, SIEVED
- 1 ½ TBSP SOURED CREAM
- APPROXIMATELY 1 ½ TSP VANILLA CASTER SUGAR, TO TASTE
- FEW DROPS ALMOND ESSENCE
- 40 G/1 ½ OZ PLAIN FLOUR
- 20 G/¾ OZ CORNFLOUR
- 12 SMALLISH RIPE PLUMS OR 12 STRAWBERRIES
- 135–175 G/4 ½–6 OZ MARZIPAN OR 12 WALNUT HALVES OR ALMONDS (OPTIONAL)
- **TO SERVE:**
- SABAYON SAUCE (SEE PAGE 357) OR COLD CUSTARD (SEE PAGE 353)

1 Beat the butter until fluffy, then gradually beat in the egg and egg yolk, then mix in the cream cheese, soured cream, sugar and almond essence. Sieve together the flour and cornflour, then, using a slotted spoon, stir into the cheese mixture and mix well until smooth. Cover and chill in the refrigerator for 30 minutes.

2 If using plums, carefully remove the stones and fill the cavities with a piece of marzipan, a walnut half or an almond, if liked.

3 On a lightly floured surface, gently roll out the dough to about 5 mm–1.25 cm/¼–½ inch thick, then cut into 12 approximately 12.5 cm/5 inch squares. Place a plum or strawberry in the centre of each. Brush the edges with a little water and fold the dough over the fruit to form a package, pressing the edges to seal.

4 Bring a wide saucepan of water to the boil, carefully lower in some of the dumplings so they are not crowded and poach for 12–15 minutes.

5 Using a slotted spoon, transfer the dumplings to a plate lined with a cloth and keep warm while cooking the remaining dumplings. Serve warm with Sabayon Sauce or cold Custard.

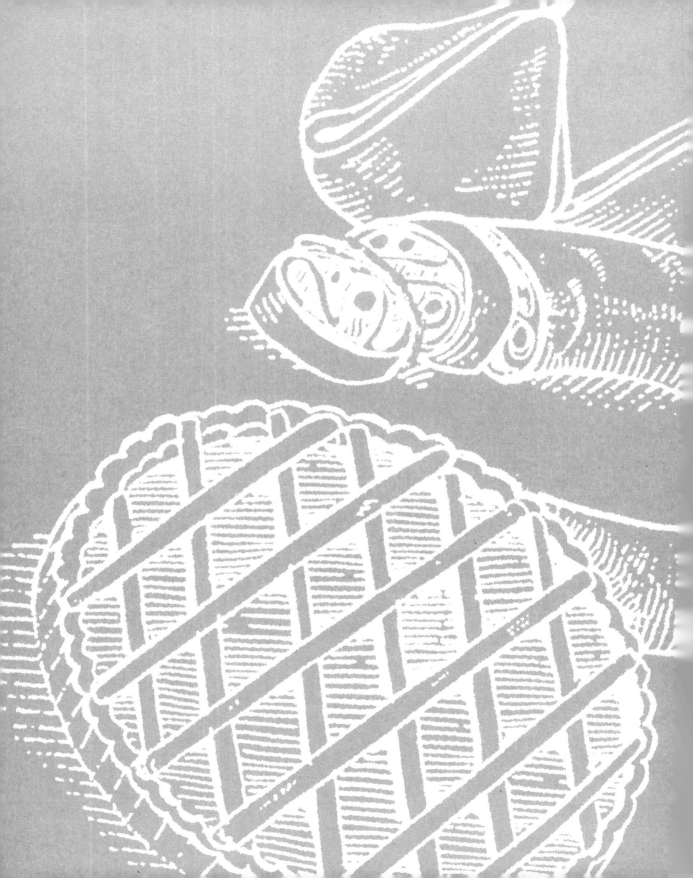

*P*ASTRIES

CHAPTER FOURTEEN

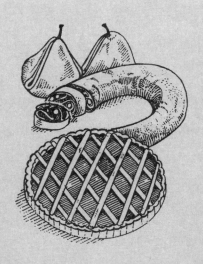

The Greeks made a very simple form of pastry from flour, honey and sesame seeds about twenty-four centuries ago. Although a very similar type of pastry is still made in the Middle East, pastry has seen many changes since then. Fat, preferably butter, is added to make it richer and more tender, eggs may also be included and the flour will be from appropriate strains of wheat. And whereas at one time the pastry was just a container for a filling, today it is just as, sometimes even more, important than the filling, for it adds taste and texture, and provides a vehicle for adding other flavours such as spices, to complement and enhance the filling. Success with pastry seems to be a question of attitude. The people who do not have any trouble seem to be those who do not expect any problems, whereas those who approach it timidly, and perhaps try too hard, seem to be the ones who experience failure. So approach it with confidence. Be aware before you start what you should be doing and understand what happens if you do not; take a little care, and feather-light, melting, crisp pastry for pies, tarts, flans, tartlets and turnovers will be yours.

PASTRIES

*Leave the flan or tart to cool
slightly, then place it centrally
on a jar. Gently ease down
the outer ring*

Shortcrust,
PÂTE SUCRÉE AND
PUFF PASTRY

☞ Recipes for pastry can vary according to the filling ingredients.

☞ Sugar in *pâte sucrée* not only makes it sweeter, but also more crisp, more difficult to handle and more likely to scorch when baked.

☞ Egg yolks add richness and enable you to patch the dough more easily, if necessary, after rolling out.

☞ Make sure the ingredients, equipment and your hands are cool before starting to make the pastry and throughout the process. If the dough becomes sticky because it is too warm, cover it and put it in the refrigerator to cool and firm up. Equipment can also be popped in the refrigerator. To cool your hands, allow cold running water to flow over them and your wrists; dry well before handling the pastry.

☞ A cool atmosphere is also important, so avoid making pastry when your kitchen is hot. In hot weather, if your kitchen becomes hot during the day, try to make the pastry in the morning before it heats up or in the evening after it has cooled down. If central heating makes it hot, try turning it off in the kitchen for a short while before making the pastry and during the process.

☞ Handle the dough quickly, lightly and sensitively, as heavy or over-handling will make the dough sticky and tough, and will prevent puff pastry rising.

☞ Cover the dough and leave it in the refrigerator for at least 20–30 minutes before it is rolled out for the final shaping and refrigerate it again afterwards for at least the same amount of time, before baking it. Puff pastry must also be chilled in between the rollings and foldings.

☞ If the dough is left so long in the refrigerator that it becomes hard, allow it to soften a little at room temperature before rolling it out.

☞ When rolling out, sprinkle a light covering of flour over the work surface and rolling pin and form the dough to the shape required, i.e. round or rectangular. Roll away from you in short, quick movements in one direction only, run a metal palette knife under the dough and then turn it.

☞ Even if the dough becomes sticky, do not sprinkle flour directly onto it, as this can produce tough pastry.

☞ When making pastry cases, always use metal, not heatproof glass, earthenware or ceramic containers.

☞ To prevent pastry from becoming soggy when filled with a cooked or liquid filling, such as a custard mixture, bake it blind first (see opposite). Once a filling has been added, the pastry must be baked immediately. Further insurance against soggy pastry is given by brushing the baked pastry with egg white and never adding a hot filling to pastry, whether raw or baked.

☞ *Pâte sucrée* and nut pastries are fragile when they are taken from the oven, so leave them to stand for a few minutes before moving them.

☞ Pastries are at their best if eaten fresh from the oven, either whilst still warm or within a few hours.

TO LINE A FLAN TIN OR RING WITH PASTRY

Butter the flan tin or a flan ring placed on a buttered baking sheet. On a lightly floured surface, using a lightly floured rolling pin, roll the dough out thinly to about 4.25–6.25 cm/1½–2½ inches larger than the diameter of the ring, depending on the depth of the sides of the tin or ring. Lightly brush away any surplus flour from the surface of the dough. Carefully roll the dough back over the rolling pin and lift it over the centre of the ring. Unroll the dough from the rolling pin and allow it to loosely fall to the shape of the ring. Working from the centre, carefully ease the dough into shape, gently but firmly pressing it into the angle between the base and the sides so that it fits snugly. If using a fluted flan ring, pay particular attention to easing the dough into the curves, especially at the base. Leave the dough to relax for 20 minutes or so, then remove the excess dough by passing the rolling pin quickly and firmly across the top of the flan ring. Lightly prick the base with the prongs of a fork, cover and chill.

The thickness of the pastry will vary according not only to the type of pastry, but also to the particular use to which it is being put – different tarts are more enjoyable with different thicknesses of pastry.

Lining tartlet tins:

Lay the pastry over the tins

TO LINE TARTLET OR BARQUETTE TINS WITH PASTRY

Group the tins together on a baking tray. Roll the pastry out thinly, fold it back over the rolling pin, lift it over the tins, then reroll it onto them. With a small ball of floured dough, ease the pastry into the shape of the tins. Roll the rolling pin firmly over the top of the tins to remove excess pastry.

Use a small ball of dough to ease in the pastry

TO BAKE PASTRY BLIND

Lay a piece of greaseproof paper on the base of the pastry case and cover with just enough dried beans or ceramic baking beans to weigh the pastry down. Bake in a preheated oven for about 10 minutes if it is to be baked further after filling or until the pastry is set and very lightly coloured. Remove the baking beans and greaseproof paper. If the pastry in the base of the case appears to be too pale, return it to the oven for a few minutes to colour a little more. If the pastry is not to be baked again after filling, return it to the oven for about 10–15 minutes after removing the lining paper until the pastry is light golden brown and completely set.

To bake pastry blind:

Cover the greaseproof paper with an even layer of baking beans

Choux pastry:

*Beat until the mixture comes
cleanly away from the sides
of the pan*

*Prick a small hole in the base
of baked choux pastries to
allow steam to escape*

☞ UNCOOKED, UNSHAPED DOUGH:
Open freeze, then wrap in heavy-duty polythene and freeze for up to 4 months. To use, thaw in the refrigerator overnight, or at a cool room temperature for about 2 hours before using.

☞ UNCOOKED, SHAPED DOUGH:
Roll the dough into shapes for pie lids, or use to line flan tins or rings, or tartlet cases. Open freeze, then remove from the container and wrap in heavy-duty polythene. Interleave pie lids with greaseproof paper and overwrap in heavy-duty polythene. Freeze for up to 4 months. To use, return pastry cases to the containers. Bake from frozen, giving them an extra 5 minutes or so in the oven. The same applies to pie lids.

☞ COOKED PASTRY:
Cool quickly, open freeze, then wrap in heavy-duty polythene and freeze for up to 3 months. To use, refresh in an oven preheated to 200°C/400°F/Gas 6 for about 10 minutes, depending on the filling.

$\mathcal{C}$HOUX PASTRY

☞ Have the flour weighed out by the hob so that it can be added immediately the liquid comes to the boil.

☞ Dice the butter so that it melts quickly.

☞ Once the butter has melted, bring the liquid quickly to the boil, then immediately remove the pan from the heat and add all the flour in one go. If the flour is added in stages it will cook into lumps.

☞ Return the pan to a low heat and cook the flour, beating with a wooden spoon or, better still, a hand-held mixer, for about ½–1 minute until it comes cleanly away from the sides and base of the pan.

☞ Allow the dough to cool slightly before adding the eggs, otherwise they will begin to cook and so be incapable of entrapping air.

☞ Beat in the eggs gradually and beat well after each addition to enable as much air as possible to be incorporated. If the eggs are added too quickly, the dough will be too soft and you will then not be able to shape it properly and it will not rise.

☞ The outside of choux pastry shapes, especially large ones, often appears cooked, while some of the dough inside is still moist, so pierce a small hole in the side of the shape to allow the steam to escape and return it to the oven with the heat turned off for a few minutes to dry out.

☞ For the best results, choux pastry really should be cooked soon after it has been made, but it can be kept for up to about 4 hours, although it will not rise so well. To prevent a skin forming on the dough, stretch a piece of cling film across the top of the saucepan.

☞ Choux pastries are at their best on the day they are made, but they can be kept in an airtight container or a plastic bag for 1 or at the most 2 days. Pop briefly in a fairly hot oven to refresh them, then allow to cool before using.

☞ Choux pastries quite quickly become soggy after being filled, so should be eaten within an hour or so.

FREEZING

Baked, unfilled choux pastry can be frozen for up to 3 months. Open freeze, then, as the pastry is fragile, pack carefully into a rigid, freezer-proof container. To use, crisp the pastry up, from frozen, on a baking sheet in an oven preheated to 200°C/400°F/ Gas 6 for 5–7 minutes.

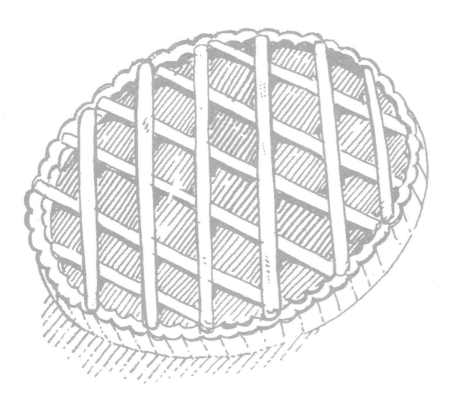

ℬASIC
SHORTCRUST PASTRY

MAKES APPROXIMATELY 375 G 13 OZ

. . .

- 225 G/8 OZ PLAIN FLOUR
- 115 G/4 OZ UNSALTED BUTTER, DICED

- COLD WATER

1 Sift the flour into a bowl, toss in the butter, then, using your fingertips, rub into the flour until the mixture resembles breadcrumbs.

2 Sprinkle about 2 tablespoons cold water over the surface of the flour mixture, then lightly mix it in using a round-bladed knife until the mixture forms large lumps; add a little more water if necessary.

3 Using your fingertips again, lightly form the lumps into a smooth ball that will leave the bowl clean, transfer to a lightly floured surface and knead lightly until smooth and free from cracks. Form into a ball, wrap in cling film and place in the refrigerator for at least 30 minutes before rolling out.

RIGHT (from top to bottom): Old English Apple Pie (see page 279); Apricot and Sesame Puffs (see page 284); Caramelized Pineapple Upside-Down Tart (see page 286).

OVERLEAF (from top to bottom): Treacle Tart (see page 285); Pears in Pyjamas (see page 283); Coconut Cream Pie in a Chocolate Case (see page 298).

*B*ASIC PÂTE SUCRÉE

MAKES APPROXIMATELY 250–300 G / 9–10 OZ

. . .

- 125 G/4 ½ OZ PLAIN FLOUR
- SMALL PINCH OF SALT
- 70 G/2 ½ OZ UNSALTED BUTTER, AT ROOM TEMPERATURE

- 2 EGG YOLKS, BEATEN
- 15–40 G/½–1 ½ OZ CASTER SUGAR

1 Sift the flour and salt onto a cold work surface and form a well in the centre. Pound the butter with a rolling pin to soften it slightly, then chop it roughly with a cold knife. Put the lumps of butter into the well with the egg and sugar, then quickly and lightly blend them together by 'pecking' at them with the fingertips until they are just beginning to come together and look rather like rough scrambled egg.

2 Sprinkle a little of the flour over the butter/egg mixture, then, as lightly and quickly as possible, draw all the ingredients together by chopping through them with a cold round-bladed knife whilst at the same time drawing free flour from the edges of the pile into the centre with a smooth, flowing action.

3 When there is no free fat or flour to be seen and the mixture resembles breadcrumbs, draw it lightly into a ball with your fingertips, then knead gently by pushing the dough away from you with the heel of one hand, then gathering up the dough with a pastry scraper or palette knife and repeating for a minute or so until the dough peels easily from the work surface. Form into a ball, wrap in cling film and place in the refrigerator for at least 30 minutes before rolling out.

*N*UT PASTRY

MAKES APPROXIMATELY 300 G / 10 OZ

. . .

- 125 G/4 ½ OZ PLAIN FLOUR
- SMALL PINCH OF SALT
- 65 G/2 ¼ OZ UNSALTED BUTTER, AT ROOM TEMPERATURE

- 1 EGG YOLK, BEATEN
- 40 G/1 ½ OZ NUTS, GROUND
- 40 G/1 ½ OZ CASTER SUGAR (OPTIONAL)

Make in exactly the same way as Pâte Sucrée, adding the nuts with the egg yolk.

Making pâte sucrée:

With the fingertips, mix together the butter, egg yolk, sugar and water

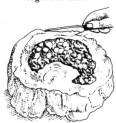

Gradually draw in the flour, using a palette knife

Chop in the flour until the mixture resembles crumbs

Knead the dough with the heel of the hand

*B*ASIC PUFF PASTRY

MAKES 450 G 1 LB

. . .

- 225 G/8 OZ PLAIN FLOUR
- PINCH OF SALT
- 1 TSP LEMON JUICE

- COLD WATER
- 225 G/8 OZ UNSALTED BUTTER, AT ROOM TEMPERATURE

1 Sift together the flour and salt, then add the lemon juice and sufficient water to form into a soft, pliable but not sticky dough. Knead it into a smooth ball, cover and place in the refrigerator for 30 minutes.

2 Place the butter between two sheets of greaseproof paper or cling film and beat it with a rolling pin until it is soft and malleable and about 1.25 cm/½ inch thick.

3 On a lightly floured surface, using a lightly floured rolling pin, roll the dough out to a square about 7.5 mm/¼ inch thick around the edges with a slightly thicker pad of dough in the centre. Place the butter on this pad and fold the corners of the dough around it, overlapping the edges very slightly, so they meet in the centre. Gently press the block of dough with the rolling pin at 1.25 cm/½ inch intervals across its surface until it has grown slightly, then roll it out to a large rectangle. Fold the two ends of the rectangle so they meet in the centre, then fold the whole piece in half so that it resembles a book. Rotate this to the normal reading position of a book with the folded side as the spine. Cover and place in the refrigerator for 30 minutes.

4 Repeat the rolling and folding five times, chilling the dough after each one for a minimum of 20–30 minutes. Then roll the dough once more before covering and chill for at least 2 hours before giving the final shaping.

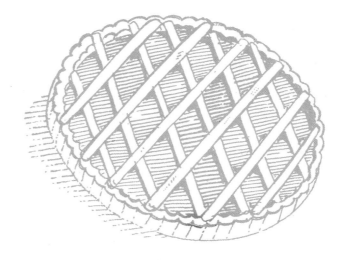

RHUBARB, SOURED CREAM AND GINGER FLAN

SERVES 4–6

*Rhubarb, held in crisp, ginger-spiked pastry and surrounded by
a creamy filling flavoured with ginger syrup, tastes heavenly.*

- 175 G/6 OZ PLAIN FLOUR
- 40 G/1 ½ OZ ICING SUGAR
- 1 ½ TSP GROUND GINGER
- 40 G/1 ½ OZ UNSALTED BUTTER
- 55 G/2 OZ FULL-FAT SOFT CHEESE
- COLD WATER
- 1 EGG WHITE, BEATEN
- **FILLING:**
- 700 G/1 ½ LB RHUBARB, CUT INTO 2.5 CM/1 IN LENGTHS

- 85 G/3 OZ LIGHT MUSCOVADO SUGAR
- 1 TBSP WATER
- 150 ML/5 FL OZ SOURED CREAM
- 4 EGG YOLKS, BEATEN
- 2–3 TBSP SYRUP FROM A JAR OF PRESERVED STEM GINGER
- **DECORATION:**
- THIN STRIPS OF PRESERVED STEM GINGER (OPTIONAL)

*Prick the base of the pastry
case with a fork, to prevent the
pastry rising during baking*

1 Sift the flour, icing sugar and ground ginger into a bowl. Cut in the butter and cheese, then lightly rub in using your fingertips until the mixture resembles breadcrumbs. Stir in sufficient very cold water to make a firm dough. Cover and place in the refrigerator for 30 minutes.

2 Butter a 22.5 cm/9 inch flan tin. On a lightly floured surface, roll out the pastry and use to line the flan tin. Prick the base of the pastry case, then cover and place in the refrigerator for another 30 minutes.

3 Meanwhile, make the filling. Gently cook the rhubarb with 1 tablespoon of the sugar and the water in a wide saucepan until slightly softened but still holding its shape. Drain and leave to cool. Boil the cooking juices until well reduced and syrupy. Cool.

4 Set the oven to 200°C/400°F/Gas 6 and put a baking sheet in the oven.

5 Place the flan tin on the baking sheet and bake the pastry case blind for 10 minutes (see page 269). Remove the paper and beans, brush the base and sides of the pastry case with egg white and return to the oven for a few minutes. Leave to cool.

6 Lower the oven temperature to 150°C/300°F/Gas 2.

7 Using a slotted spoon, transfer the rhubarb to the pastry case. Stir together the rhubarb juices, soured cream, the remaining sugar, the egg yolks and the ginger syrup. Carefully pour over the rhubarb and place in the oven for 25–30 minutes until just set in the centre. Serve warm or at room temperature with thin strips of stem ginger sprinkled over, if liked.

CANDIED PEEL TART

This is one of my mother's favourites. It is very good made from mixed candied peel that comes in a tub, but it is even better if it is made from separate, large pieces of candied orange, citron and lemon peel; remove excess sugar from the pieces before chopping and mix in roughly equal quantities.

- *PÂTE SUCRÉE* MADE WITH 175 G/6 OZ PLAIN FLOUR, 85 G/3 OZ UNSALTED BUTTER, 2 EGG YOLKS, 3 TBSP ICING SUGAR (SEE PAGE 273)
- 1 EGG WHITE
- **FILLING:**
- 2 EGGS, SIZE 2
- 2 EGG YOLKS, SIZE 2
- 150 G/5 OZ CASTER SUGAR

- 175 G/6 OZ UNSALTED BUTTER, MELTED AND COOLED
- 115 G/4 OZ CANDIED PEEL, QUITE FINELY CHOPPED
- 2 TBSP COINTREAU (OPTIONAL)
- **DECORATION:**
- ICING SUGAR, FOR DUSTING (OPTIONAL)
- TOASTED FLAKED ALMONDS (OPTIONAL)

1 Butter a 22.5 cm/9 inch flan tin. On a lightly floured surface, roll out the pastry and use to line the tin. Prick the base of the pastry case, cover and place in the refrigerator for 30 minutes.

2 Set the oven to 200°C/400°F/Gas 6. Place a baking sheet in the oven.

3 Place the flan tin on the baking sheet and bake the pastry case blind for 10 minutes (see page 269). Remove the paper and beans, brush the base and sides of the pastry with egg white and return to the oven for a couple of minutes. Leave to cool.

4 Lower the oven temperature to 180°C/350°F/Gas 4.

5 Mix together the eggs, egg yolks, sugar, butter, mixed peel and Cointreau, if using, then pour into the pastry case. Bake for about 30 minutes until very lightly set in the centre and crisp and lightly browned on top. Serve warm, dusted with icing sugar and toasted flaked almonds sprinkled on top, if liked.

Illustrated opposite page 257

$\mathscr{G}$REENGAGE AND ALMOND SHUTTLES

These pastries are called shuttles because their shape resembles the shuttles used with old-fashioned weaving looms. As it would not be worth making puff pastry specifically for this recipe, I have given the prepared weight so that you could either cut the required weight from pastry you have already made or from a piece of commercial puff pastry. When greengages are not available, substitute ripe plums.

- 55 G/2 OZ UNSALTED BUTTER, DICED
- 55 G/2 OZ CASTER SUGAR
- 1 EGG, SIZE 3, BEATEN
- 55 G/2 OZ ALMONDS, GROUND
- FEW DROPS OF ORANGE FLOWER WATER OR PINCH OF CRUSHED CARDAMOM SEEDS (OPTIONAL)

- APPROXIMATELY 225 G/8 OZ PREPARED WEIGHT PUFF PASTRY (SEE PAGE 274)
- 6 RIPE GREENGAGES, HALVED AND STONED
- 1 EGG, BEATEN, FOR GLAZING

1 Beat the butter with the sugar until light and pale. Gradually stir in the egg, then stir in the ground almonds. Flavour with orange flower water, or crushed cardamom seeds, if liked.

2 On a lightly floured surface, roll out the pastry to approximately 50 cm/20 inches square. Using a large sharp knife, trim the edges, then cut the pastry into 4 squares. Divide the almond mixture between the squares, placing it to one side of the centre and leaving a border around the edge. Nestle 3 greengage halves closely together in a single layer on the almond mixture. Brush the edges of the pastry with water, then fold the uncovered dough over the greengages and press the edges firmly together to seal. With the point of a small sharp knife, cut 3 short slashes in the top of each pastry. Place the pastries on a baking tray, cover and chill in the refrigerator for 30 minutes.

3 Set the oven to 200°C/400°F/Gas 6. Brush the pastries with beaten egg and bake for about 25 minutes until the pastry is crisp and golden. Cool slightly before serving.

Illustrated opposite page 177

*Gradually stretch the dough
over the backs of your hands*

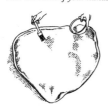

*Brush the dough with
melted butter*

*Roll up the filled dough with
the help of the sheet*

*Form into a horse-shoe shape
with the seam underneath*

BLACK CHERRY STRUDEL

SERVES 6–8

*I really enjoy making phyllo (filo) pastry. Because it takes a little
while and has to be done gently and at a quite leisurely pace, I find
it very relaxing. You will find it easier to stretch the dough if you
work it on a table that you can walk around.*

- 225 G/8 OZ PLAIN FLOUR
- 1 EGG, BEATEN
- 175 ML/6 FL OZ LUKEWARM WATER
- ½ TSP LEMON JUICE
- 115 G/4 OZ UNSALTED BUTTER, MELTED
- **FILLING:**
- 350 G/12 OZ RICOTTA OR CURD CHEESE, SIEVED
- 100 G/3½ OZ DEMERARA SUGAR
- 5–6 TBSP SINGLE CREAM
- 1 EGG, BEATEN
- FINELY GRATED RIND OF 1 LEMON
- 225 G/8 OZ RIPE BLACK CHERRIES, OR 1 × 350 G/12 OZ CAN BLACK CHERRIES IN NATURAL JUICE, WELL DRAINED
- ICING SUGAR, FOR DUSTING
- **TO SERVE:**
- VANILLA DAIRY ICE CREAM OR SINGLE CREAM

1 Sift the flour onto a work surface and form a well in the centre. Mix together the egg, water and lemon juice, then pour into the well in the flour. Using your finger tips, quickly draw the dry ingredients into the liquids to form coarse crumbs. Add a little extra water if the crumbs seem dry. Form into a fairly soft ball. Flour the work surface and knead the dough by forming it into a short sausage, picking it up by alternate ends and bringing it firmly down onto the surface, for 5–7 minutes until smooth and shiny. Cover with an upturned bowl and leave for 30 minutes.

2 Set the oven to 190°C/375°F/Gas 5. Butter a large baking sheet.

3 To make the filling, in a bowl, beat the cheese and sugar, then gradually beat in the cream, egg and lemon rind.

4 Cover the table with a clean sheet or other large piece of similar material, sprinkle it lightly with flour then roll out the dough, using a lightly floured rolling pin, to as large a square as you can make it. Cover with a damp towel and leave for 15 minutes.

5 Sprinkle flour over the backs of your hands and place them under the centre of the dough. Slowly work outwards, gradually stretching the dough evenly with both hands; do not worry if small holes appear. Repeat across the surface of the dough until it is about 1 metre/1 yard square. If the edge is very thick, cut it off. Brush the dough with melted butter, spread the cream cheese mixture over, leaving a narrow border around the edge, then cover with the cherries. Trim the edges of the dough. Roll it up with the aid of the sheet. Transfer the roll to the baking sheet, with the seam underneath, and shape it into a horseshoe. Brush with melted butter and bake for 30–40 minutes until light brown and crisp. Carefully transfer to a wire rack and dust with icing sugar. Serve sliced with vanilla dairy ice cream or single cream.

OLD ENGLISH APPLE PIE

SERVES 6

Pies of apples mixed with oranges plus dried fruits for natural sweetness were popular in Georgian times. Adjust the amounts of dried fruits, candied peel and spices if they are not to your taste.

- SHORTCRUST PASTRY MADE WITH 225 G/8 OZ PLAIN FLOUR, 115 G/4 OZ UNSALTED BUTTER AND 2–3 TBSP COLD WATER (SEE PAGE 272)
- 55 G/2 OZ PLUMP SULTANAS
- 25 G/1 OZ CURRANTS
- 55 G/2 OZ PLUMP RAISINS
- 55 G/2 OZ CANDIED PEEL, CHOPPED
- 3 TBSP RUM, BRANDY, WHISKY OR SHERRY
- 1 EGG WHITE, BEATEN
- 550 G/1¼ LB COX'S ORANGE PIPPIN OR REINETTE APPLES

- 2 ORANGES, PEELED AND SLICED
- 1 JUICY LEMON, PEELED AND SLICED, OR FINELY GRATED RIND AND JUICE OF 1 LEMON
- 55 G/2 OZ DARK MUSCOVADO SUGAR
- ½–¾ TSP FRESHLY GRATED NUTMEG
- 1–2 TSP GROUND CINNAMON
- 40 G/1½ OZ FLAKED ALMONDS
- 25 G/1 OZ UNSALTED BUTTER
- 1 EGG YOLK BEATEN WITH 1 TBSP WATER
- CASTER SUGAR, FOR DREDGING

1 Butter a 22.5 cm/9 inch pie dish. On a lightly floured surface, roll out two-thirds of the pastry and use it to line the dish. Prick the base of the pastry case, cover and place in the refrigerator for 30 minutes, along with the remaining pastry, which should be wrapped in cling film or greaseproof paper.

2 Stir the sultanas, currants, raisins, candied peel and rum, brandy, whisky or sherry together in a bowl.

3 Set the oven to 190°C/375°F/Gas 5 and place a baking sheet in the oven.

4 Place the pie dish on the baking sheet and bake blind for 10 minutes (see page 269) until set and lightly coloured. Remove the paper and beans, brush the base and sides of the pastry case with beaten egg white and return to the oven for 5 minutes.

5 Roll out the remaining pastry to make a lid for the pie dish. Peel, core and thickly slice the apples, then place in the pastry case with the orange and lemon slices, or lemon rind and juice, dried fruits and their soaking liquor, the sugar and spices. Quickly fry the almonds in the butter until golden then scatter evenly over the filling and pour over the butter. Brush the edges of the pastry case with water, then cover the pie with the pastry lid, pressing the edges well together to seal. With the point of a sharp knife, cut two slashes in the top. Use the pastry trimmings to decorate the top of the pie. Brush with beaten egg yolk, dredge with caster sugar, then bake for 35–40 minutes until the pastry is golden brown and the fruit tender. Serve warm.

Illustrated opposite page 272

REALLY GOOD LEMON
MERINGUE PIE

SERVES 6

*There are some things that one hankers for from childhood days.
For me, the type of lemon meringue pie that was popular when
I was a child is not one of them, as the filling, made from packet
ingredients, had a distinctive, rather gluey texture. Needless to say,
this pie is nothing like that. The filling resembles a clean, fresh-
tasting, light home-made lemon curd, which is highlighted by the
hint of cardamom in the pastry, and the cloud of meringue on top
has a delicious, light lemony flavour.*

- *PÂTE SUCRÉE* MADE WITH
  150 G/5 OZ PLAIN FLOUR;
  100 G/3½ OZ UNSALTED BUTTER,
  DICED; APPROXIMATELY ¾–1 TSP
  CARDAMOM SEEDS, DRY-FRIED
  THEN GROUND; 2 TSP ICING SUGAR
  AND 2 TBPS WHITE WINE OR WATER
  (SEE PAGE 273)

- **FILLING AND MERINGUE:**
- FINELY GRATED RIND AND JUICE
  OF 2 LARGE, JUICY LEMONS
- 250 G/9 OZ CASTER SUGAR
- 2 WHOLE EGGS
- 3 EGGS, SEPARATED
- 100 G/3½ OZ UNSALTED
  BUTTER, DICED
- FINELY GRATED RIND OF
  1 MORE LARGE LEMON

1 First, make the pastry. Sift the flour into a bowl, toss in the butter, then rub in until the mixture resembles breadcrumbs. Stir in the cardamom seeds, icing sugar and sufficient wine or water to make a soft but not sticky dough. Cover and place in the refrigerator for 30 minutes.

2 Butter a deep 20 cm/8 inch flan tin. On a lightly floured surface, roll out the pastry and use to line the tin. Prick the base of the pastry case, cover and chill for 30 minutes.

3 Set the oven to 190°C/375°F/Gas 5. Place a baking sheet in the oven.

4 Place the flan tin on the baking sheet and bake the pastry case blind for 10 minutes (see page 269). Remove the paper and beans and return the pastry case to the oven for 5–10 minutes until pale biscuit coloured. Leave to cool.

5 To make the filling, put the lemon rind and juice, 115 g/4 oz of the sugar and the whole eggs and egg yolks in a heatproof bowl. Place over a saucepan of hot water and gradually stir in the butter using a wooden spoon. Continue to stir for about 15–20 minutes until the mixture thickens. Leave to cool.

6 To make the meringue, in a clean, dry bowl, whisk the 3 egg whites until soft peaks form, then gradually whisk in the remaining sugar, whisking well after each addition, until the mixture is stiff and shiny. Add the rind of the extra lemon with the last addition.

7 Spoon the lemon mixture evenly into the pastry case and cover completely with the meringue, taking particular care that there are no gaps next to the pastry shell. Bake for 10–15 minutes until the meringue is lightly browned and crisp on top but still soft inside.

VARIATION:

To make a meringue nest topping, reserve 1½ tablespoons of the lemon mixture. Using a palette knife, spread two-thirds of the meringue over the lemon mixture in the pastry case to make a plateau about 1.25 cm/½ inch high. Put the remaining meringue into a piping bag fitted with a 1.25 cm/½ inch plain nozzle and pipe 8 small nests on top. Bake for 10–15 minutes. Before serving, divide the reserved lemon mixture between the nests.

Illustrated opposite page 257

$\mathcal{S}$TRAWBERRY CRÈME BRÛLÉE TART

SERVES 6

A real conversation stopper and a sure way to make sure
everyone leaves the table with happy memories.

- NUT PASTRY MADE WITH 175 G/6 OZ PLAIN FLOUR, 100 G/3 ½ OZ DICED UNSALTED BUTTER, 2 EGG YOLKS, 1 TBSP KIRSCH (OPTIONAL), 55 G/2 OZ GROUND BLANCHED ALMONDS AND 40 G/1 ½ OZ CASTER SUGAR (SEE PAGE 273)
- APPROXIMATELY 175 G/6 OZ FRESH STRAWBERRIES

- 2 TBSP CASTER SUGAR
- 1 TBSP *EAU-DE-VIE DE FRAMBOISE* OR ORANGE LIQUEUR
- 1 VANILLA POD
- 425 ML/15 FL OZ WHIPPING CREAM
- 4 EGG YOLKS
- CASTER SUGAR, FOR SPRINKLING

1 Butter a 21.5 cm/8½ inch flan tin, which is at least 2.5 cm/1 inch deep. On a lightly floured surface, roll out the nut pastry thinly and use to line the tin. Prick the base of the pastry case, cover and place in the refrigerator for 30 minutes.

2 Cut the strawberries into halves, place in a bowl and sprinkle over 1 tablespoon of sugar and the eau-de-vie or liqueur. Set aside for about 1 hour.

3 Set the oven to 200°C/400°F/Gas 6. Place a baking sheet in the oven.

4 Add the vanilla pod to the cream and heat gently to just below boiling point. Cover, remove from the heat and leave to infuse for 15 minutes.

5 Place the tin on the baking sheet and bake the pastry case blind for 10 minutes (see page 269). Remove the paper and beans, then bake the pastry for a further 12–15 minutes until lightly browned. Transfer to a wire rack to cool completely.

6 In a small bowl, stir together the egg yolks and remaining tablespoon of sugar. Uncover the cream and heat to just below boiling point again. Stir the cream onto the egg yolks, then pour back into the saucepan and heat very gently, stirring with a wooden spoon, until thickened to a smooth custard; do not allow to boil. Pour through a sieve into a bowl and leave to cool, stirring occasionally.

7 Strain off the juices from the strawberries and stir into the custard. Arrange the strawberries in a single layer in the pastry case, then pour over the custard. Smooth the top using a long spatula, then place in the refrigerator for about 2 hours.

8 About 40 minutes before serving, preheat the grill so that it becomes very hot. Sprinkle an even layer of caster sugar, about 5 mm/¼ inch thick, over the entire surface of the custard, taking particular care not to leave any gaps near the pastry. Place the tart close to the grill so that the sugar very quickly melts and becomes golden brown. Chill for 30 minutes.

$\mathscr{P}$EARS IN PYJAMAS

SERVES 4

*Crisp, buttery puff pastry makes the perfect covering for warm
pears, especially when they contain a surprise in the form of diced
dried pear (perhaps soaked in* eau-de-vie de poire Williams
*or brandy) bound in a marzipan-like mixture in lieu of a core.
Alternatively, you could use just a small piece of marzipan
or a piece of plain chocolate.*

- 1 QUANTITY PUFF PASTRY
  (SEE PAGE 274) OR
  1 × 375 G/13 OZ PACKET
- BEATEN EGG, FOR GLAZING
- 2 TSP CASTER SUGAR
- **FILLING:**
- 1 DRIED PEAR HALF,
  CHOPPED (OPTIONAL)
- 2 TBSP *EAU-DE-VIE DE POIRE
  WILLIAMS*, BRANDY OR
  WATER (OPTIONAL)

- 4 LARGE DESSERT PEARS,
  SUCH AS COMICE OR WILLIAMS
- FINELY GRATED RIND AND
  JUICE OF 1 LEMON
- 115 G/4 OZ GROUND ALMONDS
- 1 EGG YOLK
- **TO SERVE:**
- SINGLE OR WHIPPING CREAM,
  OR VANILLA DAIRY ICE CREAM

1 For the filling, soak the dried pear half in the eau-de-vie, brandy or water, if liked, for several hours.

2 On a lightly floured surface, roll out the pastry to just over 35 cm/14 inches square. Using a sharp knife, trim the edges and cut the pastry into four squares. Leave to rest.

3 Peel the pears and core them carefully from the bottom; leave the stalks on. Brush the pears immediately with lemon juice.

4 Mix together the ground almonds and egg yolk, then mix in the dried pear and any remaining soaking liquid, if used. Pack into the cavity in each pear, then stand upright in the centre of each pastry square. Brush the edges of the pastry with water, then fold the four corners up to the top of each pear. Lightly press all the seams and edges to seal, except around the stalk as there must be an outlet for the steam. Stand the pears on the baking sheet and place in the refrigerator for 30 minutes.

5 Set the oven to 220°C/425°F/Gas 7.

6 Brush the pastry with beaten egg and sprinkle with sugar. Bake for 15–20 minutes until the pastry is crisp and golden. Serve warm with single or whipping cream, or vanilla dairy ice cream.

Illustrated opposite page 273

*Fold the corners of each
pastry square up to the top of
each pear*

*Leave a small opening at the
top to allow steam to escape*

APRICOT AND
SESAME PUFFS

SERVES 4–6

*These nutty, fruity fried pastries are lighter and less sweet than
most. Instead of being soaked in a honey syrup, the syrup is simply
poured over the puffs just before they are served; the syrup is also
lightened with orange juice.*

- 175 G/6 OZ PLAIN FLOUR
- 2½ TSP SESAME SEEDS
- ½ TSP ANISEEDS,
  FINELY CRUSHED
- 2 TBSP OLIVE OIL
- 25 G/1 OZ UNSALTED
  BUTTER, MELTED
- 100 ML/3½ FL OZ SWEET
  WHITE WINE
- APPROXIMATELY 115 ML/4 FL OZ
  THICK DRIED APRICOT PURÉE

- BEATEN EGG, FOR GLAZING
- SESAME SEEDS, FOR SPRINKLING
- FLAVOURLESS VEGETABLE
  OIL FOR DEEP FRYING
- **SYRUP:**
- 1 LARGE ORANGE
- 115 ML/4 FL OZ CLEAR HONEY
- 1 TBSP WHISKY OR
  BRANDY (OPTIONAL)

1 Sieve the flour into a mixing bowl and stir in the sesame seeds and aniseeds. Form
a well in the centre. In a saucepan, gently heat together the olive oil, butter and wine
until the butter has melted, then slowly pour into the well in the flour mixture,
stirring to form a smooth dough. Turn onto a floured surface and knead lightly.
Cover and place in the refrigerator for 30 minutes.

2 Roll out the dough thinly and cut into approximately 6.25 cm/2½ inch circles.
Place about half a teaspoon of apricot purée on one half of each circle, brush the
edges of the dough with water, then fold the uncovered halves over the filling. Press
the edges well using a fork or crimping wheel, if liked, to seal. Brush the pastries
lightly with beaten egg, then sprinkle with sesame seeds and pat them in lightly.

3 To make the syrup, thinly pare the rind from the orange, then cut into strips.
Add to a small saucepan of boiling water, return to the boil then simmer for 2
minutes. Drain and rinse the rind under cold, running water. Squeeze the juice from
the orange, then gently heat in a small saucepan with the honey, stirring occasionally
with a wooden spoon, until the honey has dissolved. Add the brandy or whisky, if
using, and the orange rind. Cover and keep warm over a very low heat.

4 Half fill a deep-fat frying pan with oil, then heat to 180°–190°C/350°–375°F. Fry
the pastries in batches for about 3–4 minutes until golden. Using a slotted spoon,
transfer to absorbent kitchen paper to drain. When all the puffs are cooked, pile
them on a plate and spoon over the honey orange sauce so that all the puffs are
coated with sauce.

 Illustrated opposite page 272

$\mathcal{T}$REACLE TART

SERVES 4 – 6

The title is a misnomer as treacle tarts do not contain treacle.
They used to, until the end of the nineteenth century when the
process for refining the thick, black treacle into golden syrup was
developed. Traditionally, treacle tarts seem to have been made in
old-fashioned pie plates, so the layer of filling was fairly shallow,
but this recipe is made in a flan tin to provide
a more generous allocation.

- 175 G/6 OZ PLAIN FLOUR
- 85 G/3 OZ UNSALTED BUTTER, DICED
- 1 TBSP CASTER SUGAR
- 1 EGG YOLK
- 2½ TBSP COLD WATER
- 2 TSP FINELY GRATED LEMON RIND
- **FILLING:**
- 225 G/8 OZ GOLDEN SYRUP
- 25 G/1 OZ UNSALTED BUTTER
- GRATED RIND AND JUICE OF 1 LEMON
- 40 G/1½ OZ FRESH BREADCRUMBS
- 40 G/1½ OZ PORRIDGE OATS
- LARGE PINCH OF GROUND CINNAMON OR GINGER (OPTIONAL)
- BEATEN EGG OR MILK, FOR GLAZING

Lay the strips of pastry
over the tart to make a
lattice pattern

1 Butter a 20 cm/8 inch loose-based flan tin. Place the flour in a bowl, then rub in the butter until the mixture resembles breadcrumbs. Stir in the sugar. Mix the egg yolk with the water and the lemon rind, then lightly and quickly stir into the flour using a fork. Use your hand to quickly form into a ball. On a lightly floured surface, lightly roll out and use to line the tin. Reserve the trimmings. Place the flan tin and trimmings in the refrigerator for 30 minutes.

2 Set the oven to 190°C/375°F/Gas 5.

3 To make the filling, gently warm together the syrup, butter and lemon juice, remove from the heat and stir in the lemon rind, breadcrumbs, oats and cinnamon or ginger, if using.

4 Lightly prick the base of the pastry, taking care not to pierce right the way through. Fill the pastry case with the syrup mixture and level the surface.

5 Roll out the pastry trimmings and cut into strips. Arrange the strips in a lattice pattern over the filling, dampening the ends to seal them to the edge of the pastry case. Brush with beaten egg or milk to glaze.

6 Bake for about 25 minutes until the filling is just set. Serve the tart warm – never hot – or cold.

CARAMELIZED PINEAPPLE UPSIDE-DOWN TART

SERVES 6

This tart is a development from the French upside-down caramelized apple tart, tarte Tatin, *which in recent years has been in danger of becoming a restaurant cliché. The fresh fruitiness of the pineapple in this version makes a particularly delicious contrast to the sweet buttery topping and they are both well set off by crisp puff pastry. A good accompaniment is lightly sweetened* crème fraîche *or equal quantities of Greek yogurt and sweetened, whipped whipping cream flavoured with a few pieces of finely chopped stem ginger. Alternatively, serve with vanilla dairy ice cream.*

- 115 G/4 OZ UNSALTED BUTTER, DICED
- 115 G/4 OZ LIGHT MUSCOVADO SUGAR
- 1 PINEAPPLE, ABOUT 900 G/2 LB, PEELED, CORED AND SLICED
- PUFF PASTRY MADE WITH 150 G/5 OZ FLOUR AND 150 G/5 OZ UNSALTED BUTTER (SEE PAGE 274)

- KIRSCH (OPTIONAL)
- **DECORATION:**
- FRESH MINT SPRIGS (OPTIONAL)
- **TO SERVE:**
- VANILLA DAIRY ICE CREAM (OPTIONAL)

1 On top of the stove, gently heat the butter in a thick 21.5 cm/8½ inch flan tin or other cake tin such as a *moule à manqué* that is at least 5 cm/2 inches deep. Stir in the sugar using a wooden spoon and heat until it has melted, then continue to cook over a fairly high heat for 3–4 minutes until darkened. Remove from the heat and arrange the pineapple in the sugar-butter mixture. Leave to cool..

2 On a lightly floured surface, roll out the pastry to a 25 cm/10 inch diameter circle. Trim off the edges of the circle. Prick the pastry with a fork and place in the refrigerator for 20–30 minutes.

3 Set the oven to 220°C/425°F/Gas 7. Place a baking sheet in the oven.

4 Place the pastry centrally over the pineapple, tucking the pastry down the side of the tin. Place the tin on the baking tray and bake for 12–15 minutes, then lower the oven temperature to 180°C/350°F/Gas 4 and bake for a further 10–12 minutes until the pastry is well risen and crisp. Run the point of a knife around the edge of the pastry, leave to cool for 2–3 minutes, then place a plate that is larger than the tin over it and invert the two, shaking to unmould the tart. Sprinkle with kirsch, and decorate with mint, if using. Serve with vanilla dairy ice cream, if liked.

Illustrated opposite page 272

$\mathscr{B}$UTTERSCOTCH TART

SERVES 6

To turn this into a classic American butterscotch cream pie, cover the top with a meringue made from two size 2 egg whites and 85 g/3 oz caster sugar and bake at 200°C/400°F/Gas 6 for 8–10 minutes.

- SHORTCRUST PASTRY MADE WITH 175 G/6 OZ PLAIN FLOUR, 115 G/4 OZ UNSALTED BUTTER, 2 TSP VANILLA CASTER SUGAR, 1 EGG YOLK, AND A FEW DROPS OF COLD WATER IF THE DOUGH IS DRY (SEE PAGE 272)
- 1 EGG WHITE
- 55 G/2 OZ UNSALTED BUTTER

- 55 G/2 OZ DARK MUSCOVADO SUGAR
- 150 ML/5 FL OZ MILK
- 3 EGG YOLKS
- 1 EGG
- 1 TBSP CORNFLOUR
- 175 ML/6 FL OZ EVAPORATED MILK
- **TO SERVE:**
- WHIPPED CREAM

1 Butter a 20 cm/8 inch flan tin. On a lightly floured surface, roll out the pastry and use to line the flan tin. Prick the base and place in the refrigerator for 30 minutes.

2 Set the oven to 200°C/400°F/Gas 6. Place a baking sheet in the oven.

3 Place the flan tin on the baking sheet and bake the pastry case blind for 10 minutes (see page 269). Remove the paper and beans, brush the base and sides of the pastry with egg white and return to the oven for 10 minutes. Leave to cool.

4 Meanwhile, in a heavy saucepan, gently melt the butter, then add the sugar and heat until dissolved. Cook for another couple of minutes, then remove from the heat and slowly stir in the milk.

5 In a medium-sized bowl mix together the egg yolks, egg and cornflour, then stir in the milk mixture and the evaporated milk. Return to the saucepan and heat very gently, stirring with a wooden spoon, until thickened. Allow to cool slightly, then pour into the pastry case. Cover the surface of the filling closely with dampened greaseproof paper and leave until cold. Remove the greaseproof paper before serving the tart and serve with whipped cream.

WARM PEACH AND PECAN PIE

SERVES 6

Served warm with crème fraîche *flowing languidly around yielding peaches enlivened with a dash of spirit, and encased in a luxurious pecan pastry, this makes a very special pudding. Barackpálinka is a smooth, Hungarian peach eau-de-vie.*

- NUT PASTRY MADE WITH 225 G/8 OZ PLAIN FLOUR, 55 G/2 OZ PECANS, VERY FINELY CHOPPED, 2 EGG YOLKS, BEATEN, 85 G/3 OZ VANILLA CASTER SUGAR AND 115 G/4 OZ UNSALTED BUTTER, DICED (SEE PAGE 273)
- 1 EGG WHITE, LIGHTLY BEATEN, FOR GLAZING
- CASTER SUGAR, FOR SPRINKLING

- **FILLING:**
- 6 LARGE, RIPE PEACHES
- 1 TBSP VANILLA CASTER SUGAR
- 2 TBSP *EAU-DE-VIE DE PÊCHES*, BARACKPÁLINKA OR COGNAC
- 150 ML/5 FL OZ *CRÈME FRAÎCHE* OR 70 ML/2 ½ FL OZ DOUBLE CREAM MIXED WITH 70 ML/2 ½ FL OZ SOURED CREAM

1 Carefully peel the peaches (do this without pouring boiling water over them), then cut into quarters and remove the stones. Slice each quarter in half lengthways. Place in a dish, sprinkle over the sugar and the *eau-de-vie de pêches*, Cognac or Barackpálinka and leave for 1 hour.

2 Butter a 22.5 cm/9 inch loose-based flan tin or flan ring and place on a baking sheet. On a lightly floured surface, roll out the pastry and use about two-thirds to line the tin. Roll the other piece of pastry out to form a lid for the pie. Using an approximately 2.5 cm/1 inch cutter, remove a circle from the centre of the lid. Cover and chill the lined tin and the lid for 30 minutes.

3 Set the oven to 200°C/400°F/Gas 6.

4 Using a slotted spoon, lift the peaches from the dish and arrange the pieces in circles in the pastry case and fill in the centre of the circles with some pieces. Reserve the soaking liquid.

5 Sprinkle a little sugar over the peaches. Dampen the edges of the pastry case and place the lid centrally over the pie. Press the edges together to seal them firmly. Bake for about 20–25 minutes until the pastry is beginning to brown. Brush the top of the pie lightly with beaten egg white, sprinkle with sugar and return to the oven for about 10 minutes until the pastry is browned and crisp. Leave to stand for a few minutes, then remove the sides of the flan tin or the flan ring.

6 Mix together the *crème fraîche*, or double cream and soured cream, and the reserved soaking liquid, then carefully pour through the hole in the lid. Serve warm.

RIGHT (from top to bottom): Tangerine Syllabub (see page 333); Paskha (see page 318); Orange-Flavoured Babas with Kumquats (see page 340).

$\mathcal{K}$ING-SIZE FIG NEWTON

SERVES 8

A plump pastry bolster, bursting with moist dried fruits to which the addition of an everyday banana gives a hint of the exotic.

- 115 G/4 OZ UNSALTED BUTTER, DICED
- 55 G/2 OZ VANILLA CASTER SUGAR
- 1 EGG, LIGHTLY BEATEN
- 225 G/8 OZ PLAIN FLOUR
- **FILLING:**
- 200 G/7 OZ DRIED FIGS, CHOPPED
- 85 G/3 OZ DRIED APRICOTS, CHOPPED
- 85 G/3 OZ STONED PRUNES, CHOPPED
- 100 G/3½ OZ WALNUTS, CHOPPED
- 40 G/1½ OZ STEM GINGER, FINELY CHOPPED (OPTIONAL)
- 4 TBSP DARK RUM
- 1 LARGE RIPE BANANA
- 1 EGG WHITE, BEATEN
- 150 G/5 OZ ICING SUGAR
- ½ TSP LEMON JUICE
- 2 TBSP APRICOT JAM, SIEVED
- **TO SERVE:**
- CUSTARD (SEE PAGE 353) OR VANILLA DAIRY ICE CREAM

Chop dried fruits with scissors dipped in flour

1 Mix together the figs, apricots, prunes, walnuts, ginger, if using, and the rum for the filling, then leave to soak.

2 Meanwhile, make the pastry. Beat the butter until soft, then beat in the sugar. When well blended, beat in the egg and flour. Cover and place in the refrigerator for 30 minutes.

3 Set the oven to 190°C/375°F/Gas 5. Butter a baking sheet.

4 On a lightly floured surface, roll out the pastry to an approximately 25 cm/10 inch square. Trim the edges. Starting just under 2.5 cm/1 inch in from three sides, spread the dried fruit mixture in a strip almost 10 cm/4 inches wide over the pastry. Peel and slice the banana and lay over the dried fruit mixture.

5 Brush the pastry borders with water, then fold the uncovered dough across the dried fruits. Seal the edges firmly together, then crimp them to make them decorative. If liked, score the top of the pastry to make a diamond pattern, using the point of a sharp knife. Carefully transfer to the baking sheet.

6 In a small bowl, whisk the egg white with the icing sugar until very thick. Stir in the lemon juice, then spread over the top of the pastry. Form a small cone from a 7.5 cm/3 inch square of greaseproof paper, then spoon in the apricot jam. Cut off the tip of the cone and pipe lines of apricot across the egg white coating. Bake for about 20 minutes until golden. Turn off the oven and leave the pastry for a further 15 minutes. If the oven retains the heat very well, leave the door open. Carefully transfer the pastry to a wire rack to cool to room temperature. Cut into slices to serve, accompanied by Custard or vanilla dairy ice cream.

LEFT (from top to bottom): Banana Butterscotch Sundae (see page 321); Brown Sugar Meringue with Egg Nog Parfait and Orange Compote (see page 330); Italian Coffee Cream and Walnut Cake (see page 337).

Illustrated opposite page 256

Ease the pastry into the shape of the fluted flan ring or tin

Unroll the pastry over the tin or ring

Use the tin as a guide to the size

*A*PRICOT TART

SERVES 6

This tart reminds me of summers in the gentle Val de Loire, *where the fertile soil, warm sunshine and blue skies produce rich harvests of flavourful fruit. What bliss to picnic in a grassy spot with a tart such as this one, with its crisp pastry case and buttery custard filling over succulent apricots, and sip a cool glass of a local white wine, such as Vouvray or Côteaux du Layon.*

- *PÂTE SUCRÉE* MADE WITH 175 G/6 OZ PLAIN FLOUR, 100 G/3½ OZ UNSALTED BUTTER, 2 LARGE EGG YOLKS AND 55 G/2 OZ VANILLA CASTER SUGAR (SEE PAGE 273)
- FILLING:
- 115 G/4 OZ CASTER SUGAR
- 575 ML/1 PINT WATER

- 550 G/1¼ LB APRICOTS
- 55 ML/2 FL OZ SOURED CREAM
- 175 ML/6 FL OZ DOUBLE CREAM
- ½ VANILLA POD
- 3 EGGS, BEATEN
- 55 G/2 OZ UNSALTED BUTTER, DICED
- CASTER OR ICING SUGAR, FOR SPRINKLING

1 Butter a 24 cm/9½ inch fluted flan tin, about 2 cm/¾ inch deep, and preferably loose-based. On a lightly floured surface, roll out the pastry and use to line the tin. Prick the base of the pastry case, cover and place in the refrigerator for 30 minutes.

2 Set the oven to 220°C/425°F/Gas 7.

3 Bake the pastry blind for about 12 minutes (see page 269). Remove the paper and beans, return the pastry to the oven and bake for a further 3–4 minutes. Remove from the oven. Lower the oven temperature to 200°C/400°F/Gas 6.

4 To make the filling, gently heat 85 g/3 oz caster sugar in the water until the sugar has dissolved. Heat to just on simmering point, add the apricots and poach gently until just tender and still retaining their shape (about 5–15 minutes). Drain well and leave on absorbent kitchen paper to drain further.

5 Pour the soured cream and double cream into a saucepan, add the vanilla pod and bring to the boil. In a heatproof bowl, stir together the eggs and remaining caster sugar. Remove the vanilla pod from the saucepan. Slowly pour the boiling liquid onto the egg yolk mixture, stirring constantly, to make a smooth custard. Stir in the butter, then leave to cool, stirring occasionally to prevent a skin forming.

6 Arrange the apricots, cut-side up, in the pastry case, then pour over the custard. Bake for about 20–25 minutes until lightly set in the centre and golden brown.

7 Transfer the flan tin to a wire rack and leave until the tart is lukewarm. Remove the outer ring of the tin, sprinkle the filling with caster or icing sugar and serve.

$\mathcal{B}$LACK FOREST PUFFS

MAKES 6-8

This is a new look to the popular combination of cherries and chocolate. You will need to transfer the ice cream to the main part of the refrigerator 20–30 minutes before serving the choux puffs to give it time to soften. The tops of the choux puffs are removed, so you can pile as much ice cream as you like into the shells, but do not fill them until just before serving.

- APPROXIMATELY 225 G/8 OZ STONED RIPE CHERRIES, PREFERABLY BLACK
- 4 TBSP BRANDY OR KIRSCH
- 70 G/2½ OZ PLAIN FLOUR
- 55 G/2 OZ UNSALTED BUTTER, DICED

- 150 ML/5 FL OZ WATER
- 2 EGGS, SIZE 3, BEATEN
- APPROXIMATELY 225–300 ML/8–10 FL OZ VANILLA DAIRY ICE CREAM
- CHOCOLATE SAUCE (SEE PAGE 356)

1 Soak the cherries in the brandy or kirsch for 3 hours.

2 Set the oven to 200°C/400°F/Gas 6. Sprinkle a baking sheet with cold water.

3 Sift the flour onto a piece of paper. In a saucepan, heat the butter in the water until it has just melted, then bring quickly to the boil. Quickly remove from the heat and immediately add all the flour at once and beat vigorously with a wooden spoon until the mixture is smooth and pulls away from the sides of the pan. Return the pan to the heat and beat for 30 seconds. Remove from the heat and allow to cool slightly. Gradually beat in sufficient egg to give a dough that is shiny and soft enough to fall from the spoon.

4 Place 6 or 8 tablespoonfuls of the mixture spaced well apart on the baking sheet, then bake for 10 minutes. Increase the oven temperature to 220°C/425°F/Gas 7 and cook for a further 20–25 minutes until well risen, crisp and golden.

5 Cut a slit in the sides of the buns and, if necessary, return to the oven with the heat turned off for a few minutes to dry out. Transfer to a wire rack to cool completely.

6 Just before serving, cut off the top third or so of each choux bun, place a scoop of ice cream in each bottom portion, then cover with some cherries and spoon the juices over. Cover with the tops and pour over a little warm Chocolate Sauce. Serve the remaining sauce separately.

Illustrated opposite page 256

GÂTEAU PITHIVIERS

Uncut, this dome-shaped puff pastry looks fairly innocuous, but remove a slice while it is warm and a rich, melting almond filling will ooze out, languidly and fragrantly, to harmonize beautifully with buttery flakes of crisp pastry. The recipe for the pastry has remained unchanged from at least the beginning of the nineteenth century, and bears the name of a small town about 80 kilometres south of Paris, in the Orleannais.

- PUFF PASTRY MADE WITH 225 G/8 OZ PLAIN FLOUR AND 225 G/8 OZ UNSALTED BUTTER (SEE PAGE 274)
- 1 EGG YOLK BEATEN WITH 1 TSP COLD WATER, FOR GLAZING
- ICING SUGAR, FOR SIFTING

- FILLING:
- 85 G/3 OZ ALMONDS, GROUND
- 85 G/3 OZ CASTER SUGAR
- 85 G/3 OZ UNSALTED BUTTER, SOFTENED
- 2 EGG YOLKS, BEATEN
- 2 TBSP DARK RUM

1 For the filling, pound the almonds with the sugar to make a paste using a pestle and mortar, then spoon the paste into a bowl and work in the butter followed by the egg yolks and rum. Cover and chill very well.

2 Divide the pastry into two portions, one slightly larger than the other. On a lightly floured surface, roll out the smaller portion, using a lightly floured rolling pin, to a circle about 23.75 cm/9½ inches in diameter. Trim the edges and carefully transfer the pastry to a baking sheet making sure the shape remains true.

3 Roll out the other piece of pastry to a slightly larger circle and trim the edges. Place the almond filling on the first circle, leaving a border of about 2.5 cm/1 inch clear all the way round. Brush the border with egg glaze. Place the second circle of pastry centrally over the filling and press the pastry edges together to seal them. Form a scallop effect around the edge and make a small slit in the centre. With the point of a sharp knife, starting at the centre and working to the edge, score but do not cut right through the surface of the pastry in curved, half-moon shaped lines to give the traditional appearance. Brush the top with egg glaze, avoiding the scored lines. Cover and chill for 30 minutes.

4 Set the oven to 220°C/425°F/Gas 7.

5 Bake the pithiviers for about 20 minutes, then lower the oven temperature to 200°C/400°F/Gas 6 and bake for a further 15 minutes or so until the pastry is risen and golden brown.

6 Set the grill to its highest setting. Sprinkle icing sugar over the surface of the pastry and place under a very hot grill for a minute or two. Carefully transfer to a wire rack to cool slightly.

Illustrated opposite page 256

$\mathscr{P}$ECAN PIE

SERVES 6–8

*Feelings and loyalties run very high on the subject of pecan pie and
I would not dare to claim that this is the best, but I do know that it
is always declared as being very good. Although walnuts are
sometimes substituted for pecans, they have quite a different
flavour and texture and will produce a very different pie.
Similarly, do not hope to make a proper pecan pie by substituting
golden syrup for maple syrup – keep that for using with walnuts.*

- *PÂTE SUCRÉE* MADE WITH
  200 G/7 OZ PLAIN FLOUR,
  115 G/4 OZ BUTTER, 3 SIZE 2 EGG
  YOLKS, 55 G/2 OZ CASTER SUGAR
  AND A FEW DROPS OF VANILLA
  ESSENCE (SEE PAGE 273)
- 300 G/10 OZ PECAN HALVES
- 150 G/5 OZ MAPLE SYRUP
- 175 G/6 OZ SOFT LIGHT
  BROWN SUGAR

- 1 EGG YOLK
- 3 EGGS, BEATEN
- 1 TBSP DOUBLE CREAM OR MILK
- ½ TSP VANILLA ESSENCE
- 55 G/2 OZ UNSALTED
  BUTTER, CHOPPED
- **TO SERVE:**
- RUM- OR WHISKY-FLAVOURED
  WHIPPED CREAM, OR VANILLA
  DAIRY ICE CREAM

1 Butter a 22.5 cm/9 inch flan tin. On a lightly floured surface, roll out the pastry
and use to line the tin. Prick the base and place in the refrigerator for 30 minutes.

2 Set the oven to 200°C/400°F/Gas 6. Place a baking sheet in the oven.

3 Place the flan tin on the baking sheet and bake blind for about 10 minutes (see
page 269). Remove the paper and beans and leave to cool.

4 Chop half the pecans and scatter over the bottom of the pastry case.

5 Gently heat together the syrup and sugar, stirring with a wooden spoon, until the
sugar has dissolved, then boil for a few minutes. Allow to cool.

6 In a bowl, mix together the egg yolk, eggs, cream or milk and the vanilla essence,
then slowly stir in the syrup mixture. Heat the butter in a small saucepan over a
medium heat until it turns brown and has a nutty aroma. Pour into the syrup mixture
and mix well. Spoon over the chopped nuts, then arrange the pecan halves on top.

7 Bake for 10 minutes, then lower the oven temperature to 170°C/325°F/Gas 3 and
bake for a further 25–30 minutes until the centre is just set. Serve warm or cold with
rum- or whisky-flavoured whipped cream, or vanilla dairy ice cream.

$\mathscr{T}$OURTIÈRE AUX
PRUNEAUX ET ARMAGNAC

SERVES 6

*The memory of eating a crisp, flaky, prune-studded tourtière
that was heady with Armagnac remained with me long after my
return from an eventful trip to the south-west of France, and I
made a number of attempts to reproduce it. This is the nearest
replica I can make. The tricky part is rolling the dough sufficiently
thinly to warrant the traditional French name of* voile de mariage
*(wedding veil) for this type of pastry. The naming and exact
content is also a little difficult to fathom out – the same recipe
may be called* croustade *or* pastis *in Gascony,* gâteau Landais
*in Bordeaux, where the layers of pastry are sometimes separated
by sliced apples instead of prunes sprinkled with Armagnac.
To confuse matters further, a* pastis *may have no fruit at all,
just a sprinkling of Armagnac. Different sources, all claiming to be
authoritative, say contradictory things. Be all that as it may, this is
delicious and well worth making.*

- 36 AGEN OR LARGE PRUNES
- ARMAGNAC (OPTIONAL)
- 55 G/2 OZ MARZIPAN (OPTIONAL)
- WALNUT OIL OR MELTED
  BUTTER, PREFERABLY CLARIFIED,
  FOR GREASING
- ½ QUANTITY PUFF PASTRY
  (SEE PAGE 274)
- ICING SUGAR AND CORNFLOUR
  SIFTED TOGETHER IN EQUAL
  QUANTITIES, FOR SPRINKLING

- ORANGE FLOWER WATER
- MELTED BUTTER, PREFERABLY
  CLARIFIED, FOR BRUSHING
- 1 EGG BEATEN WITH 1 TSP
  WATER, FOR GLAZING
- 3 TBSP ARMAGNAC
- ICING SUGAR, FOR SIFTING

1 Place the prunes in a saucepan, cover with boiling water and add a few tablespoons of Armagnac, if liked, then leave the prunes to soak for about 2 hours. Bring the saucepan to just below boiling point, remove from the heat and leave to soak again for about 2 hours, by the end of which time the prunes should have softened but retained their shape and the stones be easy to remove. If necessary, repeat the heating again. Remove the stones and, if liked, divide the marzipan between the cavities of twelve of the prunes.

2 Brush a 25 cm/10 inch deep flan tin generously with walnut oil or melted butter.

3 Divide the pastry into five pieces, then form one piece into a ball. Sprinkle the work surface and rolling pin with the icing sugar/cornflour mixture, then roll the ball of pastry out on the work surface thinly to just over 30 cm/12 inches in diameter. Carefully line the tin with the rolled-out pastry. Roll out another piece of pastry in the same way to the same size. Brush the pastry lining the tin with walnut oil or melted butter and cover with the second piece of pastry. Arrange eight of the prunes near the edge of the pastry and place four around the centre. Sprinkle them with a little orange flower water and a little of the icing sugar/cornflour mix. Roll out another piece of pastry in the same way, but this time to 25 cm/10 inches in diameter. Lay this over the prunes, arrange another eight of the marzipan-stuffed prunes, if used, near the edge and four around the centre, placing them in the spaces between the prunes in the layer below. Sprinkle them with a little more orange flower water and sprinkle a little of the cornflour/icing sugar mixture over. Repeat with another portion of pastry and the remaining prunes. Finish with the last piece of pastry and glaze with beaten egg. Fold the edges of the first two layers of pastry down over the top. Cover and place in the refrigerator for 30 minutes.

4 Set the oven to 220°C/425°F/Gas 7.

5 Brush the top of the tourtière well with melted butter and bake for about 10 minutes, then reduce the oven temperature to 200°C/400°F/Gas 6 and bake for a further 20 minutes or so until the top is crisp and golden. Carefully transfer the tourtière to a wire rack, cut a small hole in the centre and pour in the Armagnac, rolling the tin from side to side so all the parts receive some. Sift icing sugar over the top and serve lukewarm.

St Clements Tart

In Britain, the name St Clements signifies the combination of oranges and lemons, after the old nursery rhyme 'Oranges and Lemons'. Here, they harmonize beautifully to make a welcomely refreshing tart. If your oven tends to be on the hot side, reduce the temperature further when cooking the filling, otherwise it may bubble over or colour too quickly.

- *PÂTE SUCRÉE* MADE WITH 125 G/4½ OZ FLOUR, 70 G/2½ OZ BUTTER, 2 EGG YOLKS AND 25 G/1 OZ CASTER SUGAR (SEE PAGE 273)
- 1 EGG WHITE, LIGHTLY BEATEN
- 3 EGGS, SIZE 3
- 1 EGG YOLK, SIZE 3
- 175 G/6 OZ CASTER SUGAR
- FINELY GRATED RIND AND STRAINED JUICE OF 2 ORANGES AND 1 LEMON

- 150 ML/5 FL OZ *CRÈME FRAÎCHE* OR DOUBLE CREAM
- **DECORATION:**
- 1 THIN SKINNED LEMON
- 1 SMALL ORANGE
- 175 G/6 OZ CASTER SUGAR
- 115 ML/4 FL OZ WATER

1 For the decoration, pare the rind very thinly from half of the orange and half of the lemon using a potato peeler, making sure that none of the white pith is included. Cut the rind into very fine shreds, then blanch three times, using fresh water each time and rinsing well after each blanching. Drain. Gently heat 70 g/2½ oz of the sugar in the water, stirring with a wooden spoon, until the sugar has dissolved, then bring to the boil without stirring. Add the orange and lemon shreds and simmer very gently until they are tender and translucent. Remove from the syrup and leave to drain on a wire rack.

2 Meanwhile, peel the lemon and the orange, making sure that all the pith has been removed, then divide into segments. Gently heat the remaining sugar in 200 ml/7 fl oz water, stirring with a wooden spoon, until the sugar has dissolved, then bring to the boil without stirring. Reduce the heat so the syrup barely simmers, then lower in the orange and lemon segments using a slotted spoon and cook gently for about 3–4 minutes. Lift from the syrup using a slotted spoon and leave to drain on a wire rack placed over a tray.

3 Butter a deep 20 cm/8 inch flan tin. On a lightly floured surface, roll out the pastry and use to line the tin. Prick the base, cover and chill for 30 minutes.

4 Set the oven to 200°C/400°F/Gas 6.

5 Bake the pastry case blind for 10 minutes (see page 269). Remove the paper and beans, brush the base of the tart with beaten egg white, then leave the pastry case to cool to room temperature.

6 Lower the oven temperature to 150°C/300°F/Gas 2.

7 Blend the eggs and egg yolk with the sugar until it has dissolved, then beat in the fruit juices and rinds and the *crème fraîche* or cream. With the tart shell still in the flan ring and on a baking tray, pour in most of the filling. Carefully place the baking tray on an oven shelf and spoon in the remaining filling. Slide the oven shelf into position and bake for about 25–30 minutes until the filling is just set (test it by shaking it gently). Leave to stand for several minutes before transferring to a wire rack to cool. Decorate the tart with the orange and lemon segments and shreds.

PASTRIES

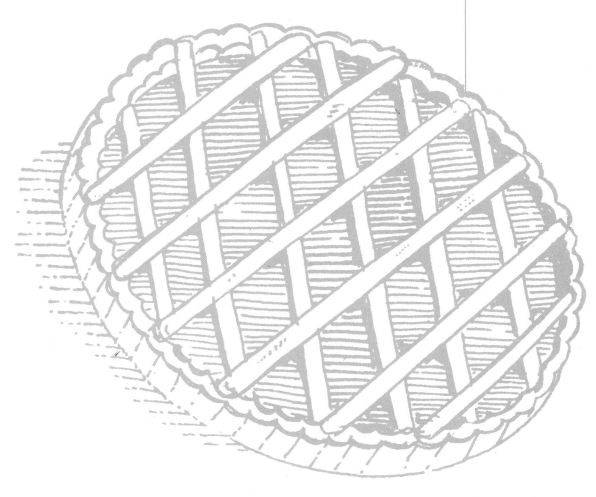

297

COCONUT CREAM PIE
IN A CHOCOLATE CASE

SERVES 8–10

This is not an American 'cream pie' (those do not actually contain cream, but a cooked custard put into a cooked pastry case), but one with coconut-flavoured cream baked in a shell of chocolate pastry so that the two fuse harmoniously together. Nestling on the pastry, surrounded by the coconut cream, a few rum-soaked cherries provide a final highlight.

CHOCOLATE PASTRY:
- 175 G/6 OZ PLAIN FLOUR
- 2 TBSP COCOA POWDER
- 4 TBSP VANILLA ICING SUGAR OR ORDINARY ICING SUGAR PLUS 2 OR 3 DROPS VANILLA ESSENCE
- 115 G/4 OZ UNSALTED BUTTER, DICED
- 1 TBSP WATER
- 1 EGG WHITE, BEATEN
- **FILLING:**
- 176 G/6 OZ RIPE CHERRIES, HALVED AND STONED

- 3 TBSP WHITE RUM
- 70 G/2½ OZ SOLID COCONUT CREAM, CHOPPED
- 500 ML/18 FL OZ SINGLE, WHIPPING OR DOUBLE CREAM, OR A MIXTURE
- 2 EGGS, BEATEN
- 4 EGG YOLKS
- APPROXIMATELY 100 G/3½ OZ CASTER SUGAR
- **DECORATION:**
- LIGHTLY TOASTED FLAKED COCONUT

1 Butter a 25 cm/10 inch deep loose-based flan tin. For the filling, leave the cherries to marinate in the rum. Put the coconut cream into a bowl. In a saucepan, gently warm the cream, pour over the coconut cream and leave until cold, stirring occasionally to dissolve the coconut.

2 To make the pastry, sift the flour, cocoa powder and icing sugar into a bowl. In a saucepan, gently heat the butter with the water until the butter has just melted, then slowly pour onto the flour mixture, stirring with a wooden spoon to make a smooth dough. Transfer to the flan tin and press evenly into the shape. Cover and place in the refrigerator for 30 minutes.

3 Set the oven to 190°C/375°F/Gas 5.

WALNUT TARTLETS

SERVES 8

*If current thinking is correct, walnuts help to lower cholesterol
levels in the blood, so as these tartlets are packed with them,
they might help to negate the effect of the butter and cream
(but dietary and nutritional claims do seem to be prone to being
revoked). If calories are your concern, sorry, there is nothing
that can ease the impact on your figure of each delicious mouthful,
so the best thing is to forget them altogether and simply enjoy
this wonderful pudding.*

- 100 G/3½ OZ FULL-FAT SOFT CHEESE
- 100 G/3½ OZ UNSALTED BUTTER, DICED
- 1 EGG YOLK
- 115 G/4 OZ PLAIN FLOUR
- **FILLING:**
- 175 G/6 OZ LIGHT MUSCOVADO SUGAR
- FEW DROPS LEMON JUICE

- 2 TBSP WATER
- 55 ML/2 FL OZ DOUBLE CREAM
- 175 G/6 OZ UNSALTED BUTTER, DICED
- FEW DROPS VANILLA ESSENCE
- 225 G/8 OZ WALNUT HALVES
- **TO SERVE:**
- ICED MASCARPONE (SEE PAGE 254) OR VANILLA DAIRY ICE CREAM

1 Put the cheese, butter and egg yolks in a mixing bowl and beat together until evenly combined, then gradually mix in the flour. Cover and place in the refrigerator for 30 minutes.

2 On a lightly floured surface and using a lightly floured rolling pin, roll out the pastry thinly and use to line eight approximately 7.5 cm/3 inch fluted tartlet tins. Prick the base of each case, then place in the refrigerator for about 30 minutes.

3 Set the oven to 190°C/375°F/Gas 5. Place a baking sheet in the oven.

4 Place the tins on a baking sheet and bake blind for 10 minutes (see page 269). Remove the paper and beans and return the pastry to the oven for 5 minutes.

5 To make the filling, gently heat the sugar and lemon juice in a heavy-based saucepan with the water until the sugar has melted, then increase the heat and boil until lightly caramelized. Remove from the heat and quickly add the cream, which will bubble a lot. Swirl the pan gently until the bubbles subside, then stir in the butter, vanilla essence and nuts.

6 Divide between the pastry cases and return to the oven for 10 minutes.

7 Leave to cool on a wire rack for a few minutes, then slip them out of the tins on to plates. Serve warm with Iced Mascarpone or vanilla dairy ice cream.

Illustrated opposite page 257

$\mathscr{W}$HAT WENT WRONG?

SHORTCRUST PATE SUCREE AND PUFF PASTRY

☞ PASTRY BECOMES STICKY:
There are three reasons for this. The dough may have become too warm, because the ingredients or equipment are warm, the atmosphere in the kitchen is warm or your hands are warm; too much water may have been added; or you have been too heavy-handed.

☞ TOUGH PASTRY:
Too much water added to the dough and rough handling are the culprits.

☞ PASTRY SHRINKS AFTER BAKING:
This is caused by too much water being added when making the dough, and/or the dough being overstretched when rolled out, and/or the dough not being allowed to rest before baking.

☞ FAT RUNS OUT DURING BAKING:
The oven was too cool or too much fat was added to the dough.

☞ SOGGY PASTRY BENEATH A FILLING:
If the pastry has not been baked blind, or sealed with beaten egg white before being filled, or sugar comes into contact with the pastry, it will be soggy.

CHOUX PASTRY

☞ THE DOUGH IS TOO SOFT:
The dough will be too soft if it was not allowed to cool sufficiently between adding the flour and beating in the eggs.

☞ THE PASTRY DOES NOT RISE:
If the dough was too soft or the oven was not hot enough the pastry will not rise.

☞ UNCOOKED DOUGH INSIDE THE BAKED PASTRY:
This is caused by insufficient baking, failure to pierce a hole in the pastry to allow the steam to escape and not returning the pastry to the oven to dry out.

COLD PUDDINGS

An advantage of serving cold puddings is that, with a few exceptions, they can be made in advance so are ready and waiting for you when you are ready for them, saving last-minute preparation, cooking and worry. Cold puddings should not be thought of as only warm-weather fare, because there are many that are as suitable for eating around a blazing open fire as when basking under a hot sun. The range is vast and varied. It includes luscious cake-type recipes; traditional dishes often associated with the nursery but nevertheless evocative and, when made well, delicious, such as honeycombe moulds and blancmange; ever-popular ice cream-based puddings; and old-fashioned favourites such as fools and trifles that never seem to lose their appeal.

RIGHT (from top to bottom): Blackcurrant and Mint Mousse (see page 316); Traditional Manor House Trifle (see page 323); Summer Pudding in a Special Jacket (see page 342).

COLD
PUDDINGS

LEFT (from top to
bottom): Chestnut
Compote with Coffee
Sauce (see page 310);
Cream Cheese Cake with
Pine Nuts and Raspberry
Sauce (see page 317);
Tiramisu with Torrone
(see page 344).

Place the bowl over a
saucepan of hot water

Squeeze sheets of gelatine to
remove excess water

$\mathcal{G}$ELATINE

☞ There are two forms of gelatine that can be used to set puddings, the more common powdered type sold weighed out in sachets and the less widely available brittle, transparent leaf or sheet gelatine.

☞ The amount of gelatine required will vary depending on the firmness of the set required, the density of the mixture and the temperature of the surroundings. As a general rule, in Britain one sachet of powdered gelatine, which is usually 3–4 teaspoons, will set 550 ml/1 pint of liquid. Leaf gelatine should be weighed, as different brands may have different weights, so check the packet to find how many sheets are needed for a given volume of liquid.

☞ Gelatine sets at 20°C/68°F and is at its best if not left in the refrigerator for more than a few hours as it will become very firm.

☞ Cover the dish while a pudding containing gelatine is in the refrigerator.

TO USE GELATINE

POWDERED GELATINE:

☞ The gelatine must be 'sponged' in a small amount of water in a small heatproof bowl first. To do this, sprinkle the gelatine over the water, usually about 3 tablespoons water for 1 tablespoon or 1 sachet gelatine, and leave until the gelatine has swollen to resemble a sponge in appearance; this takes about 5 minutes.

☞ The gelatine must then be dissolved completely. Place the bowl over a saucepan of hot, not boiling, water, leave for 5 minutes, then stir with a teaspoon. Leave until the liquid is clear.

☞ Do not add hot gelatine to a cold mixture, otherwise it will set quickly into unpleasant, rubbery strings. Remove the bowl from the saucepan, leave the gelatine to cool, then slowly stir a little of the cold mixture into the dissolved gelatine. This can then be slowly poured back into the remaining mixture, stirring constantly.

LEAF GELATINE:

☞ Soak the required number of leaves in a small amount of water for about 5 minutes or until very soft, then remove from the water and squeeze out excess moisture. Put the leaves in a small heatproof bowl, usually about 3 leaves of gelatine to 3 tablespoons water, place the bowl over a saucepan of hot, not boiling, water and proceed as for powdered gelatine.

$\mathcal{W}$ORKING WITH CHOCOLATE

☞ For advice on the choice of chocolate see page 12.

☞ If chocolate is heated to too high a temperature or for too long it will become granular when other ingredients are added.

☞ To melt chocolate, chop it, then place in a heatproof bowl placed over a saucepan of hot water; check that the underside of the bowl is not touching the water. Leave until the chocolate has melted around the edges, stir and leave until completely

Melt chocolate in a
double saucepan

melted. Remove from the heat.

☞ Steam and water can make chocolate thick and unmanageable. Should this happen, gradually stir in a little flavourless oil until the mixture is smooth.

☞ The same remedy can be used to rescue chocolate that has been overheated.

☞ Combine melted chocolate while it is warm with ingredients that are at a similar temperature. If they are much hotter or colder the chocolate may turn lumpy.

Successful Meringues

☞ Fat and water inhibit egg whites from being beaten to a stiff foam, so the bowl and whisk should be clean and dry.

☞ The temperature of the ingredients is not vital to the success of the meringue, but if the egg whites are at room temperature rather than at refrigerator temperature they will be easier to whisk to a foam.

☞ The proportion of sugar that is added determines the final texture of the meringue – 2 tablespoons of sugar per egg white produces a soft meringue, 4 tablespoons per egg white a hard one. Sugar helps to protect the meringue from drainage and collapse, but it also reduces the foaming of the egg whites, so it should not be added until the final stages of the whisking.

☞ For more than two centuries, the use of a copper bowl has been recommended for whisking egg whites because it produces a good creamy foam that is more difficult to overbeat, but just why this should be so remains a mystery. Theories that the copper gives acidity to the whites or that it establishes an electric field have not been substantiated.

☞ The addition of a small amount of an acid, such as a pinch of cream of tartar or a few drops of lemon juice or a mild vinegar, help to guard against overbeating and the overcoagulation of the egg whites, which results in lumpiness, collapse of the meringue and seeping of liquid.

☞ Although salt enhances the flavour of foods, it should not be added to meringues; it increases the time required to whisk the eggs to a foam and it decreases the stability.

Storing Cold Puddings

Puddings containing cream, milk, uncooked eggs, such as whips and mousses, and gelatine should be kept cool and eaten within a day of being made, or less if they do have to be left in a warm room. Puddings that can be refrigerated can be kept for a day longer, but they must be covered while in the refrigerator and usually should be returned to room temperature before being eaten. However, they will lose much of their former glory.

Making meringues:

Whisk the egg whites until soft peaks form

Using a large metal spoon, gently fold in the sugar

$\mathscr{P}$ASSION FRUIT WHIP

SERVES 4

*The hard, wrinkled shell of the passion fruit belies the intense,
refreshing perfume of the translucent pulp that clings to the small,
crunchy seeds inside. Combined with orange, which enhances,
and therefore 'stretches', its flavour, passion fruit makes a simple
fruit pudding that will remind you of far-away, sunny places.*

- 12 PASSION FRUITS
- 2 TBSP COINTREAU
- 6 TBSP VANILLA ICING SUGAR
- 250 ML/9 FL OZ WHIPPING
  CREAM, WHIPPED

- 2 EGG WHITES, SIZE 2
- **TO SERVE:**
- SHORTBREAD BISCUITS

1 Cut the passion fruit in half and scoop the insides into a saucepan. Heat gently, then tip into a non-metallic sieve and push the flesh through into a bowl; reserve a few of the seeds for decoration. Add the Cointreau to the passion fruit flesh and leave at room temperature for about 1 hour.

2 Stir the icing sugar into the passion fruit, then, using a cold metal spoon, fold in the cream. Cover and place in the refrigerator for 1 hour or more.

3 Just before serving, in a clean, dry bowl, whisk the egg whites until stiff but not dry, then, using a large metal spoon, gently fold into the passion fruit mixture. Spoon into chilled glasses and decorate with the reserved passion fruit seeds. Serve with shortbread biscuits.

$\mathcal{A}$PRICOT ROULADE

SERVES 8

A friend who knows how much I like dried apricots suggested the
basic idea for this pudding to me after she had been served a
similar pudding at a dinner party. And what a good idea.
The rich fruit flavour of good dried apricots wrapped around a
cool, creamy filling is given just the right 'lift' by strained Greek
yogurt. It makes the sort of end to a meal that I can't wait to reach.

Lining a cornered tin:

- 450 G/1 LB TRADITIONAL DRIED
  APRICOTS, SOAKED OVERNIGHT
- FINELY GRATED RIND OF
  1 LARGE ORANGE
- 4 EGGS, SIZE 2, SEPARATED
- 115 G/4 OZ DEMERARA SUGAR
- ICING SUGAR, FOR SIFTING

- **FILLING:**
- 115 ML/4 FL OZ STRAINED
  GREEK YOGURT
- 115 ML/4 FL OZ DOUBLE CREAM,
  LIGHTLY WHIPPED

Use the tin as a guide to cut a
paper piece, larger all round

1 Simmer the apricots in their soaking liquor with the orange rind until tender, increasing the heat towards the end of the cooking to drive off excess moisture.

2 Set the oven to 180°C/350°F/Gas 4. Line a 30 × 35 cm/12 × 14 inch Swiss roll tin with non-stick silicone paper.

Fold the edges up around the
tin, then fit snugly inside

3 Drain and reserve the last drops of juice from the apricots, then purée them with the orange rind. Add 3 tablespoons of the purée to the juice and put this to one side for the filling.

4 Whisk the egg yolks with half the sugar until thick and pale.

5 In a clean, dry bowl, whisk the egg whites until soft peaks form, then gradually whisk in the remaining sugar, whisking well after each addition, until the mixture is stiff and shiny. Using a large metal spoon, very gently fold into the egg yolk mixture in four batches, adding the apricot purée at the same time. Spoon evenly into the tin and bake for 20–25 minutes until well risen and pale golden brown.

6 Lay a sheet of non-stick silicone paper over the roulade and cover that with a damp tea towel. Leave to cool.

7 To make the filling, beat the yogurt, then stir in the reserved apricot purée and juice. Lightly fold in the double cream.

8 To finish the cake, sift icing sugar over a sheet of non-stick silicone paper, then invert the roulade onto it. Carefully peel away the lining paper, tearing it in strips to avoid tearing the cake. Spread the cream mixture over the roulade, then roll it up lengthways. Carefully transfer to a serving dish and sift over more icing sugar.

Peeling chestnuts:

Peel off the thick outer skin

*Peel and scrape off the thin,
inner skin*

CHESTNUT COMPOTE
WITH COFFEE SAUCE

SERVES 4–6

*Fresh chestnuts are set off by the rich, dark,
coffee-flavoured sauce to make a wonderful pudding.
Do not spoil the effect by using canned or reconstituted nuts. I
always buy bagfuls of fresh nuts around Christmas and freeze them,
both in and out of their shells, so that I will be able to make recipes
such as this during at least some of the rest of the year.
Peeling chestnuts can be a little fiddly, but if you do it while the
nuts are hot or warm, the shell and skin should be quite easy
to remove. It is a good idea to have a few spare nuts to hand in case
some are bad, although I have not found this a problem with
chestnuts sold by supermarkets.*

- APPROXIMATELY 32 CHESTNUTS
  (PLUS A FEW EXTRA AS
  A PRECAUTION)
- 55 G/2 OZ SUGAR
- 300 ML/10 FL OZ WATER
- 1 VANILLA POD

- **COFFEE SAUCE:**
- 3 EGG YOLKS
- 3 TBSP VANILLA CASTER SUGAR,
  TO TASTE
- 100 ML/3½ FL OZ STRONG BLACK
  COFFEE, PREFERABLY ESPRESSO

1 Cut a cross through the outer skin of the rounded side of each chestnut, then place in a saucepan of boiling water. Leave for about 2–3 minutes. Remove the pan from the heat, remove some of the nuts and peel off both the outer shell and the inner skin. Repeat until all the nuts have been peeled. If any nuts cool before they are peeled, return them to the hot water to warm again.

2 Gently heat the sugar in the water, stirring with a wooden spoon, until the sugar has dissolved. Bring to the boil, add the vanilla pod and the chestnuts and simmer for about 30 minutes until tender. Leave to cool in the liquid, then divide between 4 small serving dishes or glasses.

3 To make the sauce, place the egg yolks, sugar and coffee in a heatproof bowl, place over a saucepan of hot water and whisk until foamy and almost thick enough to support a trail of the mixture. Remove from the heat and continue to whisk for about 1 minute. Transfer to a warmed serving bowl.

Illustrated opposite page 305

$\mathcal{B}$LUEBERRY CLOUD

SERVES 4

The covering for the plump blue-black berries has just the right combination of lightness and creaminess that you neither feel as if you are eating mouthfuls of nothing, nor as if you are eating something so rich you might regret it. Cultivated blueberries are imported from North America both fresh and frozen; they freeze well, so if you are unable to find fresh berries, look in the freezer cabinet. Blueberries are also cultivated in Britain on a small scale.

- 350–450 G/12 OZ–1 LB BLUEBERRIES
- 225 ML/8 FL OZ SOURED CREAM
- 70 G/2½ OZ CASTER SUGAR
- 175 G/6 OZ CREAM CHEESE

- 2 EGGS, SIZE 2, SEPARATED
- FEW DROPS ALMOND ESSENCE
- 1 EGG WHITE
- 2 TBSP FLAKED ALMONDS
- 2 TBSP ICING SUGAR

1 Set the oven to 190°C/375°F/Gas 5. Butter a 1.2 litre/2 pint ovenproof dish and put the blueberries in the bottom.

2 Stir the soured cream and half the sugar into the cream cheese, then beat until light and fluffy. Beat in the egg yolks and a few drops of almond essence to make a thick, light mixture.

3 In a clean bowl, whisk the egg whites until soft peaks form, then gradually whisk in the remaining sugar, whisking well after each addition, until the mixture is stiff and shiny. Using a large metal spoon, gently fold into the cream cheese mixture, then pour over the blackberries.

4 Bake for about 35–40 minutes until risen and lightly set in the centre. Preheat the grill on the highest setting.

5 Sprinkle flaked almonds and icing sugar over the top of the pudding and place under the hot grill until golden. Leave to cool and serve at room temperature.

*Divide the caramel between
the dishes and immediately
swirl it around to coat the
base and sides*

$\mathscr{T}$ANGY

ORANGE CARAMELS

SERVES 4

*The bitter taste of the caramel topping both contrasts with and
complements the tang and texture of the smooth orange custard.
Whether you squeeze the oranges yourself, or buy freshly-squeezed
juice from a supermarket, really well-flavoured juice will make
all the difference.*

- GRATED RIND OF 1 ORANGE
- 300 ML/10 FL OZ ORANGE JUICE
- 3 WHOLE EGGS
- 3 EGG YOLKS
- 2 TBSP CASTER SUGAR

- **CARAMEL:**
- 115 G/4 OZ CASTER SUGAR
- 1 TBSP WATER

1 Add the orange rind to the orange juice and leave to soak.

2 Set the oven to 180°C/350°F/Gas 4. Warm 4 ramekin dishes.

3 To make the caramel, in a small, heavy-based saucepan, gently heat the sugar in the water, swirling the pan, until the sugar has dissolved, then cook until golden brown. Immediately pour a quarter into each dish and swirl them around so that the caramel coats the sides and base. Place in a baking tin.

4 Gently heat the orange juice and orange rind until just below simmering point.

5 Meanwhile, whisk the whole eggs and egg yolks with the sugar until thick, then slowly pour in the orange juice, whisking constantly. Divide between the dishes, then pour boiling water around them. Cover the dishes with greaseproof paper and cook for about 25 minutes until lightly set.

6 Remove the dishes from the baking tin and leave until cold.

7 Unmould the puddings just before serving. To do this, place a plate over each dish, hold the plate and dish firmly together, invert them and give a sharp shake. Carefully lift off the dish.

$\mathcal{C}$HOCOLATE
TRUFFLE LOAF

SERVES 6–8

*This is very rich — ambrosia for chocoholics, and very good for
many other people as well. As it contains protein, vitamins A,
B_1 (thiamine), B_2 (riboflavin), B_3 (niacin), D, E and K, iron and
calcium, this pudding could also be construed as quite nutritious!
If you would like to 'dilute' the richness, line the terrine, tin or
basin with sponge cake before filling with the chocolate mixture.*

- 300 ML/10 FL OZ WHIPPING OR DOUBLE CREAM
- 1 VANILLA POD
- 300 G/10 OZ PLAIN CHOCOLATE, CHOPPED
- 1 TBSP INSTANT COFFEE GRANULES
- 2 TBSP COGNAC
- 1 TBSP WATER
- 55 G/2 OZ UNSALTED BUTTER, CHOPPED
- 4 EGG YOLKS, SIZE 2
- **DECORATION:**
- COCOA POWDER, FOR SIFTING
- WHIPPED CREAM
- GRATED PLAIN CHOCOLATE
- **TO SERVE:**
- COLD CUSTARD (SEE PAGE 353) OR SINGLE CREAM

1 Slowly heat the cream and vanilla pod to just on simmering point, cover, remove
from the heat and leave until cold.

2 Place the chocolate, coffee granules, Cognac and the water in a heatproof bowl
placed over a saucepan of hot water and leave, stirring occasionally, until melted and
smooth. Remove the bowl from the heat and leave to cool slightly.

3 Beat the butter and egg yolks together until pale and fluffy, then, using a large,
metal spoon, gently fold in the chocolate mixture.

4 Strain the cream and whip until soft peaks form. Using a large metal spoon,
gently fold into the chocolate mixture.

5 Line a 850 ml–1.2 litre/1½–2 pint terrine, loaf tin or freezer-proof basin with
cling film. Spoon in the chocolate mixture, smooth the surface and place in the
freezer for about 2 hours until firm but not frozen.

6 Unmould the pudding, carefully remove the cling film, sift over cocoa powder
and decorate with whipped cream and grated plain chocolate. Serve with cold
Custard or single cream.

Illustrated opposite page 177

FORGOTTEN
LEMON HEAVEN

SERVES 6

*I acquired this recipe when I was at college in the mid-sixties and
it was so popular that it became the standard pudding for special
occasions when I was sharing a flat in London, at home in the
country and when I was first married. Then, as I entertained more,
I moved on to other recipes and forgot about this one, until recently.
Suddenly, I thought about the wonderful lemon flavour, the smooth
texture and how it tasted so very special without being too rich.
I could not remember, though, having seen the distinctive card
in the kitchen for years. But within about 1 minute, to my extreme
surprise, I came across it. I did not doubt that the reality would be as
good as the memory. And I was right. As the first spoonful melted
in my mouth, a whole host of memories flooded back.*

- 4 TBSP WATER
- 3 TSP POWDERED
GELATINE
- FINELY GRATED RIND AND
JUICE OF 2 LEMONS
- 3 EGGS, SEPARATED
- 115 G/4 OZ CASTER SUGAR
- 150 ML/5 FL OZ SINGLE CREAM
- 350 G/12 OZ COTTAGE
CHEESE, SIEVED

- 150 ML/5 FL OZ DOUBLE CREAM,
LIGHTLY WHIPPED
- **CRUST:**
- 8 DIGESTIVE BISCUITS,
CRUSHED
- 25 G/1 OZ DEMERARA SUGAR
- 55 G/2 OZ UNSALTED
BUTTER, MELTED
- **DECORATION:**
- CRYSTALLIZED LEMON SLICES

1 Lightly brush the sides and bottom of a 20 cm/8 inch loose-based springform cake tin with a flavourless vegetable oil.

2 To make the crust, mix the ingredients together, then spoon evenly over the base of the tin and press down lightly.

3 Place the water into a small heatproof bowl, sprinkle the gelatine over the top and leave for about 5 minutes until the gelatine becomes spongy.

4 Meanwhile, place the lemon rind, egg yolks and sugar in a mixing bowl and whisk together until pale and thick enough to support a trail of mixture when the beaters are lifted.

5 When the gelatine has become spongy, place the bowl over a saucepan of hot water and leave until the gelatine has melted, stirring occasionally. Remove the bowl from the heat and allow to cool slightly.

6 Stir a little of the single cream into the gelatine, then stir in the remaining single cream.

7 Put the cottage cheese into a bowl and stir in the single cream and lemon juice. Using a large metal spoon, lightly fold into the egg yolk mixture and leave until thick but not quite set.

8 In a clean, dry bowl, whisk the egg whites until stiff but not dry, then, using a large metal spoon, lightly fold into the egg yolk mixture in four batches, including all but 2 tablespoons of the double cream at the same time. Pour into the tin and place in the refrigerator until set.

9 Remove the sides of the tin, then, using a fish slice, carefully lift and slide the pudding onto a cold plate. Decorate with the remaining double cream and crystallized lemon slices.

Illustrated opposite page 320

ℬLACKCURRANT AND MINT MOUSSE

*A pudding that speaks loudly of summer. Blackcurrants have a
wonderful, intense, fresh-fruity flavour. Even if you do not have
a garden, mints are one of the easiest herbs to grow, in pots if
necessary, and it is worth having a selection of different flavoured
mints, such as applemint and spearmint, as each has its own
variation of the basic mint flavour. For this recipe, I chose
applemint, because it combines so well with blackcurrants.*

- 450 G/1 LB BLACKCURRANTS
- JUICE OF 1 LEMON
- 85 G/3 OZ CASTER SUGAR
- LEAVES FROM A SMALL BUNCH OF APPLEMINT
- 2 TBSP WATER
- 1 TBSP POWDERED GELATINE
- 2 EGG WHITES, SIZE 2

- 300 ML/10 FL OZ DOUBLE CREAM, WHIPPED
- 150 ML/5 FL OZ STRAINED GREEK YOGURT
- **DECORATION:**
- WHIPPED CREAM AND MINT LEAVES

1 Gently cook the blackcurrants in a covered saucepan, shaking the pan occasionally, until the juices run. Leave to cool slightly, then pour the fruit and all the juice into a food processor or blender and add the lemon juice, sugar and mint. Mix until smooth. Pour into a bowl.

2 Put the water into a small heatproof bowl, sprinkle over the gelatine and leave for about 5 minutes to soften. Set the bowl over a saucepan of hot water, stirring occasionally, until the gelatine has dissolved. Remove the bowl from the saucepan and leave to cool slightly before stirring in a little of the blackcurrant mixture, then whisk this into the remaining blackcurrant mixture. Leave until just beginning to set.

3 In a clean, dry bowl, whisk the egg whites until stiff but not dry. Whisk the blackcurrant mixture and whisk together the cream and yogurt. Using a large metal spoon, gently fold the cream mixture into the blackcurrant mixture, followed by the egg whites. Spoon into glasses or a serving dish and leave in the refrigerator for 1–2 hours to set.

4 Decorate with whipped cream, if liked, and mint leaves.

Illustrated opposite page 304

CREAM CHEESE CAKE
WITH PINE NUTS
AND RASPBERRY SAUCE

SERVES 8

The raspberry sauce provides a suitably elegant and fresh
complement to this luxurious yet simple cake. The whole pudding
is also extremely easy to make and can be made a day in advance,
although the cake is better if kept in a cool room rather than in
the refrigerator. If you do not have a sufficiently cool room and
have to refrigerate the cake, be sure to cover it, place it on the lowest
shelf of the refrigerator, and allow it to come to room temperature
before serving.

- 55 G/2 OZ UNSALTED BUTTER, SOFTENED
- 200 G/7 OZ VANILLA CASTER SUGAR
- 2 TBSP ACACIA HONEY
- 450 G/1 LB CREAM CHEESE, SIEVED
- 5 EGGS, SEPARATED
- 115 ML/4 FL OZ SINGLE CREAM
- 55 G/2 OZ PLAIN FLOUR
- 115 G/4 OZ PINE NUTS, CHOPPED
- **RASPBERRY SAUCE:**
- VANILLA ICING SUGAR, FOR SIFTING
- 700 G/1 ½ LB FRESH OR FROZEN RASPBERRIES
- ICING SUGAR AND LEMON JUICE, TO TASTE

1 Set the oven to 160°C/325°F/Gas 3. Butter a 20–22.5 cm/8–9 inch springform cake tin or loose-based cake tin.

2 Beat the butter and half the sugar together until light and airy, then beat in the honey followed by the cream cheese and egg yolks and lastly the cream. Using a large metal spoon, gently fold in the flour.

3 In a clean, dry bowl, whisk the egg whites until soft peaks form, then gradually whisk in the remaining sugar, whisking well after each addition, until the mixture is stiff and shiny. Using the metal spoon, gently fold one quarter into the cheese mixture. Fold in the remaining egg whites in three batches, adding the nuts with the last batch. Turn into the cake tin and bake for about 1 hour.

4 Leave the cake to cool in the oven with the heat turned off to prevent the cake cracking as it cools.

5 To make the sauce, Sieve the raspberries through a non-metallic sieve and add icing sugar and lemon juice to taste. Chill lightly.

6 Sift icing sugar generously over the cake and serve with the sauce.

Illustrated opposite page 305

*Place weights on the saucer
and leave to drain*

$\mathcal{P}$ ASKHA

SERVES 8

*Traditionally, Paskha is eaten by Russians at Easter and it is made
in a wooden mould shaped rather like a truncated metronome; a
clay flowerpot, even a sieve, lined with muslin can be used instead.
It will be easier to serve if you use a knife that has been dipped in
hot water. Paskha is usually served on its own, but I like to serve it
with a sauce made from sieved raspberries, strawberries or
loganberries, sweetened to taste.*

- 55 G/2 OZ CANDIED PEEL,
  CHOPPED
- 55 G/2 OZ CANDIED
  FRUITS, CHOPPED
- 55 G/2 OZ SULTANAS
- 3 TBSP WHITE RUM
- 115 G/4 OZ UNSALTED
  BUTTER, CHOPPED
- 85 G/3 OZ CASTER SUGAR
- 2 EGG YOLKS, SIZE 2
- 55 G/2 OZ BLANCHED ALMONDS,
  TOASTED AND CHOPPED

- FINELY GRATED RIND AND JUICE
  OF 1 LEMON
- FINELY GRATED RIND
  OF 1 ORANGE
- 150 ML/5 FL OZ SOURED CREAM
- 700 G/1 ½ LB RICOTTA OR
  CURD CHEESE, SIEVED
- **DECORATION:**
- WHOLE, BLANCHED ALMONDS
- CRYSTALLIZED VIOLETS

1 Soak the peel, candied fruits and sultanas in the rum overnight.

2 Wring out a piece of muslin in cold water, then use to line a conical mould, sieve or thoroughly cleaned or new flowerpot or plastic pot.

3 Beat together the butter and sugar until light and fluffy. Beat in the egg yolks, then mix in the chopped almonds, lemon rind and juice, orange rind, rum-soaked peel, candied fruits and sultanas. Using a tablespoon, fold in the soured cream and sieved cheese.

4 Stand the mould or pot on a large saucer and fill with the cheese mixture. Place a small saucer on the cheese mixture and put a weight on it. Place in the refrigerator and leave for at least 12 hours or up to 3 days.

5 Turn out onto a cold plate and carefully remove the muslin. Decorate with almonds and crystallized violets. Serve cut into thin slices.

Illustrated opposite page 288

CHOCOLATE MOUSSE CAKE

SERVES 6–8

I have many recipes for chocolate cake and I have chosen this one for this section on puddings because, unlike most, it has neither the filling nor the icing, which make more of a gâteau-type cake than a pudding. This one doesn't need embellishments and has a wonderful soft, moist centre that is like a fudgy chocolate mousse.

A raspberry sauce, made by sieving fresh or thawed frozen raspberries and sweetened to taste, does go very well with it, though.

The finely grated rind of 2 small oranges, or 1–2 tablespoons brandy, whisky or rum, or about 1 ½ tablespoons coffee granules, or about 3 tablespoons crème de menthe *or coffee liqueur can be added to flavour the cake.*

- COCOA POWDER, FOR SPRINKLING
- 175 G/6 OZ PLAIN CHOCOLATE, CHOPPED
- 175 G/6 OZ UNSALTED BUTTER, DICED

- 175 G/6 OZ CASTER SUGAR
- 5 EGGS, SIZE 2, SEPARATED
- FEW DROPS VANILLA ESSENCE
- 55 G/2 OZ PLAIN FLOUR
- 85 G/3 OZ GROUND HAZELNUTS OR WALNUTS

1 Set the oven to 180°C/350°F/Gas 4. Butter a 20 cm/8 inch round cake tin and sprinkle the inside with cocoa powder.

2 Place the chocolate in a heatproof mixing bowl placed over a saucepan of hot, but not boiling, water and leave until melted. Slowly stir in the butter until evenly combined, then remove the bowl from the heat and stir in half of the sugar. Allow to cool slightly, then gradually beat in the egg yolks and vanilla essence. Stir in the flour and ground hazelnuts or walnuts.

3 In a separate clean, dry bowl, whisk the egg whites until soft peaks form, then gradually whisk in the remaining sugar, whisking well after each addition, until the mixture is stiff and shiny. Using a large metal spoon, gently fold into the chocolate mixture in batches. Spoon into the cake tin and bake for about 40 minutes; the cake should be moist in the middle.

4 Leave the cake to cool in the tin for about 10 minutes before turning onto a wire rack to cool completely.

ℋONEYCOMBE MOULD

SERVES 4

*A clean, fresh-tasting nursery pudding that, despite its simplicity,
makes a wonderful, surprisingly special ending to a meal,
especially in summer.*

- 2 TBSP COLD WATER
- 15 G/½ OZ POWDERED
  GELATINE
- 2 EGGS, SIZE 2, SEPARATED
- 85 G/3 OZ CASTER SUGAR

- 425 ML/15 FL OZ CREAMY MILK
- 85 ML/3 FL OZ SINGLE CREAM
- FINELY GRATED RIND OF
  1 SMALL LEMON
- 4 TBSP LEMON JUICE

1 Chill a 1.2 litre/2 pint jelly mould or 4 individual moulds.

2 Put the water into a small heatproof bowl, sprinkle over the gelatine and leave for
about 5 minutes to soften. Place the bowl over a saucepan of hot water, stirring
occasionally, until the gelatine has dissolved.

3 Meanwhile, beat the egg yolks and sugar together until thick and pale. Bring the
milk and cream to the boil in a heavy-based saucepan, then stir into the egg yolk
mixture. Return to the saucepan and heat very gently, stirring with a wooden spoon,
until thickened. Remove from the heat and stir in the lemon rind and juice.

4 As soon as the gelatine has dissolved, remove the bowl from the heat. Stir a couple
of spoonfuls of the hot lemon custard into the gelatine, then stir this mixture into
the saucepan.

5 In a clean, dry bowl, whisk the egg whites until stiff but not dry. Using a large
metal spoon, gently fold into the hot custard.

6 Rinse the mould or moulds with cold water, drain well, then pour in the custard.
Leave in a cool place to set.

RIGHT (from top to
bottom): Snow Eggs on a
Caramel Lake (see page
332); Voluptuous
Chestnut, Chocolate and
Rum Cake (see page 346);
Forgotten Lemon Heaven
(see page 314).

$\mathcal{B}$ANANA
BUTTERSCOTCH SUNDAE

SERVES 4

An unashamedly childish creation that everybody loves.

- 2 RIPE BANANAS
- LEMON JUICE
- VANILLA DAIRY ICE CREAM
- APPROXIMATELY 4 TBSP
  CHOPPED PEANUTS OR WALNUTS
- GRATED PLAIN CHOCOLATE OR
  CHOCOLATE CHIPS (OPTIONAL)
- BRANDY SNAPS,
  CRUSHED (OPTIONAL)

- **BUTTERSCOTCH SAUCE:**
- 115 ML/4 FL OZ EVAPORATED
  MILK
- 55 G/2 OZ UNSALTED BUTTER
- 85 G/3 OZ DARK
  MUSCOVADO SUGAR
- 3 TBSP GOLDEN SYRUP
- 1 TBSP WATER
- SQUEEZE OF LEMON JUICE

1 To make the sauce, put the evaporated milk in a heatproof bowl. In a saucepan, gently heat together the butter, sugar and syrup until well blended, stir in the water and bring to the boil. After a few seconds, remove from the heat and gradually beat into the evaporated milk. Return to the heat and heat through gently to make a smooth sauce. Cool slightly, then add a squeeze of lemon juice.

2 Peel and slice the bananas and toss with lemon juice. Pile scoops of vanilla dairy ice cream and slices of banana into glasses, sprinkling with as many nuts, and chocolate and brandy snaps, if liked, as you want. Pour the sauce over the top and sprinkle with more nuts, and brandy snaps and chocolate, if liked. Eat immediately.

Illustrated opposite page 289

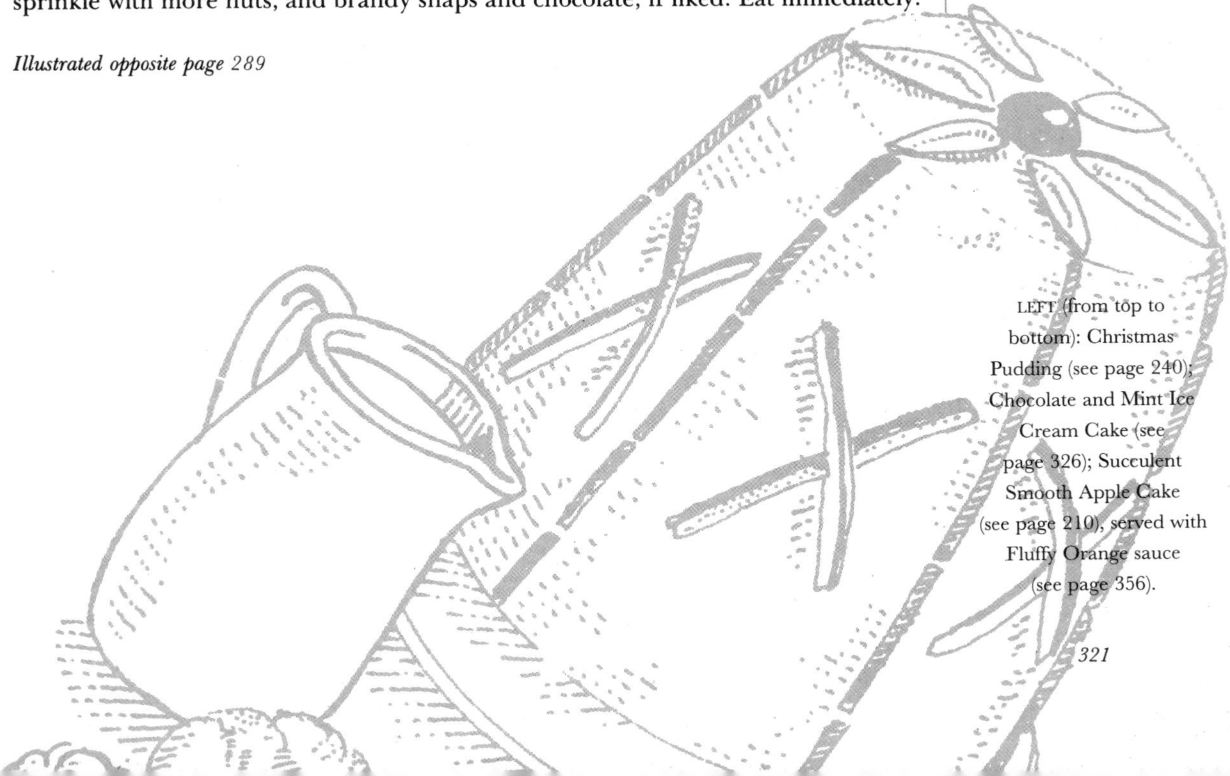

LEFT (from top to bottom): Christmas Pudding (see page 240); Chocolate and Mint Ice Cream Cake (see page 326); Succulent Smooth Apple Cake (see page 210), served with Fluffy Orange sauce (see page 356).

Sensuous, Silky
Saffron Creams

SERVES 4

*I can still remember the heady, exotic perfume that wafted
sensuously from a 1 kg/2 lb tin of saffron as it was opened in front
of me, even though it happened about seven years ago.
It was far superior to any perfume man has produced, no matter
how expensive. Saffron is costly, but the flavour and aroma are
so intense that only a small amount is needed for 4–6 people,
so the cost is not too high. Do not be tempted to buy a product that
purports to be saffron if it seems cheap, as counterfeits are far too
common; saffron threads are less likely to be adulterated
than powders.*

- SCANT ¼ TSP SAFFRON THREADS
- 4 EGG YOLKS
- 55 G/2 OZ LIGHT-FLAVOURED CLEAR HONEY

- 425 ML/15 FL OZ SINGLE CREAM

1 Set the oven to 140°C/275°F/Gas 1. Place 4 ramekin dishes or heatproof moulds in a baking tin.

2 Heat the saffron threads in a dry frying pan for 2–3 minutes, then crush them and put them into a medium-sized bowl and stir in the egg yolks and honey.

3 Heat the cream to just on simmering point, then stir into the egg yolk mixture. Return to the saucepan and heat very gently, stirring with a wooden spoon until thickened; do not allow to boil.

4 Pour into the ramekin dishes or moulds, pour boiling water around and place in the oven for 45 minutes to 1 hour until just set.

5 Remove the dishes or moulds from the baking tin and serve warm or cold.

$\mathscr{T}$RADITIONAL
MANOR HOUSE TRIFLE

SERVES 6–8

*Warning: with a syllabub on a blanket of custard laid over wine
and brandy-soaked fresh fruit and macaroons, this is one of the
most luxurious trifles there is and makes an ideal ending to a
special meal. Instead of using 5 egg yolks for the custard,
you could use 2 egg yolks and 2 whole eggs.*

- 6 LARGE MACAROONS
- 350 G/12 OZ PREPARED FRESH
  FRUIT, SUCH AS STRAWBERRIES,
  RASPBERRIES, PEACHES
  AND NECTARINES
- 150 ML/5 FL OZ DESSERT WINE
  SUCH AS BEAUMES-DE-VENISE
- 3½ TBSP BRANDY
- 425 ML/15 FL OZ SINGLE CREAM
  OR MILK

- 1 VANILLA POD
- 5 EGG YOLKS, SIZE 2
- 70 G/2½ OZ CASTER SUGAR
- FINELY GRATED RIND AND
  JUICE OF 1 LEMON
- 300 ML/10 FL OZ DOUBLE CREAM
- **DECORATION:**
- TOASTED FLAKED ALMONDS
  AND CRYSTALLIZED FRUITS

1 Put the macaroons into the base of a glass serving dish, cover with the fruit, then pour over 4 tablespoons of the wine and 2 tablespoons of brandy and leave to soak.

2 Make a custard (see page 353) with the cream or milk, vanilla pod, egg yolks and 2 tablespoons of the sugar. Allow to cool slightly, stirring occasionally, then pour over the fruit and leave to cool completely.

3 In a bowl, stir together the remaining wine, brandy and sugar and the lemon rind and juice until the sugar has dissolved. Gradually stir in the cream, then whisk until the cream holds its shape.

4 Spoon onto the custard and decorate with flaked almonds and crystallized fruits.

Illustrated opposite page 304

*E*ASY
CHOCOLATE MOUSSE

SERVES 4–6

*I have been making this recipe for almost thirty years and although
I have tasted innumerable other easy chocolate mousses, none scores
more highly than this one: the ingredients are few and
straightforward, it is easy and quick to make, and, most important
of all, it is delicious to eat, with a deep, intense chocolate flavour,
which a little coffee can enhance, and not at all sweet. If you really
want to go to town, add a couple of tablespoons of brandy or
a coffee or orange liqueur when stirring in the egg yolks
and vanilla essence.*

- 225 G/8 OZ GOOD PLAIN
  CHOCOLATE, CHOPPED
- 25 G/1 OZ UNSALTED BUTTER
- 1–2 TSP INSTANT COFFEE
  GRANULES (OPTIONAL)

- 4 EGGS, SEPARATED
- FEW DROPS VANILLA ESSENCE

1 Place the chocolate, butter and coffee, if using, in a heatproof bowl and place over a saucepan of hot water. Leave to melt, stirring occasionally, until smooth.

2 Remove the bowl from the pan and stir in the egg yolks and vanilla essence.

3 In a clean, dry bowl, whisk the egg whites until stiff but not dry. Using a large metal spoon, gently fold a quarter of the egg whites into the chocolate, then add the remaining egg whites in three batches. When just evenly combined, spoon into cold serving dishes. Place in the refrigerator for 30 to 60 minutes.

$\mathcal{T}$ANGY LIME SPONGE AND PARFAIT

SERVES 4–6

This is a moist, tangy, fragrant, cake-type pudding.
For special occasions, I decorate the parfait with glazed lime rind
(for method, see page 236) and serve the pudding with poached lime
segments (for method, see page 296).

- 2 SMALL LIMES
- 3 EGGS
- 150 G/5 OZ CASTER SUGAR
- SEEDS FROM 10 CARDAMOM
  PODS, LIGHTLY TOASTED AND
  FINELY CRUSHED
- 55 G/2 OZ UNSALTED BUTTER,
  MELTED AND COOLED
- 125 G/4½ OZ PLAIN FLOUR

- 1 TSP BAKING POWDER
- **LIME PARFAIT:**
- 2 EGG WHITES, SIZE 2
- 115 G/4 OZ CASTER SUGAR
- 4½ TBSP LIME JUICE
- 175 ML/6 FL OZ DOUBLE OR
  WHIPPING CREAM,
  LIGHTLY WHIPPED

1 To make the parfait, in a bowl, whisk the egg whites until soft peaks form. In a small saucepan, gently heat the sugar in the lime juice until dissolved. Increase the heat, bring to the boil and boil for 3 minutes. Slowly pour the mixture into the egg whites, whisking constantly. Using a large metal spoon, gently fold in the cream. Transfer to a shallow metal container and freeze for 3 hours. Transfer to the refrigerator about 20 minutes before serving.

2 Set the oven to just below 180°C/350°F/Gas 4. Well-butter a 15 cm/6 inch soufflé dish.

3 Peel the limes. Chop the pith and skin and simmer, just covered by water, in a small covered saucepan for about 35 minutes until tender. Increase the heat towards the end of the cooking time to evaporate off excess water.

4 Meanwhile, in a bowl placed over a saucepan of hot water, whisk the eggs and sugar together until very thick.

5 In a blender or food processor, purée the lime flesh with the cardamom seeds, then mix in the peel and pith and the butter. Slowly pour into the egg mixture, folding in gently with a large metal spoon. Sift the flour and baking powder over the top, then fold in lightly, using the metal spoon.

6 As soon as the ingredients are just evenly mixed, turn into the dish and bake for about 35–40 minutes, until a skewer inserted in the centre comes out clean.

7 Turn onto a wire rack to cool. Serve with scoops of parfait.

$\mathcal{C}$HOCOLATE AND MINT
ICE CREAM CAKE

SERVES 6-8

*My birthday is in July and when I was young my birthday cake was
always an ice cream one, and ever since I have had a soft spot for
ice cream cakes. For me, an ice cream cake should include a proper
cake, not just layers of different-flavoured ice creams, as there is
something magical about the combination of cake and ice cream.
This is one of my favourites, as it is suitable for any time of year
and appeals to a wide range of tastes.*

- **CHOCOLATE CAKE:**
- 200 G/7 OZ DARK SWEETENED CHOCOLATE, CHOPPED
- 5 TBSP WATER
- 5 EGGS, SEPARATED
- 150 G/5 OZ VANILLA CASTER SUGAR
- **PEPPERMINT ICE CREAM:**
- 175 G/6 OZ CASTER SUGAR
- 300 ML/10 FL OZ WATER
- JUICE OF 1 LEMON
- 2 TBSP FINELY CHOPPED MINT, PREFERABLY PEPPERMINT
- APPROXIMATELY 6 DROPS PEPPERMINT ESSENCE

- 425 ML/15 FL OZ DOUBLE CREAM, WHIPPED
- 100 G/3½ OZ PLAIN CHOCOLATE CHIPS
- **CHOCOLATE ICING:**
- 175 G/6 OZ PLAIN CHOCOLATE, CHOPPED
- 25 G/1 OZ UNSALTED BUTTER
- 1 TBSP WATER
- **DECORATION:**
- WHIPPED CREAM (OPTIONAL)
- FRESH MINT SPRIGS (OPTIONAL)
- **TO SERVE:**
- CHOCOLATE MINT SAUCE (SEE PAGE 356)

1 To make the peppermint ice cream, gently heat the sugar in the water in a heavy-based saucepan, stirring with a wooden spoon, until the sugar has dissolved, then bring to the boil and boil rapidly for a couple of minutes. Leave to cool, then pour into a shallow metal container and freeze for about 1½ hours until mushy. Tip into a cold bowl and fold in the lemon juice, mint leaves, peppermint essence, cream and chocolate chips. Taste and adjust the level of peppermint, if necessary. Spoon into a freezer-proof container, cover and freeze.

2 To make the chocolate cake, set the oven to 180°C/350°F/Gas 4. Butter two 20 cm/8 inch sandwich tins, line the base of each with greaseproof paper, then butter the paper.

3 Put the chocolate and the water into a heatproof bowl placed over a saucepan of hot water. Leave to melt, stirring occasionally, until smooth. Remove the bowl from the pan and leave the chocolate to cool slightly.

4 Meanwhile, in a separate bowl, whisk the egg yolks and half of the sugar together until very thick and pale.

5 In a clean, dry bowl, whisk the egg whites until soft peaks form, then gradually whisk in the remaining sugar, whisking well after each addition, until the mixture is stiff and shiny. Using a large metal spoon, gently fold the chocolate into the egg yolk mixture, then fold in the egg whites in four batches. Divide between the cake tins and bake for about 15–18 minutes until springy to a light touch in the centre.

6 Allow to stand for a few minutes (do not worry if they sink slightly), then turn onto a wire rack and carefully peel off the lining.

7 To assemble the cake, leave the ice cream at room temperature for about 20 minutes to soften slightly while making the icing. Put the chocolate and butter for the icing with the water into a heatproof bowl placed over a saucepan of hot water and leave to melt, stirring occasionally. Spread the ice cream over one of the chocolate cakes, then place the other cake on top and press lightly together. Quickly spread the icing over the top and sides and return to the freezer for 30 minutes to 1 hour. Decorate the top of the cake with spoonfuls of whipped cream placed in a circle with a sprig of mint in each, if liked, and serve the cake in slices with the Chocolate Mint Sauce poured over or around.

Illustrated opposite page 321

ROSE OR DAMASK

CREAMS

SERVES 4

Yet another name for this old-fashioned pudding is 'Devonshire junket', but I feared some people might not look at the recipe if it bore that title. This light, delicate, subtly-flavoured dessert makes a perfect ending to a summer meal, or a heavy one, and I urge anyone who is doubtful to try it. Chemists as well as food shops sometime sell rennet essence; on no account use junket mix.

- 550 ML/1 PINT SINGLE CREAM
- 3 TBSP CASTER SUGAR
- 2 TSP RENNET ESSENCE
- 1 TBSP BRANDY

- 4 TBSP DOUBLE CREAM
- 1—2 TSP ROSE WATER
- **DECORATION:**
- ROSE PETALS (OPTIONAL)

1 Very gently heat the cream with 2 tablespoons of the sugar, stirring to dissolve the sugar, until the temperature reaches 36.9°C/98.4°F, or it feels neither hot nor cold when tested by dipping in a clean finger.

2 Stir in the rennet and brandy, then pour into a serving dish. Leave, undisturbed, for 2–3 hours until set.

3 Stir together the remaining sugar, the double cream and rose water to taste. Carefully spoon over the top of the set junket and decorate with rose petals, if liked.

CRUNCHY OATEN HIGHLAND CREAM WITH BERRIES

SERVES 4

I always associate this type of pudding, the ingredients layered in a tall glass, with childhood treats, but I cannot remember ever being given one quite like this when I was a child.

- 55 G/2 OZ UNSALTED BUTTER
- 55 G/2 OZ LIGHT MUSCOVADO SUGAR
- 55 G/2 OZ WALNUT HALVES, CHOPPED
- 25 G/1 OZ JUMBO OATS, TOASTED AND COOLED
- 4 TBSP WHISKY

- 300 ML/10 FL OZ DOUBLE CREAM, WHIPPED
- 350 G/12 OZ FRESH RASPBERRIES OR BLACKBERRIES
- **TO SERVE:**
- LIGHTLY WHIPPED DOUBLE CREAM (OPTIONAL)

1 Oil a baking sheet.

2 Melt the butter, stir in the sugar and heat gently, stirring with a wooden spoon, until the sugar has melted. Stir in the walnuts and oats, and cook until a light golden colour. Tip onto the baking sheet, leave until cold, then roughly crush.

3 Lightly fold the nut mixture and whisky into the cream using a large metal spoon.

4 Reserve a few of the berries for decoration and layer the remainder with the cream mixture in goblets or tall glasses. Cover and chill. Return to room temperture about 30 minutes before serving. Top with extra double cream, if liked. Decorate with the reserved berries.

BROWN SUGAR MERINGUES WITH EGG NOG PARFAIT AND ORANGE COMPOTE

SERVES 4–6

Brown sugar gives the meringues a caramel taste, which takes the edge off their sweetness and forms a very good partnership with the fresh taste of the orange compote and the smooth texture of the parfait. The meringues could more simply be sandwiched together with whipped cream flavoured with Cointreau.

- 4 ORANGES
- APPROXIMATELY 5 MM/¼ IN SLICE FRESH ROOT GINGER, PEELED AND CUT INTO FINE STRIPS
- 2 TBSP WHISKY LIQUEUR
- 115 G/4 OZ CASTER SUGAR
- 150 ML/5 FL OZ WATER
- JUICE OF ½ LEMON
- **EGG NOG PARFAIT:**
- 2 EGG YOLKS, SIZE 3
- 70 G/2½ OZ CASTER SUGAR
- ¼–½ TSP FRESHLY GRATED NUTMEG

- VERY SMALL PINCH OF GROUND CLOVES
- 55 ML/2 FL OZ PALE CREAM SHERRY
- 300 ML/10 FL OZ DOUBLE CREAM, LIGHTLY WHIPPED
- **MERINGUES:**
- 2 EGG WHITES, SIZE 3
- 85 G/3 OZ LIGHT MUSCOVADO SUGAR
- 25 G/1 OZ CASTER SUGAR

1 To make the egg nog parfait, whisk together the egg yolks, sugar, spices and sherry in a medium-sized heatproof bowl placed over a saucepan of hot water until pale and thick enough to support a trail of mixture when the beaters are withdrawn. Remove from the heat and continue to whisk until the mixture is cold. Using a large metal spoon, gently fold in the cream. Spoon into a shallow freezer-proof container, cover, chill, then freeze until firm.

2 To make the compote, cut a slice from each end of each orange then stand one fruit upright on a flat plate, to catch any juice. Then, using a flexible, sharp knife and working around the orange, cut down to remove both the peel and the pith. Repeat with the remaining oranges. Slice the oranges crosswise and put the slices in a serving bowl with any orange juice collected on the plate, the ginger and liqueur.

3 Scrape the pith from the orange peel, then cut the peel into strips. Put the strips into a small saucepan, cover well with water and bring to the boil for a couple of minutes. Drain and repeat the process; this will remove some of the bitterness from the peel. Cover with water again and simmer for 25–30 minutes until just tender. Drain the peel.

4 In a small saucepan, dissolve the sugar in the water. Add the strips of orange peel and simmer for 2–3 minutes until the peel begins to look glazed and candied. Add the lemon juice then pour the strips and syrup over the orange slices. Cover and place in the refrigerator for several hours.

5 To make the meringues, set the oven to 110°C/225°F/Gas ½. Line 1 or 2 baking trays, depending on size, with non-stick baking parchment, or greaseproof paper and brush lightly with flavourless vegetable oil.

6 In a clean, dry bowl, whisk the egg whites until stiff but not dry, then gradually whisk in the sugars, whisking well after each addition, until the mixture is stiff and shiny.

7 Place dessertspoonfuls of the meringue a little distance away from each other on the baking trays and bake for about 2 hours until crisp and dry enough to remove easily from the paper. Carefully remove from the paper and place the meringues on a wire rack.

8 Transfer the egg nog parfait to the refrigerator about 30 minutes before serving. Sandwich the meringues with some of the parfait then serve with the compote. Any remaining parfait can be served separately, or eaten on some other occasion.

Illustrated opposite page 289

*Float spoonfuls of the
meringue on the milk*

*Slowly pour the milk into the
egg yolks, stirring constantly*

$\mathcal{S}$ NOW EGGS ON
A CARAMEL LAKE

SERVES 4

*These meringue 'snowballs' are usually floated on a plain vanilla
custard, but I think the addition of caramel makes a more
interesting combination, which the threads of bitter caramel on
top further enhance.*

- 2 WHOLE EGGS, SIZE 2, SEPARATED
- 55 G/2 OZ VANILLA CASTER SUGAR
- 450 ML/6 FL OZ MILK OR A MIXTURE OF MILK AND CREAM

- 115 G/4 OZ CASTER OR GRANULATED SUGAR
- 3 EGG YOLKS, SIZE 2
- **CARAMEL:**
- 55 G/2 OZ CASTER OR GRANULATED SUGAR

1 In a clean, dry bowl, whisk the egg whites until soft peaks form, then gradually whisk in the vanilla caster sugar, whisking well after each addition, until the mixture is stiff and shiny.

2 Gently heat the milk to simmering point, then, taking care not to crowd them, float teaspoonfuls or small tablespoonfuls of the meringue, depending on the size you want the 'islands', on the milk. Poach for about 30 seconds to 1 minute on each side. Lift out using a slotted spoon and leave on a tea towel or wire rack to drain. Repeat until all the meringue has been cooked.

3 In a heavy-based saucepan, gently heat the caster or granulated sugar, stirring with a wooden spoon, until the sugar dissolves to a rich golden caramel. Remove from the heat and immediately slowly pour in the milk – take care as it will spit at first. Return the saucepan to a low heat and stir until the caramel dissolves. Remove from the heat.

4 Whisk together all the egg yolks until thick, then slowly stir in the caramel-flavoured milk. Return to the saucepan and heat gently, stirring constantly, until thickened; do not allow to boil. Remove from the heat, pour into a bowl and leave to cool to lukewarm, stirring occasionally to prevent a skin forming. Pour the custard into a shallow serving dish and leave until cold. Float the meringues on top of the custard.

5 To make the caramel, gently heat the sugar until dissolved, then cook until golden brown. Remove from the heat and immediately trickle over the islands; if liked, a little of the caramel can be used to spin a 'veil' over the finished pudding.

Illustrated opposite page 320

$\mathcal{T}$ANGERINE SYLLABUB

SERVES 4

*That syllabubs were made by milking a cow into a bowl of spiced ale
or wine is fairly often mentioned, but the origins of the word
'syllabub', which I think is an unusual one, remain ignored.
The only explanation I have found so far is that it comes from
the old French for Champagne,* sille, *and the Elizabethan slang
for a bubbling drink,* bub; sille *was mixed with frothy cream
to make a 'sille bub'! It sounds plausible, if rather contrived.
No matter how it got its name, this is my favourite syllabub.*

- 700 G/1½ LB TANGERINES
  (ABOUT 6)
- 2 TBSP LEMON JUICE
- 2 TBSP COINTREAU OR
  OTHER ORANGE LIQUEUR
- 55 G/2 OZ LIGHT
  MUSCOVADO SUGAR

- 300 ML/10 FL OZ DOUBLE CREAM
- **DECORATION:**
- TANGERINE ZEST, CUT INTO
  JULIENNE (OPTIONAL)

1 Finely grate the rind from three tangerines into a small bowl; use a stiff brush to
remove all the rind from the teeth of the grater. Peel these three tangerines, divide
into segments, then carefully remove and discard the skin surrounding each
segment. Cover and place in the refrigerator to use for decorating the syllabub.

2 Halve and squeeze the remaining tangerines and pour the juice over the grated
rind. Add the lemon juice and liqueur, then cover and leave for at least 2 hours in a
cool place or in the refrigerator.

3 Stir the sugar into the fruit juices until dissolved, then stir in the cream and whip
until stiff. Spoon into glasses or individual glass dishes and chill for at least 2 hours.
Serve decorated with the tangerine segments, and tangerine zest cut into julienne.

Illustrated opposite page 288

$\mathscr{C}$HEESECAKE

SERVES 8

*After I had recovered from the initial shock of discovering that
cheesecake was not savoury, when I first went to France in the late
Fifties, I have loved cheesecake. As soon as I see a recipe,
I scrutinize it minutely. I tend to favour traditional French-style
baked versions, although I do prefer biscuit-crumb bases to pastry,
providing they are not too sweet or too much in evidence.
This recipe is one of the simplest I have among my vast collection,
and one of the ones I most enjoy. The mixture appears to be a little
soft in the centre at the end of the stated one hour's cooking time,
but it firms up as it cools.*

- 20 G/¾ OZ UNSALTED BUTTER
- 85 G/3 OZ DIGESTIVE BISCUITS, FINELY CRUSHED
- 550 G/1 ¼ LB GOOD CREAM CHEESE, SIEVED
- 150 ML/5 FL OZ SOURED CREAM
- 175 G/6 OZ CASTER SUGAR
- 4 EGGS, SIZE 3, SEPARATED
- GRATED RIND OF 2 ORANGES

- **ORANGE SAUCE (OPTIONAL):**
  - 3 LARGE ORANGES
  - APPROXIMATELY 150 G/5 OZ CASTER SUGAR
  - 2 TBSP WATER
  - JUICE OF ½ LEMON
- **TO FINISH:**
  - ICING SUGAR, GROUND CINNAMON AND FRESHLY GRATED NUTMEG, FOR SIFTING

1 Set the oven to 160°C/325°F/Gas 3. Line the base and sides of a 25 cm/10 inch loose-based or springform cake tin with greaseproof paper.

2 In a small saucepan, gently melt the butter. Remove from the heat and stir in the crushed biscuits. Transfer to the cake tin and press firmly into the base and sides to make an even shell.

3 In a large bowl, beat the cream cheese until smooth, then gradually beat in the soured cream followed by the sugar, egg yolks and orange rind.

4 In a separate, clean, dry bowl, whisk the egg whites until stiff but not dry. Using a large metal spoon, gently fold into the cheese mixture. Spoon into the cake tin and level the surface. Bake for 1 hour. Leave to cool in the tin.

5 To make the sauce, thinly pare the rind from the oranges, taking care not to include any white pith. Cut the rind into fine strips and place in a small saucepan with enough cold water to cover. Bring to the boil, then simmer until soft and slightly transparent. Tip into a non-metallic sieve to drain. In the same saucepan, gently heat the sugar in the water, stirring with a wooden spoon, until dissolved, then stir in the lemon juice, the juice of the oranges and the strips of rind. Simmer for 2 minutes, then pour into a small jug or sauceboat. Leave to cool, then chill lightly.

6 Liberally sift a mixture of icing sugar, cinnamon and ground nutmeg over the cheesecake and serve with the sauce, if liked.

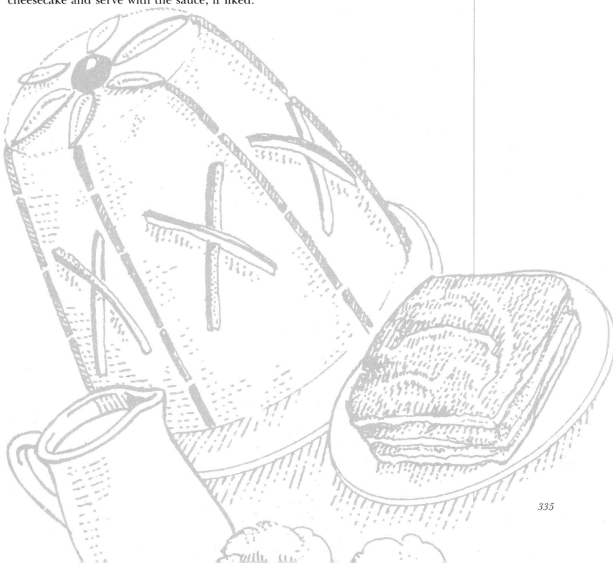

Gooseberry Fool

SERVES 4

*Fools are one of our oldest puddings. They date back to the sixteenth
and seventeenth centuries and belong to the same family as trifles
and whim whams. Fools sometimes combine just fruit and
whipped cream, but for a gooseberry fool, which is one of my
favourites and one of the least often seen, I prefer to make a creamy
custard, as I think the flavour and texture combination is superior;
the consistency is softer and the flavour fresher. In early summer,
try to get a head of elderflowers (but not from roadside bushes)
to add to the gooseberries – they add a magical muscat flavour.*

- 550 G/1 ¼ LB GOOSEBERRIES,
  TOPPED AND TAILED
- 4 TBSP DRY WHITE WINE
  OR WATER
- 2 EGG YOLKS, SIZE 3
- 25 G/1 OZ CASTER SUGAR,
  PLUS EXTRA TO TASTE

- 150 ML/5 FL OZ MILK
- 150 ML/5 FL OZ DOUBLE CREAM,
  WHIPPED
- ORANGE FLOWER WATER
  (OPTIONAL)

1 Gently cook the gooseberries in the wine or water in a covered saucepan until just tender, shaking the pan occasionally. Leave to cool in the liquid, then crush with a fork in the cooking juices; if you prefer a smooth fool, purée both the fruit and the cooking juices, then pass through a non-metallic sieve.

2 Meanwhile, whisk together the egg yolks and 25 g/1 oz sugar in a small, heatproof bowl. Bring the milk to the boil, then slowly stir into the egg mixture. Place the bowl over a saucepan of hot water and cook, stirring with a wooden spoon, until thickened. Remove the bowl from the heat and allow the mixture to cool, stirring occasionally to prevent a skin forming.

3 Gently stir the cooled custard into the gooseberries, then gently fold in the double cream, using a large metal spoon. Add sugar to taste and flavour with orange flower water, if liked. Spoon into 4 tall glasses, cover and chill lightly.

$\mathscr{I}$TALIAN COFFEE CREAM AND WALNUT CAKE

SERVES 6-8

The perennially popular partnership between coffee and walnut
is particularly enjoyable in this recipe, as the cake is light and nutty
with a delicate crumb, and the filling and topping rich and
deeply flavoured with coffee.

- 3 EGGS, SIZE 2, SEPARATED
- 115 G/4 OZ LIGHT MUSCOVADO SUGAR
- 25 G/1 OZ UNSALTED BUTTER, MELTED AND COOLED
- 125 G/4½ OZ WALNUT HALVES, GROUND
- 1 TBSP STRONG COFFEE, PREFERABLY ESPRESSO
- 1 TBSP FINE BREADCRUMBS

- **FILLING AND TOPPING**
- 1 EGG, SIZE 2, SEPARATED
- 25–55 G/1–2 OZ SUGAR
- 250 G/9 OZ MASCARPONE CHEESE
- 1½–2 TBSP STRONG COFFEE, PREFERABLY ESPRESSO
- FEW DROPS VANILLA ESSENCE
- **DECORATION:**
- COFFEE BEANS AND WALNUT HALVES

1 Set the oven to 180°C/350°F/Gas 4. Butter a 17.5 cm/7 inch springform, non-stick cake tin.

2 Whisk the egg yolks and half the sugar together until thick and light. Using a large metal spoon, fold in the butter, walnuts, coffee and breadcrumbs.

3 In a clean, dry bowl, whisk the egg whites until soft peaks form, then gradually whisk in the remaining sugar until stiff. Using a metal spoon, very gently fold into the walnut mixture. Spoon into the tin and bake for about 35 minutes until a fine skewer inserted in the centre comes out clean.

4 Leave to cool in the tin for a few minutes before turning onto a wire rack.

5 To make the filling and topping, whisk the egg yolk with the sugar in a medium-sized bowl until thick and light. Using a large metal spoon, fold in the mascarpone a tablespoonful at a time, then add the coffee and vanilla essence. In a clean, dry bowl, whisk the egg white until stiff, then, using the metal spoon, gently fold into the mascarpone mixture. Cover and place in the refrigerator.

6 About 2 hours before serving the cake, cut in half horizontally using a bread knife and spread about a quarter of the mascarpone mixture over the bottom half. Replace the top and spread the remaining mascarpone mixture over the top and sides. Decorate with coffee beans and walnut halves and keep in a cool place until required.

Illustrated opposite page 289

$\mathscr{T}$RADITIONAL WHITE BLANCMANGE WITH RED BERRIES

*The earliest known blancmanges were made in medieval times:
a mixture of cooked white meats, such as pork and chicken,
or white fish on Fridays, pounded to a pulp, then combined with
almond milk, boiled rice and sugar. By the reign of Elizabeth I,
meatless versions existed, using cream, rose water and sugar and
eggs for thickening. In the seventeenth and eighteenth centuries,
isinglass was used to set the blancmange; and arrowroot,
the precursor of cornflour, was introduced as a thickener in the
nineteenth century after it was imported from the West Indies.
In this century food companies such as Brown and Polson took
blancmange over and I should think the number of people who
made blancmange from scratch rather than use a packet could be
counted on one hand. I used to love butterscotch blancmange –
hot and in quantity. This flavour is no longer made because,
to quote, 'there is no demand'. It is impossible to replicate the taste
of the butterscotch flavouring used, so I now make a very different
type of blancmange – one that makes a very special end
to a summer meal.*

- 115 G/4 OZ BLANCHED ALMONDS, GROUND
- 450 ML/16 FL OZ MILK
- 4 TSP CORNFLOUR
- APPROXIMATELY 3 TBSP CASTER SUGAR
- 150 ML/5 FL OZ WHIPPING CREAM, WHIPPED

- APPROXIMATELY 1½ TSP ORANGE FLOWER WATER
- 375 G/13 OZ RIPE STRAWBERRIES
- 100 ML/3½ FL OZ DESSERT WINE
- ABOUT 2 TBSP ORANGE JUICE
- 250 G/9 OZ RASPBERRIES
- 1–2 TBSP FRAMBOISE LIQUEUR

1 Rinse a decorative 550 ml/1 pint ring mould with cold water, then leave upside down to drain. Line a sieve with muslin.

2 Gently heat the ground almonds and the milk to simmering point, cover and leave in a warm place for 15 minutes. Pour the mixture into a blender or food processor and process for several seconds. Pour through the sieve, pressing down well to extract all the milk.

3 In a small bowl, mix together 2 tablespoons of the milk, the cornflour and sugar. In a saucepan, bring the remaining milk to the boil, stir a little into the bowl, then pour back into the saucepan and return to the boil, stirring with a wooden spoon. Cook gently for about 3 minutes.

4 Allow the mixture to cool slightly, then, using a large metal spoon, gently fold in the cream and flavour judicially with orange flower water. Pour into the mould and leave for several hours to set.

5 Reserve about 150 g/5 oz of the strawberries. Slice or quarter the remaining strawberries, according to size, place in a bowl and pour over the wine and orange juice. Leave in a cold place for 1–2 hours.

6 To serve the pudding, dampen the centre of a cold plate, place it over the mould, then, holding the two together, invert them and give a sharp shake. Carefully lift off the mould. Drain and reserve the juices from the strawberries. Mix the berries with about 175 g/6 oz of the raspberries and pile in the centre of the blancmange. Purée the juices with the framboise liqueur, reserved strawberries and remaining raspberries. Adjust the taste with orange juice or sugar, if necessary, then trickle some over the blancmange, some over the fruit and serve the rest separately.

ORANGE-FLAVOURED
BABAS WITH KUMQUATS

SERVES 6

*With easy-blend yeasts, and food processors and mixers, cooking
with yeast has become so simple, especially when you realize that
the dough does not have to be left for a specific time in a warm
place to rise. It will in fact rise at room temperature, even in the
refrigerator — the only difference is that it will take longer.
You can, therefore, fit the rising in with your other arrangements
by purposefully selecting the appropriate place in which
to leave the dough.*

● BABAS:
● 200 G/7 OZ STRONG PLAIN FLOUR
● PINCH OF SALT
● 1 PACKET EASY-BLEND
DRIED YEAST
● 125 ML/4½ FL OZ WARM MILK
● 2 EGGS SIZE 2, BEATEN
● 1 TBSP CLEAR HONEY
● 55 G/2 OZ UNSALTED
BUTTER, SOFTENED

● SYRUP AND FILLING:
● 225 G/8 OZ CLEAR HONEY
● 2.5 CM/1 IN CINNAMON STICK
● 225 ML/8 FL OZ WATER
● 6 TBSP DARK RUM
● 3 TBSP COINTREAU
● 250 G/9 OZ KUMQUATS
● TO SERVE:
● 300 ML/10 FL OZ *CRÈME FRAÎCHE*

1 To make the syrup, in a medium-sized saucepan, gently heat the honey with the
cinnamon in the water, stirring occasionally with a wooden spoon, until the honey has
melted. Bring to the boil, simmer for a couple of minutes, then remove from the heat
and stir in the rum and Cointreau.

2 Remove the cinnamon and pour off half the syrup and reserve. Poach the
kumquats in the syrup remaining in the saucepan for about 15–20 minutes until
tender, then leave to cool in the syrup.

3 To make the babas, sift the flour and salt into a bowl, stir in the yeast and form a
well in the centre. Mix together the milk, eggs and honey, then slowly pour into the
well in the flour, drawing the dry ingredients into the liquid using a wooden spoon,
to make a smooth dough. With your hand, beat well until the dough becomes firm
and elastic. Dot the butter over the surface, cover the bowl with a damp cloth or cling
film and leave until doubled in volume — 45 minutes to 1 hour in a warm place, 1½
hours in a cool one.

4 Well butter six 9 cm/3½ inch ring moulds.

5 Turn the dough onto a lightly floured work surface and knead lightly. Divide into 6 equal portions and fit into the moulds. Cover loosely and leave until risen to the top of the moulds.

6 Set the oven to 200°C/400°F/Gas 6. Bake the babas for 10–15 minutes until risen and golden. Allow to cool slighty, then turn onto a wire rack for 5 minutes.

7 Using a slotted spoon, remove the kumquats from the syrup and slice thinly. Pour the reserved syrup back into the saucepan and heat gently without allowing it to boil.

8 Prick the babas all over with a fork, then return them to the ring moulds. Slowly spoon over the hot syrup and continue to spoon it over the babas until they are thoroughly saturated.

9 To serve, unmould the babas, place the sliced kumquats over and around. Serve with *crème fraîche* and any remaining syrup.

Illustrated opposite page 288

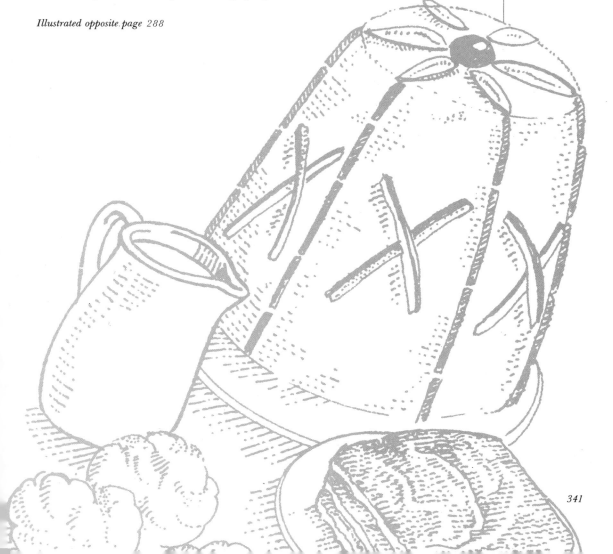

*Place the circle of sponge in
the bottom of the basin*

*Line the sides of the basin
with sponge*

Fill with fruit

*Cover with a plate or saucer;
place weights on top*

342

Summer Pudding in a Special Jacket

SERVES 6

*I love fruit, but I had a long-standing aversion to traditional
summer pudding and to its more recently popularized cousins,
autumn and winter puddings. The first summer pudding I ate was
in the late Fifties, and it had been made using sliced white bread.
I found the texture of the bread so unacceptable that I steadfastly
avoided the pudding for years. I was coaxed into trying it with
a jacket of brioche – better, I admit, but I still preferred to have
the fruit on its own. Then a friend said she used a sponge cake
to line the basin. Eureka! At last, something that was a more
suitable partner to the fruit, especially sun-ripened summer ones.
For the freshest, most fruity flavour, use a gentle heat that will
coax the juices from the fruit, and use the ripest fruit you can
to minimize the heating they need; the juice of really ripe red fruits
will run without any heating at all – just sprinkle them with sugar
and leave until the juice runs naturally. The fruits can, of course,
be varied according to personal taste and what is available.*

- 225 G/8 OZ BLACKCURRANTS
- CASTER SUGAR
- 700 G/1 ½ LB MIXED RIPE RED
  SUMMER FRUITS, SUCH AS
  RASPBERRIES, STRAWBERRIES,
  REDCURRANTS, STONED CHERRIES

- 8–10 SLICES SPONGE CAKE,
  PREFERABLY HOME-MADE AND
  NOT TOO SWEET (SEE NOTE)
- **TO SERVE:**
- FRESH FRUIT AND
  CRÈME FRAÎCHE

1 In a saucepan, mix the blackcurrants with 2 or 3 tablespoons of sugar, leave for a short while, then cover and heat gently, shaking the pan occasionally, until the fruit juices begin to run. Add the red fruits and continue to heat gently until their juices run. Add a little more sugar, if necessary, but do not forget that the cake is slightly sweet and will sweeten the juices; I sometimes like to keep the fruit unsweetened so that it makes more of a contrast to the cake.

2 Cut a circle from 1 slice of cake to neatly fit the bottom of a 1.2 litre/2 pint pudding basin. Fit the circle into the basin, then line it with most of the remaining slices, overlapping them slightly and making sure there are no gaps. Spoon the fruit and most of the juices into the basin, taking care not to dislodge the cake lining; reserve about 3 tablespoons of the juice. Cover with the remaining cake. Cover the top of the basin with greaseproof paper, then with foil and place a saucer or small plate that just fits inside the bowl on top. Place a heavy weight on the saucer or plate. Put in the refrigerator overnight.

3 To serve, run the point of a sharp knife carefully around the edge of the pudding, then invert the pudding onto a serving plate. Spoon the reserved juices over the top and place fruit around the bottom. Serve with *crème fraîche*.

N O T E : Make a Swiss roll sponge in a Swiss roll tin.

Illustrated opposite page 304

$\mathcal{T}$IRAMISU WITH TORRONE

SERVES 4–6

Tiramisu is a comparatively recent creation of the owner of the
El Toula restaurant in Treviso, Italy, but it is served so often in
restaurants (not just Italian ones), and so many recipes have been
published for it, that many people believe it is a traditional pudding.
Torrone 'nougat' is not a traditional ingredient in Tiramisu, but it does
give it that extra je ne sais quoi, *providing a good, firm, chewy nougat*
is used. Italy and Spain both produce some excellent nougats.
Christmas is a good time to look, particularly in Italian and Spanish
speciality food shops, as the nougat is a popular Christmas treat. Chop
the nougat using a food processor or blender.

- 2 EGGS, SEPARATED
- 2 TBSP SOFT BROWN SUGAR
- 300 G/10 OZ MASCARPONE CHEESE
- 115 G/4 OZ TORRONE, FINELY CHOPPED
- 150 G/5 OZ PLAIN CHOCOLATE, FINELY CHOPPED (OPTIONAL)
- 150 ML/5 FL OZ FRESHLY MADE GOOD STRONG COFFEE, PREFERABLY ESPRESSO, COOLED
- 100 ML/3½ FL OZ COFFEE LIQUEUR SUCH AS TIA MARIA OR KAHLUA
- 18 ITALIAN SAVOIARDI SPONGE FINGERS OR GOOD-QUALITY ORDINARY SPONGE FINGERS
- COCOA POWDER (OPTIONAL)

1 Whisk together the egg yolks and sugar in a large bowl until thick and pale, then gradually whisk in the mascarpone.

2 In a clean, dry bowl, whisk the egg whites until stiff but not dry, then, using a large metal spoon, gently fold into the egg yolk mixture together with the torrone and all but 2 tablespoons of the chocolate, if using. Spoon a layer over the bottom of a serving bowl.

3 In a shallow dish, stir together the coffee and liqueur. Dip one sponge finger into the dish for 10–15 seconds, turning it over so it is well soaked but does not become soggy. Place on the mascarpone mixture. Repeat with 5 more fingers, arranging them side by side. Cover with one third of the remaining mascarpone mixture. Make two more layers of fingers and mixture in the same way, then cover the top with the remaining mascarpone mixture.

4 Sprinkle the remaining chocolate, or cocoa powder if chocolate is not being used, evenly over the mascarpone. Chill in the refrigerator for at least 3 hours. Return to room temperature about 30 minutes before serving.

Illustrated opposite page 305

MUSCAT WINE JELLY AND CREAM

SERVES 4

If you think of jelly as being made from artificially-flavoured and coloured cubes from a packet and fit only for children's parties, you are in for a surprise. This one is very much for adults. The jelly is made with a wine that has a wonderful, rich, fresh, fruity, muscat flavour, with a sweetness that comes naturally from the grapes and not added by man. I often set it in sweet, juicy ripe Charentais or Ogen melons, but if they are not available, the jelly can be set in glasses and partnered by other sweet, juicy fruits.

- 310 ML/11 FL OZ WATER
- 2½ TSP POWDERED GELATINE
- 100 G/3½ OZ CASTER SUGAR
- 400 ML/14 FL OZ MUSCAT WINE, SUCH AS MUSCAT DE RIVESALTES, DE FRONTIGNAN OR BEAUMES-DE-VENISE

- JUICE OF ½–1 LEMON
- 2 SMALL, RIPE CHARENTAIS OR OGEN MELONS
- **TO SERVE:**
- APPROXIMATELY 85–115 ML/3–4 FL OZ SINGLE CREAM, CHILLED

Using a sharp knife, cut a deep zig-zag line around the circumference of the melon

1 Put 55 ml/2 fl oz water into a small heatproof bowl, sprinkle the gelatine over the top and leave for about 5 minutes until spongy. Place the bowl over a saucepan of hot water and leave until the gelatine has dissolved.

2 Meanwhile, put the sugar, wine and the remaining water into a saucepan and heat, stirring occasionally, until the sugar has dissolved.

Separate the two halves

3 Remove the bowl containing the gelatine from the pan and leave to cool slightly. Stir in a little of the wine mixture, then stir back into the remaining wine mixture. Add lemon juice to taste, then leave in a cool place until thick and syrupy.

4 Using a small sharp knife, and working around the equator of each melon, make a series of long, zigzag cuts to cut the melons in half. Scoop out and discard the seeds and fibres from the centre of each melon.

Using a spoon, scoop out the seeds

5 Reserve about one quarter of the jelly and divide the remainder between the melon shells. Place with the reserved jelly in the refrigerator to set.

6 Just before serving, whip the reserved jelly until frothy. Spoon on top of the jelly in the melon, then serve with single cream poured over.

$\mathcal{V}$OLUPTUOUS CHESTNUT, CHOCOLATE AND RUM CAKE

SERVES 8

*Chestnut trees were known as bread trees and the nuts were a staple
of many peasant communities in France, Italy and Spain because
they can be used in several different forms – fresh, dried, whole,
puréed and ground to a flour – and in many different dishes,
both sweet and savoury. But this cake certainly did not emanate
from a peasant kitchen! The complete recipe as I have given it
fully exploits the way chestnuts and chocolate enhance each other
and it is one of life's most wonderful eating experiences. The cake
on its own, with no more than a dusting of icing sugar and
cocoa powder, makes a special pudding, so the filling and icing
are really an extravagance that 'gilds the lily'. But why not?*

- 115 G/4 OZ BITTER CHOCOLATE, CHOPPED
- 55 G/2 OZ UNSALTED BUTTER, DICED
- 250 G/9 OZ UNSWEETENED CHESTNUT PURÉE
- FEW DROPS VANILLA ESSENCE
- 4 EGGS, SEPARATED
- 55 G/2 OZ CASTER SUGAR
- 1 EGG WHITE
- 4 TBSP DARK RUM
- **FILLING (OPTIONAL):**
150 ML/5 FL OZ DOUBLE OR WHIPPING CREAM

- 1 TBSP VANILLA CASTER SUGAR
- APPROXIMATELY 40 G/1½ OZ COOKED CHESTNUTS, CHOPPED (SEE PAGE 310)
- **ICING (OPTIONAL):**
- 175 G/6 OZ PLAIN CHOCOLATE, CHOPPED
- 4 TBSP WATER
- 55 G/2 OZ UNSALTED BUTTER, DICED
- **DECORATION:**
- MARRONS GLACÉS
- CRYSTALLIZED ANGELICA (OPTIONAL)

1 Set the oven to 180°C/350°F/Gas 4. Line the base and sides of a 20 cm/8 inch diameter, 5 cm/2 inch deep cake tin with greaseproof paper, then butter the paper.

2 Place the chocolate and butter in a medium-sized heatproof bowl and place over a saucepan of hot water. Stir occasionally until the chocolate and butter have melted and the mixture is smooth. Remove from the heat and sieve in the chestnut purée. Add a few drops of vanilla essence and stir to mix.

3 In a separate bowl, whisk the egg yolks and sugar until thick and pale, then, using a large metal spoon, gently fold into the chocolate mixture.

4 In a clean, dry bowl, whisk the egg whites until stiff but not dry, then, with the metal spoon, gently fold into the chocolate mixture. Transfer to the cake tin and bake for 50 minutes until springy to the touch in the centre.

5 Remove the cake from the oven and pierce holes over the top. Spoon over the rum and leave to cool in the tin.

6 Remove the cake from the tin and carefully peel off the lining paper. When cold, slice the cake in half horizontally.

7 To make the filling, lightly whip the cream with the sugar, then gently fold in the chestnuts. Spread over one half of the cake, then cover with the other half.

8 To make the icing, melt the chocolate with the water in a heatproof bowl and place over a saucepan of hot water. When smooth, remove the bowl from the saucepan and gradually beat in the butter. Leave to cool until beginning to thicken, then quickly pour over the cake and spread down the sides using a palette knife. Decorate with marrons glacés and crystallized angelica, if liked, and leave to set.

Illustrated opposite page 320

*S*AUCES

The right sauce is a valuable asset to a pudding and should complete it and be part of it, not simply an adjunct to it. This means marrying or contrasting flavours, textures and consistencies so that together they are better than the sum of their individual parts. A sauce can also, of course, moisten a pudding, but it should not swamp it — unless the sauce is superior to the pudding!

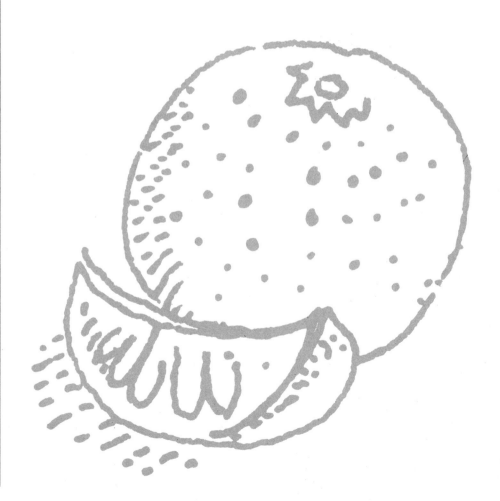

SAUCES

CUSTARD

Wooden spoon for custard:

*The corner of the spoon gets
right in to the angle between
the base and sides of the
saucepan*

*Removing seeds from a
vanilla pod:*

*For a stronger vanilla
flavour, slit the pod
lengthways, using the point
of a sharp knife*

*Scrape out the seeds and put
the seeds in the milk to heat
and infuse. Do not strain*

Custard is the most traditional and most frequently served pudding sauce. To make proper egg-based custard does not require skill, just a little patience, but this will be well rewarded by the taste and texture of the finished sauce and its effect on the pudding, and the people eating it.

☞ Use a heavy-based saucepan. I like to use one that has a non-stick coating. If using an ordinary saucepan, rinsing the pan with cold water before starting helps to prevent the milk or cream 'catching'.

☞ The base of the pan must be completely flat for even cooking.

☞ A vanilla pod can be re-used. Simply rinse and dry it after removing it from the milk or cream, then return the pod to its container.

☞ When using a vanilla pod to flavour a custard, the strength of flavour is controlled by the length of time the pod is left in the milk or cream.

☞ To ensure the heat is gentle beneath the custard as it cooks, a heat diffusing mat is useful. Some peole prefer to use a double saucepan or a heatproof bowl placed over a saucepan of hot, not boiling, water. If you use this method, check that the underside of the bowl is clear of the water.

☞ When stirring the custard, make sure you move the spoon or spatula across the entire base of the pan and reach into the angle between the base and the sides.

☞ If the custard looks as if it is beginning to cook too quickly or unevenly, remove the pan from the heat straightaway and stir hard.

☞ Custard can be made in advance and reheated if this is done in a heatproof basin placed over a saucepan of hot, not boiling, water. Stir the custard frequently while it is warming up. Custard thickens when it cools, so it may be necessary to add a little more milk or cream.

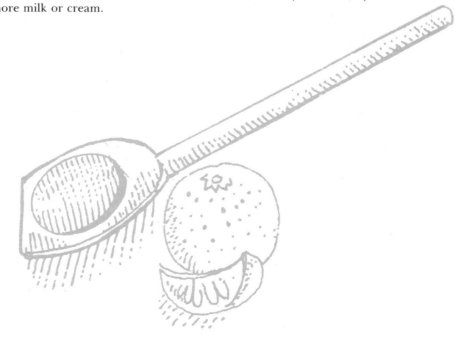

CUSTARD

SERVES 4

Many puddings benefit from being accompanied by a good custard, by which I mean custard made using eggs. Custard made from a packet mix certainly has the advantages of cost, convenience and simplicity, and many people like it, but I'm sure you'll find this version scores on flavour and texture, especially for special occasions. The richness of the custard can be altered by using single, whipping or double cream in place of some or all of the milk, and by using some whole eggs instead of all egg yolks (1 whole egg to replace 2 yolks), or even by increasing the number of egg yolks to 6 or even 8.

- 425 ML/15 FL OZ MILK
- 1 VANILLA POD OR A FEW DROPS VANILLA ESSENCE

- 5 EGG YOLKS
- APPROXIMATELY 40 G/1 ½ OZ CASTER SUGAR

1 In a heavy saucepan, gently heat the milk with the vanilla pod, if using, to simmering point. Remove from the heat, cover and leave for 15–20 minutes.

2 In a bowl, whisk together the egg yolks and sugar until thick and light.

3 Uncover the saucepan, remove the vanilla pod, if used, and the skin from the top of the milk. Bring the milk to the boil. Slowly stir into the egg yolks, then pour back into the saucepan and cook very gently, stirring with a wooden spoon, until thickened; do not allow the sauce to boil. Add vanilla essence, if using. For a really silky texture, strain through a conical sieve.

4 If serving or using the custard cold, pour it into a basin and leave to cool. To prevent a skin forming, either stir occasionally, or lay a sheet of cling film or dampened greaseproof paper on the surface of the custard, making sure there are no air bubbles.

5 The custard can be kept, covered, in the refrigerator for up to 2 days.

VARIATIONS:

COFFEE CUSTARD

At step 1, infuse 2 tablespoons of espresso coffee or finely ground dark or continental roast coffee beans with the vanilla pod in the milk. Follow the rest of the recipe as normal; do not strain the custard.

ORANGE CUSTARD

Omit step 1. Add the vanilla pod at step 2 when bringing the milk to the boil and remove it as soon as the milk reaches boiling point. Follow the remaining recipe to the end of step 3, then stir in the finely grated rind of 2 small oranges, and 1½ tablespoons of Cointreau, if liked.

CINNAMON CUSTARD

Use 1 cinnamoon stick instead of the vanilla pod and follow the recipe to the end of step 3. Add about half a teaspoon ground cinnamon.

HAZELNUT CUSTARD

Add 125 g/4½ oz ground, lightly toasted hazelnuts when the egg yolk and milk mixture has been poured back into the saucepan prior to cooking until thickened. Do not strain.

PRALINE CUSTARD

As for Hazelnut Custard, substituting crushed praline powder (see page 216).

RUM, WHISKY OR BRANDY CUSTARD

Add 3 tablespoons of rum, whisky or brandy to the custard just before serving if serving hot; add when cold if serving cold.

CHOCOLATE CUSTARD

Add 55–85 g/2–3 oz chopped plain chocolate to the milk before reheating to the boil.

*W*HAT WENT WRONG?

☞ **THE CUSTARD HAS CURDLED:**
   The custard will curdle if it is cooked too quickly at too high a temperature or it is not stirred sufficiently, especially towards the end of the cooking.
☞ **THE CUSTARD IS TOO THIN:**
   This is caused by using an insufficient number of eggs or not cooking the custard for long enough.

HOT CHOCOLATE SAUCE

SERVES 4–6

This Hot Chocolate Sauce has a good,
smooth, rich, chocolatey flavour.

- 200 G/7 OZ BITTER
  CHOCOLATE, CHOPPED
- 115 ML/4 FL OZ MILK

- 2 TBSP DOUBLE CREAM
  (OPTIONAL)
- 15 G/1½ OZ UNSALTED BUTTER

1 Put the chocolate into a small heatproof bowl, place over a saucepan of hot water and leave to melt, stirring occasionally.

2 Bring the milk and cream, if using, to the boil, then slowly stir into the chocolate. Remove from the heat and stir in the butter.

VARIATION:
For a Hot Mocha Sauce, use strong white coffee instead of the milk and add sugar to taste.

355

CHOCOLATE SAUCE

SERVES 4

*Instant coffee granules, vanilla essence, orange liqueur,
brandy, whisky or rum can be added to taste.*

- 175 G/6 OZ BITTER
  CHOCOLATE, CHOPPED
- 4 TBSP WATER

- 15 G/½ OZ UNSALTED BUTTER,
  DICED

1 Put the chocolate and the water into a small heatproof bowl placed over a saucepan of hot water and leave to melt, stirring occasionally.

2 Remove the bowl from the heat and stir in the butter. Serve warm or cold.

VARIATION:
For a Chocolate Mint Sauce, use chopped chocolate mint crisps instead of bitter chocolate.

FLUFFY ORANGE SAUCE

SERVES 4

*A billowy, tangy sauce that can be served as soon as it is made,
or made up to 8 hours in advance and served cold. The wine
not only contributes to the flavour, but also makes the sauce
a little lighter.*

- 3 EGG YOLKS
- FINELY GRATED RIND AND
  JUICE OF 2 ORANGES
- JUICE OF 1 LEMON

- APPROXIMATELY 55 G/2 OZ
  CASTER SUGAR
- 55 ML/2 FL OZ DESSERT WINE
- COINTREAU, TO TASTE
  (OPTIONAL)

1 Put all the ingredients together in as medium-sized heatproof bowl. Place the bowl over a saucepan of hot water, making sure the bottom of the bowl is not touching the water, and whisk until thick, foamy and doubled in volume; this will take about 10–15 minutes.

2 Serve immediately or remove the bowl from the saucepan and continue to whisk the sauce until it is cold.

SABAYON SAUCE

SERVES 4

*The quality and character of the wine will affect the taste,
and therefore enjoyment, of this sauce. Light-weight wines with a
fairly high acidity, such as Muscadet, are the lowest on my list;
a sauce made from a medium-sweet wine that is a bit 'flabby'
because it lacks acidity, such as Liebfraumilch, can be improved by
the addition of lemon, lime or orange juice. The sweetness of the
wine will govern the amount of sugar needed, and the sweetness of
the pudding should also be borne in mind.*

- 3 EGG YOLKS, SIZE 2
- APPROXIMATELY 40 G/1 ½ OZ
  VANILLA CASTER SUGAR

- 115 ML/4 FL OZ FRUITY-
  FLOWERY DRY WHITE WINE,
  SUCH AS CHENIN BLANC
- LEMON JUICE (OPTIONAL)

1 Put the egg yolks, sugar and wine in a medium-sized heatproof bowl, placed over a saucepan of hot water and whisk until the mixture is pale, doubled in volume and almost thick enough to support a trail; this will take about 10–15 minutes. Add more sugar and lemon juice, if necessary.

2 If serving the sauce warm, serve immediately. If serving it cold, place the bowl in a bowl of iced water and whisk until cold.

ℬRANDY BUTTER SAUCE

SERVES 4

*This is different from traditional brandy butter, as it contains
an egg yolk and cream to give a softer consistency. It has a
chameleon character, as it is just as at home with special puddings
as with simple ones, lifting them to a higher level. It can be
prepared in advance and, because it can be kept in the refrigerator
for up to 1 week, it is a useful 'store-cupboard standby' for
serving with innumerable puddings, from pancakes and waffles,
steamed and baked puddings, to fruit puddings and for stirring
into rice and similar puddings. Spirits, liqueurs and flavouring
can be varied to complement the pudding that the sauce
is to accompany.*

- 115 G/4 OZ UNSALTED BUTTER
- 115 G/4 OZ ICING SUGAR,
  PREFERABLY VANILLA FLAVOURED
- 3 TBSP BRANDY

- 1 EGG YOLK
- 4 TBSP DOUBLE CREAM
- GRATED RIND OF ½ ORANGE
  (OPTIONAL)

1 Beat the butter until pale and light, then gradually beat in the sugar alternately
with the brandy, until light and fluffy.

2 Beat in the egg yolk, double cream and fruit rind, if using.

3 Store in a covered container in the refrigerator for up to 1 week.

VARIATIONS:
*For a Rum Butter Sauce, use light muscovado sugar instead of icing sugar and substitute rum
for the brandy.*
For an Orange Butter Sauce, use Cointreau instead of brandy.
*For a Spiced Whisky Butter Sauce, use light muscovado sugar instead of icing sugar, replace the
brandy with 3 tablespoons of whisky and add the grated rind of 1 small orange, 1 teaspoon of
lemon juice, ¼ teaspoon of mixed spice and a pinch of finely crushed cardamom seeds.*

APRICOT SAUCE

SERVES 4

*Dried apricots that do not need to be soaked tend to be sweeter than
the traditional ones that need soaking, but they do not give such
a good, fresh fruity flavour. The sauce can be served hot or cold
and can be kept covered in the refrigerator for several days.*

- 175 G/6 OZ DRIED APRICOTS
- 350 ML/12 FL OZ FRUITY DRY
  WHITE WINE
- LONG STRIP OF ORANGE RIND
- HONEY, TO TASTE (OPTIONAL)

1 Put the apricots into a bowl, pour over the wine and leave to soak overnight.

2 Tip the apricots and soaking liquor into a saucepan, add the orange rind and
sufficient water to cover and simmer gently until very tender; this can take up to 40
minutes, depending on the apricots.

3 Discard the orange rind and purée the apricots and cooking liquor. Add honey to
taste, if liked.

4 If serving warm, reheat the sauce and adjust the thickness with water or wine, so
that it has the consistency of double cream.

UNITED KINGDOM

The British Sugarcraft Guild
Wellington House
Messeter Place
London SE9 5DP
Tel: (020) 8859 6943

The Cake Makers Depot
57 The Tything
Worcester
WR1 1JT
Tel: 01905 25468

Confectionery Supplies
29-31 Lower Cathedral Road
Cardiff CF1 8LU
Tel: 01222 372161
Also outlets in Bristol, Hereford
and Swansea

Culpitt Ltd
Jubilee Industrial Estate
Ashington NE63 8UQ
Tel: 01670 814545
Website: www.culpitt.com
Freephone enquiry line: 0845
601 0574
Distributor of cake decorations,
telephone for your nearest
retail outlet

Jane Asher Party Cakes
22-24 Cale Street
London SW3 3QU
Tel: (020) 7584 6177
Fax: (020) 7584 6179
Website: www.jane-asher.co.uk
Range of equipment for sale,
cake tins and wedding stands
for hire

JC Cake Supply Co
Warehouse outlet: Unit 6
Ivanhoe Industrial Estate
Off Simsby Road
Ashby de la Zouch
Leicestershire LE65 2UU
Tel: 01530 414554
Online catalogue:
www.jccakes.com
Huge range of equipment,
decorations and ingredients

London Sugarart Centre
12 Selkirk Road
London SW17 0ES
Tel: (020) 8767 8558
Fax: (020) 8767 9939
Cake tins, cake decorating
equipment and accessories

Pipe Dreams
2 Bell Lane
Eton Wick
Windsor
Berkshire SL4 6JP
Tel: (01753) 865682
Tools, accessories, cake stands
and tins

Renshaw Scott Ltd
229 Crown Street
Liverpool L8 7RF
Tel: (0151) 706 8200
Websites:
www.renshawscott.co.uk
or www.supercook.co.uk
Manufacturers and distributors
of cake decorations and baking
supplies, including the
Supercook brand

Special Occasions
39 High Street
Kirkaldy
Fife
Scotland
KY1 1LB
Tel: (01592) 267 635
Large selection of equipment

Squire's Kitchen
International School of Cake
Decorating and Sugarcraft
Squire's House
3 Waverley Lane
Farnham
Surrey GU9 8BB
Tel: (01252) 734309
Fax: (01252) 714714
Website:
www.squires-group.co.uk
Courses in cake decoration

SOUTH AFRICA

The Baking Tin
52 Belvedere Road
Claremont 7700
Cape Town
Tel: (021) 671 6434

South Bakels
55 Section Street
Paarden Eiland 7420
Cape Town
Tel: (021) 511 1381

South Bakels
235 Main Road
Martindale 2092
Johannesburg
Tel: (011) 673 2100

Chefs and Ices
Shop 3, Lower Level
Sandton City
Sandton 2196
Johannesburg
Tel: (011) 783 3201

Party's, Crafts and Cake Decor
Shop 4, East Rand Mall
Rietfontein Road
Boksburg 1459
Johannesburg
Tel: (011) 823 1988

Chocolate Den
Glen Dower Shopping Centre
99 Linksfield Road
Glen Dower
Edenvale 1609
Johannesburg
Tel: (011) 453 8167

The Baking Tin
Shop 108, Glenwood Village
Cnr Hunt & Moore Road
Glenwood 4001
Durban
Tel: (031) 202 2224

South Bakels
125 Pat Mullin Street
Bloemfontein 9301
Tel: (051) 435 7224

The Baking Tin
Rochel Road
Perridgevale 6001
Port Elizabeth
Tel: (041) 363 0271

South Bakels
41 Patterson Road
North End 6001
Port Elizabeth
Tel: (041) 484 2878

AUSTRALIA

Cake Art Supplies
Kiora Mall
Shop 26 Kiora Rd
MIRANDA
NSW 2228
Tel: (02) 9540 3483

Hollywood Cake Decorations
52 Beach St
KOGARAH
NSW 2217
Tel: (02) 9587 1533

The Cake Decorating Centre
36 Timwilliam St
GOODWOOD
SA 5034
Tel: (08) 8271 1171

Susie Q
Shop 4/372, Keilor Rd
NIDDRIE
VIC 3042
Tel:(03) 9379 2275

Cake and Icing Centre
651 Samford Rd
MITCHELTON
QLD 4053
Tel: (07) 3355 3443

Petersen's Cake Decorations
370 Cnr South St and
Stockdale Rd
OCONNOR
WA 6163
Tel: (08) 9337 9636

Gum Nut Cake and Craft
Supplies
SORELL
TAS 7172
Tel: (03) 6265 1463

NEW ZEALAND

Auckland:
Chocolate Boutique
5 Mokoia Road
Birkenhead
Tel: (09) 419 2450

Innovations Specialty Cookware
52 Mokoia Road
Birkenhead
Tel: (09) 480 8885

Milly's Kitchen Shop
273 Ponsonby Road
Ponsonby
Tel: (09) 376 1550

Spotlight
(branches throughout New
Zealand)
19 Link Drive
Glenfield
Tel: (09) 444 0220
www.spotlightonline.co.nz

Wellington:
Starline Distributors Ltd
28 Jessie Street
Wellington
Tel: (04) 385 7424

Christchurch:
Hitchon International Ltd
220 Antiqua Street
Christchurch
Tel: (03) 365 3843

Icing Specialists Equipment
Shop 6, Church Corner Mall
Riccarton
Tel: (03) 348 6828

$\mathcal{I}$NDEX